Tourism and Religion

MIX
Paper from
responsible sources
FSC
www.fsc.org
FSC® C014540

ASPECTS OF TOURISM

Series Editors: **Chris Cooper** *(Oxford Brookes University, UK)*, **C. Michael Hall** *(University of Canterbury, New Zealand)* and **Dallen J. Timothy** *(Arizona State University, USA)*

Aspects of Tourism is an innovative, multifaceted series, which comprises authoritative reference handbooks on global tourism regions, research volumes, texts and monographs. It is designed to provide readers with the latest thinking on tourism worldwide and in so doing will push back the frontiers of tourism knowledge. The series also introduces a new generation of international tourism authors writing on leading edge topics.

The volumes are authoritative, readable and user-friendly, providing accessible sources for further research. Books in the series are commissioned to probe the relationship between tourism and cognate subject areas such as strategy, development, retailing, sport and environmental studies. The publisher and series editors welcome proposals from writers with projects on the above topics.

All books in this series are externally peer-reviewed.

Full details of all the books in this series and of all our other publications can be found on http://www.channelviewpublications.com, or by writing to Channel View Publications, St Nicholas House, 31-34 High Street, Bristol BS1 2AW, UK.

ASPECTS OF TOURISM: 83

Tourism and Religion

Issues and Implications

Edited by

Richard Butler and Wantanee Suntikul

CHANNEL VIEW PUBLICATIONS
Bristol • Blue Ridge Summit

DOI https://doi.org/10.21832/BUTLER6454

Library of Congress Cataloging in Publication Data

A catalog record for this book is available from the Library of Congress.

Names: Butler, Richard, 1943- editor. | Suntikul, Wantanee.

Title: Tourism and Religion: Issues and Implications/Edited by Richard
Butler and Wantanee Suntikul.

Description: Bristol, UK: Blue Ridge Summit, PA: Channel View Publications,
2018. | Includes bibliographical references and index.

Identifiers: LCCN 2017044015| ISBN 9781845416447 (pbk: alk. paper) | ISBN
9781845416454 (hbk: alk. paper) | ISBN 9781845416485 (kindle)

Subjects: LCSH: Tourism–Religious aspects. | Travel–Religious aspects.

Classification: LCC G156.5.R44 T68 2018 | DDC 203/.51–dc23 LC record available
at https://lccn.loc.gov/2017044015

British Library Cataloguing in Publication Data

A catalogue entry for this book is available from the British Library.

ISBN-13: 978-1-84541-645-4 (hbk)
ISBN-13: 978-1-84541-644-7 (pbk)

Channel View Publications

UK: St Nicholas House, 31-34 High Street, Bristol, BS1 2AW, UK.

USA: NBN, Blue Ridge Summit, PA, USA.

Website: www.channelviewpublications.com

Twitter: Channel_View

Facebook: https://www.facebook.com/channelviewpublications

Blog: www.channelviewpublications.wordpress.com

The policy of Multilingual Matters/Channel View Publications is to use papers
that are natural, renewable and recyclable products, made from wood grown in
sustainable forests. In the manufacturing process of our books, and to further
support our policy, preference is given to printers that have FSC and PEFC Chain of
Custody certification. The FSC and/or PEFC logos will appear on those books where
full certification has been granted to the printer concerned.

Typeset by Deanta Global Publishing Services Limited.

Printed and bound in the UK by Short Run Press Ltd.

Printed and bound in the US by Edwards Brothers Malloy, Inc.

Contents

List of Contributors

Richard Butler, Strathclyde Business School, University of Strathclyde, Glasgow, UK

Noga Collins-Kreiner, Department of Geography and Environmental Studies, University of Haifa, Haifa, Israel

Simon Curtis, Department of Property and Construction, University of Westminster, London, UK

Kevin Griffin, School of Hospitality Management and Tourism, Dublin Institute of Technology, Dublin, Ireland

Rami Isaac, Academy for Tourism, NHTV Breda University of Applied Sciences, Breda, The Netherlands

Pushkar Kanvinde, School of Planning and Architecture, Bharatiya Kala Prasarini Sabha's College of Architecture, Pune, India

Kristel Kessler, Leeds Business School, Leeds Beckett University, Leeds, UK

John King, Australian Tourism Export Council and Pacific Asia Tourism Association, Birchgrove, Australia

Nimrod Luz, Department of Sociology and Anthropology, The Western Galilee College, Acre, Israel

David Mercer, School of Global, Urban and Social Studies, RMIT University, Melbourne, Australia

Yuji Nakanishi, Department of Humanities and Culture, Faculty of Integrated Arts and Social Sciences, Japan Women's University, Tokyo, Japan

Kevin O'Gorman, School of Management and Languages, Heriot Watt University, Edinburgh, UK

Daniel Olsen, Department of Geography, Brigham Young University, Provo, Utah, USA

Elina Ostrometskaia, School of Hospitality Management and Tourism, Dublin Institute of Technology, Dublin, Ireland

Razak Raj, Leeds Business School, Leeds Beckett University, Leeds, UK

Amos Ron, Department of Tourism Studies, Ashkelon Academic College, Ashkelon, Israel

Mark Saunders, Birmingham Business School, University of Birmingham, Birmingham, UK

Caroline Scarles, School of Hospitality and Tourism Management, University of Surrey, Guildford, UK

Silvia Aulet Serrallonga, Faculty of Tourism, University of Girona, Girona, Spain

Deborah Shmueli, Department of Geography and Environmental Studies, University of Haifa, Haifa, Israel

Wantanee Suntikul, School of Hotel and Tourism Management, The Hong Kong Polytechnic University, Hong Kong

Matina Terzidou, Business School, Middlesex University, London, UK

Dallen Timothy, School of Community Resources and Development, Arizona State University, Phoenix, Arizona, USA

Binumol Tom, Department of Architecture, Rajiv Gandhi Institute of Technology, Kottayam, India

Corah Wong, The Institute for Tourism Studies, Macau

List of Figures

List of Tables

Acknowledgements

We are very grateful to the contributors of this volume for their support and cooperation and particularly for their chapters. The relationships between tourism and religion are complex, sensitive and often personal, and the authors have responded to our requests for contributions on specific topics in true academic spirit. We are also appreciative of their patience and positive responses to queries over the preparation of the volume. We trust that our editorial adjustments have not distorted the meanings of their texts and have not exceeded our responsibilities. Errors and omissions remain our responsibility.

We also wish to thank the staff at Channel View Publications, particularly Elinor and Sarah, for their support for and patience with the project, from the initial proposal to the final submission of the completed manuscript. They have been an excellent group of colleagues with whom to work.

Finally, we thank our families for their patience and support during what became a rather longer than anticipated project; their tolerance and encouragement are much appreciated.

1 Tourism and Religion: Origins, Interactions and Issues

Wantanee Suntikul and Richard Butler

Introduction

Recent years have seen a rise in the numbers of issues recorded between tourism and religion. These have related to a range of subjects including politics, religious fundamentalism, environmental and social impacts, inter-faith and within-faith disputes and numbers and actions of visitors to religious sites. Many of these issues, disagreements and conflicts have featured in the general media (for example: Beaumont, 2017; Coghlan, 2015; Hider, 2011; Tomlinson, 2015; Trew, 2015), and have not been confined to academic publications. The relationship between tourism and religion has outgrown the original topic of pilgrimage and its links with tourism, religious sites and organisations. Now, the often problematic relationship is far more extensive and complex, reflecting the changes in the scale and nature of tourism, and different beliefs and reactions among the various faiths. It is this nexus or interaction that is the primary focus of this volume, reflecting the fact that in the 21st century the common ground between tourism and religion has moved beyond what has been termed 'religious tourism'. This term has become confusing and possesses little meaning today, as religious tourism suggests tourism that is motivated by religion or faith, and while this is certainly a still significant segment of tourism, tourism to religious sites now encompasses many more facets of tourism and is subject to more and varied motivations than spiritual obligation or need. Accordingly, this volume is focused on the much wider topic of tourism to what may be viewed as places (locations, sites, artefacts) of religious or faith significance and the implications and consequences of such visitation. In so doing, it moves beyond discussions of the sacred and profane, or of traditional pilgrimage, to throw light on how religious bodies and agencies are dealing with tourism, and how modern travel interacts with what are often ancient sites with generally conservative management. While many of the issues and problems raised are common to tourist visitation to all destinations, religious sites are imbued with

1

additional complications of politics, nationalism, emotion, obligation and belief, as well as traditional roles of welcoming and offering hospitality and sanctuary to travellers.

The increase in overall tourist numbers (UNWTO, 2016) over the past half century has been reflected in the increased numbers of visitors to religious locations, accentuating already existing tensions and difficulties which many such sites have faced in managing their faithful (Sarddar, 2016). These concerns are illustrated in the large number of books and articles that have appeared in the last decade addressing some of these issues. The *International Journal for Religious Tourism and Pilgrimage*, for example, has begun its fifth year of publication and a special issue of the *International Journal of Tourism Anthropology* (Di Giovine & Garcia-Fuentes, 2016) focused on the links between pilgrimage and heritage, recognising the vastly wider scope of pilgrimage in the present day. A steady number of articles are being published in other established tourism journals (see for example Creighton-Smith *et al.*, 2017) on a variety of aspects of religious tourism, and Leppakari and Griffin (2016) and Raj and Griffin (2017) have recently produced books on management and conflict, respectively, relating to tourism to religious locations. Recent (2016 and 2017) decisions at the international level (UNESCO) on the designation of World Heritage Site status for religious sites in Israel and Palestine reflect the complicated political as well as religious forces that become involved with the tourist implications of such designations. Thus, it is timely to explore both how specific religious faiths have been and are currently involved in tourism, and also how individual countries, destinations and organisations deal with the problems that have emerged from this interaction. The focus in this volume comes from a tourism rather than a religious perspective, which makes it somewhat unique in that regard. Much of the literature that is discussed focuses on religious tourism, particularly pilgrimage, and thus also issues such as beliefs, commitments, obligations and dogmas, rather than on more specific and current problems such as the use of tourism to religious sites for political reasons, the economic benefits and costs of incorporating tourist visitation with religious site management, and issues of marketing tourism to religious sites in troubled destinations, which are discussed in this volume.

As well as the current increased interest in the above topics as expressed in publications, there has also been an increase in the numbers of meetings organised by bodies ranging from the World Tourism Organisation (UNWTO), which held its first conference on Tourism and Pilgrimage in 2014 at Santiago de Compostela, Spain, attended almost entirely by people from spiritual organisations to specific academic meetings such as the annual conferences on Religious Tourism and Pilgrimage. In October 2016 in Utrecht, the Netherlands, a conference titled 'Religious Heritage Tourism: How to increase religious heritage tourism in a changing society' was jointly organised by UNWTO and the Cultural Heritage Agency of the Netherlands. This conference was one of the first to raise questions such as: 'How can we further develop the social and economic impact of religious heritage tourism?', 'How can we further develop religious heritage sites as tourist destinations?' and 'From which good practices can we learn to bring religious heritage tourism forwards?'. Much of the emphasis in the above meetings has been on spiritual discussions and what the role of religious organisations should be with respect to tourism, rather than examining the issues from the primary perspective of tourism.

This book is not focused on purely conceptual or spiritual approaches, but examines both general issues and more specific problems stemming from the interactions between religion, travel and tourism with hospitality and culture in general, as well as the implications for site management and interpretation. Thus, while this volume explores aspects of the oldest form of religious tourism, pilgrimage, from its original form to the multiple variations, spiritual and secular, in which it exists today, it goes much further in examining the links between tourism and religion. Tourism to religious sites and features in the modern world is far broader than pilgrimage, and incorporates historical and cultural interests which may be divorced from the spiritual, including aspects of personal homage and faith, religious festivals that attract not only believers but also non-believers, as well as purely hedonistic use of religious features, including sightseeing with no spiritual dimension or motivation at all. This range of motivations of visitors and purposes of visits makes the interaction of tourism and religion extremely volatile and complex. Accordingly, the chapters contained herein address various issues and conflicts arising from the collision of religion, philosophy, psychology, behaviour, geography, culture, politics and tourism, and the impact of tourism and tourists on religious features, communities and phenomena, including those arising from the deliberate involvement of some religious agencies with tourism.

Tourism and Religion

Religion has been a motivation for travel for centuries, if not millennia, and continues to account for a significant, growing and highly developed segment of the tourism market around the world (Digance, 2003; Olsen & Timothy, 2006; Wall & Mathieson, 2006). Improvements in tourism infrastructure and the increasing accessibility of religious sites play roles in spurring this popularity, as well as the strategic marketing and development of these sites as visitor attractions by authorities in the destinations and countries in which they are sited (Vukonic, 2002). Pilgrimage, a journey to a site of special spiritual significance within one's religious tradition for the purposes of spiritual growth (Glazier, 1992), is one of the oldest forms of religious-motivated tourism, and is still practiced by millions of tourists of various faiths every year. The hajj, the annual Muslim pilgrimage to Mecca, and the journeys of spiritual visitors to India's Ganges River are among the best-known and largest of these practices in the modern day.

Not all tourism to sites of religious significance is necessarily inspired, in part or whole, by spiritual motivations, however (Smith, 2009). As many religious sites tend to have heritage structures and artefacts, and host cultural events of different sorts, they also attract tourists who are interested in them for their cultural significance, architectural importance, aesthetic beauty or historic value, independent of their religious value (though religious tourism can be considered as a subset of cultural tourism [Jackson & Hudman, 1995]). Some such sites – for example, Notre Dame Cathedral in Paris or the Temple of the Emerald Buddha in Bangkok – are among the iconic sights of those destination cities, included in the itineraries of the most mainstream and generic of mass tourism products. In practice, many sites of religious significance now function as 'multi-purpose places' (Shuo *et al.*, 2009; Vukonic, 2006) reflecting the need to cater to the range of tourists that visit them.

Given that there is no clear and agreed-upon distinction between terms such as 'religious tourism', 'faith tourism', 'sacred tourism' and 'spiritual tourism' in the literature (Smith, 2009: 74), one aim of this volume is to explore the diverse range of trips encompassing these and other related perspectives and the problems of accommodating the increasing numbers of tourists at religious sites. While religious tourism is defined in terms of having to do with spiritual beliefs rather than hedonistic motivations, or secular or worldly concerns, as a realm of practice in tourism it becomes intertwined with other economies and aspirations. Religious tourism can account for a major part of the economy of countries with important pilgrimage destinations like India (Singh, 2006). Also, because of the hybrid nature of many of the destinations for religious tourism, the development of this niche of tourism can also contribute to the conservation of cultural heritage assets (Raj & Griffin, 2015), while at the same time creating problems of conservation and protection of those sites.

To date, pilgrimage has been the major focus of most of the relevant literature on religion and tourism, and this topic has been addressed by many authors, particularly from anthropology and sociology (e.g. Badone & Roseman, 2004; Eade, 2015; Eade & Sallnow, 1991). Other related texts on this subject include Barber (1993), Maddrell (2014), Reader and Walter (1993) and Turner and Turner (1969, 1978). In terms of a more geographical viewpoint, there are books by Ivakhiv (2001), Margry (2004), Stoddard and Morinis (1997) and Vukonic (1996), and most recently, Timothy and Olsen (2006), the latter focusing specifically on religious journeys, including pilgrimage. Reader (2013), while also writing on pilgrimage, presents a different focus, that of the marketplace, rather than the more general issues resulting from the interaction of religion and tourism. Perhaps the most unique of recent books dealing with aspects of religion and tourism is that of Ross-Bryant (2012) who discusses the relationship between religion and nature in the United States, particularly in the context of national parks. However, a good number of the works on religion and tourism are a decade or more old, so that during the time since their publication great changes have occurred in this challenging relationship. None of the above-cited books takes a comprehensive view of the multiple issues and problems that have emerged in recent years, in particular those caused by the growth in the volume and nature of tourism and the diverging and complex transformations occurring in many of the world's faiths and their interactions with each other and with other sociocultural factors.

The pressures of tourism on religious communities, sites and features are multiplying exponentially, along with negative reactions in some places to the presence and impacts of tourism and tourists, leading to measures to reduce the touristification of such sites. However, as will be discussed later in this volume, there are also cases in which religious institutions are choosing to become even more involved in tourism and leisure, and actively encouraging visitation by tourists, religiously motivated and otherwise, to their sites. Some churches in the UK, for instance, have introduced new tourism products and activities such as 'champing', i.e. camping in churches. Though such initiatives are often undertaken in the interest of finding new revenue channels to fund conservation, they are not without controversy. There has been some debate within various religious establishments as to whether such commercialisation of sacred places is appropriate. There is also often resistance from factions of local communities who believe that such actions denigrate the sacredness of churches or other religious sites. There is clearly a need for a review and to take stock of the overall relationship between tourism and religion and the implications of such relationships.

Structure and Content

This book contains both historical and contemporary perspectives on the relationship between religion and tourism, ensuring that the topic is examined in a way that is historically situated as well as current and applicable in the modern context. It is also broadly international in terms of the examples, issues and perspectives represented. The chapters encompass all major faiths, and the mix of contributing authors is multidisciplinary. This makes for a collection of writings that takes in various paradigms and approaches, and the examples discussed are topical and highly relevant to today's world. The volume is structured in three parts, each with a short introduction, bracketed by this introductory chapter at the beginning and a conclusion at the end.

The first and longest of this book's three parts, 'Faiths and Tourism', incorporates seven chapters on examples of issues that have arisen between the world's major religious beliefs and travel and tourism. The section begins with Chapter 2, 'Indigenous Tourism: The Most Ancient of Journeys', in which John King discusses the confrontation between modern tourism and indigenous belief systems as tourism impinges on sites and landscapes held sacred by Australia's aboriginal population. In Chapter 3, 'Origins of Hospitality in Monastic and Christian Orders', Kevin O'Gorman reveals that many of the principles of hospitality operations in tourism have their roots in ancient practices of the Christian ethos of hospitality in the context of pilgrimage, while Chapter 4, 'Inspiration for Muslims to Visit Mosques' by Razaq Raj and Kristel Kessler, explores the roles of mosques in motivating travel among Muslim religious tourists as well as their wider role in Muslim communities. In 'Judaism and Tourism over the Ages: The Impacts of Technology, Geopolitics and the Changing Political Landscape' (Chapter 5), Noga Collins-Kreiner and Nimrod Luz look at the effects of geopolitics on the changing patterns and practices of religiously motivated travel in the case of Judaism. Chapter 6, 'Shintoism and Travel in Japan' by Yuji Nakanishi, explains the changing position of the Shinto religion in Japanese culture over the years, and the accompanying shifting of the practices and significance associated with travel to visit Shinto shrines. In Chapter 7 'Hinduism and Tourism', Pushkar Kanvinde and Binumol Tom explain the enduring religious significance of travel in Hindu spiritual life, and how it is linked to the sacred geography of India and its many holy sites. In the final chapter of this section (Chapter 8), Cora Wong presents a discussion of 'The Monks and Nuns of Pu-Tuo as Custodians of Their Sacred Buddhist Site', offering insights into the tactics by which Buddhist monks and nuns accommodate the incursion of tourism into the space and routines of their sacred domain.

The five chapters that make up the next part, 'Issues and Problems', delve deeper into the conflicts that can arise with the entanglement of religion and tourism. In Chapter 9, 'The Vow and Tourist Travel', Matina Terzidou, Caroline Scarles and Mark Saunders explore the historical roots of the relationship between the religious and the touristic, and articulate the ways in which both the sacred as well as the secular components of the religious tourism experience contribute to the 'becoming' of religious tourists, as tourists and as believers. They provide a review of the relevant literature on the relationship between the orientation and focus of tourists to religious sites and their feelings of religiousness or spirituality and provide a framework illustrating the links and differences between tourism and believers involved in travel to religious sites. These differences can manifest themselves in disputes and conflicts in many forms and in Chapter 10 'Politics, Tourism, Religion and Conflicts: A Suggested Framing Framework', Noga Collins-Kreiner and Deborah Shmueli draw on a case study in Israel to suggest a general framework for understanding the mechanisms of such conflicts involving politics and state involvement. Rami K. Isaac, in Chapter 11, 'Religious Tourism in Palestine: Challenges and Opportunities', shows the ways in which political and security issues in the Palestinian territories impact on the practices of both tourism in general and religious tourism specifically to these areas, illustrating other examples of political disputes affecting tourism to religious sites. In Chapter 12 on 'Marketing Myanmar: The Religion/Tourism Nexus in a Fragile Polity', David Mercer shows how internal conflicts with religious dimensions underlie inequities in the tourism industry and the selective way in which religious sites are being developed for tourism in this Southeast Asian nation. This chapter also illustrates the political manipulation of both tourism and religion in that troubled country. This part is rounded out by Elina Ostrometskaia and Kevin Griffin's Chapter 13, 'Religious Tourism and Pilgrimage in Russia', in which they discuss issues surrounding the resurgence of religiously motivated tourism and the restoration of religious tourism sites in Russia following the fall of the Soviet Union. Again, changes in political structure and ideology have had significant impacts on religious activity and tourism to religious sites.

The final part of this book is titled 'Secular Tourism in Sacred Places', and presents five chapters relating to the hybrid nature of many tourism sites of religious significance, which also attract tourists without spiritual motivations. In Chapter 14, 'Spiritual Tourism in Europe: The SPIRIT-Youth Project', Silvia Aulet Serrallonga examines the distinctions between 'religious' and 'spiritual' in the context of travel, through a review of the relevant literature on this topic. The context is provided by a particular endeavour to develop a product aimed at youth-oriented spiritual tourism which is described in the second part of the chapter. In this discussion, she explores the relationship between nature-based experiences and spirituality in tourism, especially for young Europeans and the issues involved in making spiritual tourism more relevant and attractive to the younger generation. Chapter 15, 'Religious Routes, Pilgrim Trails: Spiritual Pathways as Tourism Resources', by Dallen J. Timothy and Daniel H. Olsen, traces the history of the Way of Saint James (Camino Santiago de Compostela) and other pilgrim trails as both sacred routes and their potential as economic engines for communities along their routes. Chapter 16, 'Reaching Out – Engagement Through Events and Festivals – The Cathedrals of England', by Simon Curtis, addresses the practices put in place by the Anglican church's decision to intentionally promote selected sacred sites as attractions for non-sacred tourism activities and some of the difficulties that ensue. Daniel H. Olsen and Dallen J. Timothy present a New World example in the following chapter (Chapter 17), 'Tourism, Salt Lake City and the Cultural Heritage of Mormonism', showing how the development of tourism, economy and faith in harmony have been successfully combined in the seat of the Mormon religion and how followers of that faith engage in a variety of forms of tourism. Finally, the closing chapter of this part, Amos S. Ron's Chapter 18, 'Religious Needs in the Tourism Industry: The Perspective of Abrahamic Traditions', focuses on three major areas with respect to the religious needs of travellers, whether pilgrims or other travellers, namely food, ritual and atmosphere, and the implications for those providing services and hospitality to travellers, relating back to O'Gorman's chapter (Chapter 3) on early Christian hospitality for travellers.

A concluding chapter by the editors synthesises the insights presented in the various chapters and proposes implications for the theorisation of the interactions between tourism and religion and for future practices in tourism operations and policy, and indeed beyond tourism into the political, cultural and social realms.

References

Badone, E. and Roseman, S. (eds) (2004) *Intersecting Journeys: The Anthropology of Pilgrimage and Tourism*. Champaign, IL: University of Illinois Press.

Barber, R. (1993) *Pilgrimages*. London: The Boydell Press.

Beaumont, P. (2017) UNESCO adopts controversial resolution on Jerusalem holy Sites. *The Guardian*, 7 July, p. 33.

Coghlan, T. (2016) We're ready to fight Iran Saudis say in Haj row. *The Times*, 16 September, p. 44.

Creighton-Smith, B.A., Cook, M. and Edginton, C.R. (2017) Leisure, ethics and spirituality. *Annals of Leisure Research* 20, 1–17.

Digance, J. (2003) Pilgrimage at contested sites. *Annals of Tourism Research* 30 (1), 143–159.

Di Giovine, M.A. and Garcia-Fuentes, J-M. (eds) (2016) Sites of religion, sites of heritage: Exploring the interface between religion and heritage in tourist destinations (Special Issue). *International Journal of Tourism Anthropology* 5 (1-2).

Eade, J. (2015) *International Perspectives on Pilgrimage Studies*. Routledge: London.

Eade, J. and Sallnow, M.J. (eds) (1991) *Contesting the Sacred: The Anthropology of Christian Pilgrimage*. London: Routledge.

Glazier, S.D. (1992) Pilgrimages in the Caribbean: A comparison of cases from Haiti and Trinidad. In E.A. Morinis (ed.) *Sacred Journeys: The Anthropology of Pilgrimage* (pp. 135–147). Westport, CT: Greenwood Press.

Hider, J. (2011) UNESCO decision to give Palestinians membership ignites row over holy sites. *The Times*, 7 October, p. 47.

Ivakhiv, A.J. (2001) *Claiming Sacred: Pilgrims and Politics at Glastonbury and Sedona*. Bloomington, IN: Indiana University Press.

Jackson, R.H. and Hudman, L. (1995) Pilgrimage tourism and English cathedrals: The role of religion in travel. *Tourist Review* 50 (4), 40–48.

Leppakari, M. and Griffin, K. (2016) *Pilgrimage and Tourism to Holy Cities: Ideological and Management Perspectives*. Wallingford: CABI.

Maddrell, A. (2014) *Journeying to the Sacred*. London: Routledge.

Margry, J.P. (ed.) (2008) *Shrines and Pilgrimage in the Modern World: New Itineraries into the Sacred*. Amsterdam: University of Amsterdam Press.

Olsen, D. and Timothy, D. (2006) Tourism and religious journeys. In D. Timothy and D. Olsen (eds) *Tourism, Religion and Spiritual Journeys* (pp. 1–22). Abingdon: Routledge.

Raj, R. and Griffin, K. (2015) Introduction to sacred or secular journeys. In R. Raj and K. Griffin (eds) *Religious Tourism and Pilgrimage Management: An International Perspective* (pp. 1–16). Wallingford: CABI.

Raj, R. and Griffin, K. (2017) *Conflicts, Religion and Culture in Tourism*. Wallingford: CABI.

Reader, I. (2013) *Pilgrimage in the Marketplace*. London: Routledge.

Reader, I. and Walter, T. (1993) *Pilgrimage in Popular Culture*. Basingstoke: Macmillan.

Ross-Bryant, L. (2012) *Religion and Nature in the United States*. London: Routledge.

Sarddar, Z. (2016) *Mecca: The Sacred City*. London: Bloomsbury.

Shuo, Y.S., Ryan, C. and Liu, G. (2009) Taoism, temples and tourists: The case of Mazu pilgrimage tourism. *Tourism Management* 30 (4), 581–588.

Singh, R. (2006) Pilgrimage in Hinduism: Historical context and modern perspectives. In D.J. Timothy and D.H. Olsen (eds) *Tourism, Religion, and Spiritual Journeys* (pp. 220–236). London: Routledge.

Smith, M.K. (2009) *Issues in Cultural Tourism Studies*. London/New York: Routledge.

Stoddard, R.H. and Morinis, A. (1997) *Sacred Places, Sacred Spaces: The Geography of Pilgrimages*. Baton Rouge, LA: Geoscience Publications, Louisiana State University.

Timothy, D.J. and Olsen, D.H. (eds) (2006) *Tourism, Religion and Spiritual Journeys*. London/New York: Routledge.

Tomlinson, H. (2015) Pilgrims chastised over selfies at Mecca. *The Times*, 3 February, p. 33.

Trew, B. (2015) Jihadists target Egypt tourist trade with suicidal attack on Luxor temple. *The Times*, 11 June, p. 33.

Turner, V. and Turner, E. (1969) *The Ritual Process*. London: Routledge.

Turner, V. and Turner, E. (1978) *Image and Pilgrimage in Christian Culture*. New York: Colombia University Press.

UNWTO (2016) *Tourism Barometer* Madrid: UNWTO.

Vukonic, B. (1996) *Tourism and Religion*. London: Elsevier.

Vukonic, B. (2002) Religion, tourism and economics: A convenient symbiosis. *Tourism Recreation Research* 27 (2), 59–64.

Vukonic, B. (2006) Sacred places and tourism in Roman Catholic tradition. In D.J. Timothy and D.H. Olsen (eds) *Tourism, Religion and Spiritual Journeys* (pp. 237–253). London/New York: Routledge.

Wall, G. and Mathieson, A. (2006) *Tourism: Change, Impacts and Opportunities*. Harlow: Pearson Education Limited.

Part 1: Faiths and Tourism

In this first part of the book, we include chapters that discuss specific involvement and relationships between the major faiths of the world and tourism. In view of the immense literature on religious tourism, it was not felt necessary to have a discussion of the formal viewpoint of each faith on tourism and travel, but rather to illustrate some of the issues and links between tourism, travel and specific faiths.

The first chapter is unique in the book in that it is not an invited chapter written especially for this volume, but the transcript of a speech given by John King, who at that time (2014) was chairman of the Australian Tourism Export Council, and it deals with traditional beliefs and customs of Australian Aboriginal peoples, some dating back 40,000 years and predating all of the current established conventional religious faiths. It is included here because of the relative lack of material on the interaction between tourism and indigenous peoples in places and features sacred to the latter (Butler & Hinch, 2007) and it illustrates the issues raised by tourism to sites of religious and cultural importance to indigenous peoples and how such sites can be managed to respect the still-held beliefs and customs of the traditional owners and occupiers of those sites. The example King uses is that of Uluru in Northern Australia. An iconic tourist attraction and a World Heritage Site, this feature has been the centre of controversy over the practice of tourists climbing (walking) to the top of the rock against the wishes of the local Aboriginal inhabitants who regard Uluru as sacred. In recent years, this practice has declined out of respect for those views, but in April 2016 the chief minister of the Northern Territory, a man of Aboriginal descent, argued that Aborigines should drop their opposition to tourists climbing Uluru on the grounds that tourism offers jobs and cash to the local community. Not surprisingly, this statement aroused opposition, including from an Aboriginal member of parliament who commented that Uluru was 'one of the most culturally and spiritually significant places in Australia. It's not just a place with a nice view' (Lagan, 2016: 37). This situation illustrates a number of issues that are discussed in subsequent chapters in this volume, in particular the frequent differences of opinion between local (sometimes indigenous) residents in or near sacred sites, the perpetual tension between sometimes profane tourist behaviour and the need for respect for sacred spaces, and the need for management of such sites involving all concerned parties.

The second chapter in this section by O'Gorman, focuses on the key role of the Christian church in developing the principles of hospitality to travellers, principles that still underlie the operating models of many enterprises in the hospitality and tourism industries. Hospitality is, of course, not confined to Christian churches and organisations, it is a feature of many indigenous cultures and other religions, but given the importance of Western traditions in the development of modern tourism, the Christian church's involvement in providing hospitality to travellers is particularly relevant in this volume. This chapter provides an interesting and appropriate context for the later chapter by Ron on the efforts of contemporary accommodation providers to meet the needs of current religious travellers. The next chapter, by Raj and Kessler, discusses the driving forces and motivations behind Muslims travelling to mosques and the roles of mosques in Islamic communities. Such travel may be both long distance, as in the case of the hajj, or local to neighbouring mosques, with the buildings strengthening community and faith links between adherents and representing a long tradition of movement driven by faith. Raj and Kessler note the multiple roles and contributions of mosques to Muslim life and also some of the issues that can arise when mosques are used for political and prestige purposes rather than their community and faith functions, thus raising again the problems of the politicisation of religious features.

Somewhat in contrast, Collins-Kreiner and Luz examine the impacts of more recent developments on travel by followers of Judaism. As well as dealing with technological innovation and development, they also discuss the impact of geopolitical forces that shape and often disrupt potential travel by the faithful of all religions. Travel to and within Israel and the Holy Land has long been beset by political, religious and military problems and the ongoing threat of violence, dating from before the Crusades almost a thousand years ago (Beveridge & O'Gorman, 2013). The juxtaposition of highly sacred and important sites in contested situations makes this situation even more problematical than in many other areas. They note that Jewish pilgrimage has broadened from initially being solely religious in motivation to also becoming increasingly heritage motivated and thus part of mainstream tourism, a balance that varies with the presence or absence of conflict (Krakover, 2013). The discussion of travels to sacred sites associated with Shintoism in Japan, presents a relevant review of changing beliefs and behaviour in that country and the growth of tourism and leisure visitation to Shinto shrines and temples. In this chapter, Nakanishi explains how what may be termed 'pilgrimage' in the context of Shintoism is different to that practiced in some other faiths, and how the place and role of Shintoism within Japanese society has changed significantly since its inception. There has become a greater emphasis on travel and less on religion and sacred obligation, and this trend has increased in recent years, with much more visitation being related to leisure in the broadest sense rather than religion. Shintoism has become more of a folk religion with its distinctive practices and motivations.

Kanvinde and Tom, however, reveal that there is still a great significance placed on more conventional pilgrimage and visitation to holy sites in the Hindu homeland of India, with clear routes and expectations of the behaviour of the faithful. They note the great importance, as in the case of Islam, with visiting temples and shrines, and also the significant role of architecture in the design and construction of temples. The morphology of the temples themselves is important, as is their relative location, and the formal routes taken by the faithful on journeys of devotion described in the chapter encompass the most sacred sites in selected regions. They note the increasing problems these sites experience in managing the continually increasing numbers of visitors, both sacred and secular. Finally, in this part, Wong discusses the management approach of Buddhist monks to tourist visitation and how such disturbance is accommodated within their religious life and setting. She notes how some major Buddhist sites are also becoming tourist attractions and the problems of combining tourist use with religious practice. She notes that various coping mechanisms are employed by the monks in dealing with the different types of visitors and their varying behaviour. She makes the important argument that it is critical to recognise these personal variations in dealing with tourist-related issues rather than assuming a universal management approach, reflecting the variety of tourists and sites being visited and the variation in the nature of the encounters between hosts and guests.

This part sets the context in which further discussions in later chapters examine specific issues and problems, some relating specifically to one faith, many being relevant to most faiths. In this part, there is clear evidence that all faiths have had to make adjustments when accommodating the pressures of tourism, some have been more welcoming than others, some facing levels of disturbance and conflict that pose major problems for continued religious observance at specific sites. All faiths, however, have been involved with religious travel for many centuries, and more lately, conventional tourism, and are still having to adjust to the potential clash between the sacred and the sometimes profane tourism.

References

Beveridge, E. and O'Gorman, K. (2013) The Crusades, the Knights Templar, and Hospitaller: A combination of religion, war, pilgrimage and tourism enablers. In R.W. Butler and W. Suntikul (eds) *Tourism and War* (pp. 39–48). Abingdon: Routledge.

Butler, R.W. and Hinch, T. (2007) *Tourism and Indigenous Peoples Issues and Implications*. Oxford: Elsevier.

Krakover, S. (2013) Developing tourism alongside threats of wars and atrocities: The case of Israel. In R.W. Butler and W. Suntikul (eds) *Tourism and War* (pp. 132–142). Abingdon: Routledge.

2 Indigenous Tourism: The Most Ancient of Journeys[1]

John King

Introduction

Aboriginal Australians, like many other indigenous peoples and cultures, have highly complex belief systems that interconnect their land, their spirituality, law, society and their regard and care for the environment in which they live. These belief systems, for Aboriginal Australians, flow from their beliefs of creation, from when the world was a featureless void and when ancestral spirits in human and other life forms emerged from the earth and sky, creating all living things, the landscape, the seasons and all natural phenomena.

While creation beliefs and the customary practices and observances that stem from them may vary across the vast land mass of the country and from one language group to another, they are all based on ancestral beings and events that took place in the 'Dreamtime'. Dreamtime ancestors created songlines as a part of the creation. These songlines are still very much recognised and used today.

Because of the interconnection between the land and spiritual belief, and the belief that all landscape features have been created by Dreamtime beings, songlines encompass law, culture and spirituality. However, in their physical form, they also link a few or many landscape features whose origins are also linked to the Dreamtime. Accordingly, they are observed, maintained and travelled today, important not only in maintaining the connection to creation, but also in ensuring the continuity of all living things. The songlines, sometimes called Dreaming tracks, are paths across the land or sky, which mark the tracks taken by the localised creator beings, and whose paths are recorded by way of song, stories, dance and paintings.

Learned elders and traditional owners of the land and song are able to navigate from one landscape feature to another by singing the songs. These songs, believed to have been sung by the ancestral beings themselves, have been handed down from one generation and one custodian to the next over eons. The routes they define and describe sometimes traverse relatively short distances, while others cover many hundreds of kilometres and the lands of other tribal and language groups. Archaeological studies of paintings and relics of spiritual observance associated with the creation stories and the songlines suggest that many have been followed, observed and used in an unbroken line for at least 40,000 years.

Significant Areas to Aboriginals and Their Management

Two areas of special significance to Aboriginal, as well as other Australians, are today included in the national parks of Uluru-Kata Tjuta and Kakadu, both in Australia's Northern Territory. Both were declared World Heritage Areas in the 1980s in recognition of their natural and cultural significance. Following the historic granting of native title in Australia, these areas were leased by the traditional owners to the Australian government in the 1980s to be operated as National Parks and World Heritage Areas, and are jointly managed with the traditional owners to protect and promote their significant natural and cultural values.

This author is immensely privileged to have been involved with both areas. In the case of Kakadu, I worked with the traditional owners and other stakeholders to develop a joint vision and strategy for jointly managing, promoting and preserving the values the park. In the case of Uluru-Kata Tjuta, I worked as a member of the board of management, both parks having a similar system of joint management.

At Uluru-Kata Tjuta, joint management commenced in October 1985 when the lease of the land by the Aboriginal owners to the Australian government was formally signed. At that time, a board of 12 people was appointed to manage the park – eight of whom were Anangu representatives elected from among the traditional owners, the remaining four members comprised the director of Parks Australia, two other nominees of the federal government (with tourism and environmental experience) and one nominee of the Northern Territory government. Significantly, these last three nominees are subject to the approval of the Anangu board member before they are entitled to take their place on the board. Meetings are bilingual – interpreted each way between English and Pitjantjatjara, the local language. Through the board of management, Nguraritja (traditional owners) and Parks Australia share decision-making for the management of Uluru-Kata Tjuta National Park.

Many places in the more than 1300 square kilometre park are of enormous spiritual and cultural importance to Anangu. The park also contains features such as Uluru and Kata Tjuta (previously known as Ayers Rock and the Olgas, respectively) which have become major symbols of Australia. The Aboriginal traditional owners of Uluru-Kata Tjuta National Park (Nguraritja) have looked after and, in turn, have been looked after by the land for over 1000 generations.

One of the roles of the joint board is the development and management of a comprehensive 10-year plan of management which results from extensive input by stakeholders and broad consultation and approval by the Anangu community. The final draft is subject to a further 6-month review before being tabled in federal parliament and becoming law for its 10-year duration. Joint management brings together cultural and scientific knowledge and experience, and interweaves two law systems – Piranpa (white man) law and Tjukurpa. Working together means learning from each other, respecting each other's cultures and finding innovative ways to bring together different ways of seeing and interpreting the landscape and its people and their culture. Most importantly, however, from a sustainable tourism point of view, it ensures that the values of the place are preserved, that the stories and significance of the place are accurately interpreted and that the experience of the visitor is both authentic and relevant to the place he/she is visiting.

Larrakia Declaration and Indigenous Rights

This leads to my third key point – the need for fully cooperative, equitable and mutually beneficial participation of indigenous peoples in any activity that involves their culture, land or intellectual property. As a tourism leader in my country and in the Asia Pacific Region (where there is the greatest concentration of indigenous cultures in the world), I believe that the tourism industry has not only a great opportunity to embrace indigenous culture, but also a great responsibility to ensure that indigenous peoples are provided with opportunities for advancement and inclusion and are not exploited and subjugated through tourism. In March 2012, I was honoured to convene the first Pacific Asia Indigenous Tourism Conference, held on the traditional lands of the Larrakia people in Northern Australia, and attended by over 190 delegates from 16 countries. One of the important outcomes of this conference was the development and adoption of the Larrakia Declaration.

This declaration has since been adopted by the Pacific Area Travel Association and supported by the World Tourism Organisation (UNWTO). Its foundation is based on the United Nations Declaration on the Rights of Indigenous Peoples adopted on 7 September 2007.

The Larrakia Declaration recognises that:

- While tourism provides the strongest driver to restore, protect and promote indigenous cultures, it also has the potential to diminish and destroy those cultures when improperly developed.
- As the world becomes increasingly homogeneous, indigenous cultures will become increasingly important for tourism to provide differentiation, authenticity and the enrichment of visitor experiences.
- For indigenous tourism to be successful and sustainable, indigenous tourism needs to be based on traditional knowledge, cultures and practices and it must contribute to the well-being of indigenous communities and the environment.

- Indigenous tourism provides a strong vehicle for cultural understanding.
- Universal indigenous values underpin intergenerational stewardship of cultural resources and understanding, social interaction and peace.

The declaration thereby resolved to adopt the following principles:

- Respect for customary law and lore, land and water, traditional knowledge, traditional cultural expressions and cultural heritage that will underpin all tourism decisions.
- Indigenous culture, and the land and waters on which it is based, will be protected and promoted through well-managed tourism practices and appropriate interpretation.
- Indigenous peoples will determine the extent and nature and the organisational arrangements for their participation in tourism, and that their governments and multilateral agencies will support the empowerment of indigenous peoples in that regard.
- That governments have a duty to consult and accommodate indigenous peoples before undertaking decisions on public policy and programmes designed to foster the development of indigenous tourism.
- The tourism industry will respect indigenous intellectual property rights, cultures and traditional practices, the need for sustainable and equitable business partnerships and the proper care of the environment and communities that support that.
- That equitable partnerships between the tourism industry and indigenous peoples will include the sharing of cultural awareness and skills development which support the well-being of communities and enable enhancement of individual livelihoods.

Conclusion

In the context of the First UNWTO International Congress on Tourism and Pilgrimages 2014, I believe I can draw many parallels with many of the discussions and contributions I heard.

It is important in discussing either pilgrimage tourism or indigenous tourism that we are not just talking about ancient monuments, historic events or past beliefs. We are first and foremost talking about and dealing with living cultures, current and strongly held beliefs and real and contemporary values.

Note

(1) This chapter is the text of a presentation made to the UNWTO Conference on Tourism and Pilgrimage held in Santiago de Compostela, Spain, from 17 to 20 September, 2014.

3 Origins of Hospitality in Monastic and Christian Orders

Kevin O'Gorman

Introduction: Following in the Footsteps of Egeria

Egeria (also known as Etheroiua or Aetheria) was a Spanish woman, possibly a nun, who travelled to Jerusalem and the surrounding country in early AD 380, just 50 years after the death of Constantine, and her manuscript is the earliest detailed account of its kind. Her writing, known as the *Itinerarium Egeriae*, is a long letter addressed to her 'dear ladies', a circle of women in her spiritual community at home in Spain. Written at the end of her journey, this text is considered to be the earliest account of Christian pilgrimage; she describes her journey to Mount Sinai from Byzantium (now Istanbul, Turkey), then staying three years in Jerusalem and visiting Mount Nebo and the tomb of Job in Carneas (now Al-Shaykh Saad, Syria) and the Hagia Thekla near Seleucia Isauriae (now Silifke, Turkey), particularly venerated by women. Since Egeria, Christianity has been characterised by pilgrimage along recognised routes to the main centres of Jerusalem, Rome and Santiago. A massive industry grew up to support these pilgrims, the monasteries offering hospitality, while religious knights offered travel, banking and security.

Monasticism: Giving Hospitality to the Pilgrim

Monasticism itself was not a particularly novel concept; the Christian ascetic tradition on which the movement was founded can be traced directly back to the teachings of the New Testament (Matthew 19:21). There are pre-Christian examples to be found dating from the second century BC, with parallels in early Buddhist and Hindu writings. For example, Hindu merchants had an established and prosperous colony in Alexandria, the principal commercial and intellectual centre in the Mediterranean, if not the Western world (Clement, *Stromateis*, 1.71). The rapid growth of Christian asceticism coincided with the last of the great Roman persecutions of Christians to take place in Egypt; under the emperors Decius in AD 240 and Diocletian in AD 304, when many hundreds, if not

18

thousands, fled from the cities to avoid martyrdom. It is not unreasonable to assume that they would have formed the nuclei of what would quickly evolve into loosely organised communities.

In the 4th century, when St Basil organised Greek monasticism, he insisted upon community life, with meals, work and prayer, in common. With him the practice of austerity, unlike that of the Egyptians (Chaumartin, 1946), was to be subject to the control of the superior. He considered that wearing out the body with austerities, making it unfit for work, was a misconception of the scriptural precept of penance and mortification. His idea of the monastic life was the result of the contact of primitive ideas, existing in Egypt and the East, with European culture and modes of thought.

St Benedict is considered the founder of Western monasticism; he was born at Nursia, (better known by its Italian name 'Norcia') about AD 480 and died at Monte Cassino in AD 543. The only authentic life of Benedict of Nursia was that contained within the second book of St Gregory's 'Dialogues' (Migne, 1896). Benedict had lived the life of an eremite in the extreme Egyptian pattern; therefore, he was fully cognisant of the unsuitability of much in the Egyptian systems to the times and circumstances in which he lived (Regnault, 1990). Instead of attempting to revivify the old forms of asceticism, he consolidated the coenobitical life, emphasised the family spirit, discouraged all private venture in austerities and emphasised the importance of hospitality for pilgrims (Vogüé, 1977). He produced his Rule which provides the first principles of hospitality to be offered to travellers arriving at a Benedictine monastery.

Significance of the Rule

Benedict wrote the first ever 'Rule' for the organisation of large-scale hospitality. The most obvious principle, of course, is emblazoned at the very head of the chapter in the saying of Jesus, quoted from Matthew 25: 'I was a stranger and you took me in'; an encounter with Christ has to be expected in encounters with strangers and wayfarers. Two areas are key in Benedict's Rule: treatment of guests and management practice. Sensitivity must be shown to the guests and their needs, they are to receive a cordial welcome, be led into the centre of community life and given the opportunity to eat as honoured guests; the needs of the guests are of paramount importance. He also indicates that everyone has to be treated with kindness, but not all are to receive equal treatment, *'congruus honor'* i.e. greater honour is due to some, discrimination is based on ontological being; those who have committed themselves to be more like Christ have to be treated better, and this could be reflected in a hierarchy of accommodation. The posture of the monk before the guest is one of humility and receptivity. It is clear that the monk is there to aid the guest, who must not be seen as a hindrance to the lifestyle of the monastery. The reception of guests must not disrupt community life for those not directly involved with their care. Guests will be received on the community's terms; however, the rule of life of the monks may be altered slightly to accommodate the needs of the guest.

Benedictine hospitality as defined by Benedict

In Benedict's Rule, chapter 53 is entitled '*De Hopitibus Suscipiendis*' – 'The Reception of Guests' (see Figure 3.1; placing significance on the family spirit of the monastery and the reception of 'all' guests). In the second verse, there is the first of the qualifications regarding 'all'. *Congruus*

All guests who arrive should be received as if they were Christ, for He himself is going to say: 'I came as a stranger, and you received Me'; and let due honour be shown to all, especially those who share our faith and those who are pilgrims. As soon as a guest is announced, then let the Superior or one of the monks meet him with all charity, and first let them pray together, and then be united in peace. For the sign of peace should not be given until after the prayers have been said, in order to protect from the deceptions of the devil. The greeting itself, however, ought to show complete humility toward guests who are arriving or departing: by a bowing of the head or by a complete prostration on the ground, as if it was Christ who was being received. After the guests have been received and taken to prayer, let the Superior or someone appointed by him, sit with them. Let the scripture be read in front of the guest, and then let all kindness be shown to him. The Superior shall break his fast for the sake of a guest, unless it happens to be a principal fast day; The monks, however, shall observe the customary fasting. Let the Abbot give the guests water for their hands; and let both Abbot and monks wash the feet of all guests; after the washing of the feet let all present say this verse: 'We have received Your mercy, O God, in the midst of Your church'. All guests should be received with care and kindness; however, it is when receiving the poor and pilgrims that the greatest care and kindness should be shown, because it is especially in welcoming them that Christ is received. There should be a separate kitchen for the Abbot and guests, so that the other monks may not be disturbed when guests, who are always visiting a monastery, arrive at irregular hours. Let two monks who are capable of doing this well, be appointed to this kitchen for a year. They should be given all the help that they require, so that they may serve without murmuring, and on the other hand, when they have less to occupy them, let them do whatever work is assigned to them. And not only in their case but a similar arrangement should apply to all the jobs across the monastery, so that when help is needed it can be supplied, and again when the workers are unoccupied they do whatever they are required to do. Responsibility for the guesthouse also shall be assigned to a holy monk. Let there be an adequate number of beds made up in it; and let the house of God be managed by wise men and in a wise manner. On no account shall anyone who is not so ordered associate or converse with the guests, but if he should meet them or see them, let him greet them humbly, as we have said, ask their blessing and pass on, saying that he is not allowed to converse with a guest.

Figure 3.1 *De Hopitibus Suscipiendis* (Source: O'Gorman, 2010)

honor 'proper or due honour' means that not all receive the same honour; those in whom Christ is more readily recognised receive greater honour. There are two categories of person due particular honour: *domesticus fidei* and *peregrinis*. *Domesticus fidei* literally 'those who share our faith', the phrase appears at first sight to contrast Christians and non-Christians (cf. Galatians 6:10), but the phrase probably should be taken, in a narrower sense, to refer to clerics and monks. The Rule of Pachomius explicitly directs that clerics and monks are to be received with greater honour and that the phrase includes these and pious laymen – in fact, all who are connected with the house of God (monastery) 'by a certain connaturality with its religious ideal and the type of life led there' (Fry, 1981: 256).

The other category of person to whom particular honour is due are the *peregrini*. *Peregrinis* can mean 'pilgrim', 'visiting', 'strange' and 'foreign'. The context seems to favour the more technical meaning of 'pilgrim'; one who could possibly be understood as a subdivision of the *domestici fidei*. In verse 15 above, the fact that people were on a holy journey could single them out for special attention. Although pilgrimage, as a form of popular spiritual exercise, peaked after St Benedict's time (Leclereq, 1968), there is good evidence before his time for pilgrimage to the tombs of the martyrs and saints, especially at Rome, and to the Holy Places (Böckmann, 1988). In verse 15, the *peregrini* are associated with the poor in contrast to the rich, suggesting that they should be considered socially disadvantaged by being far from their own land and should therefore be the objects of special concern (Fry, 1981: 257).

Omni officio caritatis 'all charitable service' probably refers to cordial words and facial expressions, rather than concrete acts of hospitality. These latter will be described in the succeeding verses, but the former are extremely important for the morale of the guest. The duty of caring for the physical need of the guest actually counts for little, if it is carried out in an insensitive manner (Kardong, 1996: 423). Benedict then gives instruction on how a guest has to be received. *Primitus* 'first' is not a throwaway word, priority is given to prayers; emphasis is on the primacy of the spiritual in the dealings of monks with outsiders. The guest is received on the monastery's terms, not his own; when the monks put aside their religious character to deal secularly with seculars, the cloister is breached and true monastic hospitality is falsified.

Once purified by prayer, hospitality is truly a welcome given to Christ. The monks, who have followed Christ out of the world, recognise Christ in those who come from the world. Nowhere does Benedict repudiate the principle of withdrawal from the world, which requires that a protective membrane be maintained around the community. When this barrier is physically opened to admit a visitor, it is still kept in place by subtler means. *Socientur* is a very strong word, indicating a union of comrades (*socii*). Benedict sometimes uses it to mean incorporation into the monastic community (RB 61.6,8), but not in this context. It can still mean a spiritual bond on a deep level; the hospitality offered to strangers should not be merely a superficial crossing of paths but a real sharing of spiritual gifts (Kardong, 1996: 423).

From the 14th-century Congregation of Strasburg:

> Abbots are to guard against treating guests by imitating worldlings, and on the pretext of hospitality or regard for dignity, entertaining them lavishly or extravagantly. Toward all there should be proper consideration for the guest's state in life, as well as for monastic poverty and sobriety. (Sause, 1962: 600)

Prayer came before the peace; the reading of scripture precedes the meal. The guest is granted the supreme honour of being treated as a spiritual person, interested primarily in the word of God. The guest is being led deeper into the building and into the life of the community. Even though guests are not allowed into the cloister, to pray with the monks is to penetrate to the very centre of their life. Breaking the fast on his account, comes down to stating implicitly that he represents the bridegroom, in whose company there may not be fasting (Matthew 9:15).

From its earliest origins, monasticism considered hospitality so important as to override asceticism. This is made clear in many stories of the lives of the desert monks (Holzherr, 1982). However, the bending of the Rule when there are guests should not be allowed to disrupt community life. The washing of feet is a mark of hospitality, not uncommon in the early Church (1 Timothy 5:10; cf. Luke 7:44-45). This section closes with a specific mention of the poor; those in most need of hospitality.

The rest of the chapter, verses 16 to 24, is more pragmatic, even restrictive. It would seem that guests are never in short supply and can arrive at any time, but the monks need to try to minimise the disturbance to the community. There are three additional matters that are dealt with in this conclusion to the chapter: the guest's kitchen, their accommodation and communications with monks.

Verse 22 has two practical suggestions. *Ubi sint lecti strati sufficienter* 'let there be sufficient beds made up', the guesthouse should always be ready for travellers arriving fatigued from their journey; long delays in preparing the guesthouse would be a hardship for them. *Sapientibus et sapienter administretur* 'wisely managed by wise persons', the wisdom needed is not theoretical, but in the service of practical charity. This is not to deny, though, that in a given monastic situation, the guest master may give spiritual counsel. The term *administretur* 'managed' is important, for it contrasts with proprietorship: God is the owner of the house; the monks merely manage it (Kardong, 1996: 430).

From the 15th-century Congregation of Bursfeld:

In the guest rooms everything is to be kept clean, but simple, lest in striving too hard to please we displease. Without explicit permission, none of the brethren is to visit guests; permission is not granted to anyone for visits after Compline. (Sause, 1962: 600)

The chapter concludes with a strict instruction to the monks about contact with the guest, *ullatenus societur neque colloquatur* 'not to visit or speak with them'. This seemingly harsh restriction seems quite out of harmony with the spirit of the first half of the chapter. On the one hand, monasteries that are overrun by guests need to protect their monks from the curious. While on the other hand, there are garrulous monks in need of a sympathetic ear. Guests who come to the monastery for solitude should not have to provide that kind of listening service (Kardong, 1996: 431).

Evolution of Monastic Hospitality for Pilgrims

In the centuries immediately after Benedict, the hospitality afforded by monasteries was comprehensive as well as caring for pilgrims: it included lodging for travellers, accommodation and treatment for the sick and charitable services for the poor. There were few urban centres, and monasteries were the most stable and well-endowed institutions in the countryside and were needed for safe accommodation for long-distance travellers. The Rule of St Benedict has left its stamp upon all subsequent developments of monastic rule. The prominence of the guesthouse for pilgrims in all monastic buildings, beginning with the famous plan of St Gall in the 9th century, attests indirectly to how scrupulously this tradition was respected (Lenoir, 1856). In the Rites of Durham, there is an account of the splendour of their guesthouse and of the hospitality practised therein. The usual period during which hospitality was freely provided was two complete days; and some similar restriction, upon the abuse of hospitality, seems to have been prescribed by most of the orders, of friars, as well as monks (Thurston, 1910: 484).

Hospitality for pilgrims extended beyond the monastery into the great households, which, whether they were ecclesial or not, were responsible for providing hospitality; the level usually being governed by the status of the guest. Bishops, for example, have always enjoyed and enjoined a role in overseeing hospitality and directing poor relief. For example, if any priest was found to be lacking in hospitality, he could not be ordained a bishop (Gratian, *Distinctio XLII*; see Friedberg, 1879). There was a very close connection between clerical hospitality for pilgrims and the relief of the poor:

The word 'hospitality' is of some importance because the phrase most commonly used by the medieval canonists to describe the poor relief responsibilities of the parish clergy was tenere hospitalitatem - they were obliged, that is, to 'keep hospitality'. The primary sense of the word referred to the reception of travellers [pilgrims], the welcoming of guests, but the canonists very often used it in a broader sense to include almsgiving and poor relief in general. (Tierney, 1959: 68)

This led to abuses of hospitality with the pilgrims being forgotten. Hospitality was given in excess at one end of the spectrum, but it was also being forgotten about at the other. At a local level, clergy were working with minimal resources. In his work *Medieval Poor Law*, Tierney (1959) gives examples of exhortations to provide adequate hospitality and relief, and examples of concern that pastoral care included feeding the hungry and receiving guests. Parishioners were expected, but not forced, to pay tithes to the church from which funds for hospitality and relief for the poor were taken. Clergy were required to provide hospitality, but the record of their work was mixed. There were, of course, even more grave problems, as in many parishes the clergy were simply absent.

The Rise of the Knights: Developments in Religious Hospitality

The Benedictines were not the only religious order to concentrate on hospitality; certain orders like the Knights Hospitallers of St John of Jerusalem and the Knights Templar were largely given up to works of charity, hospitality, security and banking for pilgrims. After the (re) capture of Jerusalem in 1099, pilgrims travelled in greater numbers than ever before to visit the biblical sites of great religious significance, arriving first in Jaffa, but when travelling further afield they risked the open road and exposure to bandits and robbers. The route between Ramallah and Jerusalem was particularly dangerous; according to the Fulcher of Chartres 'the populace lived in a state of perpetual insecurity, always attentive to the trumpet blast which warned them of danger' (as cited in Barber, 1994: 3). Daniel, a Russian abbot, travelling the region during the period offers this description:

> . . . this place is very dreadful and dangerous. Seven rivers flow from this town of Bashan and great reeds grow along these rivers and many tall palm trees stand about the town like a dense forest. This place is terrible and difficult of access . . . And lions are found here in great numbers. (Wilkinson, 1988: 126)

The wilder regions of what is now called Jordan were often endured by pilgrims so that they could reach other prominent religious sites and consequently they ran a high risk of robbery and violence. This chaos combined with the pilgrim's needs for food, drink and accommodation underpinned the foundation of the Knights Templar and the Knights Hospitaller.

The Knights of St John, known as the Knights of the Order of the Hospital or Hospitaller Knights, were formed around 1050 in Jerusalem during the First Crusade, and after the conquest of Jerusalem, became a military order under its own charter. It exists today as 'The Sovereign Military Hospitaller Order of Saint John of Jerusalem of Rhodes and of Malta', also known as the Sovereign Military Order of Malta; the world's oldest surviving order of chivalry. It is headquartered in Rome and is widely considered by many countries to be a sovereign subject of international law and has been granted permanent observer status at the United Nations. Today, the order has about 13,000 members, 80,000 permanent volunteers and 20,000 medical personnel including doctors, nurses, auxiliaries and paramedics. The goal is to assist the elderly, handicapped, refugees, children, homeless, those with terminal illnesses and leprosy in five continents of the world, without distinction of race or religion. The Knights provided medicine and shelter to pilgrims, initially at the Hospitaller infirmary near the Church of the Holy Sepulchre in Jerusalem, but the order extended soon after to provide an armed escort, which grew into a substantial force (Barber, 1994). Despite the occupation of Jerusalem in July 1099 there were deficiencies in the occupational authority and this was most prevalent in an 'inability to secure the safety of travellers and pilgrims in the regions supposedly under Frankish control' (Barber, 1994: 3).

It is commonly held, although details and evidence are lost to history, that the Knights Templar were founded on Christmas Day 1119, in the Holy Sepulchre of Jerusalem. They named themselves 'The Poor Fellow-Soldiers of Christ and of the Temple of Solomon' (*Pauperes commilitones Christi Templique Solomonici*) and were commonly known as the Knights Templar, the Order of the Temple. Their founding charism and central purpose was 'to protect pilgrims along the perilous pilgrimage routes of the Middle East' (Reston, 2001: 12). The Templars entrusted that by undertaking this endeavour, they were purchasing their eternal salvation and defending the Pope; they believed that 'the Templar dead who had attained eternal life . . . had "consecrated their hands to God in the blood of the unbelievers"' (Partner, 1987: 9). This understanding and practice was derived from the teachings of St Bernard of Clairvaux where killing in the name of Christ was 'malecide not homicide' and thus to 'kill a pagan is to win glory for it gives glory to Christ' (Reston, 2001: 12).

It was St Bernard who validated and vindicated the hospitable practices of the Order of the Temple as 'men whose bodies were protected by iron and whose souls were clothed in the breastplate of faith' (Haag, 2009: 145).

This belief is echoed in the Fulcher of Chartres cited in Bongars 1905: 513 writing of Pope Urban II's speech: 'Let those . . . who are accustomed to wage private wars wastefully even against Believers, go forth against the infidels in a battle worthy to be undertaken now and finished in victory. Now, let those, who until recently existed as plunderers, be Soldiers of Christ'. The Order's initial success is clear from the Council of Troyes in 1128 where their work is acclaimed and followed by full papal recognition in 1129 (Partner, 1987). The Templars' existence was tied closely to the Crusades; when the Holy Land was lost, support for the Order faded. Deliberate rumours about the Templars' secret initiation ceremony created mistrust, and King Philip IV of France who was deeply in debt to the Order, took advantage of the situation. In June 1308, a papal inquiry into the Templars was held in the French city of Poitiers. Under interrogation, most probably including torture, 72 knights confessed heresy to Pope Clement V (*Inquisitiones contra Templarios in Romana Curia*, 1308a, 1308b, 1308c). Many of the Order's members in France were arrested, tortured and burned at the stake. The abrupt disappearance of the Order has, unsurprisingly, caused great speculation and corresponding legends to grow and develop which have kept the 'Templar' name alive. There is clear evidence in the Vatican Secret Archives contained in a document known as the 'Chinon Parchment' (1308) dated 17–20 August 1308 (wrongly filed in 1628 and rediscovered in 2001), that Pope Clement absolved the Templars of all heresies in 1308 before formally disbanding the Order in 1312 (Frale, 2004). With the publishing of the documents pertaining to the trial of the Templars (*Archivum Secretum Vaticanum*, 2007), the Catholic Church holds that the medieval persecution of the Knights Templar was unjust.

The Knights Templar provided safe passage and protection to pilgrims who, under their protection received hospitality, and in return the Templars saw this as a means of direct passage to heaven, exercising hospitality to their fellow Christians by considering their lives expendable to ensure the pilgrims' safety (Migne, 1899). Although the Templar Order began as a disparate collection of impoverished knights who pitied Christian pilgrims, they took up arms to defend them and excelled in their task. Their increasing immersion in commerce allowed for the establishment of a merchant fleet used to ship 'pilgrims, soldiers and supplies between Spain, France, Italy, Greece and Outremer' (Haag, 2009: 137). As their economic power grew, so did the tasks they took on; one account of carrying pilgrims from Marseille speaks of ships carrying 'up to a maximum of 1,500 pilgrims and any number of merchants' (Barber & Bate, 2002: 129). This saw the beginnings of the organised mass movement of pilgrims under the collaboration of the Templars and the Hospitallers, offering security, shelter and safety while travelling to an occupied land during turbulent and dangerous times (O'Gorman, 2013).

The Templars' international structure and considerable resources allowed them to initiate what became a European-wide banking system. Unsurprisingly, this 'use of the Temple for the deposit and transmission of funds gave it a new and unanticipated importance among feudal princes' (Partner, 1987: 11). Banking, the protection of assets and money, became a natural complement to their activities in the Holy Land, allowing them to protect pilgrims more fully. There was no stratification regarding who could use the Order's banking facility, and the Templars allowed borrowing too. For example, King John of England borrowed at the time of the *Magna Carta* in 1215; the last Latin Emperor of Constantinople, Baldwin II borrowed huge sums against supposed relics of the 'True Cross'; and Louis VII of France also borrowed to join the Second Crusade alongside the Templar Order. This led to the Templars effectively becoming the French monarchy's treasurers (Haag, 2009) as well as holding 'papal subsidies' and political donations towards their own endeavours in the Holy Land, a fateful role which ultimately led to their end. Their establishment as bankers was not only indicative of their trustworthy status in medieval society but conveyed their progressive thinking towards the task they had taken on in defending pilgrims. They moved on from not just protecting large volumes of pilgrims, but escorting them from docks on Western shores to the occupied lands in the East and ensuring the protection of their valuables until their arrival in Jerusalem, thus removing all threats and impracticalities inherent in carrying all one's personal valuables halfway around the known world on a road crawling with brigands. Instead, they allowed travellers to deposit their belongings for which they received a receipt bearing the Templar seal. In return, they could carry this to any other Templar bank and withdraw the amount denoted on the receipt, thus facilitating not only the physical movement of pilgrims into the Holy Land but also financial mobility that can be attributed to the Templars.

Reformation and the Decline of Religious Care for Pilgrims

In 1536 in England the act for the Dissolution of the Lesser Monasteries ordered the suppression of all religious houses which had an annual income of less than £200; it also covered, retrospectively, any previous suppressions; while the 1539 act for the Dissolution of the Greater Monasteries, vested all monastic property in the monarch. These two acts effectively ended monastic hospitality in the British Isles; this did not happen in isolation. In Germany and her Austrian dominions, the Treaty of Westphalia saw the confiscation of religious property to the benefit of Protestant princes and in later centuries a similar situation was to arise throughout the Iberian Peninsula, France and what would be considered modern-day Italy.

The Protestant reformers were attempting to redefine the practice of hospitality. They offered unrelenting critiques of the extravagance, indulgence and waste associated with late medieval hospitality. Heal (1990) emphasises that the clergy were also part of the ruling class, and had a particular role to play in affairs of state. Cardinal Wolsey was a bishop, but he was also King Henry VIII's Lord Chancellor, therefore his extravagance would have been expected as the King's principle minister. According to Pohl (1999), in their studies of scripture, Luther and Calvin gave limited but explicit attention to hospitality and to how it should be practiced in their own day. One of the beliefs of the Reformation was supposedly an enhanced appreciation for the value of so-called ordinary life. The Protestant reformers did not see, in the ancient sources, an apposite understanding of the church as an important location for hospitality; instead, they identified hospitality with the civic and the domestic spheres. 'The sacramental character of hospitality was diminished and it became mostly an ordinary but valued expression of human care' (Pohl, 1999: 53). The Protestant Reformation was to have a transforming effect on hospitality, hospitals, poor relief and responsibility to refugees. These became separated from their Christian roots as the state increasingly took over more responsibility.

> At the same time, the domestic sphere became more privatised; households became smaller, more intimate, and less able or willing to receive strangers. With little attention to the church as a key site for hospitality, the institutional settings for Christian hospitality diminished and the understanding of hospitality as a significant dimension of church practice nearly disappeared. (Pohl, 1999: 53)

An ecumenical council of the Roman Catholic Church which was convened in Trent and other towns for a period of about 40 years, in its 25th solemn session, decreed as a doctrine of faith:

> all who hold any ecclesiastical benefices, whether secular or regular, to accustom themselves, as far as their revenues will allow, to exercise with alacrity and kindness the office of hospitality, so frequently commended by the Holy Fathers; being mindful that those who cherish hospitality receive Christ in the person of their guests. (Denzinger & Schönmetzer, 1997: 75)

The Catholic Church and the counter-reformation within was emphasising the importance of hospitality. Nevertheless, the monasteries were on the decline and other forms of accommodation for travellers needed to be found.

Commercial hospitality was not born out of the decline of the monasteries; however, its growth and development has been inexorably linked to religion. In the gospel of Luke 2:7, *kataluma* can mean a room or 'dwelling', whereas *pandocheion* is used for an inn, a tavern or even a brothel. In the Gospel of Luke 10:35, for example, the 'Good Samaritan' brought the man, whom he had rescued, to a *pandocheion*. The parable makes clear that this *pandocheion* was a 'for profit' hostelry, as the Samaritan left money with the innkeeper to pay for the care of the invalid guest. The term *pandocheion* continued to be used later, in the Byzantine world, though it appears less frequently than the word *xenodochein*, which referred to a charitable hostelry for lodging strangers and the poor. Some of the *xenodocheia* association with good works seem to have been incorporated into the understanding of the Byzantine *pandocheion*, since, unlike those from antiquity, later *pandocheia* sometimes provided charitable hospitality. Others, however, continued to function as ordinary inns. Many Byzantine *pandocheia* were privately owned, though some were built in conjunction with churches or monasteries to lodge needy travellers (O'Gorman, 2010).

Polybius, while travelling in southern Italy, gives an early example of the perceived good value associated with commercial hospitality:

> ... the cheapness and abundance of all articles of food will be most clearly understood from the following facts: travellers in this country, who put up in inns, do not bargain for each separate article they require, but ask what is the charge per diem for one person. The inn-keepers, as a rule, agree to receive guests providing them with enough of all they require for half an as per diem, i.e. the fourth part of an obol, the charge being very seldom higher. (Polybius, cited in White, 1968: 23)

There has always been a link between pilgrimage and hospitality; Jerusalem and the Holy Places were not the only locations for pilgrimages. Canterbury was a famous centre of pilgrimage and there were a number of pilgrim inns, though traces of only a few of them can be found today. In 1299, the Germanic ambassador stayed in one such inn, on the occasion of the marriage of Edward I to his second wife Margaret, sister of Philip IV of France. The ambassador commented that 'the inns in England are the best in Europe, those of Canterbury are the best in England, and The Fountain, wherein I am now lodged as handsomely as I were in the King's Palace, the best in Canterbury' (cited in Borer, 1972: 32).

Until the decline of the monasteries and the improvements in the roads, lack of custom was holding up development of the inn before the 15th century. While pilgrims and vagrants enjoyed free charity and the nobility expected free hospitality, there could not be much general demand for good inns, given the comparatively few middle-class travellers. The decline of the monasteries was not the only factor in the growth of commercial hospitality; evolution in the transportation infrastructure was to play a large part in its development. In 1285, during the reign of Edward I, a statute was passed that stated:

> That Highways leading from one Market-Town to another shall be enlarged, where bushes, woods, or dykes be, so that there be neither dyke, underwood, nor bush whereby a Man may lurk to do hurt, within Two Hundred Foot of the one Side, and Two Hundred Foot of the other Side of the Way . . . that Offenders may not pass, ne return to do evil. (Edward I R, cited in Ruffhead, 1786: 114)

It is remarkable to note that this was the first legislation that dealt with roads that was enacted in the British Isles since the departure of the Romans in around AD 480. From that time, there had been no central authority to maintain the roads; most villages being connected by rough tracks, which became so muddy in winter that they were almost impassable. The roads between towns were no better; in Hertfordshire, the roads were so dangerous that the Abbot of St Albans provided a special armed patrol to accompany travellers on their way from St Albans to London.

Conclusion

The combined improvement in both coaches and roads led to the establishment of regular stagecoach services. These regular stagecoach routes in turn led to the evolution of 'coaching inns' and 'posthouses' on major routes servicing the coaching and mail industries. Originally, an inn would have been a farmhouse set by the roadside, and as such was self-supporting. 'Posthouses' took their name from the system of fixed posts in the ground that marked regular stopping places on main roads. From these posts, the farmers/innkeepers were able to anticipate the number of guests they would have to feed and predict the time of their arrival, but the smaller inns on less regular routes had greater difficulty with housekeeping. Already, location was to play an important part in the hospitality industry, as the fixed routes were to supply a steady flow of customers. Housekeeping and guest accommodation were important features; 'Fires must be made in empty rooms to keep them aired. Linen and blankets and bedding must be turned and dried. Windows and shutters, and candles and oil lights kept clean and bright for the influx of travellers, who would come in a bunch-suddenly-without warning' (Hartley, 1954: 410). It is also observed that there were even human resource management difficulties at that time 'for if one employed an ugly ill-favoured wench to serve, the travellers grumbled; and if one employed a pretty, lively wench, she got married!' (Hartley, 1954: 412). Thus, commercial and geographical factors had assumed priority over religious charity in the provision of hospitality.

Note

Biblical Quotations: New Testament quotes are translated from *Nestle-Aland Novum Testamentum Graece* (Nestle & Aland, 2006) which is the critical scholarly work redacted from over 5400 complete or fragmented Greek manuscripts. The most recent edition (2006) shows a nearly exhaustive list of variants but includes only the most 94 significant witnesses for each variant. It is from this edition that the quotes are translated.

(1) In recent years there has been a trend for monasteries and convents to offer commercial accommodation to tourists; the website www.monasterystays.com lists over 500 such places (Claworthy, 2016) suggesting old habits die hard, combined with generally lower prices at such institutions.

References

Archivum Secretum Vaticanum (2007) *Processus Contra Templarios*. Status Civitatis Vaticanae: Scrinum.

Barber, M. (1994) *The new knighthood. A history of the order of the temple.* Cambridge: Cambridge University Press.

Barber, M. and Bate, K. (2002) *The Templars: Selected Sources Translated and Annotated.* New York: Manchester University Press.

Böckmann, A. (1988) Xeniteia-Philoxenia als Hilfe zur Interpretation von Regula Benedicti 53 im Zusammenhang mit Kapitel 58 und 66. *Regulae Benedicti Studia 14/15*, 131–144.

Bongars, *Gesta Dei per Francos*, 1, pp. 382 f., trans in Oliver J. Thatcher, and Edgar Holmes McNeal, eds., *A Source Book for Medieval History*, (New York: Scribners, 1905), 513–17.

Borer, M.C. (1972) *The British Hotel Through the Ages*. London: Lutterworth Press.

Chaumartin, H. (1946) *Le Mal des Ardents et le Feu Saint-Antoine*. Vienne la Romaine: Les Presses de l'Imprimerie Ternet-Martin.

Chinon Parchment (1308) *Archivum Secretum Vaticanum Call No.: Archivum Arcis Armarium D 217*. Unpublished manuscript, Status Civitatis Vaticanae.

Claworthy, B. (2016) A heavenly way to see Italy's cities. *The Times*, 10 September, p. 31.

Denzinger, H. and Schönmetzer, A. (1997) *Enchiridion symbolorum definitionum et declarationum de rebus fidei et morum*. Freiburg/Basel/Rome/Vienna: Herder.

Frale, B. (2004) The Chinon Chart: Papal absolution to the last Templar, Master Jacques de Molay. *Journal of Medieval History* 30 (2), 109–134.

Friedberg, E. (ed.) (1879) *Decretum Magistri Gratiani: Corpus Iuris Canonici, Volume 1*. Leipzig: Bernhard Tauchnitz.

Fry, T. (1981) *RB 1980: The Rule of St. Benedict, In Latin and English with Notes.* Collegeville, PA: Liturgical Press.

Haag, M. (2009) *The Templars History and Myth*. London: Profile Books.

Hartley, D. (1954) *Food in England: A Complete Guide to the Food that Makes Us Who We Are*. London: Little, Brown.

Heal, F. (1990) *Hospitality in Early Modern England*. Oxford: Oxford University Press.

Holzherr, G. (1982) *Die Behediktsregel: Eine Anleitung Zu Christlichem*. Leben: Benziger.

Inquisitiones contra Templarios in Romana Curia (1308a) *Archivum Secretum Vaticanum Call No.: Archivum Arcis Armarium D 208*. Unpublished manuscript, Status Civitatis Vaticanae.

Inquisitiones contra Templarios in Romana Curia (1308b) *Archivum Secretum Vaticanum Call No.: Archivum Arcis Armarium D 209*. Unpublished manuscript, Status Civitatis Vaticanae.

Inquisitiones contra Templarios in Romana Curia (1308c) *Archivum Secretum Vaticanum Call No.: Archivum Arcis Armarium D 210*. Unpublished manuscript, Status Civitatis Vaticanae.

Kardong, T.G. (1996) *Together Unto Life Everlasting: An Introduction to the Rule of Benedict*. Richardton, ND: Assumption Abbey Press.

Leclereq, J. (1968) *The Spirituality of the Middle Ages*. London: Burns and Oates.

Lenoir, A. (1856) *Architecture Monastique*. Paris: Imprimerie Nationale.

Migne, J.P. (1896) *Sancti Gregorii Papæi cognomento Magni, opera omnia: ad manuscriptos codices Romanos, Gallicos, Anglicos emendata, aucta, et notis illustrate accurante J.P. Migne*. Paris: Garnier Fratres.

Migne, J.P. (1899) *Willelmi Malmesburiensis monachi opera omnia quæ varii quondam editores, Henricus Savilius et al. in lucem seorsim emiserunt Willelmi scripta, nunc primum, prævia diligentissima emendatione, prelo in unum collecta mandantur: accedunt Innocentii II et al. opuscula, diplomata, epistolæ*. Paris: Garnier Fratres.

Nestle, J. and Aland, K. (2006) *Nestle-Aland Novum Testamentum Graece*. Berlin: Deutsche Bibelgesellschaft.

O'Gorman, K.D. (2010) *The Origins of Hospitality and Tourism*. Oxford: Goodfellow.

O'Gorman, K.D. (2013) The Crusades, the Knights Templar, and Hospitaller: A combination of religion, war, pilgrimage, and tourism enablers. In R.W. Butler and W. Suntikul (eds) *Tourism and War* (pp. 39–48). Abingdon: Routledge.

Partner, P. (1987) *The Knights Templar and Their Myth*. Vermont, NE: Destiny Books.

Pohl, D.C. (1999) *Making Room: Recovering Hospitality as a Christian Tradition*. Grand Rapids, MI: Eerdmans.

Regnault, L. (1990) *La Vie Quotidienne de Pères du Désert en Egypte au IVe Siècle*. Paris: Hachette.

Reston, J. (2001) *Warriors of God*. New York: Broadway.

Ruffhead, O. (1786) *The statutes at Large: from Magna Charta to the end of the reign of King Henry the Sixth to which is prefixed a table of the titles of all the publick and private statues during that time [the Union of Great Britain and Ireland]*. London: Mark Basket.

Sause, B.A. (1962) *The Principles of Monasticism*. St Louis, MO: Herder.

Tierney, B. (1959) *Medieval Poor Law: A Sketch of Canonical Theory and Its Application in England*. Berkeley, CA: University of California Press.

Vogüé, A. (1977) *La Règle de saint Benoît, VII, Commentaire Doctrinal et Spiritual*. Paris: Les editions du Cerf.

White, A. (1968) *Palaces of the People: A Social History of Commercial Hospitality*. London.

Wilkinson, J. (ed.) (1988) *Daniel. The Life and Journey of Daniel, Abbot of the Russian Land*. London: Hakluyt Society.

4 Inspiration for Muslims to Visit Mosques

Razaq Raj and Kristel Kessler

Introduction

This chapter will discuss religious tourists' motivations for visiting mosques. The chapter will attempt to discuss, through research, how Muslim visitors are attracted to mosques and what they seek for themselves in modernity from a visitation to holy sites.

Within ever-changing global political landscapes, religion has retained a significant place as a social movement with a complexity of structures and functions that pervades cultures and traditions. The revival and visitation to pilgrimage sites have been witnessed in the world today. The rediscovery of pilgrimage to religious sites has changed the thinking and beliefs in the secular public space and introduced thinking in new forms to find spirituality and develop alternative religious movements.

The emerging notion of Islamic tourism is newly recurrent in the religious tourism literature and often offers interesting and challenging themes comprising outstanding ramifications. Its definition is in itself a justification to critically analyse and understand its components and meanings. Many researchers have attempted to define and characterise Islamic tourism by detailing its features and by distinguishing to whom this type of tourism actually caters. More recently, it has been defined by its purpose and scope, which seem to offer a better understanding of its significance. Indeed, the notion is presented as 'Muslims travelling to Muslim friendly destinations offering halal tourism options combining religious and cultural tourism oriented attractions' (Kessler, 2015: 23) encompassing a type of tourist, a place of travel, a way to travel and tourist activities.

The term *mosque tourism* has been legitimised as a religious tourism practice featuring religious- and non-religious-motivated visits to mosques incorporating several processes: Muslims visiting mosques as tourist attractions while travelling; Muslims attending prayers while travelling; and non-Muslims visiting mosques as tourists or knowledge seekers.

Scholars have published significant literature on the relationship between tourism and Islam in recent years (Al-Hamarneh & Steiner, 2004; Aziz, 2001; Battour *et al.*, 2010a, 2010b; Din, 1989; Raj, 2012; Sanad *et al.*, 2010; Stephenson, 2014; Timothy & Iverson, 2006; Zamani-Farahani &

Henderson, 2010). When considering Islam, it is important to present not only its principles but also its followers. Muslims currently represent 23% of the global population, totalling about 1.6 billion Muslims in 2010 and this figure is expected to rise to 2.2 billion by 2030. The largest number of Muslims can be found in Asia (60%), the Middle East and North Africa (20%), while significant Muslim minorities are recorded in other regions and countries: Europe (38.1 million), United States (8 million) and Canada (1 million) (Asif, 2011; Pew Forum, 2011). Muslim numbers are growing worldwide; they are perceived as a valid consumer group and represent a market with significant buying power, especially when considering the spending power of consumers from Gulf countries such as Saudi Arabia and the United Arab Emirates (UAE). Marketers have recognised their significance and have acknowledged their specific needs and requirements as a distinctive market, which is heavily led by faith. Indeed, Islam has an important place in Muslims' life regardless of their religiosity level. The principles of Islam provide followers with clear guidelines by which to live their lives while fully embracing their beliefs, following certain rituals, whereby their spiritual and secular lives are united under sharia law.

Muslim communities and their rituals are often misunderstood because of negative media headlines linking Islam to terrorist attacks or to terrorist groups such as Al Qaeda, ISIS, ISIL or DAESH, who, though unrepresentative of Islam and its teachings, proclaim themselves as The Islamic State, while following an extreme interpretation of sharia law through violence. This has had the effect of associating Islam with fanaticism, radicalism and anti-Western ideologies. Consequently, Muslims and Muslim countries are often misjudged and feared. This has huge impacts on the global tourism map and has changed the pattern of holiday destinations of Western, Muslim and Middle Eastern tourists. Indeed, Western tourists have increasingly selected non-Muslim destinations, especially after September 11 and the Arab Spring, while at the same time, Muslim tourists, feeling targeted themselves, have decided to travel regionally and turned to neighbouring countries or other Muslim countries in increasing numbers (Al-Hamarneh & Steiner, 2004). Intra-Arab and intra-Muslim travels have created and reinforced Islamic tourism. Accordingly, tourism developers have joined in by promoting and developing tourism and leisure products specifically targeted at Muslim communities, leading to the concept of Islamic tourism (see Chapter 11, this volume).

Muslim Communities

The term *Muslim* refers to a person who follows the religion of Islam, which is one of the three main monotheist religions along with Judaism and Christianity. Koeing *et al.* (2001: 18) defined religion as 'an organized system of beliefs, practices, rituals and symbols designed to facilitate closeness to the sacred or transcendent (God, higher power, or ultimate truth/reality)'. Consequently, religion is a very personal matter with the degree of practice varying greatly from one follower to another depending on one's level of religiosity (Delener, 1994; Essoo & Dibb, 2004; Sood & Nasu, 1995). Religion and human civilisation have a close relationship as they both often define a nation, its values, its institutions and its people (Fam *et al.*, 2004; Vukonic, 1996). Religiosity is another important notion in spirituality that is often mistaken with religion. The difference lies in the fact that religion is a continuum of commitment and beliefs representing a particular faith, while religiosity involves the level of importance and assiduity that one is willing to apply to the practice of his/her religion (Eid & El-Gohary, 2015; Weaver & Agle, 2002). We can therefore argue that religion shaped the world but that religiosity focuses on the followers' daily lives by shaping their attitudes, values, behaviours, practices, rituals and how they want to utilise them to give meaning to their existence and life in general (Eid & El-Gohary, 2015). Consequently, religion and religiosity are powerful in influencing human behaviour and decisions as well as potentially having significant impacts on tourism development and tourists' selections of places to visit (Delener, 1994; Essoo & Dibb, 2004; Sood & Nasu, 1995).

Muslim communities are diverse and complex, depending on the country in which they are based, the branch of Islam that they follow and also cultural, social, historical and personal variables. However, they agree on certain aspects, which define their beliefs and practices. The Quran, the Sunnah and sharia law are three crucial elements in the lives of Muslims and the organisation of their communities:

- *The Quran* is the holy book corresponding to Islam, which is considered to be the verbatim word of God as revealed to their main prophet Muhammad. The Quran is more than a religious or holy book; it is a manual for life for all Muslims.
- *The Sunnah* is comprised of Hadiths, which are collections of reports of teachings, deeds and sayings of the Prophet Muhammad.
- *Sharia law* is significant in Muslims' religious and secular practices, which are inextricable (Frishman & Khan, 2002; Ibrahim, 1997; Newby, 2002).

Indeed, the particularity of Islam is that religious and secular beliefs and domains are completely linked and fused with each other, which is very well illustrated by sharia law. 'Sharia' originally meant *'path leading to the water'*, which really has to be understood as *'way to the source of life'*. Sharia law is comprehensive and touches on all human activities by combining Western civil and criminal law, whereby human actions are categorised as obligatory, meritorious, indifferent, reprehensible and forbidden (Frishman & Khan, 2002). These have an important place in Islam as they guide the daily life of Muslims by providing a clear code of conduct to adopt in many areas (Saeed *et al.*, 2001). Officially, this is an Islamic legal system derived from the Quran and the Hadith. Consequently, Islam has a strong influence on its followers' life, as it is omnipresent and transcendent. It basically affects their spiritual and secular life by impacting on their way of life as individuals, communities and consumers.

Muslims strictly follow the five pillars of Islam, which are:

- Acceptance of the *Shahada*, a declaration that proclaims that *'there is no God but God* (and) *Muhammad is the messenger of God'*.
- Performing five *Salat* (prayers) a day.
- The act of *Zakat* which consists of donating 2.5% of annual income to charity.
- The act of *Sawm* (fasting), particularly during the holy month of Ramadan, which consists of abstaining from eating, drinking, smoking and sexual relations from sunrise to sunset. All Muslims are required to fast during the ninth lunar month of the Islamic calendar.
- Undertaking a pilgrimage to Mecca (Muhammad's birthplace) from the age of puberty at least once in a person's life if one is physically and financially fit to do so.

Whether followers have a high or a low level of religiosity, the five pillars are key to all Muslims and summarise clearly their beliefs and also their duties (Ali, 2003; Frishman & Khan, 2002; Ibrahim, 1997; Newby, 2002). Muslims have been recognised as a growing market and are now clearly labelled as consumers, consequently branding and marketing to gain and retain the Muslim market are required. As Power and Abdullah (2009) mention, Muslim consumers want brands that speak to them. Accordingly, branding for Muslim tourists should follow religious principles, enshrined in sharia law, which can be seen as an *Islamic code of life* establishing a social structure and providing moral guidelines for daily activities. This clearly states what is permissible or *halal*, and what is forbidden or *haram* (Al-Hamarneh & Steiner, 2004; Henderson, 2003; Sanad *et al.*, 2010; Stephenson, 2014). We have established that religion is an active element of Muslim consumers' choices; logically impacting on their tourist choices. Indeed, Islam consciously and unconsciously affects Muslims' selection of activities, transportation modes, accommodation, attractions and restaurants.

Islam and Tourism

The second most influential element in their tourist choices is linked to the worldwide geopolitical climate. Islam and Muslims have been at the centre of many media headlines, often of a negative nature as they are frequently associated with conservatism, fanatics, oppression, terrorism and anti-Western sentiment (Armstrong, 2001; Henderson, 2003). The September 11 attacks, the April 2013 Boston Marathon bombing, Boko Haram massacres and ISIS crimes, the 2015 attacks in Paris and Nice and the 2017 attacks in London have all been linked to Islam and Islam followers in the media, creating anti-Arab and anti-Muslim tendencies, which have been recorded by many scholars (Al-Hamarneh & Steiner, 2004; Henderson, 2003). These tendencies can be referred to as 'Islamophobia', which is defined as an irrational fear of Muslims, hatred of Islam and hostile behaviour toward Arab and/or Muslim individuals and communities. This growing anti-Muslim sentiment has a communitarianism effect, as Muslim communities feel unsafe and targeted and prefer to congregate within the Muslim sphere. This is directly affecting their residential, employment, education, social, leisure and travel choices (Stephenson & Ali, 2010).

Even though this phenomenon focuses on Muslim communities, it affects all countries as Muslim communities are growing in number and are located in all continents, and also because they are a powerful market which is in constant growth and holds significant purchasing power. For instance, in the travel and tourism industry, Muslims as a market represent US$126.1 billion, or 12.3% of the total global outbound tourism market for 2011 (Chinmaneevong, 2015). The Middle East and North Africa markets represent 60% of the total global Muslim tourist outbound expenditure in 2011, with Saudi Arabia as number one, followed by Iran, the UAE, Indonesia and Kuwait. In recent times, these Muslim tourists are changing their travel habits and redirecting their choices towards Muslim-friendly destinations, enabling them easy access to halal-friendly products and services and also to guarantee a genuine feeling of safety and freedom to be themselves on holidays, escaping from the increasing Islamophobia.

Islam is often perceived as a rather strict and rigorous religion involving many constraints, but it is important to realise that Islam and tourism are compatible. Indeed, Islam is not opposed to tourism, as the act of *travelling*, which can nowadays be associated with the notion of *tourism*, is clearly mentioned in several chapters of the Quran (Surah). Actually, *travelling* is explicitly encouraged and is perceived as a tool to acquire knowledge and contemplate the beauties of the world under certain conditions; this is why the acts of hajj (pilgrimage to Mecca, which is one of the five pillars of Islam), umrah (pilgrimage to Mecca and Madinah) and ziyarat (other religiously motivated trips to mosques, graves, caves or battlefields) are of great importance in Islam (Aziz, 1995; Hamza *et al.*, 2012; Henderson, 2003; Jafari & Scott, 2010; Zamani-Farahani & Henderson, 2010).

It is also important to mention that Islam is not incompatible with Muslim countries welcoming tourists from other countries and religions (Carboni *et al.*, 2014); however, conservative countries such as Saudi Arabia, Libya, Brunei and Iran have developed tourism mainly focusing on Muslim travel in order to preserve their cultural and religious values as well as limiting the potential immoral influences that Western tourism might have on the local communities (Aziz, 1995; Baum & Conlin, 1997; Din, 1989; Mansfeld & Winckler, 2008; Mathieson & Wall, 1990; Ritter, 1975; Robinson & Meaton, 2005; Sadi & Henderson, 2005; Zamani-Farahani & Henderson, 2010). Indeed, in the Quran it is mentioned that the traveller should be treated with compassion, as 'the conduct of Prophet Muhammad, both as host and guest, enjoins traits of humility, compassion, and a magnanimous degree of tolerance. Travellers, as the Prophet repeatedly said, must be accorded with the most selfless generosity' (Din, 1989: 18), implying that welcoming tourists in one's country is permitted and charitable. (See Chapter 3, this volume, for a comparison with the concept of hospitality in Christian religious communities.) Consequently, the Quran permits Muslims to travel to Muslim and non-Muslim countries for entertainment, religious and educational purposes as well as allowing Muslim countries to host tourists whether they are Muslims or not. Frequently, Western tourism is associated with lavishness, permissiveness and decadence, which can be in contradiction to some of the Islamic principles and way of life. Consequently, Islamic tourism, which is a fairly recent and emerging concept, seems like a positive alternative to the hedonic Westernised interpretation of tourism (Sonmez, 2001: 127). Thus, the relationship that tourism has with Islam is complex as are the ways that Islam influences tourism. This is why creating tourism products in response to the Muslim communities' needs is not an easy task and involves tangible and intangible elements, which can be classified under the broad concept of Islamic tourism (Henderson, 2010; Weidenfeld & Ron, 2008).

The Mosque as a Central Feature of Islamic Tourism

Mosques are linked to Islam and its rituals, thus it is important to fully understand the principles of Islam in order to realise the significance and purpose of mosques for Muslims and Muslim communities. Praying is an important part of every religious person; in Islam, prayers are one of the five pillars, which means that they are compulsory and very important in a Muslim's life.

The first obligation of a Muslim is to undertake worship on a regular basis in his/her house, mosque or any suitable place. This means observing the salaat five times a day at the proper times stated and prescribed in the Quran. The manner in which it is performed comes from the Sunnah of Prophet Muhammad. One of the essential principles to remember is that the salaat was given to the Prophet Muhammad by the Lord of the worlds (Allah) during the night of Miraj (Journey to heaven). It was a present to Prophet Muhammad (pbuh) from Allah, with the binding duty of undertaking salaat 50 times a day at the beginning, which was reduced to five times a day at the end – at the begging of the Prophet Muhammad (pbuh) during the night of Miraj on the advice of Prophet Moses. After the appeal of Holy Prophet Muhammad, Allah showed his mercy and blessing by announcing good news to the Holy Prophet Muhammad, reducing it to five daily prayers.

Ibn Maja, Ikametu's-Salah (p. 194) reports that Allah said:

O the Prophet (pbuh)! Allah abides by His word. You will get reward of fifty for the five.

The Holy Prophet Muhammad after returning from Miraj, announced to his people that Allah had given him the gift of five daily prayers for his followers:

Allah said: 'I enjoined the five daily prayers on your people. There is a pledge by Me. I will surely place those who perform the five daily prayers in time into the paradise. And there is no pledge by Me to those who do not keep these prayers'. (Ibn Maja, Ikametu's-Salah, 194)

These five daily prayers are a fundamentally important part of Muslim belief. There is a very clear wisdom behind undertaking the five prayers at specific times of the day. They are divided into different times to offer spiritual and bodily benefits for human beings, provided that the person who is offering the prayer is serious and is suitably prepared before standing to offer the prayer. Allah says in the Quran:

So (give) glory to Allah, when you reach eventide and when you rise in the morning; to him be praise, in the heavens and on earth; and in the late-afternoon and when the day begins to decline. (Surah Al Ar-Rum 30: 17–18)

The salaat consists of recitations from the Holy Quran and other glorifications of God by undertaking various bodily postures during all five salaats. Figure 4.1 outlines the five daily prayers.

These times correspond with the organisation of an individual's time around various activities that he/she performs during the day. The purpose of salaat is a multifaceted act of worship to keep the individual's relationship with his/her creator very close by offering salaat regularly. The salaat can be performed anywhere – in a mosque, at home, in one's place of work, outdoors or in any other clean place. It is essential for individuals

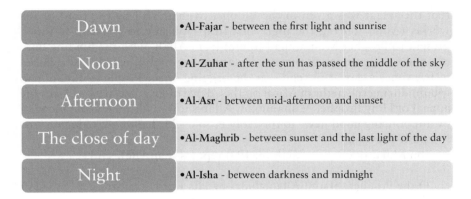

Figure 4.1 Names and times for daily prayers

to address and obey the obligatory acts of salaat. Figure 4.2 highlights the principle acts of salaat which need to be carried out by the individual during each offering of prayer.

The salaat can be offered either individually or in congregation. Congregational prayer is preferred to individual salaat because of its obvious aspects of brotherhood and solidarity. Muslims around the world have established mosques for congregational worship. The rewards of congregational prayers increase 25–27 times when the mercy of God descends. Praying in a mosque is considered preferable by the Messenger of Allah (upon him be peace). Ibn 'Abbas (may Allah be pleased with him) relates:

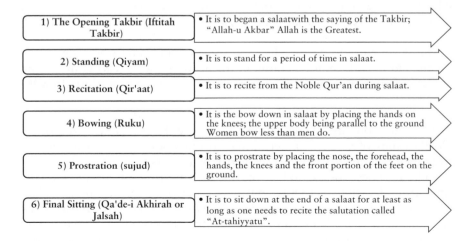

Figure 4.2 Principle acts of salaat

Mosques are the houses of Allah on the earth. They shine up to the inhabitants of the heavens just as the stars in the sky shine down to the inhabitants of the earth. (Tabarânî)

Once a mosque is erected and built by the local community, it will always be a mosque and the property of Allah. It cannot return to being the property of any person or community even those who may have paid to establish it. Mosques are very special places of worship, which cannot be sold for financial gain by individuals. The Messenger of Allah (upon him be peace) said,

All the earth will disappear on the Day of Judgment with the exception of the masjids for they will join with one another. (Suyûtî, Jâmi' al-Shaghîr)

Mosques are iconic Islamic edifices (AbulQaraya, 2015). The first mosque built was the Quba Mosque in Madinah (Saudi Arabia) by the prophet himself, which is currently one of the holiest mosques to pray in as part of a holy pilgrimage, bringing considerable reward to the person offering salaat (Raj, 2012). Prayers follow certain rituals and can be undertaken in a house, mosque or any suitable place that is considered 'clean', even if praying in a mosque is usually preferred. They can be performed individually or collectively; however, congregational prayers are encouraged as these bring forward the notions of brotherhood and solidarity among the Muslim community adherents called 'ummah' (Raj, 2012). They are supposed 'to offer benefits for human spiritually and bodily' (Raj, 2012: 98) because they can bring God's forgiveness and life's pleasure when properly performed. This duty is mandatory even when travelling but can be condensed from five daily prayers to two shortened ones. Consequently, the availability and easy access to mosques are of great importance to Muslim tourists.

Apart from being a place of worship, mosques are also social and gathering locations within a neighbourhood as well as being utilised as education centres (Taib & Rasdi, 2012). Building a mosque is an important event within a community and needs to follow certain criteria in terms of site planning and design. The mosque should ideally be located within a residential area easily accessible by public transportation with its entrance visible from the street, adjacent to parking facilities and located on elevated land easily expandable in the future if required (Kahera et al., 2009). Unfortunately, many modern mosques have lost their essence and original purpose, which was to cater for a community, because of political and social changes within modern Muslim society. Indeed, nowadays, mosques are built as iconic buildings and landmarks as a nation's statement of its grandeur, architectural supremacy and power, with emphasis on aesthetics rather than functionality (Frishman & Khan, 2002; Spahic, 2002; Taib & Rasdi, 2012). Mosques following their original purpose and therefore their function in the Quran are labelled as 'sustainable mosques' as they combine sustainable communal mosque design and sustainable multifunctional communal usage in order to enhance the quality of life of the community by reflecting the true teachings of Islam as stipulated in the Quran and Hadith, regardless of the fact that they are located in a Muslim or non-Muslim country (Baharudin & Ismail, 2014). The building itself and its architecture are important as a mosque is the Islamic building par excellence, and as such the key to Islamic architecture (Hillenbrand, 1994). A mosque is characterised by the presence of a dome, a minaret, a mihrab and a minbar, which cannot be omitted, as it would distort the main function of the building and therefore tarnish its sacredness (Frishman & Khan, 2002; Taib & Rasdi, 2012). As a result, mosques can be compared to a community centre where their purpose is to serve a community and answer their needs. In modern society, their purpose has slightly evolved with the development of facilities within each city and focus more on aesthetics than functionality in an effort to make a statement by building a grand iconic building symbolising a nation and its capabilities (Frishman & Khan, 2002; Spahic, 2002; Taib & Rasdi, 2012). Nonetheless, according to the Quran, mosques should cater for and serve their community (AbdulQaraya, 2015; Taib & Rasdi, 2012) and should be labelled 'sustainable mosques' (Baharudin & Ismail, 2014) when they achieve a 'sustainable communal mosque design, sustainable multi-functional communal usage in order to enhance the quality of life of the community' (Kessler, 2015: 24). It used to be a place to teach religious and secular subjects, to settle community disputes, to use the library, to rest in a clean and safe environment and to provide food, water and shelter for the poorest. It was also a place where news and regional or international information were announced as well as being a place for celebrations. In time, as Muslim nations and their communities became bigger and mosques started to be built in greater numbers in each city, their role started to change. Indeed, in Muslim countries those roles are now left to the largest mosques. In the West, interestingly, while Muslim communities may have an abundance of 'Muslim-friendly' or 'halal-friendly' facilities such as schools, shopping areas or restaurants, mosques are places that maintain their sense of identity forming an Islamic centre containing religious, community and teaching facilities. They are places that bring Muslims together to develop their sense of identity and belonging as well as enabling them to create a bond with God and to keep their spirituality alive. Consequently, mosques are central to the Arab world, the Muslim world and Muslims in general not only as a place in itself but also as a symbol of a faith that brings people together and serves a community.

A great example of a 21st-century mosque blending tradition with modernity is the Sultan Qaboos Grand Mosque in Oman, which opened in 2001. The Grand Mosque is open to Muslims and non-Muslims, who can use the well-appointed library with modern equipment to facilitate research and knowledge distribution and learn Arabic and Islam. It allows Muslims to pray and offers seminars and lectures on religious and some secular topics as well as allowing tourists (Muslims or not) to visit the mosque premises outside of prayer times. Tourists are welcome to enter the visitor centre to talk with the mosque volunteers on topics related to Islam, Oman, their way of living or any other topics that such a visit might raise. A wide variety of mosque designs and styles exist in the world based on their location since mosques serve as the single most important visible representation of Muslim identity and values (Frishman & Khan, 2002). A mosque is a building and a functional space: the building is a prayer house catering for Muslim followers but essentially it carries out the functions of a community centre for the ummah. It is a grand building, a symbol of Islam and its teachings, and consequently attracts people of diverse interests.

According to AbulQaraya (2015), mosques have three main functions: monotheistic, socialisation and communicative. The core of a mosque is its monotheistic function as it is primarily a religious and spiritual building representative of the followers of Islam, which is one of the three monotheist religions, with Judaism and Christianity. This function is linked to the notion of worship, adoration and prayer and is divided into three levels: individual, national and global with specific goals and a target audience. The individual level promotes monotheism and its main principles including the teaching and ritual involved in Islam. The national level relates to the notion of ummah, which refers to the Muslim community as a whole, which could be described as a group of people united on a brotherly journey in Islam. This sense of community is reinforced by the mandatory Friday prayers, collective prayers and Eid prayers. Finally, the global function is an invitation to the world, especially non-Muslims, to understand Islam and its message. Secondly, the mosque has a socialisation function and is presented as a centre to gather for educational activities that benefit its community. This is a place enabling knowledge and values to be transferred 'Through . . . tolerance'. Not only does it help to gain knowledge but it also produces it, which can be regarded as being the equivalent to modern universities. Lastly, the final function involves social communication by linking knowledge seekers and individuals belonging to different social classes: it's a tool that allows social barriers to be broken. Accordingly, the mosque is an important Islamic edifice with a central place in Islam, in Muslim countries and non-Muslim countries with Muslim neighbourhoods and communities. It can be seen as an instrument attracting visitors to pray, to gain and spread knowledge, to promote Islam and its values, to unite the ummah and to provide a multipurpose gathering space. Consequently, it has religious, social, educational and intellectual purposes.

Similarly, Kessler (2015: 23) argues that the mosque and its various functions can be found on every axis of Islamic tourism as detailed below:

- Economic axis: The Muslim market, meaning the Muslim community is attached to the mosque as a place of worship and the centre of the Islamic city or the centre for the Muslim diaspora residing in non-Muslim countries.
- Geographic axis: Mosques are an omnipresent feature of the Arab and the Muslim world and can be found in large numbers in all those destinations.
- Religious axis: Mosques are a key element in Islam and are crucial to Muslims' practice of their faith.
- Cultural axis: Mosques are a symbol of Islam and the spread of Islam. They are part of history and are important heritage sites of architectural, historical, aesthetic and artistic value.

Hence, a mosque is a lighthouse for moderation and religious tolerance used as channels to transmit the values and virtues of Islam by accurately portraying cultural and religious practices. This promulgates the mosque as a tool to interpret and understand a nation, its people and their lifestyles (AbulQaraya, 2015). This is why it has considerable tourist potential to attract Muslim and non-Muslims tourists and enables a wide range of activities on its grounds. This concept has been labelled 'mosque tourism' and includes all tourists' visits to mosques while travelling away from home, especially when they can be categorised as Islamic tourism practices.

Legitimising the Term 'Mosque Tourism'

Mosques are sacred buildings in Islam and entering or simply 'being' in a mosque outside of prayer times counts as a 'good deed' (Frishman & Khan, 2002). Spanning many centuries of history and an undeniable symbol of beauty, architectural splendour and devotion, mosques are found in every neighbourhood in Muslim countries and in the main cities of non-Muslim countries. Many are only open to Muslims but some can be visited by non-Muslims outside of prayer times. They are part of those countries' heritage and landscape and can for the Western eye be visual wonders full of mystery and oriental myth. The scale and grandeur of some mosques have transformed those sacred community centres into tourist landmarks and 'must-see' attractions, part of exploring a tourist destination, reflecting the country's cultural, historical and architectural aspects. Consequently, tourists often visit a mosque as part of their holiday without religious motivation, even if the primary purpose of the mosque is a spiritual one. Interestingly, even tourists who do not physically enter a mosque to visit it are touched by their presence as mosques in Muslim countries form part of the scenery and the sense of place (Henderson, 2003). One of its most visible and audible elements is the minaret, the tower where the call to prayer 'Adhan' is performed, which can be compared to church bells in countries of Christian tradition, to summon the faithful to prayer (Frishman & Khan, 2002: 11). Mosques are composed of various elements that are important for religious rituals and are recognisable by their architectural features. Mosques have the following features:

- The prayer hall: A demarcated space partly roofed and partly open to the sky to accommodate the congregation at prayer times.
- The Qibla wall: A prayer hall must have a wall facing Mecca.
- The Mihrab: A niche, which is the central and most decorated feature of the mosque, usually located in the centre of the Qibla wall.
- The Minbar: A pulpit positioned at the right of the Mihrab allowing the Iman leading the prayer to deliver his oration.
- The Qubba: A dome that is the symbolic representation of the vault to heaven.
- The ablution area.
- The Minaret: A tall tower from which the call for prayer 'adhan' is performed.

Additionally, mosques are decorated with calligraphy, geometric patterns and Quranic quotations, which serve to indicate that the building is sacred and to convey a spiritual message to passers-by and people coming to pray. Decorative geometric patterns serve to enrich and beautify the interior. Such patterns create an atmosphere favouring meditation and prayer as well as having metaphysical significance (Frishman & Khan, 2002).

Henderson (2003) suggests that a mosque itself may be considered a tourist attraction if it is unique and outstanding. Indeed, throughout the Muslim world many mosques known for their majesty have become tourist attractions. Some of those tourist mosques are no longer houses of prayers but some manage to establish a dual usage and purpose. The Grand Mosque of Paris, which opened in 1926, is the oldest mosque in France and is a focal point for the French Muslim community as well as being a famous Parisian landmark visited by tourists. It comprises a library, a conference hall, a madrassa (school), a prayer hall, a 3500 square meter garden and annexes include an oriental restaurant, a teahouse, a woman-only hammam and a shop. Adults and children are able to learn Arabic, Quran and Islam principles in its madrassa. In addition, it hosts many events such as book fairs of Muslim literature in Arabic and French, religious conferences and lectures, Muslim community celebrations as well as having a halal service centre informing and training on what is permitted in halal product consumption. Finally, tourists are welcome to visit the mosque and its gardens, which benefit from gorgeous mudejar architecture and calligraphy decorations, following the Iberian style influenced by the Moors.

All of the Organisation of Islamic Cooperation (OIC) top halal destination countries have engaged in different tourism development strategies featuring different types of tourism and tourist policies. But, they all have one feature in common: mosques. As Muslim countries, mosques are part of their landscapes and of their history. It would be impossible to visit Djerba in Tunisia, which is principally a beach resort island, without passing by 1 of its 365 mosques scattered across its 514 square kilometres. They are part of each country and its essence. From a tourist point of view, many of them are key landmarks and central tourist points of interest. Figure 4.3 lists the main mosques that are tourist attractions in the top OIC halal-friendly destinations, to illustrate the importance of this building as a tourist attraction. Indeed, many of the listed mosques are 'must-see' attractions and well-known landmarks as well as being symbols for Muslim communities of those countries. In addition, the three most sacred religious tourism and pilgrimage sites for Muslim communities are Mecca, Medina and Jerusalem, which are sites built around a holy mosque that is a primary attraction of religious tourists on their ground. Mosques are therefore essential sacred sites in Islamic tourism.

Top Halal Travel destinations	Key Mosques
Brunei	Jame Asr Hassanil Bolkiah Mosque / Sultan Omar Ali Saifuddin Mosque
Egypt	Mosque of Ibn Tulun / Al Hakim Mosque / Al-Azhar Mosque / Sultan Hassan Mosque / Alabaster 'Mohammad Ali' Mosque / El Mu'ayyad Mosque 'Red Mosque' / Abdel Monaem Read Mosque / The citadel of Saladin (including 3 mosques)
Indonesia	Istiqlal Mosque 'Independence Mosque' (Jakarta) / Cut Mutiah Mosque (Jakarta) / Baiturrahman Grand Mosque 'Masjid Raya' (Sumatra)
Jordan	King Abdullah I Mosque / The mosque of Mazar / King Hussein Bin Talal Mosque / Abu Derwish Mosque
Malaysia	Putra Mosque / Crystal Mosque / Kota Kinabalu city Mosque / State Mosque / National Mosque 'Masjid Negara' / Putrajaya Mosque / Zahir Mosque / Masjid Jamek / Masjid Ubudiah 'Perak's Royal Mosque' / Masjid Bahagian Kuching
Morocco	Hassan II Mosque Casablanca / Kutubiyya Mosque in Marrakesh
Qatar	Blue 'State Grand' Mosque, Katara Mosque / the Golden Mosque / Sheikh Muhammad Ibn Abdul Wahhab Mosque
Saudi Arabia	Al Masjid Al Nabawi the prophet's Mosque / Al-masjid Al-Haram (Hosts the Kabba in Mecca = Most sacred site in Islam) / Jeddah Floating Mosque / Jawatha Mosque / Masjid al-Qiblatain (Medina) / Madina Quba Mosque (Oldest mosque in the world)
Tunisia	Qairawan Great Mosque 'Sidi Oqba' / Mosque of the Barber 'Zaouia Sidi Sahab' Kairouan / Kairouan Mosque of three doors 'Djeema Tleta Bibane' / Kairouan Mosque of the Sabres 'Zaouia Sidi Amor Abbada' / Sousse Great Mosque of Sousse / Tunis Al Zaytuna Mosque.
Turkey	Aya Sofya Mosque (Istanbul) / Blue Mosque (Istanbul) / Istanbul new Mosque / Suleymaniye Mosque (Istanbul)/ Green Mosque / Eyup Sultan Mosque (Istanbul) / Aslanhane Mosque (Ankara) / Beyazit Mosque (Istanbul) / Sultan Ahmed I Mosque (Istanbul) / Sehzade Mosque
UAE	Sheikh Zayed Grand Mosque (Abu Dhabi) / Al Bidyah Mosque (Fujairah) / Jumeirah Mosque (Dubai) / Alnour Mosque (Sharjah).

Figure 4.3 Key sacred sites mosques in the OIC top halal tourist destinations

It is interesting to note that many World Heritage Sites of cultural importance listed by the United Nations Educational, Scientific and Cultural Organisation (UNESCO) are mosques, reinforcing their importance on historical, architectural, religious and tourist bases. Historic Cairo features the Al Azar Mosque and Morocco, the Kutubiya, which are beautiful buildings full of history. The Suleiman Mosque and Selimiye Mosque in Istanbul are well-known landmarks; similarly, the great city of Kairouan in Tunisia is called the city of 50 mosques and is referred to as the spiritual house of all Tunisians and the fourth most holy city after Mecca, Medina and Jerusalem. Certainly, mosques are central features in Islam and the Arab world. Long-standing tourist destinations such as Egypt and Tunisia have always recognised the importance of their mosques from a tourist point of view and have promoted them to tourists by including them in their cultural itineraries and excursions portfolio. Recently developed tourist destinations have also understood the importance of those iconic buildings in their scenery and tourist attraction development.

Indeed, each Gulf country has built a colossal mosque, a symbol of their grandeur and their ability to master the construction of a huge and magnificent building, often competing with their Khaleeji neighbours. Oman built the Sultan Qaboos Grand Mosque in 2001, which was at the time the biggest mosque in the Middle East with a capacity of 20,000 worshippers, setting a world record for the world's second-largest hand-woven carpet and chandelier. Six years later, this was dethroned by Sheikh Zayed Grand Mosque in Abu Dhabi, which can currently host 40,000 worshippers. Most of those mosques have a dual usage as they are used by worshippers for prayers and other activities, while they also cater for tourists at specific times, outside of prayer times. Accordingly, the Sultan Qaboos Grand Mosque in Oman can be visited free of charge from 8am to 11am from Saturday to Thursday and features an 'information centre' managed by volunteers, where tourists can ask questions about the mosque and learn about Islam, Oman and its inhabitants. Coffee, fresh mineral water and Omani dates are served and free books and CDs in various languages are distributed on topics such as women and Islam, understanding the Quran, the prophets and similarities and differences of Islam with Judaism or Christianity, in a very informal and welcoming atmosphere (El Amrousi & Biln, 2010).

Conclusion

This chapter is a valuable step in presenting the term 'mosque tourism' and the mosque itself as a central element in Muslims' lives. Undeniably, Muslims' inspirations to visit mosques are to undertake religious tourism and cultural tourism, to use its community gathering mechanism and to openly display pride in those accomplishments.

Mosques have been central buildings through history with the spread of Islam and are still central elements in today's Muslim world. They are the tools of Islam transmission and stand majestically as a bounding instrument within Muslim communities. Their main purpose is to be a prayer house for Islam followers and, as such, mosques are religious sites of a sacred nature with great spirituality and religiosity. However, similarly to the transcendence of Islam, mosques effortlessly combine sacred and secular domains in an effort not only to represent but also to serve the Muslim communities in Muslim and non-Muslim countries.

Therefore, Muslims have several motives to visit mosques and their inspirations are multidisciplinary. Consequently, Muslims primarily visit mosques to pray and perform religious rituals to sustain a certain level of religiosity and religious duty. This also allows them to be close to God and to the ummah when attending congregational prayers or functions. Mosques are iconic buildings of Muslim nations, which take pride in building and promoting the grandeur of their edifices symbolising the capacity and values of the nation.

Their educational and gathering features seem to attract Muslims who are very eager to engage with the ummah and learn in a spiritually welcoming atmosphere. They visit mosques to use the on-site facilities such as the library, computer labs and gardens as well as to attend religious- and non-religious-related conferences, lectures, exhibitions and classes; thus, mosques are of great personal, community, political and religious significance, as well as sometimes being tourist attractions.

References

AbulQaraya, B. (2015) The civic and cultural role of Sheikh Zayed Grand Mosque. *Procedia – Social And Behavioral Sciences* 211 (1), 488–497.

Al-Hamarneh, A. and Steiner, C. (2004) Islamic tourism: Rethinking the strategies of tourism development in the Arab world after September 11th 2001. *Comparative Studies of South Asia, Africa and the Middle East* 24 (1), 173–182.

Ali, A.Y. (2003) *The Holy Qu'ran* (translation). New Delhi: Goodword Books Pvt. Ltd.

Armstrong, K. (2001) *Islam: A Short History*. London: Phoenix Press.

Asif, A.S. (2011) Opinion: Pakistan export potential in global halal market. Halal Focus. See http://halalfocus.net/opinion-pakistan-export-potential-in-global-halal-market/ (accessed 15 May 2015).

Aziz, H. (1995) Understanding attacks on tourists in Egypt. *Tourism Management* 16, 91–95.

Aziz, H. (2001) The journey: An overview of tourism and travel in the Arab Islamic context. In D. Harrison (ed.) *Tourism and the Less Developed World: Issues and Case Studies* (pp. 151–160). Wallington: CABI.

Baharudin, N.A. and Ismail, A.S. (2014) Communal mosques: Design functionality towards the development of sustainability for community. *Procedia – Social and Behavioral Sciences* 153, 106–120.

Battour, M.M., Ismail, M.N. and Battor, M. (2010a) The impact of destination attributes on Muslim tourist's choice. *International Journal of Tourism Research* 13 (6), 527–540.

Battour, M.M., Ismail, M.N. and Battor, M. (2010b) Toward a halal tourism market. *Tourism Analysis* 15 (4), 61–70.

Baum, T. and Conlin, M. (1997) Brunei Darussalam: Sustainable tourism development within an Islamic cultural ethos. In F. Go and C. Carson (eds) *Tourism and Economic Development in Asia and Australasia* (pp. 91–102). London: Cassell.

Carboni, M., Perelli, C. and Sistu, G. (2014) Is Islamic tourism a viable option for Tunisian tourism? Insights from Djerba. *Tourism Management Perspectives* 11, 1–9.

Chinmaneevong, C. (2015) TAT ready to welcome Muslim visitor. *Bangkok Post*, 2 March. See http://www.bangkokpost.com/print/486250/ (accessed 15 March 2017).

Delener, N. (1994) Religious contrasts in consumer decision behavior patterns, their dimension and marketing implication. *European Journal of Marketing* 28 (5), 33–36.

Din, K.H. (1989) Islam and tourism: Patterns, issues, and options. *Annals of Tourism Research* 16 (4), 542–563.

Eid, R. and El-Gohary, H. (2015) The role of Islamic religiosity on the relationship between perceived value and tourist satisfaction. *Tourism Management* 46, 477–488.

El Amrousi, M. and Biln, J. (2010) Muscat emerging: Tourism and cultural space. *Journal of Tourism and Cultural Change* 8 (4), 254–266.

Essoo, N. and Dibb, S. (2004) Religious influences on shopping behaviour: An exploratory study. *Journal of Marketing Management* 20 (7–8), 683–712.

Fam, K.S., Waller, D.S. and Erdogan, B.Z. (2004) The influence of religion on attitudes towards advertising of controversial products. *European Journal of Marketing* 38 (5/6), 537–555.

Frishman, M. and Khan, H. (2002) *The Mosque: History, Architectural Development & Regional Diversity*. London: Thames & Hudson.

Hamza, I.M., Chouhoud, R. and Tantawi, P. (2012) Islamic tourism: Exploring perceptions and possibilities in Egypt. *African Journal of Business and Economic Research* 7 (1), 85–98.

Henderson, J.C. (2003) Managing tourism and Islam in Peninsular Malaysia. *Tourism Management* 24 (4), 447–456.

Henderson, J.C. (2010) Sharia compliant hotels. *Tourism and Hospitality Research* 10 (3), 246–254.

Hillenbrand, R. (1994) *Islamic Architecture*. Edinburgh: Edinburgh University Press.

Ibrahim, I.A. (1997) *A Brief Illustrated Guide to Understanding Islam* (2nd edn). Darussalam: Houston.

Jafari, J. and Scott, N. (2014) Muslim world and its tourisms. *Annals of Tourism Research* 44, 1–19.

Kahera, A., Abdulmalik, L. and Anz, C. (2009) *Design Criteria for Mosques and Islamic Centres. Art, Architecture and Worship*. London: Routledge.

Kessler, K. (2015) Conceptualizing mosque tourism: A central feature of Islamic and religious tourism. *International Journal of Religious Tourism and Pilgrimage* 3 (2), 11–32.

Koeing, H.G., McCullough, M.E. and Larson, D.B. (2001) *Handbook of Religion and Health*. New York: Oxford University Press.

Mansfeld, Y. and Winckler, O. (2008) The role of the tourism industry in transforming a rentier to a long-term viable economy: The case of Bahrain. *Current Issues in Tourism* 11 (3), 237–267.

Mathieson, A. and Wall, G. (1990) *Tourism, Economic, Physical & Social Impacts*. Harlow: Longman.

Newby, G.D. (2002) *A Concise Encyclopedia of Islam*. Oxford: One World.

Pew Forum (2011) The future of the global Muslim. See http://www.pewforum. org/2011/01/27/the-future-of-the-global-muslim-population/ (accessed 15 May 2015).

Power, C. and Abdullah, S. (2009) Buying Muslim. *Time South Pacific* (Australia, New Zealand edition) 173 (20), 31–34.

Raj, R. (2012) Religious tourist's motivation for visiting religious sites. *International Journal of Tourism Policy* 4 (2), 95–105.

Ritter, W. (1975) Recreation and tourism in the Islamic countries. *Ekistics* 40 (236), 149–152.

Robinson, A.J. and Meaton, J. (2005) Bali beyond the bomb: Disparate discourses and implications for sustainability. *Sustainable Development* 13 (2), 69–78.

Sadi, M. and Henderson, J.C. (2005) Tourism in Saudi Arabia and its future development. *Journal of Business and Economics* 11, 94–111.

Saeed, M., Ahmed, Z.U. and Mukhtar, S.M. (2001) International marketing ethics from an Islamic perspective: A value-maximization approach. *Journal of Business Ethics* 32 (2), 127–142.

Sanad, H.S., Kassem, A.M. and Scott, N. (2010) Tourism and Islamic law. In N. Scott and J. Jafari (eds) *Tourism and the Muslim World: Bridging Tourism Theory and Practice* (pp. 17–30). Bingley: Emerald.

Sonmez, S. (2001) Tourism behind the veil of Islam: Women and development in the middle east. In Y. Apostolopoulos, S. Sonmez and D.J. Timothy (eds) *Women as Producers and Consumers of Tourism in Developing Regions* (pp. 113–142). Westport, CT: Praeger.

Sood, J. and Nasu, Y. (1995) Religiosity and nationality: An exploratory study of their effect on consumer behavior in Japan and the United States. *Journal of Business Research* 34 (1), 1–9.

Spahic, O. (2002) *Studies in The Islamic Built Enviroment*. Kuala Lumpur: International Islamic University Malaysia.

Stephenson, M.L. (2014) Deciphering 'Islamic hospitality': Developments, challenges and opportunities. *Tourism Management* 40, 155–164.

Stephenson, M.L. and Ali, N. (2010) Tourism, travel and Islamophobia: Post 9/11 journeys of Muslims in non-Muslim states. In N. Scott and J. Jafari (eds) *Tourism in the Muslim World* (pp. 235–251). Bingley: Emerald Group Publishing Limited.

Taib, M.Z. and Rasdi, M.T. (2012) Islamic architecture evolution: Perception and behaviour. *Procedia – Social and Behavioral Sciences* 49, 293–303.

Timothy, D.J. and Iverson, T. (2006) Tourism and Islam: Consideration of culture and duty. In D.J. Timothy and D.H. Olsen (eds) *Tourism, Religion and Spiritual Journeys* (pp. 186–205). Oxford: Taylor & Francis Group, Routledge.

Vukonic, B. (1996) *Tourism and Religion*. New York: Pergamon.

Weaver, G.R. and Agle, B.R. (2002) Religiosity and ethical behavior in organizations: A symbolic interactionist perspective. *The Academy of Management Review* 27 (1), 77–98.

Weidenfeld, A. and Ron, A. (2008) The religious needs in the tourism industry. *Anatolia: An International Journal of Tourism and Hospitality Research* 19 (2), 357–361.

Zamani-Farahani, H. and Henderson, J.C. (2010) Islamic tourism and managing development in Islamic societies: The cases of Iran and Saudi Arabia. *International Journal of Tourism Research* 12 (1), 79–89.

5 Judaism and Tourism Over the Ages: The Impacts of Technology, Geopolitics and the Changing Political Landscape

Noga Collins-Kreiner and Nimrod Luz

Introduction

What are the connections between Judaism and tourism? Indeed, one may question the very idea of wedding these two concepts. One may wonder if Judaism, as a creed and a religious frame of reference, holds any particular understanding that serves and guides its adherents' 'touristic' approach. Further, what is religious tourism and how does it differ from non-religious tourism? Does pilgrimage as a religious journey to a sacred centre differ greatly or easily disenables from a non-religious journey to the same sacred site?

These are indeed relevant and pertinent questions that call for a conceptual, theoretical and surely practical clarification. In recent years, these questions have been met in the field and valiant efforts have been made to explore them and arrive at a better understanding of these intricate connections (Badone, 2014; Badone & Roseman, 2004; Coleman & Eade, 2004; Collins-Kreiner, 2010; Eade, 1992; Eade & Sallnow, 1991; Margry, 2008).

To be clear, tourism and religion are distinct and yet, in our times, overlapping realities (Stausberg, 2011). In the modern world and against current technologies, these two are interconnected and not mutually exclusive as may be seen through a variety of themes and activities. Therefore, it is incumbent on us to try and make sense of this situation and define, albeit briefly, what constitutes for us in this short survey of tourism in Judaism our main goals and fields of interest against the scope of theoretical questions that may be relevant to the subject.

In this chapter, we explore the connections and dramatic changes in pilgrimage and religious tourism in Judaism and among Jewish pilgrims and tourists within a longue durée. We hold this approach germane to explain the vicissitudes in Jewish perceptions of pilgrimage and the nature and types of religious tourism from their inception to the present. This approach holds particular relevance for efforts to understand current trends in Jewish tourism and their relationship with religion and religiosity in the context of modernity and against prevailing technologies. By that we infer the types of transportation mostly but also new emerging virtual technologies which allow for digital visitations and remote encounters with pilgrimage sites. Thus, we will embark on a survey of pilgrimage in Judaism in history and end with contemporary manifestations of a variety of religious tourism phenomena.

It is our intention to contribute to the current literature by investigating a topic that has thus far evaded thorough exploration: the sensitive and complex relationship among Judaism, tourism, pilgrimage, heritage, culture and politics. Understanding the context in which these elements have developed and interacted within Jewish culture enables us to better explain these complex relationships in their past and present formats. In order to explain these developments, we analyse them from a cultural-political-ecological approach. Hence, we explore themes that loosely fall under the category of tourism in Judaism over the ages mainly through three lenses: the changes in technology and methods of pilgrimage, the impact of the prevailing political machination and the changes in the political status of Jews namely from a marginalised minority to a hegemonic majority in a Jewish nation state.

In light of the above, the chapter consists of three sections: pilgrimage in Judaism from its origins to the late 19th century, Jewish pilgrimage tourism in modernity and current manifestations of Jewish heritage tourism (JHT). This structure is based on the premise that, although Jewish pilgrimage constituted the initial building block of Jewish tourism and for this reason must be the first element considered, we aim to broaden our understanding in the ways in which Jewish tourism has developed over the years from a religion-based duty to heritage-rooted popular visitation. Whereas past research on Jewish tourism has typically considered Jewish pilgrimage solely from a religious perspective, it is now clear that the phenomenon must also be explored in the context of heritage, culture and politics.

The chapter's first section contextualises a few seminal terms that are essential to our understanding of the contemporary research on Jewish travel. Following is a section that considers the main attributes and sites of Jewish pilgrimage in the pre-modern periods. Our next section explores the dramatic changes in Jewish pilgrimage during the modern period, particularly as part of the emergence of Jewish society within the state of Israel against technological and other changes brought forth by modernity. It also highlights the reflexive relationship between Jewish-Israeli nationalism and religious behaviour, and how these two phenomena have altered the nature, volume and destinations of Jewish tourism in contemporary Israel. The last section deals with Jewish pilgrimage heritage tours from both a supply and demand perspective as tourism in Judaism cannot be understood solely as deriving from a religious impetuous, but also from the perspective of the mixed motives of religion, culture and heritage in the current era.

We conclude the chapter with a discussion of our main argument that Jewish tourism is not a *thing* but rather a *process*, which continues to change as the 21st century progresses and as the conceptual boundaries between 'sacred' and 'profane' are becoming more fluid, indeed with the sacred increasingly coming to encompass practices and sites that are not necessarily religious (e.g. tourism, war memorials and sites of tragic death). Rigid dichotomies between pilgrimage and tourism no longer appear tenable in the shifting world of postmodern travel.

Pilgrimage Travel in Judaism

Pilgrimage, as a movement towards a sacred centre aimed at being exposed to God's presence (Coleman & Elsner, 1995), is located at the very core of Jewish belief. The biblical text is unequivocal about the importance of this journey and the religious imperative of performing this ritual on both physical and metaphorical levels:

> Three times a year all your men must appear before the Lord your God at the place he will choose: at the Festival of Unleavened Bread, the Festival of Weeks and the Festival of Tabernacles. No one should appear before the Lord empty-handed: Each of you must bring a gift in proportion to the way the Lord your God has blessed you. (Deuteronomy, 16: 16–17)

Following the ascendancy of Davidic traditions, Jerusalem and its religious centre (the Jewish Temple) became supreme, and all other existing pilgrimage centres were shunned. The ending of Jewish autonomy, symbolised mainly by the destruction of this sacred site in 70 CE, only intensified Jerusalem's symbolic role. The period of Jerusalem's ascendancy is of crucial importance, as this pilgrimage map and imaginative geography served as the platform for the pilgrimage made by Jesus himself, which culminated in his crucifixion. The Christian traditions regarding Jesus's death and resurrection established Jerusalem as a central pilgrimage centre for Christians as well, adding to the saturated hagiographic pilgrimage map of Jerusalem and the entire Holy Land (MacCormack, 1990; Markus, 1994; see also Chapter 11, this volume).

Jews continued to perform pilgrimage to Jerusalem and its environs with certain restrictions during the Roman period. After the Crusader period, and especially during the Mamluk period (between the 13th and 16th centuries), Jewish pilgrimage, as well as accounts of Jewish voyages, intensified and expanded far beyond Jerusalem to other sites within the Land of Israel (Prawer, 1988; Reiner, 2014). This process was shaped by periodic constraints imposed by local authorities, as well as by reaction and contestation, with the sometimes contested proliferation of Christian and Muslim sacred centres and traditions. Like those of other religions, Jewish perspectives on pilgrimage have changed over time. Nevertheless, Solomon (2013: 42) suggests a stark difference between Judaism and other known (or at least monotheistic) religions: If you were to pick a Christian at random in the street and ask what he or she could say about pilgrimage, you could reasonably expect a coherent reply, maybe with a reference to Rome or Jerusalem or Santiago; a Muslim similarly button-holed might mention Mecca, a Hindu Varanasi. If you were to stop a Jew and pose the same question, you would more likely get a puzzled look, perhaps a remark on the Pilgrim Festivals in Ancient Israel, or even a statement to the effect that 'we don't do pilgrimages'. Is this a difference of substance or just a difference of vocabulary?

Solomon certainly has a point, but the difference between Judaism and its counterparts (Christianity and Islam) in the region is not an essential one; rather, Judaism presents a different take or emphasis on the importance of ritual (Limor, Reiner & Frankel, 2014). Furthermore, if a rejection of pilgrimage ever prevailed, it has long since succumbed to a plethora of pilgrimage sites and a dramatic rise in both its sociopolitical and religious importance. Thus, as in other religious perceptions, Jewish pilgrimage plays a key role in the search for the holy and the maintenance of a community of believers (Singer & Adler, 1964, 35, including for example, Hasidic pilgrimages to Brooklyn to visit the site of the Chabad founder (see Kravel-Tov & Bilu, 2008).

As noted above, following the biblical creed, Jews were expected to 'appear before the Lord your God at the place he will choose'. According to the prevailing Jewish narrative constructed by canonised texts that largely follow Judean literature, after its inauguration by King Solomon in 970 BCE, the Jerusalem Temple became the most important and revered Jewish pilgrimage site. Although this narrative has come under increasing scrutiny (Eliav, 2005, 2008; Finkelstein & Silberman, 2001), there is ample evidence to support the growing role of the Jerusalemite temple as the focal point of Jewish pilgrimage (Aliyah Laregel) during the Second Temple period (Eliav, 2005). Under King Herod (37–34 BCE), the compound underwent a massive and highly ambitious renovation and refurbishment project, which, among other things, involved the construction of four gargantuan retaining walls. This construction project transformed the temple into a separate urban entity, which since then has been known as the Temple

Mount. Following the temple's destruction by the Romans, the western retaining wall became the most iconic Jewish pilgrimage site.

The topocide of this central Jewish pilgrimage site and the cessation of the liturgy therein unleashed a lengthy philosophical debate regarding the status of the former temple and pilgrimage to it (Feldman, 2005). Initially, Jewish scholars were of the opinion, much like in early Christianity, that until the compound was restored to its former glory and function, Jerusalem and its temple were to be erased from the pilgrimage map and the biblical creed of *Aliya Laregel* (literally, 'ascending by foot') to the house of God was null and void. This *axis mundi*, however, was too strong to be ignored and remained the ultimate object of Jewish yearning and a symbol of future redemption (*geula*) and of the end of the diaspora and life in exile.

Over time, the city, particularly the Western (Wailing) Wall (as the most important relic of the former temple), regained its mythic and central importance. Jews continued to make pilgrimages to Jerusalem that culminated, if political circumstances permitted them to do so, with a visit to the Wailing Wall (Prawer, 1998). Thus, a convoluted and meandering historical process that originated in biblical times, began in earnest during the Second Temple period, and was finalised after the Roman conquest in 70 CE. Jerusalem and its temple were transformed from ideas that symbolised the Jewish presence in Eretz Israel into spiritual and metaphysical symbols that came to constitute the very essence of Jewish existence.

Hence, from late antiquity (the 4th to the 6th centuries CE) onward, Jewish pilgrims were no longer engaged with the canonical *Aliya Laregel* but rather performed rituals that are better translated as (and bear a greater semblance to) the Latin term *peregrination*, or 'pilgrimage' (Reiner, 2014). Jews also went on pilgrimage to other sites in the Holy Land, which Jewish travellers and chroniclers referred to as Eretz Israel, namely the Land of Israel. The Galilee region in general and, more specifically, the Upper Galilee city of Safad, became a major Jewish sacred centre where new lunar months (*rashei hodesh*) were proclaimed. The Galilee region also emerged as an important centre for Jewish sages and poets, and Safad and Tiberias emerged as two of the four Jewish holy cities. The growth and diversification of Jewish pilgrimage sites are readily apparent in Jewish travellers' itineraries from the 12th century onward (Bar, 2010). Another important development was the absorption of Christian and Muslim traditions and the embracing of non-Jewish sites as legitimate Jewish ones, such as the tomb of David on Mount Zion and the tomb of Rachel in Bethlehem (Limor, 1988, 2007; Sered, 1998).

It would seem that Jewish intellectuals opposed this growing phenomenon of grave visitations. The illustrious Maimonides (1138–1204) was quite adamant and outspoken against this type of pilgrimage: 'Graves are to be marked, and a memorial is built over the grave. But a memorial is not to be built over the graves of the righteous, for their words are their memory. Nor should a person visit graves' (Eevel, 4, 4). Doctrine aside, it is clear from the emerging hagio-geographic layout of Jewish pilgrimage sites of the last 800 years that even his authoritative voice could not quench the thirst for these visits. By the end of the 19th century and the eve of the national struggle between Jewish and Arab communities, a wide range of Jewish pilgrimage sites and a highly variegated sacred map had already emerged therein. This map became the foundation and base against which dramatic changes would soon take place with the creation of the independent Jewish state of Israel.

Jewish Pilgrimage: Tourism in the Modern Period

As we embark on an analysis of the changes in Jewish pilgrimage in the modern period, it is incumbent upon us to highlight the contribution of two notable phenomena to the variation, and the exponential growth in the numbers of both pilgrims and pilgrimage sites since the late 19th century. The first one concerns the impacts of the new development of transportation technologies. The move from walking on foot or riding beasts of burden towards the sacred to the possibility of traveling by cars, boats, trains and later on planes, inevitably enabled a wider audience to perform pilgrimage. These transport technologies allowed for better accessibility, a shortening of the travel time and the ability to perform these religious activities several times annually. The second change concerns a new phase in Jewish pilgrimage tourism due to the sociopolitical changes that ultimately led to the emergence of Israel as a Jewish state within the geographical setting of the biblical Holy Land. The 20th century, particularly following the creation of Israel in 1948, witnessed a dramatic growth in pilgrimage sites (whether old, new or renewed) and a soaring increase in the volume of Jewish pilgrims, along with significant trends of religious radicalisation and religious resurgence (Bar, 2004, 2009; Bilu, 1998, 2010; Sered, 1986, 1989, 1991, 1998). Against this background, one may understand better the nature and vast changes in Jewish tourism. These changes in Jewish pilgrimage have encouraged the emergence of a voluminous, varied and lively field of research.

Israel, as the geopolitical entity that emerged from the Jewish ideological concept of the Holy Land or Eretz Israel, has undergone dramatic and riveting transformations, resulting in a cornucopia of sacred sites and newly invented pilgrimage routes. These changes have involved state attempts to consecrate the land as part of the ongoing conflict with Palestinians from inside and beyond the Green Line, as well as religious resurgence and radicalisation within Jewish-Israeli society (Luz, 2004, 2008, 2012).

Arguably, the Wailing Wall and its environs have together constituted the most iconic landmark and the fulcrum of the processes that have played a role in the increasing importance of the religious sphere in contemporary Israel. As we have seen, Jews yearned for and venerated the site for centuries before it once again became accessible to Jewish pilgrims after the 1967 Arab–Israeli war (known in Israeli historiography as the Six Day War). The state took an active part in transforming the site by transforming its spatiality, including the demolition of a former Muslim neighbourhood. The changes were designed not only to produce a central pilgrimage site for Jews but also to reflect an emergent religious nationalist understanding (Nitzan-Shiftan, 2011). The centrality of this site and its canonical status as the most important national and pilgrimage icon must also be understood in the context of everyday Jewish Israeli attitudes towards a mythologised past, manifested in the geographical concept of Eretz Israel as the 'historical' foundation of modern-day Israel.

Today, the holy sites dating from historical periods consist primarily of the burial places of saintly figures (Sered, 1998), including, among others, the tomb of Rachel the Matriarch in Bethlehem, the cave of the Patriarchs in Hebron and the tomb of Maimonides in Tiberias to name but a few. It must be noted, however, that most of these sites are recognised as saintly graves based on later traditions and do not necessarily mark the saintly figure's (*zaddik*) exact burial location. Indeed, as previously mentioned, pilgrimage to these saints' graves was neither cultivated nor authorised by religious authorities (Bilu, 1998, 2010). From a purely theological perspective, the question of intercessionary prayer to the dead (that is, grave visitations and prayers therein) touches on a wide range of issues in the domain of Jewish religious life: the links between the living and the dead; the relationship between popular practice and religious authority; the impact (whether positive or negative) of impinging religious traditions; and surely the philosophical discussion on the 'true' nature of Jewish monotheism. However, as we discuss below, in various strains of Judaism, both among Ashkenazi groups and their Sephardi counterparts, pilgrimage to graves (a form of sacred sites) for the purpose of prayer and asking intercession has become a prevalent practice of piety in the modern period.

Our analysis of these activities and the widespread pilgrimage sites draws on Cohen's (1992) distinction between formal and popular pilgrimage centres. Formal centres are usually more rigorous and are under the scrutiny of orthodox leaders. The rituals at these centres are highly formalised and decorous, and are conducted in accordance with orthodox precepts. Despite the presence of folkloric elements, these play a secondary role in contrast to popular centres and sometimes are even suppressed by the authorities. At popular centres, folkloric activities assume greater importance and may even take precedence over more serious and sublime activities. The pilgrim's principal motive for the pilgrimage, if not just a pretext for recreation or entertainment, is typically a personal request or the fulfilment of a vow. The requests of pilgrims are often simple and concrete and most commonly include success in business, luck in life and love, and good health or healing. Indeed, popular centres, rather than formal ones, often acquire a reputation for fulfilling requests and providing succour to individual worshippers.

While formal sites are growing and are well funded, popular shrines have also rapidly expanded. Several of the Galilee sites became important pilgrimage centres after the Roman conquest prevented Jerusalem from functioning as a religious hub and the focal point of Jewish political-religious activity was forced to move northward to this mountainous region. Places like Bet Shearim, Tiberias and Sepphoris served not only as administrative centres and significant Jewish cities but also harboured a variety of highly popular pilgrimage sites. Although these sites no longer serve as seats of political power, they continue to play a role as pilgrimage shrines (Reiner, 2014). In terms of Israel's current sociopolitical structure, they can be understood as peripheral 'centres out there', although they were not established as such, unlike the minor shrines, which emerged during the second half of the 20th century and will be discussed below.

The most important of the peripheral centres is the tomb of Rabbi Shimon Bar-Yochai, located on Mount Meron near Safad. Shimon Bar-Yochai lived during the 2nd century CE and preached against the Romans. He is also believed to have written the Zohar (*The Book of Splendour*), the most important book of Jewish mysticism, and to have performed miracles. Pilgrims visit the shrine throughout the year, but mass celebrations occur only during the festival of Lag Ba'omer (the thirty-third day after Passover). Whereas approximately 1.5 million people visit the shrine annually, it is estimated that approximately 500,000 people come to the site for this one-day festival. The site is also a major tourist attraction, drawing individuals from all segments of Jewish-Israeli society and imbuing the site with a largely popular character. Other major peripherally located pilgrimage centres in Israel include the tombs of Rabbi Yonatan Ben-Uziel near Safad, Rabbi Meir Ba'al Hanes near Tiberias, Rabbi Akiva in Tiberias, Honi Hameagel at Hatzor Haglilit and Rabbi Yehuda Bar Ilai near Safad (Collins-Kreiner, 2006). This short list is but a fraction of the plethora of places that have been consecrated in recent years throughout Israel. The emergence of new touristic pilgrimage sites is the outcome of dramatic changes in Israeli society and politics. Among the key reasons we may note here are: the empowerment of hitherto marginal groups in Jewish society, namely the Mizrhai-Sephardi population, and the general desecularisation of Israeli society.

Since the 1980s, new shrines for Jewish saints have been established, or 'discovered', in several Israeli development towns. Sered (1986, 1989, 1991, 1998) forcefully argues that the development of these cults in contemporary Israel reflects, among other things, the popularity of devotion to holy men in North Africa, the role of the charismatic rabbi in Hasidic sects and a national wish to strengthen the sense of historical belonging to the land (Sered, 1998: 28). Weingrod (1990, 1998), Ben-Ari and Bilu (1992, 1997) and Bar (2004, 2009) reflect on the reasons for this new kind of marginal pilgrimage site and conclude that the sociocultural and political changes within Israeli society, influenced by the Jewish immigrants arriving during the 1950s primarily from Muslim North Africa, were the major factors leading to the emergence of these sites. The immigrants brought with them the popular Muslim tradition of '*ziyara*', or pilgrimage to the sacred graves of holy figures. About 10 of these new popular pilgrimage sites currently exist across Israel, and their numbers are growing. Most have only a limited following, but some are popular throughout the entire country and attract a large number of visitors throughout the year, especially on Jewish holidays and the '*hillulot*', which are marked by a gathering at the saint's grave on the anniversary of his death. The most popular site of this kind is the tomb of Baba Sali in the town of Netivot, located in the Negev desert region of southern Israel. A similar pilgrimage site is Rabbi Chaim Chouri's Tomb in Beer-Sheva (Weingrod, 1990).

Many sites located in North Africa – Morocco, Tunis, the island of Djerba and Egypt – also attract visitors, who visit them as pilgrims (Ben-Ari & Bilu, 1992; Carpenter-Lahiri, 2012). An intriguing manifestation of this trend may be found in the formation of new pilgrimage sites in peripheral Israeli cities. These newly 'invented' sites owe their naissance to local impresarios. Some of them have prevailed since their emergence in the 1970s and some have vanished from the pilgrimage map (Bilu, 2010). Stadler and Luz (2014, 2015, and see http://sacredplaces.huji.ac.il) have been exploring newly emerging popular sites in their charismatic stage through a comparison between the three dominant religions in Israel.

The Jewish pilgrimage tourism map has changed dramatically since 1948, and particularly since the 1970s (Bar, 2008, 2010). In addition to the revitalisation, renovation and reconstruction of established official sites, new popular shrines have also been constructed, mythologised and appropriated. Part and parcel of this process has been the intensifying relationship between Zionism and pilgrimage. Although Zionism is a highly secular modern ideology, from its beginnings it targeted the Land of Israel as a platform for national resurrection based solely on the Jewish collective memory of Eretz Israel (Raz-Krakotzkin, 2007). It also adopted the religious concept of *Aliya Laregel* as a doctrine referring primarily to Jews' return to their homeland. Against this background, the highly venerated historical pilgrimage sites have been subjected to a new mythologised nationalistic understanding. Thus, these sites conjointly form a voluminous secularist-cum-religious nationalistic pilgrimage map (Abu al-Hajj, 2001; Ben Yehuda, 1995; Zerubavel, 1995).

In recent years, amid widespread religious resurgence in Jewish-Israeli society, intriguing links have been forged between Zionism as a national secularist theory (although some might challenge the idea of Zionism as a secular phenomenon as it is based on biblical sources) and various Jewish religious manifestations. Thus, Aliya (literally, ascending) interpreted as a movement towards the land of Israel, has acquired a new meaning among religious Zionist circles and is used as an umbrella term for various activities aimed at reconstructing the temple and engaging in pilgrimage to the site (Chen, 2014). The number of pilgrims has continually increased and new platforms are being used to increase public knowledge and awareness about this burgeoning practice. Social media, internet forums, general information websites and websites of specific sites are becoming increasingly widespread, reflecting not only a proliferation and an increasing number of pilgrimage sites but also the more general religious resurgence that is currently underway throughout Israel.

In sync with global trends, we are beginning to witness changes in religious Jewish tourism affected by the new technologies brought forth by the digital revolution. Thus, new possibilities are emerging that allow for eTourism, eReligion and their intersection, ePilgrimage (UNESCO, 2016). This type of religious tourism is as yet under researched but we may safely say that the new possibilities that are already being exploited, for the sake of religious Jewish tourism, are legion. In recent years, webcams were installed at the Wailing Wall which allows 'pilgrims' from around the world to participate, observe and experience prayers and rituals therein year-round (http://www.aish.com/w/46127727.html). Thus, online media is beginning to be used as a supplement for a concrete and tangible visit.

Additionally, one may find growing use of social media in the promotion and sustaining of pilgrimage sites. The site of Rabi Meir in Tiberias boasts an 'official' page on Facebook, which is used to inform pilgrims about special events, donation possibilities, celebrities visitations and so forth (https://www.facebook.com/קרבר-יבר-ריאמ-בעל-הנס-1656703877947944/).

Websites and Facebook pages are also used as billboards to promote Hilulut and other festive occasions in these sites. Thus, eReligion and eTourism are advancing the commercialisation and commodification of these sites. Digital platforms are increasingly being used to enhance the pilgrim experience, to relay information and, as the case may be, to create an eCommunitas in a variety of pilgrimage and heritage locations. In our surveys of and visits to these sites, we witnessed the increasing usage of digital media devices by pilgrims not only to record and commemorate their own visit but in a variety of creative ways to enable eParticipation from far and wide.

Jewish Heritage Tourism

The term 'heritage tourism' has been used to denote the interest of large numbers of visitors in attributes related to a nation's history, archaeology, culture, religion and art, and even its natural landscape (Prentice, 1993). This meaning is consistent with the definition of heritage as the cultural expression of what makes humans what they are, their spiritual DNA (Boniface & Fowler, 1993). JHT is defined as the supply of, and demand for, sites and activities connected to the Jewish faith, culture and tradition, including both relics of the past and products of the present. JHT is a product offered to visitors in many European towns and cities (Gruber, 2002; Krakover, 2013) with a comprehensive segmentation of the demand side spanning heritage tours, interaction tours, solidarity missions and ritual tours (Collins-Kreiner & Olsen, 2004).

Pilgrimages to memorial sites or concentrations camps, pilgrimages of nostalgia and heritage tours have been on the rise since the turn of the millennium (Biran *et al.*, 2011; Feldman, 2005; Ioannides & Ioannides, 2002; Stone, 2006; Stone & Sharpley, 2008). A prominent example of such phenomena has been 'The March of the Living', an annual educational programme established in 1988 and run in conjunction with the Israel Youth Hostel Association, which brings students from all over the world to Poland on Holocaust Memorial Day. Participants march silently from Auschwitz to Birkenau, the largest Nazi German concentration camp complex built during World War II. The object of the march, as formulated in its organisers' vision statement (Solomon, 2013), is to 'strengthen the Zionist awareness and identity of Jewish youth and impart knowledge about Judaism and Jewish culture'.

Over the past few decades, and particularly since the dissolution of the Soviet Union in 1989–1991, Europe has witnessed a growth of interest in elements related to Judaism, Jews, Jewish culture and the Holocaust, which is increasingly recognised as part of national history and culture. As part of this trend, Jewish culture, or what is perceived or defined as Jewish culture, has become a visible component of 'heritage' and 'identity', even in countries where Jews themselves are now practically invisible. It is a Europe-wide phenomenon, observable in countries whose citizens were perpetrators, victims and bystanders of the Holocaust. In most countries of Europe, this trend has been manifested in Klezmer festivals, synagogue restorations, the opening of Jewish museums, the construction of Holocaust memorials, the production of films and the composition of novels (Valley, 1999).

Jewish heritage sites, in Israel and abroad, are usually visited by visitors based on motivations such as remembrance, nostalgia and curiosity (Ioannides & Ioannides, 2002). Jewish heritage sites in Europe are also characterised by small non-monumental exhibits that appeal to special interest groups of tourists who have some links to, or at least curiosity regarding Jewish culture. These sites are usually promoted by cultures outside the Jewish faith, and their development often encounters states of cognitive dissonance vis-à-vis the local culture (Tunbridge & Ashworth, 1996).

Jewish-themed tourism has become a well-established niche in the vast tourist market, promoted on the private level and also strongly backed by state, city and regional authorities (Gruber, 2002). Jewish guidebooks, brochures, heritage maps, posters and other materials have been published, and new travel agencies specialising in Jewish tours have opened their doors. Responding to this growing interest, old Jewish quarters are under development as in the case of tourist attractions and gentrification areas in cities such as Seville, Cordoba, Venice, Budapest, Prague, Cracow, Lublin and Vilnius. Similarly, Jewish museums have opened in Berlin, Frankfurt, Warsaw, Moscow, Vienna, Paris, Munich, Copenhagen, Thessaloniki and Budapest, as well as in smaller towns and rural villages in many countries, from Romania to France (Gruber, 2007; Krakover, 2013).

Holocaust sites, from Dachau to Auschwitz-Birkenau, are visited by millions of people every year (Thurnell-Read, 2009). Jewish-style shops, galleries, cafes and restaurants have been opened in several cities, in many cases by non-Jews. Jewish-themed souvenirs of various materials and origin are sold in these locations and establishments. Since the current Jewish presence in most of these cities and countries is negligible, the vast majority of visitors, customers and audiences are non-Jews (Heitlinger, 2013). However, Jews themselves have not been immune to this phenomenon. In parallel to the development of a non-Jewish embrace of 'things Jewish' in Europe, there has also been an internal Jewish rediscovery of roots and heritage, particularly since the fall of the 'Iron Curtain'. Indeed, the embrace of Jewish culture by mainstream society has proceeded side by side with efforts by Jews themselves to recover or redefine personal Jewish identities and to revive or enrich Jewish communities, Jewish life and internal Jewish culture in various countries (Krakover, 2016).

Considering the experiences of revitalisation and commodification of Jewish neighbourhoods, this process has reflected both positive and negative aspects. On the one hand, there are negative attitudes towards the commercialisation of the sacred sites in Poland and Germany among Jewish communities worldwide, and the controversial commercial exploitation of

Jewish heritage in some European cities was even described as a 'Jewish Disneyland' in Berlin, and the 'Jurassic Park of Judaism' or 'Circus of the Dead' (Corsale & Vuytsyk, 2015; Gruber, 2009). On the other hand, the rehabilitation of Jewish heritage sites in the aforementioned cities has turned Jewish neighbourhoods into vibrant urban spaces and boosted the physical development of once dilapidated and depressed areas (Krakover, 2012).

Discussion

This chapter has shed light on the primary aspects that have characterised the changing relationship between Judaism and tourism from the 10th century BCE to the present. First, we have observed that pilgrimage to holy sites in general and Jerusalem in particular was the most prominent feature of Jewish tourism in the past and remains so today. Second, there appear to be several motives, and different combinations of religious, heritage and cultural reasons, for traveling in the context of Jewish tourism. Whether or not Jews feel a personal affinity with Israel or with Judaism, their current travel patterns suggest that their cultural and religious identity have a strong influence on their touristic activities. Third, this trend is consistent with the current literature regarding the growing differentiation among pilgrimage, religious tourism and heritage tourism, as well as between the 'sacred' and the 'profane', with the 'sacred' coming increasingly to encompass practices and sites that are not necessarily religious. Our fourth observation is that against the growing implications of modernity, the commodification of national identity has been one of the most distinctive features of Jewish tourism development over the past decades. One motivation for this commodification process has been an increased interest, among Jewish communities and individuals, in uncovering more about their collective pasts and identities by discovering family roots and expanding their awareness of past historical events and places. Lastly, the impacts of the digital revolution have already begun to be noticeable in a variety of ways in pilgrimage, heritage and other sites which constitute Jewish tourism. These media platforms allow for pilgrims and visitors to experience the sites in innovative ways previously unknown. They enable the sites' impresarios to reach larger audiences and construct virtual communities which not only visit but also promote the sites and at times donate and help sustain them. Webcams, Facebook pages and internet sites are the most visible outcomes, but as we keep observing in the field, new developments and previously unimaginable products are emerging almost daily. These are calling for new research methodologies and will surely keep challenging the field in years to come.

References

Abu al-Hajj, N. (2001) *Facts on the Ground: Archaeological Practice and Territorial Self-Fashioning in Israeli Society*, Chicago, IL: University of Chicago Press.

Badone, E. (2014) Conventional and unconventional pilgrimages: Conceptualizing sacred travel in the twenty-first century. In A. Pazos (ed.) *Redefining Pilgrimage: New Perspectives on Historical and Contemporary Pilgrimages* (pp. 7–32). Farnham/Burlington, VT: Ashgate.

Badone, E. and Roseman, S. (eds) (2004) *Intersecting Journeys: The Anthropology of Pilgrimage and Tourism*. Champaign, IL: University of Illinois Press.

Bar, D. (2004) Re-creating Jewish sanctity in Jerusalem: The case of Mount Zion and David's Tomb between 1948–1967. *The Journal of Israeli History* 23 (2), 233–251.

Bar, D. (2010) Jewish holy places in Israel: Continuity and change. *Zmanim* 110, 92–103.

Bar, G. (2008) Reconstructing the past: The creation of Jewish sacred space in the State of Israel, 1948–1967. *Israel Studies* 13 (3), 1–21.

Bar, G. (2009) Mizrahim and the development of sacred space in the state of Israel, 1948–1968. *Journal of Modern Jewish Studies* 8 (3), 267–285.

Ben Yehuda, N. (1995) *The Masada Myth: Collective Memory and Mythmaking in Israel*. Madison, WI: University of Wisconsin Press.

Ben-Ari, E. and Bilu, Y. (1992) The making of modern saints: Manufactured charisma and the Abu-Hatseiras of Israel. *American Ethnologist* 19 (4), 672–687.

Ben-Ari, E. and Bilu, Y. (1997) *Grasping Land: Space and Place in Contemporary Israeli Discourse and Experience*. New York: State University of New York.

Bilu, Y. (1998) Divine worship and pilgrimage to holy sites as universal phenomena. In R. Gonen (ed.) *To the Holy Graves: Pilgrimage to the Holy Graves and Hillulot in Israel* (pp. 11–26). Jerusalem: The Israel Museum, Jerusalem (in Hebrew).

Bilu, Y. (2010) *The Saints' Impresarios: Dreamers, Healers, and Holy Men in Israel's Urban Periphery*. Israel/Brighton, MA: Academic Studies Press.

Biran, A., Poria, Y. and Oren, G. (2011) Sought experiences at (dark) heritage sites. *Annals of Tourism Research* 38 (3), 820–841.

Boniface, P. and Fowler, P.J. (1993) *Heritage and Tourism in 'the Global Village'*. Chicago, IL: Routledge.

Carpenter-Lahiri, D. (2012) The ghriba on the island of Jerba or the reinvention of a shared shrine as a metonym for a multicultural Tunisia. In G. Bowman (ed.) *Sharing the 'Sacra': The Politics and Pragmatics of Intercommunal Relations around Holy Places* (pp. 7–32). Oxford/New York: Berghahn Books.

Chen, S. (2014) Visiting the Temple Mount: Taboo or Mitzvah. *Modern Judaism* 34 (1), 27–41.

Cohen, E. (1992) Pilgrimage and tourism: Convergence and divergence. In A. Morinis (ed.) *Sacred Journeys: The Anthropology of Pilgrimage* (pp. 47–61). New York: Greenwood Press.

Coleman, S. and Elsner, J. (eds) (1995) *Pilgrimage: Past and Present in the World Religions*. Cambridge, MA: Harvard University Press.

Coleman, S. and Eade, J. (eds) (2004) *Reframing Pilgrimage: Cultures in Motion*. London/New York: Routledge.

Collins-Kreiner, N. (2006) Graves as attractions: Pilgrimage-tourism to Jewish holy graves in Israel. *Journal of Cultural Geography* 24 (1), 67–89.

Collins-Kreiner, N. (2010) Researching pilgrimage: Continuity and transformations. *Annals of Tourism Research* 37 (2), 440–456.

Collins-Kreiner, N. and Olsen, D.H. (2004) Selling diaspora: Producing and segmenting the Jewish diaspora tourism market. In T. Coles and D.J. Timothy (eds) *Tourism, Diasporas and Space* (pp. 279–290). New York: Routledge.

Corsale, A. and Vuytsyk, O. (2015) Jewish heritage tourism between memories and strategies. Different approaches from Lviv, Ukraine. *Current Issues in Tourism.* doi: 10.1080/13683500.2015.1103210.

Eade, J. (1992) Pilgrimage and tourism at Lourdes, France. *Annals of Tourism Research* 19, 18–32.

Eade, J. and Sallnow, M. (eds) (1991) *Contesting the Sacred: The Anthropology of Christian Pilgrimage.* London/New York: Routledge.

Eliav, Y. (2005) *God's Mountain: The Temple Mount in Time, Space, and Memory.* Baltimore, NJ: Johns Hopkins University Press.

Eliav, Y. (2008) The Temple Mount in Jewish and early Christian traditions: A new look. In T. Mayer and S. Mourad (eds) *Jerusalem: Idea and Reality* (pp. 47–66). London/New York: Routledge.

Feldman, J. (2005) The experience of communality and the legitimation of authority in Second Temple pilgrimage. In O. Limor and E. Reiner (eds) *Pilgrimage: Jews, Christians, Muslims* (pp. 88–109). Rananna: Open University/Yad Ben Zvi.

Finkelstein, I. and Silberman, N. (2001) *The Bible Unearthed: Archaeology's New Vision of Ancient Israel and the Origin of Its Sacred Texts.* New York: Simon and Schuster.

Gruber, R.E. (2002) *Virtually Jewish: Reinvention of Jewish Culture in Europe.* Berkeley, CA: University of California Press.

Gruber, R.E. (2007) *Jewish Heritage Travel. A Guide to Eastern Europe.* Washington, DC: National Geographic Society.

Gruber, R.E. (2009) Beyond virtually Jewish: New authenticities and real imaginary spaces in Europe. *Jewish Quarterly Review* 99 (4), 487–504.

Heitlinger, A. (2013) *In the Shadows of the Holocaust and Communism: Czech and Slovak Jews since 1945.* Bloomington, IN: Indiana University Press.

Ioannides, D. and Ioannides, M.W. (2002) Pilgrimages of nostalgia: Patterns of Jewish travel in the United States. *Tourism Recreation Research* 27 (2), 17–25.

Krakover, S. (2012) Coordinated marketing and dissemination of knowledge: Jewish heritage tourism in Serra da Estrela, Portugal. *Journal of Tourism and Development (Revista Turismo & Desenvolvimento)* 17–18 (1), 11–16.

Krakover, S. (2013) Generation of a tourism product: Jewish heritage tourism in Spain. *Enlightening Tourism* 3 (2), 142–168.

Krakover, S. (2016) A heritage site development model: Jewish heritage product formation in south-central Europe. *Journal of Heritage Tourism.* doi:10.1080/17438 73X.2016.1151430.

Kravel-Tov, M. and Bilu, Y. (2008) The work of the present: Constructing messianic temporality in the wake of failed prophesy among Chabad Hasidim. *American Ethnologist* 35 (1), 64–80.

Limor, O. (1988) The origins of a tradition: King David's tomb on Mt. Zion. *Traditio* 44, 453–462.

Limor, O. (2007) Sharing sacred space: Holy places in Jerusalem between Christianity, Judaism and Islam. In I. Shagrir, R. Ellenblum and J. Riley-Smith (eds) *Laudem Hierosolymitani: Studies in Crusades and Medieval Culture in Honour of Benjamin Z. Kedar* (pp. 219–231). Aldershot: Ashgate.

Limor, O., Reiner, E. and Frenekl, M. (eds) (2014) *Pilgrimage: Jews, Christians, Muslims.* Rananna: The Open University of Israel Press.

Luz, N. (2004) *Al-Haram Al-Sharif in the Arab-Palestinian Public Discourse in Israel: Identity, Collective Memory and Social Construction.* Floersheimer Institute for Policy Study, Jerusalem: Achva Press [Hebrew].

Luz, N. (2008) The politics of sacred places. Palestinian identity, collective memory, and resistance in the Hassan Bek mosque conflict. *Society and Space: Environment and Planning D* 26 (6), 1036–1052.

Luz, N. (2012) The Islamic movement and the lure of the sacred: The struggle for land through sacred sites. In E. Rekhess and A. Rudnitzky (eds) *Muslim Minorities in non-Muslim Majority Countries: The Test Case of the Islamic Movement in Israel* (pp. 75–84). Tel Aviv: Eyal Press.

MacCormack, S. (1990) Loca sancta: The organization of sacred topography in late antiquity. In R. Oustershout (ed.) *The Blessed of Pilgrimage* (pp. 7–40). Urbana and Chicago, IL: University of Illinois Press.

Margry, P. (ed.) (2008) *Shrines and Pilgrimage in the Modern World: New Itineraries into the Sacred*. Amsterdam: Amsterdam University Press.

Markus, R. (1994) How on earth could places become holy? Origins of the Christian idea of holy places. *Journal of Early Christian Studies* 2/3, 257–271.

Nitzan-Shiftan, N. (2011) Stones with a human heart: On monuments, modernism and preservation at the Western Wall. *Theory and Critic* 38–39: 65–100.

Prawer, J. (1988) *The History of the Jews in the Latin Kingdom*. Oxford: Oxford University Press.

Prentice, R. (1993) *Tourism and Heritage Attractions*. London: Routledge.

Raz-Krakotzkin, A. (2007) Jewish memory between exile and history. *The Jewish Quarterly Review* 97 (4), 530–543.

Reiner, E. (2014) Jewish pilgrimage to Jerusalem in late antiquity and the Middle Ages. In O. Limor, E. Reiner and M. Frenkel (eds) *Pilgrimage: Jews, Christians, Muslims* (pp. 46–130). Rananna: The Open University of Israel Press.

Sered, S. (1986) Rachel's Tomb and the Milk Grotto of the Virgin Mary: Two women's shrines in Bethlehem. *Journal of Feminist Studies in Religio* 2 (2), 7–22.

Sered, S. (1989) Rachel's Tomb: Societal liminality and the revitalization of a shrine. *Religion* 19, 27–40.

Sered, S. (1991) Rachel, Mary, and Fatima. *Cultural Anthropology* 6 (2), 131–146.

Sered, S. (1998) A tale of three Rachel's, or the cultural history of a symbol. *Nashim: A Journal of Jewish Women's Studies & Gender Issues* 1, 5–41.

Singer, I. and Adler, C. (1964) *The Jewish Encyclopaedia*. New York: Ktav Publishing.

Solomon, N. (2013) Jewish pilgrimage and peace. In A. Pazos (ed.) *Pilgrimages and Pilgrims as Peacemakers in Christianity, Judaism and Islam* (pp. 36–92). Farnham/Burlington, VT: Ashgate.

Stadler, N. and Luz, N. (2014) The veneration of womb tombs: Body-based rituals and politics at Mary's Tomb and Maqam Abu al-Hijja. *Journal of Anthropological Research* 70 (2), 183–205.

Stadler, N. and Luz, N. (2015) Two venerated mothers separated by a fence: Iconic spaces and borders in Israel: Palestine. *Journal of Religion and Society* 6, 127–141.

Stausberg, M. (2011) *Religion and Tourism: Crossroads, Destinations and Encounters*. London/New York: Routledge.

Stone, P.R. (2006) A dark-tourism spectrum: Towards a typology of death and macabre related tourist sites, attraction and exhibition. *Tourism* 52 (2), 145–160.

Stone, P. and Sharpley, R. (2008) Consuming dark-tourism: A thanatolological perspective. *Annals of Tourism Research* 35 (2), 574–595.

Thurnell-Read, T-P. (2009) Engaging Auschwitz: An analysis of young travellers' experiences of Holocaust tourism. *Journal of Tourism Consumption and Practice* 1 (1), 26–52.

Tunbridge, J.E. and Ashworth, G.J. (1996) *Dissonant Heritage: The Management of the Past as a Resource in Conflict*. Chichester: Wiley.

UNESCO (2016) Pilgrims in the digital age: A research manifesto. *International Journal of Religious Tourism and Pilgrimage* 4 (3), Article 3. See http://arrow.dit.ie/cgi/viewcontent.cgi?article=1129&context=ijrtp (accessed 31 July 2016).

Valley, E. (1999) *The Great Jewish Cities of Central and Eastern Europe.* Northvale, NJ: Jason Aronson.

Weingrod, A. (1990) *The Saint of Beersheba.* New York: SUNY Press.

Weingrod, A. (1998) The Saints Go Marching On. In O. Abuhab, E. Hertzog, H. Goldberg and E. Marx (eds) *Local Anthropology* (pp. 625–640). Tel Aviv: Cherikover (in Hebrew).

Zerubavel, Y. (1995) *Recovered Roots: Collective Memory and the Making of Israeli National Tradition.* Chicago, IL: The University of Chicago Press.

6 Shintoism and Travel in Japan

Yuji Nakanishi

Introduction

Shinto refers to the belief in and rituals devoted to the indigenous gods of Japan, or *kami*. It is centred around Shinto *jin-ja*, hereafter referred to as shrines. Deeply related to Japanese folk beliefs, Shintoism is an animist religion in which natural phenomena like mountains, forests, waterfalls and islands are recognised as *kami* (or gods). This chapter offers a summary of Japanese religious history and the current state of religion in Japan, locating Shintoism in Japanese culture and looking historically at the relationship between Shintoism and tourism.

Overview of Shintoism and religion in Japan

According to a 2014 survey by the Agency for Cultural Affairs of the Japanese government, there are currently around 81,000 Shinto shrines in Japan and 77,000 Buddhist temples, in addition to Christian churches and facilities of 'new religions' (religious organisations established since the middle of the 1900s). This puts Shinto at 46.8%, Buddhism at 42.6%, Christianity at 2.6% and other religious sects at 8.0%, making Shinto and Buddhism the central religions of Japan (www.bunka.go.jp/tokei_hakusho_shuppan/tokeichosa/shumu/pdf/h26kekka.pdf).

Japanese villages have many additional small shrines (*hokora*) devoted to *kami* (ancient deities) and temples devoted to Buddhist deities that are not included in the survey above, and many families in rural areas have household shrines as well. Thus, in actuality there are many more structures devoted to gods and *kami* than those included in the agency's survey above.

In religious terms, Shinto is something of a folk religion, differing at a basic level from Christianity and Islam. Shinto has no founder, and there are no scriptures that adherents must follow. Shinto shrines are at the centre of the religion; towns and villages in Japan have local shrines devoted to *kami* called *ujigami* or *chinju*, which are guardians of a particular place. There are also large-scale shrines known as *jingu* or *taisha* where religious services are performed by specific organisations. The Ise Jingu Shrine, which was visited by G7 heads of state at the G7 Ise-Shima Summit in 2016, is said to house the *kami* that are the ancestors of the imperial family, while the

Kasuga Taisha Shrine in Nara, a World Heritage Site, houses the *kami* of the Fujiwara family, a powerful imperial family in medieval times (see Figures 6.1 and 6.2). There are also shrines for people of a particular profession. Shrines can thus be symbols of certain regions, families or associations.

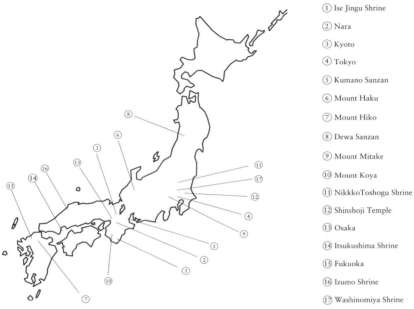

① Ise Jingu Shrine

② Nara

③ Kyoto

④ Tokyo

⑤ Kumano Sanzan

⑥ Mount Haku

⑦ Mount Hiko

⑧ Dewa Sanzan

⑨ Mount Mitake

⑩ Mount Koya

⑪ NikkkoToshogu Shrine

⑫ Shinshoji Temple

⑬ Osaka

⑭ Itsukushima Shrine

⑮ Fukuoka

⑯ Izumo Shrine

⑰ Washinomiya Shrine

Figure 6.1 Location in Japan of cities, Buddhist temples and Shinto Shrines

Figure 6.2 Ise Jingu Shrine

Kami thought to be enshrined at each shrine are basically the native deities of Japan, supposedly the ancestors of the imperial family. The first written references to *kami* are in the *Kojiki* (712) and *Nihon Shoki* (720). However, certain *kami* have come in and out of popularity over the ages. In the Edo period (1603–1867), for example, when the samurai still controlled the political system and Japan had not yet become a modern nation state, the development and flourishing of the economy and various industries led to the popularity of *kami* devoted to commerce. The representative shrine of this trend is Fushimi Inari Taisha Shrine in Kyoto, which in recent years has become very popular with tourists from outside Japan.

Shinto's relative lack of doctrine and scripture reflects its nature as a folk religion. Shinto priests are called *kan-nushi*, *guji* and *negi*, most of them are male, and compared with Buddhist monks and Christian priests they are burdened with very few restrictions or formal taboos in their daily life. Today, many local Shinto priests have secular professions (working as teachers, civil servants or company employees) in addition to their primary role in carrying out religious services at their shrine. During these services, they perform chants addressed to *kami* called *norito*.

The few rules in Shinto govern ritual purity when visiting a shrine. Generally speaking, someone who has just lost a close relative should not visit a shrine for a fixed amount of time. Although this is uncommon in cities, there are still many rural areas where this rule is strictly followed. There is also a taboo against women visiting shrines while menstruating, though this too has grown weaker in recent years. The former is referred to as 'black impurity' while the latter is referred to as 'red impurity', and it is thought that these impurities must be avoided when standing before the *kami*. For example, in front of Japanese shrines there is a *torii*, a type of gate marking the shrine's entrance (Figure 6.3). To the side there is often a large stone basin with water inside, which conscientious visitors use to wash their hands and rinse their mouth. This signifies ritual cleansing of oneself before entering the shrine. As women are considered impure, their participation at shrine festivals is often limited.

Shinto has also deeply permeated people's day-to-day lives in Japan. Especially in the agriculture, fishing and forestry industries, there is a deep connection between labour and rituals at shrines. For example, in the process of growing rice, a central part of Japanese agriculture, people often perform rituals at shrines before the rice season begins, after planting finishes, during summer weeding and after the harvest, based on the idea that *kami* can bring an abundant harvest. This shows the way that rituals at shrines always correspond to the cycles of community life throughout the year.

Figure 6.3 Torii (Washinomiya Shrine in Saitama Prefecture)

At multiple times throughout the year, the dates are decided for larger ceremonies called *taisai*, or major festivals. These are carried out by *ujiiko*, a term for local people whose *ujigami* are housed in a given shrine. They carry *mikoshi* (portable shrines to transport deities) and perform various forms of traditional art and entertainment. These Shinto shrine festivals and the extremely wide variety of traditional art performed there are a unique part of Japanese folk religion, not found in other cultures of East Asia. Additionally, unlike the situation in other East Asian nations, there are many shrine festivals performed by urban residents such as the Gion Matsuri Festival in Kyoto and the Sanja Matsuri Festival in Tokyo's Asakusa district.

If one were to categorise in terms of the secular and the sacred, religion falls squarely in the realm of the sacred. However, Japanese people mainly take part in Shinto through rituals and have relationships with individual shrines, these shrines' establishing the important points in their day-to-day life, their lives overall and in the yearly schedule for the community. For Japanese people, visiting shrines and participating in festivals are a part of daily life, often not consciously recognised as a form of religion. This tendency is especially strong in Shinto, and this, too, can be recognised as a unique feature of religions in Japan.

The Concept of Pilgrimage in Japan

One could say that tourist activities in the modern day are composed of three components. First is the receiving of information about a destination and the resulting desire to go there. Second is the maintenance of infrastructure to reach the destination and to dwell while there. Transportation by cars, trains and airplanes has been a crucial part of modern tourism, and the same goes for hotels. The final aspect is returning to one's place of origin, with which tourist activities come to a close.

Turner's (1966) theory of rituals is cited throughout Smith (1977), an early collection of essays on the anthropology of tourism. Turner's theory describes the structure of rituals by focusing on the 'round trip' to a sacred space outside of everyday life, which Smith shows can also be applied to modern-day tourism. This is very useful when considering the role of religion in the history of tourism in Japan. *Junrei*, or pilgrimages, were the first form of 'round trip' in Japan, according to the above definition. In the 11th century, the Buddhist ascetics called *hijiri* were already performing pilgrimages, travelling to the sacred sites of 'Kanzenon' bodhisattva (Avalokitaisvara).

In a Buddhist framework, these trips to holy sites by monks could be seen as the beginning of the practice of pilgrimage in Japan, but these were not confined to holy people; laypeople were also going on pilgrimages during this period. One well-known example is the Pilgrimage to Kumano, a journey to three holy sites in present-day Shingu in Wakayama Prefecture (the sites are referred to together as Kumano Sanzan, which means 'the three mountains of Kumano'). Old roads and religious facilities related to the Pilgrimage to Kumano were registered as a World Heritage Site in 2004 and formally designated 'Sacred Sites and Pilgrimage Routes in the Kii Mountain Range'. They are now visited by many tourists from inside and outside Japan (these are similar to other religious routes and trails as discussed in Chapter 15, this volume).

Here, it is appropriate to clarify the idea of 'pilgrimage' in Japanese. 'Pilgrimage' in the World Heritage Site description above is a translation of the Japanese word *sankei*, but in Japanese there are two words which translate as pilgrimage – *junrei* and *sankei* – and they differ slightly in nuance. *Sankei* refers to visiting temples or shrines but without the strong inference of religious practice. *Junrei*, on the other hand, originates as a Buddhist term for a practice performed by monks. In historical materials, visiting Ise Jingu Shrine is described as *sankei*, and unrelated to *junrei*. The difference between the terms can be described simply as follows. When the people making a pilgrimage are monks or other followers of Buddhism, and they are visiting multiple temples or shrines for religious purposes, the word *junrei* tends to be used. However, when those on the pilgrimage are laypeople and they are making the journey in order to have a desire or wish fulfilled, the word *sankei* tends to be used. Additionally, the destination in *sankei* is often a place where *kami* are enshrined. It is this *sankei* type of pilgrimage, moreover, that would evolve into modern-day tourism.

Later, in the Edo period, *sankei* began to show more similarities with modern tourism. The Pilgrimage to Kumano was the beginning of large-scale *sankei* in Japan, and the term was also later used for trips to Ise Jingu Shrine; this shows that the origins of tourism in Japan can be found in these journeys to Kumano. When the term 'pilgrimage' is used in this chapter, it refers mainly to what is termed *sankei* in Japanese – that is, secular pilgrimage – while *junrei* within the religious framework will be referred to as religious pilgrimage.

Pilgrimage to Kumano and the medieval religious system

From the 11th to the 12th century, the imperial court and nobility in Kyoto went on pilgrimages together to Kumano Sanzan. Emperor Go-Shirakawa (1127–1192) was passionate about this, completing the pilgrimage as many as 33 times over the course of his life. Kumano Sanzan is made up of three shrines: Kumano Hongu Taisha Shrine, Kumano Hayatama Taisha Shrine and Kumano Nachi Taisha Shrine. Thus, the pilgrimage might seem Shinto in nature; however, this was not the case. The origins of this pilgrimage actually stem from Japan's unique views on *kami* and Buddhism.

From the 10th to the 11th century there were changes to the way *kami* were worshipped in Japan. Buddhism is said to have arrived in the mid-6th century, and in the 8th century it became the national religion. Esoteric Buddhism, which arrived in the early 9th century, would exert a major influence on later religions in Japan as well. From the 11th century onwards, Buddhism developed into a major political force thanks to the large-scale feudal system, and *kami* would be redefined within the Buddhist system. *Honji suijaku* ('Manifestation Theory'), which was developed during the medieval period (the 11th to 16th centuries, broadly speaking), is a famous theory about the relationship between Japanese *kami* and Buddhism in the medieval period. The theory explains *kami* in a Buddhist context, stating that Japanese *kami* are a temporary transformation taken on by the Indian Buddha in order to rescue the Japanese people. In the 10th to 11th centuries, the original Buddhist deities (*honji*) were thus thought to manifest as *kami*. For example, an important *kami* called Amaterasu is enshrined at Ise Jingu Shrine. This deity is of the imperial family and were thought to be a reincarnation of Mahavairocana (Dainishi Buddha); that is to say, Mahavairocana was the *kami*'s true form as a Buddhist deity.

This theoretical system is generally referred to as *shinbutsu-shugo*, or the syncretism of *kami* and Buddhism. Buddhists created this ideology, and Buddhist priests were the ones to enshrine *kami* in the medieval period, continuing until the Edo period. The syncretism was part of the Buddhist system, and especially in medieval times was part of the core ideology of Buddhism. As the fundamental ideology of major medieval temples and shrines, it is referred to as *kenmitsu* (exoteric-esoteric) Buddhism. Kumano Sanzan, mentioned earlier, was a sacred ground within the religious framework of *kenmitsu* Buddhism.

What then was the reason for the belief in Kumano's *kami* by the imperial court and nobility? This is related to *jodo* (pure land, paradise), a Buddhist concept regarding the rebirth that spread throughout Japan starting in the 10th century. The afterlife had been a dirty place in the 8th-century world view expressed in the *Kojiki* and *Nihon Shoki*, described in what could be considered a negative light. However, with the introduction of the idea of *jodo*, people in the medieval period began to believe that they could go to a Buddhist utopia after death, guided by the Buddhist deities. Kumano Sanzan represented a temporary *kami* manifestation of Buddhist deities, and by forming a relationship with these *kami* pilgrims could ensure that they would go to the pure land, or *jodo*, after death. This made pilgrimages to Kumano Sanzan very popular, almost as if Kumano Sanzan itself was the pure land.

In this way, tourism – that is, going on a round trip to a sacred area – began in Japan with the ritual services for kami in *kenmitsu* Buddhism. From then until the Meiji period which began in 1868, shrines were, with the exception of Ise Jingu Shrine and a few others, managed by Buddhist monks. Shinto shrines are often seen as traditional symbols of Japan's long and unique history, but, in reality, most currently existing shrines were reconstructed after 1868 to minimalise and even eradicate Buddhism's influence. This meant that monks were expelled from shrines, Buddhist facilities within shrines were taken down and dismantled and Buddhist images were discarded. Accordingly, Shinto shrines look different now than they did up until the end of the Edo period; this can be seen as an example of the 'invention of tradition' during the Meiji period (Nakanishi, 2010).

Finally, one unique feature of the medieval Pilgrimage to Kumano is that, as a form of tourist activity, this pilgrimage was wholly operated by the religious sector. The guides used the religious titles *sendatsu* and *oshi*, and these terms and their organisational structures were also used later in pilgrimages to Ise Jingu Shrine. On the long journey from Kyoto to Kumano, shrines referred to as the *kujuku oji* were set up along the way as rest areas and places for lodging. One could say that the religious sector served the role of modern-day travel agencies. In this sense, belief in Kumano Sanzan and pilgrimages there, can be seen, in more terms, as a business model used by the religious sector, turning faith into a packaged commodity of pilgrimage.

Shinto and the popularisation of the pilgrimage

In the case of the Pilgrimage to Kumano, belief in the rituals carried out for *kami* fit into the framework of *kenmitsu* Buddhism. Among Japanese historians, some believe that while rituals for the gods have existed since ancient times, in the medieval period they were absorbed into *kenmitsu* Buddhism, and, furthermore, the liberation of these rituals from *kenmitsu* Buddhism is the origin of the Shinto known today (Dobbins & Gay, 1999). There is room for further investigation in this area, but at the very least it can be said that Shinto was organised into a religious system no earlier than the 13th century.

Those who made pilgrimages in medieval times were members of the imperial court and nobility, in other words high-ranking people in society. However, this practice became widely popular when the samurai seized power in the Edo period (1603–1867). In this era, the major political and economic power holders of the medieval period – temples and shrines, the imperial court and the nobility – faded, while the warrior class arose as the new centre of the political system, and Japanese society underwent major economic development. Religious organisations – especially large-scale temples and shrines – naturally changed to accommodate the demands of the general public, a prime example being the flourishing of pilgrimages among the general public. Travel was generally restricted during the Edo period, but pilgrimages to temples and shrines were an exception. The popularity of pilgrimages was also given a significant boost by the Edo shogunate's creation of networks of roads across the country.

Ise Jingu Shrine is representative of the Edo period pilgrimages, and such pilgrimages were referred to as *okagemairi*. Though the Ise Jingu Shrine had been partially related to Buddhism in the medieval period, the shrine tended to keep its distance from Buddhism. The rise in the popularity of pilgrimages to Ise Jingu Shrine was a dramatic change, symbolic of the times, as religious pilgrimages to shrines had never previously been considered a formal duty in Shinto. Thus, the increase in pilgrimages in this period is indicative of their secularisation and popularisation, a phenomenon that reflects changes in Japanese concepts about religion. There are theories that group pilgrimages to Ise Jingu Shrine by the general public originated in the 14th to 16th centuries, but in any case, they became more common from the 17th century onwards. Some 3.3–3.7 million people visited the Ise Jingu Shrine in only two months in 1705, while 2 million visited in 1771 and around five million people visited over approximately a six-month period in 1830 (Kokushi Daijiten Hensan Iinkai [ed.], 1980). This pilgrimage was arguably the first kind of 'tourist trip' experienced by the Japanese public.

The motive for pilgrimages in the Edo period was generally to pray for abundant harvests, commercial prosperity, good health or recovery from disease – in other words, safety in day-to-day life. This pursuit of worldly benefits through religious faith, referred to as *gense riyaku*, is another folk belief developed in Japan. However, as is clear from research in this area, these pilgrimages were in a sense simply excuses for other things, with pilgrims' real goals closer to modern-day tourism: sightseeing, going to the theatre and eating delicious food (cf. Guichard-Anguis, 2009; Ishimori, 1995).

However, far from taking a hands-off approach to these tourist pilgrimages, religious organisations promoted group pilgrimages as package deals, or at the very least tolerated them. Pilgrimages to sacred mountains were extremely popular in the Edo period, as the medieval system used in the Pilgrimage to Kumamoto became accessible to the general public. As a result, there was an explosive increase in pilgrimages to other local sacred mountains (Dewa Sanzan in Yamagata Prefecture, Mount Hiko in Fukuoka Prefecture and Mount Haku, which lies on the border between Ishikawa, Fukui and Gifu Prefectures, for example). These originated from *shugendo*, a part of medieval *kenmitsu* Buddhism, and many of the sacred grounds drew on both Shinto and Buddhism. Practitioners of *shugendo*, called *yamabushi* and *shugenja*, outwardly resembled esoteric Buddhist monks, but they worshipped *kami* more as laypeople with shamanistic religious activities. These *yamabushi*, acting as what would nowadays be recognised as talented salesmen, helped spread faith in the mountains and supported the mass popularity of sacred mountains in the Edo period.

Finally, as an example of selling pilgrimages as 'package deals', the *on-shi* (usually pronounced *oshi* but in Ise pronounced *on-shi*) around Ise Jingu Shrine should not be overlooked. *On-shi*, officially Shinto in nature, managed hotels and restaurants, arranged excursions and acted as local guides for pilgrims. *Ko*, organisations of members of a religion that were created all over Japan, played a major role in the popularisation of pilgrimages to Ise Jingu Shrine in the Edo period as well, each *ko* organising pilgrimages in coordination with specific *on-shi* in the area. The pilgrims paid for Shinto rituals and charms through the *on-shi* and expended large sums of money for luxury lodging facilities, foods and various amusements prepared by the *on-shi* (Kanamori, 2004). The gate at Ise Jingu Shrine marked the entrance to a separate world that could well be called a 'tourist destination'. To describe the popularity of Ise Jingu Shrine in contemporary tourism terms, it was a packaged tourism product that became wildly popular, created by fringe members of a religion called *on-shi*.

Shinto, Tourism and Modernisation

With the Meiji Restoration in 1867, the shogunate political system controlled by the samurai collapsed, and a new Meiji government aimed at modernising the nation came to power. The Meiji period (1867–1912) was a time of major upheaval for religion in Japan. The government established a national system around the emperor, which had major repercussions for the world of *kami*. Shrines were at the centre of this order because they were places where *kami*, the ancestors of the imperial family, were enshrined (this is also called 'State Shinto'). The syncretism of Shinto and Buddhism that had been at the core of faith since medieval times was now banned, and policies were made to remove Buddhist elements from Shinto (1868). *Shugendo*, which had helped mountain pilgrimages flourish in the Edo period, was banned by the government in 1872 (though later lifted in 1945). Although religious freedom was generally pursued during the Meiji period (with the ban on Christianity being lifted in 1873), Shinto was deemed outside the category of 'religion', and considered instead to be a system of rituals, manners and customs deeply permeating Japanese society. Shrines were not religious institutions but rather part of a national institution, while Shinto priests were repositioned as government officials. This classification ended with Japan's defeat at the end of World War II (1945), and afterwards, Shinto organisations were formally recognised as religious organisations once more.

The religious policies of the Meiji period had a major impact on religion across Japan (Yasumaru, 1979), while also affecting pilgrimages by the general public to shrines and temples. The *yamabushi* of the once popular sacred mountains were forced to return to secular life by the ban on *shugendo*, and thus compelled to seek employment outside the realm of religion. The organisations of temples and shrines around the sacred mountains abandoned Buddhism during this period and chose to be affiliated with Shinto instead. The fact that the religious organisations affiliated with the sacred mountains mentioned earlier – Kumano Sanzan, Dewa Sanzan, Mount Hiko and Mount Haku – are now considered to be Shinto was heavily influenced by political measures in the early Meiji period. The government's management of Shinto also led to the abolition of the *on-shi* system, and in Ise and other pilgrimage sites across Japan, *on-shi* towns and settlements fell into decline. A village at the summit of Mount Mitake in the mountains west of Tokyo is probably the only *on-shi* community remaining from the Edo period.

The area around Ise Jingu Shrine was affected similarly and lost the prosperity it had enjoyed during the Edo period. However, pilgrimages to temples and shrines would later make a comeback in a different form, as the private financial sector began to participate in pilgrimages. The first modern travel agency in Japan, the Nippon Travel Agency, began by offering services between Mount Koya (a holy ground in Shingo esoteric Buddhism located in Wakayama Prefecture) and Ise Jingu Shrine (www. nta.co.jp/recruit/company/history.html). Also, the development of railways in Japan starting in the late 19th century, especially private railways, would serve as a means of transforming pilgrimages into modern tourism.

The private railways created throughout Japan in this period connected urban centres with areas in the outskirts. In the case of major cities like

Tokyo and Osaka, terminal stations existed in city centres, but the issue was the terminal stations in local areas. A notable feature of Japanese private railways is that many pilgrimage sites popular since the Edo period are now terminal stations or other stations along the way. One can take Tobu Railways, which extends from Tokyo to northeast Japan, to Nikko's Toshogu Shrine, while Keisei Electric Railway, extending to the east, takes passengers to Narita's Shinshoji Temple, a pilgrimage site once very popular with people living in Kyoto.

The biggest private railway company in Japan, Kinki Nippon Tetsudou, based in Osaka, opened a route in 1914 between Osaka and Nara, a tourist city with many ancient shrines and temples. Then, in 1931, a limited express train line was created between Osaka and the Ise region, making possible day trips from Osaka to Ise Jingu Shrine. Thus, the private financial sector's contributions to pilgrimages helped bring about a revival in pilgrimages made by the general public.

Tsushima (2012) has carried out detailed research on the links between private railways in the Kinki region – principally Kyoto and Osaka – and pilgrimages. During the second half of the 19th century, and the construction of railways that linked metropolitan and rural areas, private railways and temples/shrines had a shared interest because pilgrims were also users of the railways. It was, however, the pilgrims who really made this arrangement work. At the beginning of the 20th century, private railways created new rail lines for pilgrimages and organised events related to the pilgrimages. Tsushima notes that these railways were not simply transporters of pilgrims, arguing instead that they were important engines for introducing pilgrims to temples and shrines, in the manner of the pre-modern *Oshi*. Tsushima (2012: 55) thus calls these private railways 'secular religious coordinators'.

One phenomenon that encapsulates the relationship between railway companies and Shinto is *hatsumode*, when people make their first visits to shrines at New Year. *Hatsumode* is a custom that began relatively recently, with many Japanese people making these pilgrimages between 1 and 3 January. For example, more than three million people are said to visit Meiji Shrine in Tokyo during this time, while around 2.7 million visit Kyoto's Fushimi Inari Taisha Shrine. According to the National Police Agency's calculations, 90 million people around Japan made *hatsumode* visits in 2010. *Hatsumode* may appear to be a traditional event, but according to historian Takagi (1997), it has only been practiced by the general public since the Meiji period, and it was not until the 20th century that it became the kind of large-scale event that it is today. According to Takagi, one reason for the expansion of *hatsumode* is the marketing efforts made on behalf of private railway companies.

In short, pilgrimages were initially managed under the umbrella of religion, then went through the populist boom of the Edo period and finally reached a form resembling modern tourism as they came under the control of the private financial sector in the 20th century. This process is related to religion's spread among the Japanese public, which increased the importance of Shinto and the enshrinement of *kami*. Shinto was a secular religion, a direct extension of people's daily lives, and the connection between pilgrimages and tourism was an inevitable result of the popularisation of Japanese society and religion.

Re-creation of Tradition

Even today, Shinto has major significance in tourism. The economic effects of this are illustrated by the number of people going on *hatsumode*, as described above. Also, many of the registered World Heritage Sites in Japan are shrines: Itsukushima Shrine in Hiroshima Prefecture, Nikko Toshogu Shrine in Tochigi Prefecture and the shrines of Kyoto and Nara not only receive large numbers of tourists from within Japan but also many inbound tourists from abroad. Shrine festivals are certainly important for domestic tourism, but there is no denying that they are now also major tourist attractions for foreign tourists. The Sanja Matsuri Festival held every May in Asakusa in Tokyo, the Gion Matsuri Festival at Kyoto's Yasaka Shrine in July and the Hakata Gion Yamakasa Festival held at Fukuoka's Kushida Shrine are traditional urban festivals that draw many tourists both domestic and foreign even today.

These shrine festivals can become influential events, as seen in the example of the *shikinen sengu* (regular shrine removal) ceremony held at Ise Jingu Shrine in 2014. There is a rule that every 20 years the shrine must be rebuilt, and the series of rituals and ceremonies affiliated with this are referred to by the general public as *shikinen sengu*. As an example, 14.2 million people came to Ise City to see this when it happened in 2014, an increase in visitors by about 177% over the previous year (www.city.ise. mie.jp/secure/12124/25kankotoukei.pdf).

There are also some special cases that have attracted tourists – modern-day pilgrims, that is – and given new meaning to shrines. The area of Shimane Prefecture known as Izumo appears in Japanese legends and contains the Izumo Taisha Shrine, which is very old and one of the most important large-scale shrines. In recent years, its significance as the home of a matchmaking deity has been emphasised, and there has been a rapid increase in visitors, especially women. In addition, areas considered 'power spots' have become popular. 'Power spot' is a Japanese term constructed from English loanwords referring to a location (spot) supposedly filled with spiritual power, and many Shinto shrines have been described in the media as power spots.

In the modern day, many Japanese people visit shrines seeking monetary profit. The idea that there is profit to be gained through shrine visits has been promoted in the print media, on television and on the internet. Thus, the impact of media on pilgrimages in the modern era is exceedingly large. One unique example is Washinomiya Shrine in Kuki City, Saitama

Prefecture, located in a suburb of Tokyo. The area in front of the shrine was the setting for a popular anime television show, resulting in a sudden increase in the number of people visiting for *hatsumode* in 2008. When people visit modern Japanese shrines, they often write their wishes on wooden boards called *ema*, which are then hung in a certain place inside the shrine, the wishes supposedly fulfilled by *kami*. Usually many of these *ema* have traditional Japanese designs printed on them, but the ones in Washinomiya Shrine also have, in addition to people's handwritten wishes, illustrations from the anime drawn by young people. These have earned the special nickname *ita-ema* (see Figure 6.4).

Figure 6.4 Ita-ema (Washinomiya Shrine in Saitama Prefecture)

Looking at a phenomenon like this, it may appear that a completely new, modern relationship has been established between shrines and the public. Shinto, however, lacking any complicated doctrine and serving as an extension of people's everyday lives, has always existed in this manner. Shinto and its shrines have existed in a form that responds to the society and times, experiencing various transformations. In the Edo period, as a result of commercial development, shrines for material prosperity were built. Now, as a result of the rising popularity of anime, Washinomiya Shrine has, though by chance, become akin to a holy ground for anime fans. Interestingly, Washinomiya Shrine and the surrounding community are trying to use this popularity to benefit the region.

Shinto and its shrines have been regarded as part of Japanese traditional culture. However, because religion only gains meaning from its supporters, it will most likely continue to change in the future. It will be interesting to see what new changes occur in Shinto and at shrines in the context of these changing phenomena.

References

Dobbins, J.C. and Gay, S. (1999) Shinto in the history of Japanese religion: An essay by Kuroda Toshio. In G.J. Tanabe Jr. (ed.) *Religions of Japan in Practice* (pp. 451–467). Princeton, NJ: Princeton University Press.

Guichard-Anguis, S. (2009) Introduction: The culture of travel (*tabi no bunka*) and Japanese tourism. In S. Guichard-Anguis and O. Moon (eds) *Japanese Tourism and Travel Culture* (pp. 1–15). London/New York: Routledge.

Ishimori, S. (1995) Tourism and religion: From the perspective of comparative studies. In T. Umesao and H. Befu Suita (eds) *Japanese Civilization in the Modern World*, IX: *Tourism* (pp. 179–194). Senri Ethnological Studies 38. Osaka: National Museum of Ethnology.

Kanamori, A. (2004) *Ise mode to edo no tabi (Pilgrimage to Ise and Travel in the Edo Era: Price of Travel in the Travelogue)*. Tokyo: Bungei-Shunju. (In Japanese.)

Kokushi Daijiten Hensan Iinkai (Editorial Board of Encyclopedia of Japanese National History) (ed.) (1980) Okagemairi. In *Kokushi Daijiten [Encyclopedia of Japanese National History]* (Vol. 2; p. 728). Tokyo: Yoshikawa Kobunkan. (In Japanese.)

Nakanishi, Y. (2010) Magical power of 'real articles': Issues in the historical discourse about old temples and shrines tourism in Japan. *Encounter* 1, 21–25.

Smith, V.L. (ed.) (1977) *Hosts and Guests: The Anthropology of Tourism*. Philadelphia, PA: University of Pennsylvania Press.

Takagi, H. (1997) *Kindai ten-no sei no bunkashiteki kenkyu: Ten-no shunin girei, nenchu gyoji, bunkazai (Cultural-Historical Studies of Modern Emperor System in Japan: Emperor Inauguration Ceremony, Annual Rituals and Cultural Property)*. Tokyo: Asakura-shoten. (In Japanese.)

Tsushima, M. (2012) Tetsudo to Reijo: Shukyo coordinator to shiteno kansai shitetsu (Railway and religion: Private railway companies in West Japan as religious coordinator). In H. Yamanaka (ed.) *Shukyo to Tourism: Seinaru monono jizoku to hen-yo [Religion and Tourism: Persistence and Transformation of the Sacred]* (pp. 32–57). Kyoto: Sekai shiso sha. (In Japanese.)

Turner, V.W. (1966) *The Ritual Process: Structure and Anti-Structure*. London: Routledge and Kegan Paul.

Yasumaru, Y. (1979) *Kamigami no Meiji ishin: shinbutsu bunri to haibutsu kishaku* [*Meiji Restoration of Deities: Separation of Buddhism and Shintoism and a Movement to Abolish Buddhism*]. Tokyo: Iwanami-shoten. (In Japanese.)

Websites

Agency for Cultural Affairs, Government of Japan, *Statistical Survey about Religion* (in Japanese). See http://www.bunka.go.jp/tokei_hakusho_shuppan/tokeichosa/shumu/pdf/h26kekka.pdf.
History of Nippon Travel Agency, *Nippon Travel Agency* (in Japanese). See https://www.nta.co.jp/recruit/company/history.html.
Tourism Statistics of Ise City, *Ise City in Mie prefecture* (in Japanese). See http://www.city.ise.mie.jp/secure/12124/25kankotoukei.pdf.

7 Hinduism and Tourism

Pushkar Kanvinde and Binumol Tom

Religion

India is a country with a rich tradition based on religion. In religion lies the vitality of India and here not only does it provide Indians with a way of life, but it also forms the 'asthithwa' or the very existence of people. Each religion that originated in India created its own architectural language which became symbolic of each religious group. The idea to have a place for public worship led to the rise of places of worship built generally through a regal commission for use by a community of people. The spiritual foundation, upon which the marvellous monuments of glory to God and charity to all beings have been built, stands unshaken, strong as ever according to swami Vivekananda. The Indian philosophical spatial concepts of the centre, axis and human relatedness to the cosmic reality are followed conspicuously in the making of the temples. However, the implementation of the temple built form follows the Vedic religious practices.

The spatial organisation of a temple is dictated by the symbolism of the vertical axis joining the nether world (hell) with the sky (heaven) and the horizontal axis following the cardinal directions. Religious architecture is a celebration of life as it manifests ideas, encodes messages and emotes feelings in believers. It communicates through spatial tools and forms a microcosm in the cosmos connecting the sensorial, experiential and associational levels of contact between 'Atman' and 'Brahman', the fundamental basis of any existence.

Three religions now stand in the world that have come down to us from prehistoric times. They are Hinduism, Zoroastrianism and Judaism. 'Hindu' is a term used to broadly denote the dominant culture of India, initially encompassing a wide range of different people who are neither Muslim, Sikh, Jain or Christian. It originated from a Persian word for people inhabiting the region beyond the Indus River and is found in 16th-century Sanskrit and Bengali texts. According to Hindus, the whole world of religions is only a voyage of men and women through various conditions and circumstances to the same goal of reaching 'Brahman', the supreme reality. As it is meant in the most important and famous prayer of Hindus, ॐ भूर्भुवः स्वः । ॐ तत्सवितुर्वरेण्यम्भर्गो देवस्य धीमहि धियो यो नः प्रचोदयात् ॥ 'Let us meditate on the glorious effulgence of that supreme being who has created the universe. May she enlighten our hearts and direct our understanding'.[1]

Culture, Religion and Architecture

Every culture inspires a type of architecture that can range from landmarks to everyday homes. History has proved that the various architectural styles have developed in response to the climate, lifestyle, geography and geology of a place, the religious philosophy of the people and the availability of building materials. Religion and lifestyle seem to be the most common influences overall. Culture, in fact, underlines the important role that economics, politics, religion, heritage and the natural environment play in shaping the built environment.

Religion has created various streams of thoughts, customs and practises. This, in turn, called for building magnificent abodes of gods and goddesses. The idea of having a place for public worship led to the rise of temples built generally by a collective endeavour under the patronage of various kings. Various languages of architecture also developed for building the abodes of gods and goddesses.

Religion is understood as a universal phenomenon that has endured over time due to a belief in a visible/invisible, supernatural power, object or presence that regulates individuals' relationship, both with each other and with their surroundings through several sacred practices. Such beliefs laid the foundation of the specific manifestation of built forms to showcase the sacred. Architectural and anthropological thinkers such as Lewis Morgan and Amos Rapoport introduced the sociocultural perspectives of rich architectural heritage. Each culture is unique and the more we learn about them, the more we appreciate our surroundings and understand why certain things appeal to us. Architecture is indeed a cultural artefact that cannot be understood outside its cultural context and is dependent on the state of the cultural evolution of the social group to which it belongs. According to Rapoport (1969), religion is an essential part of all cultures starting from the most primitive and pre-industrial ones and is closely linked with and inseparable from their social life and needs. He places emphasis on culture by stating that a building is a cultural phenomenon; its form and organisation are greatly influenced by the cultural milieu to which it belongs.

Without doubt, architecture is a part of culture. It is certainly part of how we see ourselves, and part of how we see the world. The unique aspect of architecture is that in its physical incarnation of buildings, it may last for hundreds of years. Architecture is created by people. The most successful architecture goes beyond just being a shed or a box to live in. The most important examples of architecture as we look back over history are buildings or environments that have done so much more in a variety of ways – be that innovation in building and construction or buildings that have pushed the discipline to get us to think about our environment in different ways or just incredibly beautiful buildings that have lifted the human spirit in addition to housing our activities and our lives.

To every Hindu, Hinduism is more a way of life than a religion. In olden times, every action a person performed and every building he/she constructed were governed by his/her strong religious beliefs. In the erection of a temple or a house, the selection of the site, the measurements, the date of commencement of the work, the materials employed, the orientation of the structure, its layout and other, all had religious connotations that, if overlooked, were believed to displease the gods and bring ill luck to people. Regardless of the most severe physical constraints and technological limitations, people built in ways so strikingly diverse that they can be attributed to choice, which deliberately comes from the culture. Any temple town in India gives testimony to the fact that an active cultural universal such as religion can give shape to a whole urban conglomeration with the abode of God as the focal point.

Temples: The Places of Worship in Hinduism

The abodes of Hindu gods in India present a unique architectural language, exhibiting excellence in the creation of the temple form, its structural clarity, stylistic tradition and symbolism characterised by a high level of craftsmanship and building skill. Though based on the genetic code stipulated by the science of architecture, followed in India as Vastushastra, temples display many regional variations as a result of the broad geographical, climatic and ethnic differences. The temple architecture in India developed over 2000 years of dedicated works of the sthapathis (local nomenclature for craftsmen involved in the construction of buildings), and occurred within the rigid frameworks derived entirely from religious and ritualistic thoughtfulness. One finds an overwhelming richness of architectural vocabulary created by the elements, sculptural forms and decorative ebullience making each famous temple complex a heaven on earth. This, in fact, is a magnet that promotes tourism. The canonical texts on Indian architecture classify temples into three main orders: the Indo Aryan of Nagara (north Indian style), the Dravidian (south Indian style) and the Vesara (mixed style), in addition to the definite regional variety of styles of Bengal, Kerala and the Himalayan areas.

Some of the finest examples of the Indo Aryan style of temple architecture are found in the Khajuraho group of temples in Madhya Pradesh, which are famous for their architectural symbolism and their erotic sculptures, such as the Sun Temple at Modhera in Gujrat and the Sun Temple at Konark in Orissa (Figures 7.1–7.3). The best examples of the south Indian style are the temples of Brihadeshwara at Tanjore

(Figure 7.4), Meenakshi at Madurai, temple complexes at Pattadakkal, Aihole and Badami, the Hoysaleswara Temple at Halebidu (Figure 7.5) and Kanchipuram. The essential parts of a temple are the sanctum sanctorum (garbhagriha) which contains the main deity, adorned by a vimana over it, a hall attached (ardhamandapa) or detached (mahamandapa) in front of the garbhagriha, circumambulatory paths (pradakshinapatha), enclosing walls and four entrance towers (gopurams) at the four cardinal directions. In addition, there are dancing halls, eating halls, tanks, wells and shrines for minor gods and goddesses.

Figure 7.1 Khajuraho Temple

Figure 7.2 Sun Temple Konark

Figure 7.3 Sun Temple Konark at Orissa

Figure 7.4 Brihadeshwara Temple at Tanjore

Figure 7.5 A closer profile of Halebidu Temple

The highly acclaimed Khajaraho and Halebidu temples stand as the most befitting climax of the Indian master sculptor working on stone creating a dramatic scene of closely knit sculptural compositions, continuous mouldings, borders, cornices and friezes depicting various postures of kamasutra and various stories of purana enveloping the analogous voluminous spaces inside. The sculptural detailing found in these temples remind one of the fact that Dharma (virtuous living), Artha (material prosperity) and Kama (desire) are aims of everyday life, while Moksha (salvation/liberation) is to be sought to release oneself from the cycle of death and rebirth. The dynamics of the sculptural architectonics of these temples are in contradiction to the cold purity of the architectural form developed on solid platforms. The temples are mostly enveloped by walls that carry skilfully carved sculptures. These sculptures represent the beauty of the most sensual male and female bodies and they stand as a celebration of the human body, an integral part of being one with the sacred. The magnetism of the curvaceous female body is explicitly seen in the sculptures that are not just adorning the wall but forming an essential part of the temple's skin and structure. Many tourists flock to enjoy the enchanting architectural disposition of the temples of India.

Religious Tourism

The relevance of religious tourism lies in the fact that modern-day life is filled with activities related to daily chores and one finds it difficult to spare time for one's own self. In the words of Jay Lakhani, 'In this busy life, carrying out daily religious rituals is a short break to pause and be with yourself, think about higher things, at least for a short time. It also gives you reminder of a God and higher things in existence' (transcript from video). Pilgrimage or religious tourism is a long break from routine when one learns about different locales, geography, climate, people and practices and language, and in return, understands oneself better and returns a wiser person with greater enthusiasm for life and ultimate reality. In olden days, with no activities promoting tourism of any kind, pilgrimage was the only way to explore and learn about the world outside one's domain.

Hindu Religious Tourism in India

Tourism and Hinduism have a very close relationship in India. Since ancient times, religious tourism has been promoted in Hinduism and other Indic religions as a way of life. The idea is to introduce change from routine and be refreshed. It must also include learning about different geographies, climates, social groups, cultures, languages and cuisines. In olden days, with slower modes of transport, such travels must have been tedious but enriching and life-fulfilling experiences for commoners.

Since Hinduism is a practice in search of human resolution that organises the conditions we live in, it makes an effort to understand the rules and regulations that control all happenings in this universe in which we live. It is a religion with a vast number of gods and goddesses promoting ritualistic living. Beyond a religion, and as a way of living, Hinduism has a mature, pluralistic tradition. This tradition has called for various ways of leading a healthy spiritual and mental life. Thus, it gave birth to various festivals designed to suit the rituals that the tradition demands. Hindu mythological frameworks were mostly merged with the traditions of sacred places belonging to a variety of local contexts.

Rivers, the life-givers for communities, are considered very sacred in this religion. Hence, many pilgrimages are associated with rivers. One of the greatest religious festivals that brings the greatest number of tourists is the Grand Pitcher Festival, regionally known as 'Kumbhmela', which takes place once every 12 years at four different locations in India. This festival witnesses the largest human gathering at a sacred location along the holy rivers Ganges, Godavari and Kshipra. Most famous and elaborate, where over 70 million people gather, is the one that takes place on the banks of the holy river Ganges, near its confluence with the river Yamuna and the invisible river Saraswati, 15 kilometres from the city of Allahabad, for more than a month of bathing rituals. The rituals are intended to wash away sins and hasten the people's progress towards nirvana (salvation).

The Teerthyatras (pilgrimages)

Yatra, a sanskrit word meaning journey when used as *Teerthyatra* in Hindi, means a pilgrimage to holy places such as those referred to in the great epics viz. Mahabharata and Ramayana, the holy hills as well as the confluences of rivers that are considered holy. A dip in such holy waters and the penance of travelling to distant places and the temples found in such divine regions are usually undertaken by the religious in groups. Belief in the salvific power of certain places becomes the major dimension that supports religious tourism, and specific locations become salvific spaces. Salvific spaces gain their strength from religious narratives, rituals, history and structures as they have become central ideas in the Hindu traditions of pilgrimage, and concern the ability of space, especially sites associated with bodies of water such as rivers and lakes, to grant salvific rewards to the devotee.

Various pilgrimage circuits connect such salvific spaces and structures, such as Char-dham, 12 Jyotirlingas, Shaktipeethas, Astavinayaka and 11 Marutis, where devotees visit in groups, promoting religious tourism in India. Of these, Char Dham is considered to be of the highest importance and also the most difficult to go through. It requires the devotee to visit holy places located at four extreme ends of the Indian subcontinent, as discussed below.

There are many similar smaller circuits mentioned above that the pilgrims visit. Ashtavinayaka means eight Ganeshas, referring to a pilgrimage route to the eight holy temples dedicated to Lord Ganesha in the state of Maharashtra in India. It is believed that these eight idols are self-originated or 'swayambhu' and a religious tour visiting all eight temples is considered very auspicious. Other than the Char Dham regular circuit, another smaller circuit called Chotta (Mini) Char Dham is also considered auspicious. It consists of a visit to the temples of Badrinath and Kedarnath and the origins of the river Ganges at Gangotree and Yamuna at Yamunotree, all located in the Himalayas, close to each other.

Similar to the Ashtavinayaka, the 11 Marutis also forms a religious circuit that is often referred as 'Vaariche Maruti' or Akra Maruti (अकरा मारुती), established in the 17th century by Shri Swami Samarth Ramdas around Satara dedicated to Lord Hanuman. The Ashtavinayak temples are Moreshwar Temple in Morgaon, Girijatmaj Temple in Lenyadri, Vighnahar Temple in Ozar, Mahaganapati Temple in Ranjangaon and Chintamani Temple in Theurall located in Pune district, Siddhivinayak Temple in Ahmednagar, Ballaleshwar Temple in Pali (Raigad) and Varadavinayak Temple Mahad near Khopoli, again in Raigad district. The 11 Maruti temples are located at Shahapur near Karad (built in 1644), Masur near Karad (built in 1645), ChaphalVirMaruti Temple near Satara (1648), Chaphal Das Maruti Temple near Satara (1648), Shinganwadi near Satara (1649), Umbraj near Masur (1649), Majgaon near Satara (1649), Bahe near Sangli (1651), Manapadale near Kolhapur (1651), Pargaon near Panhala (1651) and Shirala (1654).

12 Jyotirlingas

The etymology of Jyotir Lingam is the 'radiant sign of almighty Shiva' with Jyoti meaning 'radiance' and Lingam the 'image or sign' of Shiva. The Jyotirlingam is a devotional object representing the Supreme God, Shiva. There are 12 traditional Jyotirlinga shrines in India, 6 in Maharashtra while 2 are in Madhya Pradesh and the rest are in Gujrat, Andhra Pradesh, Jharkhand and Tamilnadu.

Shaktipeethas

The Shaktipeethas or Shakti Pithas are temples that are scattered in the regions of present-day Pakistan, India, Sri Lanka and Bangladesh. The concept behind Shaktipeethas is that when the goddess Parvati, also known as Sati Devi or Shakti, was killed, her body was chopped into pieces and thrown to various geographic regions around the Indian subcontinent. Preserving the mortal relics of famous and respected individuals was a common practice in ancient India. Hence, wherever a portion of her body fell, temples were erected and venerated.

Char-dham

'Char Dham' is literally translated as 'the four abodes' and the term is coined in reference to the four widely revered sacred abodes of Hinduism – Badrinath Temple in Uttarakhand, Jagannatha Temple Puri in Orissa, Ramanatha Swamy Temple Rameshwaram in Tamilnadu and Dwarakadheesh Temple Dwarka in Gujrat (Figure 7.6). Geographically, these four temples are located in the northern, eastern, southern and western regions of the Indian subcontinent. Three are Vaishnavite temples while Ramanatha Swamy Temple in Tamilnadu located in the south follows the Shaivite philosophy of Hinduism. Traditionally, the Char Dham circuit starts from the eastern point at Puri, proceeding in a clockwise direction to Rameshwaram in the south, Dwarka in the west and finally to Badrinath in the north, concluding at Puri, the point of origin.

Chardham

Figure 7.6 Chardham

This religious circuit is considered a highly sacred journey that ensures the path towards 'moksha' (salvation) – the transcendent state of enlightenment. Devotees from all over the world embark on this holy voyage to experience eternal bliss. It also provides the traveller with varied experiences of travelling through different climatic zones. At one end, one enjoys the sea breezes and at the other end the picturesque surroundings of the mountainous region filled with silent and tranquil locales enrich one with salvific powers.

Kashi Yatra

Varanasi, also called Kashi or Benaras, is one of the oldest and holiest cities located on the banks of the Ganges in Uttar Pradesh, north India. It is believed to be a life-fulfilling experience for every Indian to make a pilgrimage to Kashi, known as Kashi Yatra. The importance of this yatra is depicted in Kashi-Khand of Skaanda Puranam. The Kashi religious circuit consists of various subcircuits such as the Panchkrosi Parikarma, Jal Tirth Yatra, Navagraha Yatra, Shivayatan Yatra, Durga Devi Yatra, Gauri Yatra, Antargrihi Yatra and Ekadasha Maharudra Yatra. All these religious voyages help devotees attain mukti (salvation). Tradition holds that Varanasi is the site at which the universe was created and will be destroyed. Annually, more than 40,000 cremations are conducted at Manikarnika, Varanasi's most prestigious cremation ghat, reflecting the belief that this is the place where corpses will be immolated at the end of time.

Amarnath Yatra

This is an annual pilgrimage of Hindu devotees in large numbers to Amarnath cave, a shrine located at an altitude of 3888 metres in Jammu and Kashmir. This shrine, which is actually a snow-clad cave, is considered the holiest one in Hinduism and is dedicated to Lord Shiva. The cave, as it is covered with snow most of the year, is open to pilgrims only for a short period of time in summer. Yet, about 300,000 pilgrims visit the shrine following the yatra and pay obeisance at this cave each year. The annual pilgrimage to the Amarnath cave is through challenging mountainous terrain to pray to the Shiva Linga located inside the 40-metre-high cave. This is a stalagmite formed out of freezing drops of water that fall from the cave roof and grows up vertically. The religious claim that the lingam grows and shrinks with the phases of the moon, reaching its height during the summer festival, although there is no scientific evidence for this belief.

Ratha Yatra

Also called the festival of chariots, this pilgrimage is conducted in commemoration of the annual visit of Lord Jagannatha of Puri in the state of Orissa to Gundicha Mata's Temple. Large numbers of pilgrims come to Puri during the festival to pull the Lord's chariots with ropes. On this day, even non-Hindus are allowed on the premises of Puri Temple.

Kailas-Mansarovar Yatra

This pilgrimage involves a 201-km-long trek through rugged terrain at high altitudes of up to 19,500 feet, around Mount Kailas, which is considered a very sacred place in Hinduism as it is believed to be the abode of Lord Shiva. Circumambulating the mount on foot is considered a very holy ritual by Hindus. Devotees who chant Om Namah Shivaaya have to pass through places such as Sirkha, Gala, Bundi, Kalapani, Gunji, Navidhang and Lipulekh before reaching Taklakot (Tibet border), and have to climb at least 4444 stairs to reach their destination. Many domestic as well as foreign tourists are attracted to this yatra.

Pandharpur yatra

In Maharashtra, even today there exists a tradition that is more than 700 years old, of travelling together in a huge group for an annual pilgrimage from many different places to Pandharpur. This is known as the famous Wari or Pandharpur yatra, where the voyage is to Vitthal Temple, and is held twice a year during the Hindu month of Ashadha (June and July) and again in the month of Kartik (October and November). Although many different groups originating from various places in Maharashtra and Karnataka participate in this pilgrimage, those originating from the towns of Dehu and Alandi near Pune to Pandharpur 250 kilometres away are the most significant and important (Figures 7.7 and 7.8). The pilgrimage is referred to as 'Wari' and the pilgrims are referred to as Warkaris. More than half a million Warkaris participate in this annual pilgrimage. The barefoot Warkaris carry Padukas (symbolic footwear) of Saint Tukaram from Dehu and Saint Dnyaneshwar from Alandi, both renowned devotees of Lord Vitthal, a form of Lord Vishnu, in a palkhi (palanquin) to Pandharpur in procession that lasts for more than three weeks. Upon reaching Pandharpur, the devotees take a deep dip in the holy river Chandrabhaga and visit Vitthal Temple for darshan to conclude the pilgrimage.

Wari route 1 Dnyaneshwar Maharaj

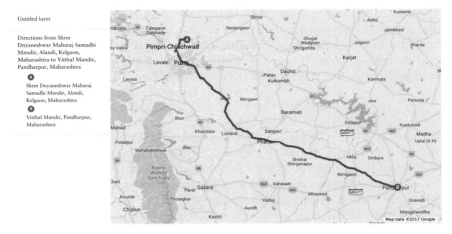

Figure 7.7 Wardi route 1: Dnyaneshwar Maharaj

Wari route 2 - Tukaram Maharaj Palkhi

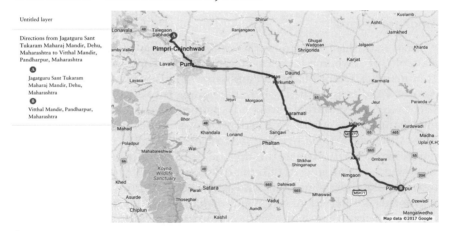

Figure 7.8 Wardi route 2: Tukuram Maharaj Palkhi

Deoghar Yatra

The literal meaning of Deoghar is the abode of gods and goddesses. It denotes the Baidyanath Dham or Baba Dham, situated in the eastern part of the state of Jharkhand. Regarded as 1 of the 12 Lord Shiva Jyothirlingam in India, it is a highly sought-after pilgrim trail for devotees. The ritual is to carry the holy water of the river Ganges from Sultanganj and offer it to the Jyotirlinga of Lord Shiva at Deoghar. In addition to the yatras mentioned above, a great number of single destination point journeys are undertaken by Hindus throughout India.

Present Issues, Trends and Implications

Pilgrimage trails, temples and their precincts are all manifestations of beliefs and aspirations of humanity that contain both tangible and intangible cultural values. Every change in belief can lead to loss of the cultural value of the religious voyage as well as the temple complex. Today, religious sites have become destination points of high-end tourism. In today's fast-paced world, the uncertainty of all aspects of life and the resultant stress are taking their toll on human beings. Submission to god is a way to get some psychological relief and also keep alive hope for a better tomorrow. Compared to the 1960s and 1970s, we can see tremendous growth in the number of devotees visiting religious places of all religions. This is further supported by communication and transportation revolutions that have made planning and undertaking journeys to religious places less tedious than in the past; thus, we have seen tremendous growth in religious tourism during the last 30 years. Temples that were visited by barely a few devotees are now thronged by thousands of them.

This sudden rise in the number of visitors and religious tourists has led to many different issues. Foremost is the lack of infrastructure. The visiting devotees, in addition to transportation infrastructure, also need places to rest or stay, facilities to have food and related sanitary conveniences. Many religious places do not have adequate facilities, which often leads to chaotic situations. Management of the stream of visitors crowding temple precincts is another issue that requires immediate attention. Many devotees may be disabled and their comfort and convenience need to be prioritised. Paying respect and devotion to gods is the right of people and hence steps need to be taken to provide safe and secure accessibility to such tourist spots.

At most places of pilgrimage, the temples receive large sums of money through offerings made by devotees. Temple complexes and managing trusts have become wealthy through receiving such funds. Many of these trusts and bodies are now helping the local authorities by providing monetary support to create facilities for tourists. However, intervention by local authorities is often restricted to upgrading urban infrastructure in terms of facilitating the availability of water, sewerage, transportation and security as well as maintenance of these services. Other infrastructure facilities including places to stay and obtain food and the management of a queueing system (wherever required) have to be managed by a trust or the managing body of the temple or by other private entrepreneurs. Conflict often exists among corporate groups to spend money on decorating certain temples to please God. Of course, such corporate magnanimity is reserved only for a few temples to the envy of other struggling places of worship. Perhaps there is a class distinction among gods too.

Owing to the increasing numbers of visitors and the relative shortage of infrastructure, many managing trusts and bodies have resorted to offering privileges and priorities to devotees by charging fees. Gods and their blessings are made available in packages sold at higher prices. Tourism is a double-edged sword, meaning that the utmost care must be taken when including temples and religious trails among tourist destination points, otherwise the cultural value of the temples and the religious circuits could suffer. A new surge of cosmopolitanism is evident in a few of the most sought-after temples and circuits.

Today, Hindu pilgrimages are becoming increasingly popular, with an upsurge of religious crowds to such places. Although travel to pilgrimage places in India is becoming easier and more comfortable, some physical exertion is still involved in such journeys. This, in turn, demands more infrastructure including new buildings such as sarais or hotels (resting places), eating halls, restaurants, shelter for people standing in queues for darshan and other temporary accommodation. The post-independence scene in India presents dual diverse trends, one of which is derived from the modernistic style of life, with an emphasis on concrete as the medium of construction with linear, cubical and curvilinear shapes expressing forms no different from what can be seen all over India, even in traditional religious precincts and Hindu circuits. The alternate stream may be rooted in an enquiry into the traditional style of construction and the revival of functional architecture. The use of indigenous materials, the adoption of traditional techniques and the matching of climatic needs are the features of this trend in architecture. Architecture across all ages has been an expression of social values. It is ever changing yet a distinct regional character has evolved in every region in India, influenced by the local materials, climate and aesthetic values, but still based on the code defined by the science of Vastu known as VastuShastra. This has been propagated from time immemorial through the tradition of *gurushishyaparampara* (master disciple legacy). What is found in contemporary architectural scenes are the pangs of a conflict or perhaps a synthesis of evolved architecture and the innovations in technology. Whether the regional character will still be preserved or not depends on the intrinsic worth of the traditional technology and the inherent strength of the social values of simplicity, functional perfection and subtle aesthetics.

The physical form of most of the religious precincts and temple complexes has undergone major changes, due to constant maintenance, renovation works and rapid urbanisation, followed by increased pilgrim traffic. The modern layers created in and around the temple precincts do not generally follow the traditional construction systems and material vocabulary. The replacement of vernacular building materials with cement and steel is causing considerable harm to the existing built fabric and has become a threat to the cultural value of these resources and their environments. Insensitive repair works, additions and alterations to allow catering to religious tourists are, by and large, causing serious damage to the holiness of these places. Today, some of the most ethnic and serene religious places have been transformed into concrete jungles. Contemporary construction mostly follows contradictory paths. Hence, every development in this regard needs to be focused on inclusiveness and responsiveness. The safety of women pilgrims needs to be brought into the mainstream of policy formulation and implementation. Further, the special needs of elderly people and the disabled need to be given critical importance.

Religious heritage architecture is a celebration of life as it manifests ideas, encodes messages and emotes feelings in believers. It communicates through spatial tools and forms a microcosm in the cosmos connecting the sensorial, experiential and associational levels of contact between Atman and Brahman, the fundamental basis of any existence. It also nourishes emotionally as well as spiritually, and enhances the sacred progression from the corporeal to the spiritual world. This experience should be a product of perception by the devotee as a consequence of his/her imaginative devotional associations provoked by the all-existing symbolism linked with a temple and its related circuits. Sacred sites are extremely sensitive as there is always an unquantifiable apparent heritage associated with them that can only be appreciated through experience.

Conclusion

Hinduism is possibly the oldest living religion, dating back to 2500 BC. It is known as a most complex yet tolerant religion and has given birth to many religious voyages. Over the millennia, Hindus have developed a very large number of pilgrim sites and pilgrim circuits, as well as pilgrimage-related practices. The purposes fulfilled by such voyages are taking darshan of deities, austerities and undertaking penances, listening to talks and receiving advice on spiritual life, participating in worship and glorification (e.g. kirtan), performing specific rites (such as shraddha), circumambulation of holy places and giving charity to priests and temples. Fortunately, when it comes to pilgrims and pilgrimages, their aspirations are derived from their own faiths and beliefs and this makes them more likely to adjust to the services and facilities that are available. Travelling for religious purpose is an essential part of the evolution of tourism and thus pilgrimage remains among the most practised forms of tourism. Hence, the developments along the pilgrimage paths should be controlled and made sensible as well as responsive.

Pilgrim paths, temples and their precincts function as magnets for every community and hence undergo major changes due to hurried modernisation accelerated by the ever-increasing pilgrim traffic. The commercialisation and rapid modern development of these environments brought about by the growth of religious tourism can degrade the 'intactness and wholeness' of the holy sites, destroying the intrinsic value of the tangible and intangible heritage held by those sites. In 2002, the government of India launched a campaign 'Incredible India', that often features religious sites such as temples. Hence, any intervention needs to be undertaken with the utmost sensitivity and seriousness, so that both the tangible and intangible cultural values of these sacred places remain well preserved and can be handed over to the next generation in the manner in which they are deserving.

Note

(1)   Gayatri Mantra is the famous prayer of Hindus that has its origins in Rigveda (mandala 3.62.10). It is a prayer to Sun or energy without which there could be no life.

References

Albanese, M. (2001) *India: Treasure from an Ancient World*. Vercelli: White Star.
Basham, A.L. (1967) *The Wonder That was India*. London: Sidgwick & Jackson.
Carrington, D. (2001) 'Kumbh Mela'. *New Scientist*. January. See http://www.newscientist.com/issue/2272 (accessed on 12 September 2016).
Lakhani, J. (2014) *Talks on Hinduism*. London: Hindu Academy.
Rapoport, A. (1969) *House Form and Culture*. Englewood Cliffs, NJ: Prentice Hall.

8 The Monks and Nuns of Pu-Tuo as Custodians of Their Sacred Buddhist Site

Cora Un In Wong

Introduction

Despite the fact that a number of Chinese Buddhist monastery sites have become important cultural tourism resources, little research has been done to reveal how the Buddhist monastic order copes with tourism development while at the same time maintaining the sanctity of their sacred places. Unlike many Judeo-Christian sites that are protected against tourists' inappropriate or destructive behaviour by lay security guards or volunteers, Buddhist monasteries and nunneries in China are typically protected by monks and nuns on guard duty. While conventional visitor management at many sacred sites focuses on controlling the visitors in a variety of ways, the spirit of Buddhism emphasises the respect of the free will of all. Such an apparent conflict leads one to wonder how Buddhist monasteries are managed by their monks in a way that is in line with the spirit of Buddhism, in particular when they have to confront visitor misconduct, sometimes intentional and sometimes not (Wong *et al.*, 2013). This chapter discusses the Buddhist way of managing a sacred site, Pu-Tuo-Shan, that comprises a number of monasteries, nunneries and other religious buildings, and now hosts some 6 million visitors a year. Unlike some previous studies on visitor management that adopt a structural quantitative approach to examine the research phenomenon, the current chapter reports on an ethnographic study of visitor management as practiced at Pu-Tuo-Shan and concentrates on understanding the Buddhist-inspired approach that its resident monastic members adopt to safeguard their sacred site and to cope with tourist numbers.

Overview of Visitor Management Techniques

Urry (1990) argues that tourists are motivated by the desire to see unusual and extraordinary scenery and objects, distinct from those in their daily life, when they travel; it is therefore not surprising that many historical and cultural attractions are tourism magnets of many different destinations. Many ancient religious and sacred sites, for example, are popular attractions that attract not only believers, but also a large numbers of non-believers motivated by reasons other than faith (Rinschede, 1992). Gutic *et al.* (2010), for example, report that few of the visitors to Chichester Cathedral in England are religiously motivated. Woodward (2004) documents how a Buddhist pilgrimage site in Sri Lanka, now routinely included in generic bus tours of the country, is losing its religious character. Joseph and Kavoori (2001) describe a similar phenomenon at a Hindu site in India. At those religious sites, leisure tourists considerably outnumber religiously motivated visitors, just as is the case at Pu-Tuo-Shan. In extreme cases, such as the Sistine Chapel in the Vatican, some nominally religious sites have for all practical purposes become first and foremost tourist attractions (Anon, 2012).

It is well documented in tourism studies that a situation where believers and non-believers 'co-exist' simultaneously in a sacred religious place may create 'conflicts of interest' and lead to potential competition for the limited space and resources on-site (Pfaffenberger, 1983; Shackley, 2001, 2002). Conventionally, believers are presumed to be dignified visitors who behave respectfully when at 'their' religious sites, while tourists who seek a cultural and pleasurable experience may sometimes behave otherwise. Rinschede (1992) gives a general presentation of religious tourism, and Nolan and Nolan (1992) provide a classic discussion of the pilgrim/tourist distinction. Whether or not tourists are actually solely or mostly responsible for compromising the gravitas of sacred sites and damaging them, the literature tends to concentrate on them. Consequently, much discussion centres on how to preserve the sanctity of religious sites by minimising the negative impact of tourism development (Joseph & Kavoori, 2001; Singh, 2005).

It is worth taking note of Shackley's (2001) observation that it is not only non-believers who misbehave at a religious sacred site, but believers also have a tendency to behave undesirably, as some can be fanatical about taking home mementos of the physical fabric (such as tiles or the limestone of a pillar) of the sacred site. Shackley (2001) analyses the possible negative impacts generated *in situ*, not only by leisure tourists but by all visitors, including pilgrims. She lists eight categories of negative consequences for religious/sacred sites, including theft of artefacts, vandalism/ graffiti, accidental damage, physical pollution, noise pollution, littering, microclimate change, as well as overcrowding. She also gives examples of the challenges being created by the actions of very devout pilgrims, such as touching or kissing a holy object, acts that typically would not be performed by tourists but rather by pilgrims who, driven by religious fervour, have an urge for physical contact with religious artefacts (Shackley, 2001: 37–38).

Religious sites that are tourist attractions typically use a combination of proactive and reactive measures to control the behaviour of visitors

(Mason, 2005; Shackley, 2001, 2002, 2006). Proactive measures include the imposition of an entrance fee, combined possibly with the use of pay perimeters, the prohibition of some activities or behaviour, a dress code, CCTV cameras, uniformed guards, physical protection of the site's physical assets, control of visitor flow, with possibly the imposition of a prescribed route, and queue control. Differential fees may be charged for visiting the different parts of a site. Shackley (2001, 2002) mentions that visitor management measures have been adopted in some Catholic churches, such as creating restricted zones reserved for pilgrims to separate and 'protect' them from tourists. In short, the literature suggests that tourists tend to misbehave at religious sites or simply overcrowd them and that, as a reaction, some of the space or resources of such sites are often reserved for pilgrims. At the same time, rules and codes of conduct are imposed on tourists to prevent them from indulging in destructive or unbecoming behaviour. The common message of these scholarly works is that tourists can become a burden for a sacred site if they are too numerous or if they do not behave respectfully, and that all too often they fail to do so.

As regards reactive measures, many sacred sites need the constant presence of staff to watch over visitors to deter vandalism, theft, physical damage and inappropriate behaviour. Woodward (2004) provides an account of the army of paid and volunteer stewards who guard St Paul's Cathedral in London. The case of Pu-Tuo-Shan is different. The 'guards' who safeguard the monasteries and nunneries in Pu-Tuo-Shan are the resident monks and nuns themselves. The purpose of this chapter is to relate how the Buddhist monks and nuns themselves cope with challenges created by visitors at their sacred sites. The locus of the current research is Pu-Tuo-Shan, a Buddhist pilgrimage site in China with more than a thousand years of history that today attracts many religious visitors and tourists.

Pu-Tuo-Shan and Its Visitors

Pu-Tuo-Shan is a small island (12.5 square kilometres) belonging to Zhejiang Province of China. For centuries, it has been a sacred Buddhist site and a traditional pilgrimage destination exclusively dedicated to Bodhisattva Avalokitesvara. With Jiu-Wa, E-Mei and Wu-Tai, Pu-Tuo is one of the four Buddhist sacred mountains of China. Because of its proximity to large cities and year-round moderate weather, it attracts a particularly large number of visitors; in 2015 it recorded over 6.78 million visits (Pu-Tuo-Shan Tourism Bureau, 2015), many more than the other sacred mountains. Of these visitors, a majority can be categorised as tourists, in that they require overnight accommodation on the island (Wong, 2011).

From a religious perspective, Pu-Tuo-Shan is particularly renowned as an important Chinese Buddhist pilgrimage destination because it is related in Buddhist scriptures that Pu-Tuo-Shan is Potalaka, the home in *samsara* (the existing world) of Bodhisattva Avalokitevsara, where the Great Being preached the Dharma of Buddhism. Apparitions of the Great Being at Pu-Tuo-Shan were recorded many times (Bao & Bai, 2008; Fang & Wang, 2005; Wang, 1999). As a result, many Chinese Buddhists go to Pu-Tuo for devotions in a quest for favours or to fulfil a vow. In addition to its religious significance, Pu-Tuo-Shan is visited because of its historical and cultural value; its large assortment of ancient religious structures appeals to cultural tourists. Furthermore, its natural scenic beauty and beaches offer visiting tourists the possibility of leisure activities. All these characteristics make Pu-Tuo-Shan an interesting object of study in itself and a good example for other sacred sites in China that have similar features. Pu-Tuo-Shan was accordingly selected as the investigation site, with the research aim of understanding how its resident monks and nuns, numbering more than a thousand, cope with the rapid tourism development that is taking place on the island and yet manage to preserve the sacredness of their sites and homes without compromising their monastic life.

There are 28 monasteries, nunneries and shrines on Pu-Tuo-Shan. They receive thousands of visitors daily, and particularly large crowds during religious festivals. The larger monasteries that attract the most visitors consist of a number of halls, other monastic buildings, courtyards and park areas. Except at times when they are being used for a *puja* (a Buddhist 'mass' during which scriptures are recited and mantras chanted), the halls are open to the public. The grounds of the monasteries, nunneries and shrines are enclosed, and thus access can be controlled at their gates. They are closed outside of visiting hours.

An approximate idea of the composition of the population of visitors who go to Pu-Tuo-Shan can be gathered from the survey of a large number of visitors reported in Wong *et al.* (2013). About 53% of the surveyed visitors described their visit as having the purpose of '*hsu yan* and *huan yuan*', meaning, respectively, to make wishes to the divinities and to thank them for granted wishes. The monks and nuns call those visitors *Xiankes*, meaning literally 'incense burners', as their worshiping involves a great deal of incense burning (Wong, 2011; Wong *et al.*, 2013, 2014). While the *Xiankes* are religiously motivated, the monks and nuns do not consider them real Buddhists, but rather people ignorant of the tenets of the religion who actually come to a Buddhist site to perform religious but folkloric rites. In their survey, Wong *et al.* (2013) note that only 10.5% of the surveyed visitors reported that they came 'to learn Buddhism and unearth their innate Buddha-hood'. These visitors are called *Jushis* by the monks and nuns who regard them as true Buddhists. The group that can be considered as tourists, those who said that they came 'primarily for relaxation and sightseeing' represented 31.4% of the sample. The remainder (5.3%) described their motivation as being partly religious and partly touristic. Less than 3% of the sample consisted of visitors from abroad; Pu-Tuo-Shan is thus visited almost exclusively by Chinese people living in China, as is typical of the Chinese sacred mountains in general.

Methodology

In Judeo-Christian religions the mundane task of enforcing the visitation rules of religious sites open to the public is generally delegated to lay people, volunteers or professional security guards (Shackley, 2001). Things are different at Pu-Tuo-Shan, where it is the Buddhist monks and nuns themselves who guard the monasteries/nunneries, a common practice at Buddhist sites in China. Mostly junior monks and nuns spend several hours a day in charge of visitor control on the grounds of their monasteries/ nunneries. They position themselves by the halls and in the open areas and intervene if a visitor behaves in an undesirable way. These monastic members are therefore expert informants who can provide reliable testimony about how visitors are managed and controlled in a Buddhist way on the basis of their extensive hands-on experience. The corpus of data was accordingly derived from interviews with those monastic members. On-site observations and thematic interviews with monks and nuns involved in visitor management were the main sources of data. The author also had the opportunity to make observations about visitor behaviour at the sites and about how the monasteries are safeguarded by the monastic members. Those observations were useful to suggest topics to be discussed in the course of the interviews.

Nineteen monks and six nuns were selected to participate in the research through convenience sampling when the fieldwork was conducted. Monks and nuns attached to large, small, central or remotely located monasteries and nunneries were all included to obtain a representative sample of sites. Interviews were used as the research tool because they allow rich contextual data to be revealed through interactions and conversations between the researched and the researcher (Patton, 2002). The open-ended question, 'Could you share with me some experiences you had in dealing with visitors?' was used to initiate each interview. Responses were then further probed as the conversations proceeded, to obtain clarification of some specific statements or to elicit a deeper understanding. Follow-up questions included 'What visitor behaviours do you consider inappropriate?' and 'How do you react when you witness such behaviour?'. The interviews, which lasted for an hour on average, were individually conducted and audio-recorded. All names attributed to informants in what follows are pseudonyms. In all cases, the many on-site observations of the researcher were consistent with the responses of the interviewed monks and nuns. The analytical process follows the steps suggested by Marshall and Rossman (2006), of which the first step is to organise the raw field data and the second step is to immerse oneself in the data. The third step is to generate categories and themes from the corpus of data. The fourth step, in particular, individual quotes were carefully studied and statements of a similar nature across case studies were identified and assigned to existing or newly created categories. Categories perceived of the same nature were further assigned into one theme. The fifth step is to offer meanings about certain phenomena based on the themes identified from the raw field data. The sixth and seventh steps are to assess and review carefully the interpretations. The eighth and ninth steps are to write, edit and revise the coherent text based on the emergent understanding of the underlying story of the research phenomenon.

The Buddhist way: Detachment and compassion

Very limited proactive measures of visitor control are in place in the monastic sites of Pu-Tuo-Shan and the protection of the site relies mostly on reactive interventions by its monastic custodians on guard duty. This leaves them a large degree of discretion when they have to intervene on a case-by-case basis and the interviews show that how monks and nuns react to visitors' misbehaviour varies from person to person. Reported visitor behaviour that creates challenges include noise, incense smoke, antagonistic attitudes towards monks and nuns and disrespectful or undignified conduct inside the monasteries and nunneries. Some informants were found to use *detachment*, one of the key Buddhist virtues, as the frame of mind governing their interaction with problematic visitors. Detachment in a Buddhist context is defined as the ultimate understanding of the true nature of all forms of existence of objects and phenomena on earth: the recognition of the fact that they are simply illusions and that they are not real in an absolute sense. The Venerable Karmapa (2008: 52–53) said, 'External objects exist only at the moment our mind creates them and clings to them. When one has reached a stable focused mind and acquired the ability to establish and maintain the proper balance within one's mind, then one is detached from illusions and it is the beginning of achieving enlightenment'.

In contrast to expectations based on findings of previous investigations (Digance, 2003; Joseph & Kavoori, 2001; Smith, 1989); the majority of monks and nuns at Pu-Tuo-Shan were not found to be hostile to visitors and were not aggravated by the large number of tourists on site. They remained detached for the sake of their concentration on achieving enlightenment by mentally isolating themselves from the external world. This Buddhist mentality influences the way they live with the situation of constantly having a crowd of tourists at their religious site and home. When asked about their feelings on this matter, they mostly professed detachment from it all, as the following quotes show:

> **Monk Ming Sheng**: They [the tourists] just come in and go and their presence is of no concern to me at all. I don't really have any comment or remember anything in particular . . . I don't let this get into my mind. Having many tourists or having no tourists is the same. I am happy with whatever task is being assigned to me. It is because, no matter what I am working with, I am still practicing Buddhism.
>
> **Monk Zhao Mun**: Whether they [the tourists] come or not in fact does not concern me. I don't care about things which are none of my business. I concentrate on practicing and meditating, which are the only things that I am concerned with and dedicated to.
>
> **Monk Yuan Guang**: . . . what people do, how people behave is not something that should bother a monk's mind; that is why I tell you that whether they come or not or how many come has no effect on me . . . I am here to learn Buddhism, to seek serenity and enlightenment.

In addition to professing no interest in or concern for tourists, informants also use detachment as a method to deal with misunderstandings or problems created by visitors.

> **Monk Lian Yi**: We have the same routine anyway; monastic life is every day the same and so is what you are supposed to do. I wanted to become a monk because I wanted to be free from sorrows and burdens, to live freely. Then, why do I have to care about how people comment on me? It does no good to my Buddhist practice. What I can do is to focus on my own learning; this is the most practical thing and the only thing that I care about. To be a monk is to seek enlightenment and ultimately have no need to be reborn. To care about things that are unnecessary will only make you mess with those unnecessary karmic causes and effects. Then why do you have to do something that prevents you from achieving your enlightenment goal?

By looking at the excerpts derived from the above quotes, such as 'I don't care about things that are none of my business', 'What people do, how people behave is not something that should bother a monk's mind', 'Why do you have to do something that prevents you from achieving your enlightenment goal?', it is clear that, to these informants, what is paramount is retaining their serenity and concentration for the sake of achieving enlightenment. They use detachment as an instrument to help them remain focused on their practice of Buddhism and preserve their inner serenity, even at times when they are facing the antagonistic attitudes of some tourists. As a matter of fact, one of the monks was interrupted during the interview by a visitor asking for direction to a particular hall. The male visitor asked his question without addressing the monk properly, expressed himself in a commanding abrupt manner and left without expressing even token gratitude. The monk was then asked by the researcher to share how he felt being treated this way and whether such a situation happened often. He calmly replied:

> I don't feel anything. You get used to it and people are like this. You cannot control how people treat you. Whether they want to show respect to us or not is their business. We are here to serve people; so, whoever come to us, we help them and we don't care whether they are polite and pay respect to us or not. Who they are, how they behave, has nothing to do with us, and there is no need to care whether they are polite to us or not. It is their choice.

Several informants also testified of their Buddhist duty of *compassion* towards all sentient creatures. These monks and nuns do not deny that tourists intrude, yet they do not choose to completely ignore these challenges by simply adopting a detached attitude. Rather, they take a compassionate world view in which tourism is viewed as a channel to preach Buddhism even if at the cost of being subjected to some amount of distraction and inconvenience. When facing challenges, they do not choose to ignore them or simply bear with them, but they practice forgiveness towards peoples' ignorance and adopt a compassionate manner to handle them. The following quotes illustrate the supportive attitude of some informants towards tourism from the standpoint of being compassionate.

> **Nun Ming Yuan:** Having tourists come to Pu-Tuo will provide them with a chance to make good knots and plant good seeds in this life time. Different individuals come to this place for different reasons, but they all have good seeds and they get the chance to come over . . . So tourism is a medium to let people have a chance to get closer to Buddhism. But at the individual level, having many tourists is sometimes inconvenient and disturbing to our monastic lives, but this is something inevitable. We use what we learned from Buddhism to overcome the challenges. At the same time, if there are more people who believe in Buddhism because of the visits they pay to Pu-Tuo, we are also doing something good.
>
> **Nun Yin Yi:** Having tourists come here has its good and bad sides. The good side is that it is good for the economy of this island. That many tourists come can also sustain the finances of the monasteries. The bad side is that having tourists definitely has an influence on the quality of our monastic lives and practice of Buddhism. Yet, at the same time, what is bad for us is in fact a good thing for those who come. It is because even

though tourism brings inconveniences and interruptions to our practices, tourism development allows more people from everywhere to come to Pu-Tuo and have a chance to make good ties with Buddhism, even if it is just a beginning, just a start. Those who come have already planted their seed in Buddhism; they make a knot with Buddhism . . . your seed in Buddhism will germinate and flourish in the future; it is just a matter of time.

Nun Yin Yi's quote shows compassion and sympathy for lay people. Though she is aware of the possible inconveniences brought about by tourism, she is still supportive because, as she said, despite the interruptions to monastic practices, tourists are given a chance to learn Buddhism and she continued by pointing out that helping them to do so is what a Buddhist should do. A similar message is found in the following:

Abbot Zhong Zhi: . . . to serve people, to solve people's problems, to preach Buddhism to people, to guide them onto the right path, are duties for a Buddhist monk. Having tourists around will affect a monk's practices; at the same time, we should be able to practice all the time, even at times when we solve other people's problems, even at times when we face challenges; this is all part of Buddhist training. If you take a look at it from another perspective, having tourism and tourists come over to Pu-Tuo creates an opportunity for us to get more people to believe in Buddhism. People come over to your monastery, to give you the chance to preach Buddhism, and you no longer need to wander around to look for them. Then why should you not be happy?

The above quotes illustrate the attitudes of the monks and nuns towards receiving visitors and their state of mind when interacting with tourists in their role as custodians. Typically, they acknowledged the fact that tourists in their monasteries represent a form of intrusion. Some informants though, complained harshly about those tourists who misbehave and indicated that they preferred not to have much contact with them. Still, a majority of monks and nuns perceived tourists and having to interact with them in a positive light, with a combination of detachment and compassion. The comments of an 80-year-old nun display how a highly enlightened Buddhist thinks about tourism. To her, tourism is a sign of peace and bliss rather than an instrument to generate profit for the nunnery. She is happy to have visitors come to Pu-Tuo-Shan and she did not perceive any intrusions even at the time, during the interview, when a nearby group of tourists were laughing, talking loudly and taking photos on their way to the inner hall of the nunnery. She was still smiling gently while resting in the sun and explained slowly to the researcher why it was good to have tourism. She said:

. . . The fact that they can come to Pu-Tuo means that our country is getting richer, more stable; people are getting richer, and so they have time and money to travel. If it was in the war time, people could not afford to travel, everyone would have to suffer. People can travel now; it means that the country is at peace, people are rich and this is very good. The place where Buddha Shakayamuni talked about the world of Nirvana is also a peaceful place where people have no sorrows, no sufferings, but happiness only. Buddha's aim is to teach people to leave suffering, to create a world where there is peace. You can see that people come here happily; it is a good sign . . . it is good for them to come in and have a look, to plant their seeds in Buddhism. In the future, the seeds will germinate and eventually they will grow. It is good to let people have a chance to get close to Buddhism.

A typology

Two main principles thus appear to be adopted by the monks and nuns at Pi-Tuo in coping with challenges created by visitors: detachment and compassion. These two guiding principles are to an extent contradictory and it is for each individual monastic member to choose the extent to which he/she is willing to sacrifice detachment for the sake of compassion in his/her dealings with tourists. This appears very clearly from the interviews. The interviews also provided some evidence to suggest that the monks and nuns who tend to resent any grief that the visitors may cause them see it as an indication of their own lack of enlightenment. Taking these considerations into account suggests a model of an *ideal type* of behavioural coping mechanisms of the monks and nuns, as expressed by them, based on their level of enlightenment and the Buddhist virtues adopted to deal with problematic visitors. *Ideal type* is a methodological device first introduced by Max Weber (Shils & Finch, 1949). In this chapter, the ideal types provide a typology of possible behavioural coping mechanisms adopted by monks and nuns in receiving visitors and tourism. The ideal types, as Weber cautions, are not meant to be a perfect description. Monks and nuns, in other words, are not 'boxed' in any one type of behavioural coping mechanisms; on the contrary, one may adopt more than one behavioural coping mechanism in different situations. Figure 8.1 represents the ideal types of behavioural coping mechanisms of the informants based on the analysis of their responses.

In Figure 8.1, the vertical axis measures the degree to which an informant's behavioural coping mechanism, when dealing with visitors' intrusions, corresponds to a Buddhist or a mundane world view. The axis might be interpreted as a measure of the extent to which the monastic member has achieved enlightenment. The caption at the top

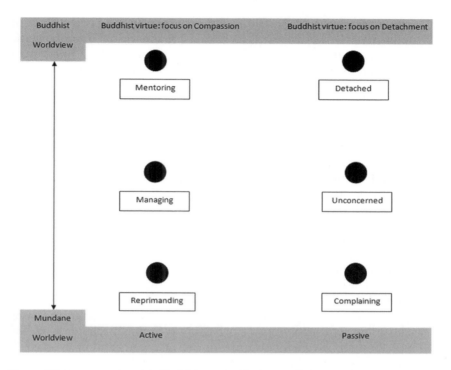

Figure 8.1 A conceptual model of Buddhist monks' ideal types of behavioural coping mechanisms towards visitors

of the two columns corresponds to the two central Buddhist virtues of compassion and detachment. The lower caption of the two columns describes the actual concrete behavioural coping mechanisms taken when facing challenges posed by visitors, corresponding to compassion and detachment, respectively. With respect to compassion, the behavioural coping mechanism consists of being active, taking charge, assuming one's responsibility and trying to solve the problem in as empathetic a way as possible, towards all concerned (the culprit, the other visitors and the monastery). With respect to detachment, one has the behavioural coping mechanism of being passive, not acting, implicitly not assuming responsibility. Each is discussed below.

(1) Reprimanding. A monk or nun holding a behavioural coping mechanism close to this ideal type is mostly driven by the mundane world view (reflecting a low level of enlightenment) and is more compassionate than detached. He/she will take his/her responsibility in his/her functional role inside monasteries/nunneries seriously and

will explicitly instruct visitors not to misbehave, scolding them if necessary. He/she will tend to have a preference for unproblematic visitors, in particular Jushis (Buddhist practitioners). Nun Jing Yung's comment, as shown below, appears to put her close to this ideal type.

> . . . they don't really respect the rules and even after they have been told many times, they still do whatever they want to do, they don't listen. We cannot let them do whatever they want . . . the area here is so small and if someone brings incense sticks in, others will follow and it can be very dangerous. But they just do not listen to what you say. Even though we have talked to them nicely and told them what the rules are, they simply ignore you . . . so I tell them to go back home to use their own ways to worship to their own statues!

(2) Complaining. Similar to the reprimanding attitude, a monk or nun holding a behavioural coping mechanism close to this ideal type is mostly driven by the mundane world view, but detachment dominates compassion. He/she will tend to consider that having many visitors can be a burden to their monastic life and that visitors are annoying, particularly those who misbehave. Yet, unlike the monks and nuns who adopt reprimanding as a behavioural coping mechanism, he/she will not directly confront unruly tourists, if it can at all be avoided. A statement made by Monk Jing Xuan may serve to exemplify this ideal type of behavioural coping mechanism. He said:

> We won't argue with them, but if they really undertake some destructive actions and do not listen to what we say, there are lay workers here and they will come over to talk to those people and ask them to leave the monastery . . . of course you feel angry, upset, but we are monks; our identity is different; we do not argue with them and will not fight with them. If we do that, it will not be good for our image.

From Monk Jung Xuan's comments, one can see that he is holding a behavioural coping mechanism different from the one of Nun Jin Yung because, though he complains, he chooses not to have direct confrontation with visitors.

(3) Managing. A monk/nun holding a behavioural coping mechanism which is close to this ideal type is driven by a blend of Buddhist and mundane world views. Due to the Buddhist view that all are equal, such a monk/nun will tend not to have personal preferences for some type of visitors over others. He/she will generally welcome all visitors to Pu-Tuo as long as they behave well. He/she also appreciates that tourism brings financial advantages to a monastery/nunnery. When

visitors misbehave, he/she does not take it personally but does his or her work of enforcing the rules. Monk Pu Huang, a senior monk who oversees a large monastery gives a comment that constitutes a good example. He says:

> . . . if the challenge threatens only ourselves, we should use tolerance, Bodhi-wisdom, to tame our minds and handle the challenge. If it is something destructive to the monastery, then of course we have to tell people explicitly that such behavior is wrong and ask them to stop . . . you don't need to have any feeling or get angry personally, lay people misbehave because their own understanding of Buddhism is not clear. It is important that we have a big and forgiving heart such that we always treat all the sentient beings on an equal basis.

(4)   Unconcerned: A monk/nun adopting this behavioural coping mechanism is close to the last ideal type and shares its mixture of Buddhist and mundane world views, but is more concerned with preserving his/her detachment than in finding a compassionate solution to a problem that may arise. Such monks and nuns tend not to mind much having visitors. In fact, they often ignore visitors and rely on others to correct any problem. This mechanism corresponds to the responses given by some monks and nuns to the effect that 'they [tourists] just come in and go away and their presence is of no concern to me at all'; 'whether they come or not, whatever they do, has nothing to do with me'; 'I don't feel anything [about tourists' presence]'; 'You get used to it and people are like this. Who they are, how they are, have nothing to do with me and there is no need for me to care'. Such monks and nuns commonly choose to focus their minds on studying Buddhism and prefer not to have much contact with visitors, if possible. Monk Zhao Mun is a typical example of a Buddhist monk with this attitude. He said, 'I don't care about things that are none of my business; I concentrate on practicing and meditating, which are the only things that I am concerned with and dedicated to'.

(5)   Mentoring. A monk/nun adopting a behavioural coping mechanism which is close to this extreme ideal type is very enlightened and adopts the Buddhist world view to look at visitors and tourism. He/she perceives tourism positively because he/she sees that the presence of visitors and the resulting opportunities to interact with them provide him/her with the opportunity to preach Buddhism and provide the visitors with a chance to learn about it. Monks and nuns who rely on this type of behavioural coping mechanism are primarily eager to help visitors cultivate their Buddhist seeds. They will gladly help whether their needs are related to Buddhism or not, and they consider

that helping people is a part of being a Buddhist. Being compassionate and forgiving towards visitors' ignorance are the principles that guide them when facing challenges created by visitors. They aim at a positive outcome that will help more people make good ties with Buddhism. The 80-year-old nun exemplified this kind of ideal type. She said she was happy to receive tourists because 'it is good to let people have a chance to get close to Buddhism' and she sees tourism 'as a sign of peace'.

(6) Detached: A monk/nun relying on a behavioural coping mechanism close to this ideal type is both highly enlightened and detached. When facing visitors' misbehaviour, his/her reaction, if any, is minimal, and an engagement with a problematic tourist, if it cannot be avoided, does not affect his/her serenity. Ultimately, such a monk/nun believes that a troublesome visitor's Buddhist seed will eventually germinate by itself in due time and thus the visitor's inappropriate conduct will naturally cease. Monk Lian Yi's comment is very representative. He said:

> Things will fall into place naturally. You cannot force people to stand still and listen to you about what they should do and what they should not do inside the monastery. If they have good seeds and want to learn Buddhism, want to know what are the correct and respectful things to do inside the monastery, they will naturally come and approach you, to learn more from you . . . in any case, you cannot change people's behavior; you cannot force them . . . they have their way of thinking and you cannot really change them. They are the only ones to decide if they want to change or not; when they will mature, they will understand what they should do. Buddhism cannot save those who do not want to be saved; likewise, you cannot preach Buddhism to those who snub learning.

Conclusion

The results of the interviews suggest that before proceeding to discuss how a religious/sacred site can or should be managed, it is necessary to take into account the influence of the religion itself on the religious hosts at the site. The Buddhist mentality is found to provide, to varying degrees, a normative guidance to monks and nuns at Pu-Tuo on how to deal with tourists. Two tenets of the religion, detachment and compassion, seem to constitute the foundation of their behaviour when acting as custodians of their sacred land. Most of the informants perceive tourism positively and they view it as a channel that allows more people to learn about the religion.

Only a few members expressed that they were not comfortable with having tourists around. Such a finding contrasts with some tourism studies that describe tourism as detrimental to the sanctity of religious/sacred places and as being perceived negatively by the religious hosts (Digance, 2003; Joseph & Kavoori, 2001; Smith, 1989).

The findings also suggest a set of ideal types of behavioural coping mechanisms that are adopted by Buddhist monks and nuns as ways of dealing with tourists, and how the mechanisms vary with both their level of enlightenment and the extent to which compassion dominates detachment, or vice versa. At the same time, just as there are different kinds of visitors at sacred sites, it is also possible to have different types of religious hosts and different ways of dealing with tourists. This issue is mostly neglected in the existing literature. When considering how religious hosts deal with visitors, the literature often emphasises the view of the religious community as a homogeneous institution rather than the perspective(s) of its individual members (Joseph & Kavoori, 2001; Nolan & Nolan, 1992; Pfaffenberger, 1983; Shinde, 2007b; Singh, 2004). Nonetheless, it is the individual members who have to deal with visitors and tourism in practice, and, as evidenced in the quotes, they do not all behave in the same way.

References

Anon (2012) Vatican Row over 'Drunken Tourist Herds' Destroying Sistine Chapel's Majesty. *The Observer*, London, 29 September.
Bao, H. and Bai, H. (2008) *The Legend of Pu-Tuo-Shan*. Beijing: Tong-Iong Printing Press.
Digance, J. (2003) Pilgrimage at contested sites. *Annals of Tourism Research* 30 (1), 143–159.
Fang, L.X. and Wang, D.X. (2005) *The Monograph of Pu-Tuo-Shan, China*. Pu-Tuo: Hai Chao Press.
Gutic, J., Caie, E. and Clegg, A. (2010) In search of heteropia? Motivations of visitor to an English cathedral. *International Journal of Tourism Research* 12 (6), 750–760.
Joseph, C.A. and Kavoori, A.P. (2001) Mediated resistance: Tourism and the host community. *Annals of Tourism Research* 28 (4), 998–1009.
Karmapa, O.T.D. (2008) *Heart Advice of the Karmapa*. Sidhpur: Altruism Press.
Marshall, C. and Rossman, G.B. (2006) *Designing Qualitative Research* (4th edn). Thousand Oaks, CA: Sage.
Mason, P. (2005) Visitor management in protected areas: From 'hard' to 'soft' approaches? *Current Issues in Tourism* 8 (2 and 3), 181–194.
Nolan, M.L. and Nolan, S. (1992) Religious sites as tourism attractions in Europe. *Annals of Tourism Research* 19 (1), 68–78.
Patton, M.Q. (2002) *Qualitative Research & Evaluation Methods* (3rd edn). Thousand Oaks, CA: Sage.
Pfaffenberger, B. (1983) Serious pilgrims and frivolous tourists: The chimera of tourism in the pilgrimages of Sri Lanka. *Annals of Tourism Research* 10 (1), 57–74.
Pu-Tuo-Shan Tourism Bureau (2015) Statistics on tourist arrivals at Pu-Tuo 2015. See http://www.putuo-tour.gov.cn/news/html (accessed 5 March 2016).
Rinschede, G. (1992) Forms of religious tourism. *Annals of Tourism Research* 19 (1), 51–67.
Shackley, M. (2001) *Managing Sacred Sites: Service Provision and Visitor Experience*. London/New York: Continuum.

Shackley, M. (2002) Space, sanctity and service: The English cathedral as heterotopia. *International Journal of Tourism Research* 4 (5), 345–352.

Shackley, M. (2006) Empty bottles at sacred sites: Religious retailing at Ireland's national shrine. In D.J. Timothy and D.H. Olsen (eds) *Tourism, Religion and Spiritual Journeys* (pp. 94–103). London/New York: Routledge.

Shils E.A. and Finch, H.A. (1949) *Max Weber on The Methodology of the Social Sciences.* Illinois: The Free Press of Glencoe.

Shinde, K.A. (2007b) Pilgrimage and the environment: Challenges in a pilgrimage centre *Current Issues in Tourism* 10 (4), 343–365.

Singh, S. (2004) Religion, heritage and travel: Case references from the Indian Himalayas. *Current Issues in Tourism* 7 (1), 44–65.

Singh, S. (2005) Secular pilgrimages and sacred tourism in the Indian Himalayas. *GeoJournal* 64 (3), 215–223.

Smith, V. (1989) *Hosts and Guests The Anthropology of Tourism* Philadelphia: University of Pennsylvania Press.

Urry, J. (1990) *The Tourist Gaze: Leisure and Travel in Contemporary Societies.* London: Sage Publications.

Wang, L.X. (1999) *The Monograph of Potalaka.* Shanghai: Shanghai Ancient Script Press.

Woodward, S.C. (2004) Faith and tourism: Planning tourism in relation to place of worship. *Tourism and Hospitality Planning and Development* 1 (2), 173–186.

Wong, C.U.I. (2011) Buddhism and tourism at Pu-Tuo-Shan. PhD thesis, University of Waikato.

Wong, C.U.I., McIntosh, A. and Ryan, C. (2013) Buddhism and tourism: Perceptions of the monastic community at Pu-Tuo-Shan, China. *Annals of Tourism Research* 40, 213–234.

Wong, C.U.I., Ryan, C. and McIntosh, A. (2013) The Monasteries of Putuoshan, China: Sites of secular or religious tourism? *Journal of Travel & Tourism Marketing* 30 (6), 577–594.

Wong, C.U.I., McIntosh, A. and Ryan, C. (2014) Visitor management at a Buddhist sacred site. *Journal of Travel Research* 55 (5), 675–687.

Part 2: Issues and Problems

As noted in Chapter 1, the relationships between tourism and religion are numerous and complex, and often highly dynamic. Conflicts over religion have often affected travellers, both secular and religious, depending on location, time period and local and national conditions. Almost inevitably, political issues have involved religion and conflict, with impacts upon travel and tourism to specific locations. In the first chapter in this part, Chapter 9: The Vow and Tourist Travel, Matina Terzidou, Caroline Scarles and Mark Saunders review the literature on the nature of the experience being sought by tourists to religious sites in order to discuss the similarities and contrasts between secular tourists and spiritual believers when visiting such locations. They examine the origins of the relationship between the varied participants in such travel and if and how the experience gained affects the nature and emotions of those involved, i.e. their 'becoming' a religious tourist and believer. They provide a framework illustrating the links and differences between tourism and believers involved in travel to religious sites and the process of change involved.

Collins-Kreiner and Shmueli (Chapter 10) propose a framework by which to analyse problems and issues arising from the interplay of politics, religion, tourism and conflict. The focus of their study is Israel, and they use three religious sites in Haifa, Nazareth and Jerusalem for the application of their framework. Their review of the development of the issues involved in the three cases allows them to identify and frame the key problem areas that emerge. They conclude that three specific frames, namely issues, process and values, prove useful to categorise such conflicts and enable the development of a typology that may help resolve some of the often seemingly unfathomable problems which can result from disputes over religious sites. Many such disputes involve not only secular visitors, but also visitors from different faiths who regard the sites as sacred to more than one religion, a problem not limited to the particular context of the Middle East, but one which is unfortunately universal.

Chapter 11 by Isaac also discusses such issues in Israel and Palestine, in the context of religious tourism to Palestine, and in particular, the Holy Land. He reviews the situation and also examines the phenomenon of growing Islamic tourism to the sacred Muslim sites in Palestine, despite the problems involved with Israeli control of entry to Palestine. Future growth of tourism to Palestine and its religious sites greatly depends on the resolution of security issues and a political settlement in the region. Isaac provides a further example of the difficulty in dealing with already complex problems when political issues add another dimension to the issue. In this troubled location, as in others, the results of the combination of politics and religion make travel and tourism to such areas dangerous and subject to fluctuations reflecting the level of conflict or the onset of peace.

Myanmar represents another state in which the development of tourism has been dramatically affected by religious and political actions. In Chapter 12, Mercer notes how the advent of military rule and religious bigotry had reduced the tourism industry in Myanmar to a very low level, partly as a result of effective external boycott campaigns aimed at foreign tourists. As the military have relinquished at least partial control of the country and endeavoured to stimulate tourism, increased development of facilities and infrastructure has taken place and the numbers of foreign visitors increased. However, the developments that have occurred have often involved the removal of local residents and the use of forced labour (often of minority faiths and ethnic groups) to restore temples and monuments of the dominant faith, and antagonism and opposition to the ruling authority have made parts of the country unsafe for visitors. Thus, the marketing and promotion of Myanmar include religious artefacts and symbols to a large degree, but only of the dominant Buddhist faith, making the relationship between tourism and religion both fragile and vulnerable.

The final chapter (Chapter 13) of this part, by Ostrometskaia and Griffin, examines modern pilgrimage and religious travel and tourism in present-day Russia, placed in the context of a past when religion was suppressed under a policy of 'irreligion' in the former Soviet Union. This topic, and indeed tourism to religious sites and in general in Russia represent aspects of tourism that have been virtually ignored in the English language literature. The collapse of communism has meant that there has been a renewed interest in, and commitment to, religious practice in Russia, as shown by the rebuilding of churches and an increasing pilgrimage industry. Thus, the change in political ideology has resulted in significant changes in the levels of both secular tourism to Russia in general, and in tourism to religious sites in particular. Russia contains a mix of faiths, and while the Russian Orthodox faith is the primary one, there are large numbers of Muslims, Buddhists, other Christian sects and other beliefs living in Russia, making a complex scene with a great variety of sites of religious interests to visitors but with many local issues needing to be addressed before the full potential benefits of this form of tourism can be maximised.

Thus, a common theme running through all of the chapters in this part is that when political interests become involved in religious issues, the end result is often conflict, and the overall impact on tourism of any type is almost inevitably negative. There are many issues and difficulties to be overcome to have successful tourism visitation to religious and sacred sites, and political intervention is rarely helpful in attempts to successfully resolve such problems.

9 The Vow and Tourist Travel

Matina Terzidou, Caroline Scarles and Mark Saunders

Introduction

In this chapter, the role of religion and tourism within the context of religious understanding is renegotiated, moving from a study of textuality (Badone, 2007) and strict categorisation of travellers (Andriotis, 2009; Ron, 2009) towards the essential embodiment and materiality of the tourist world (Edensor, 2009; Rakic & Chambers, 2012). Within this, it is argued that religion and tourism are highly connected within the religious context since a religious-oriented tourist or pilgrim is a performer in both the realm of religion and of tourism. The first part of the chapter critiques the relationship between religion and tourism. Within this realm, religious-oriented tourists are understood as performers, who act simultaneously in two settings that intertwine and interact – the religious and the touristic – both contributing to the religious experience. As will be shown, this relationship is intensified within the context of vows that often require believers to travel. The second part reviews the performative side of the religious experience, addressing issues of tourism spaces, embodiment and the unpredictable becoming, tourism proving the stage to experience religiousness.

Religion and leisure have a long relationship with each other (Heintzman, 2003; Vukonic, 1996). Historically, travellers have often combined their journey with a stopover in religious places (Jackson & Hudman, 1995; Smith, 1992) as almost all religions through processes of authentication (Cohen & Cohen, 2012) encourage their adherents to travel to religious sites that are perceived to be the 'Centre of the World' (Eliade, 1969). Yet, while tourism is a universal and diachronic phenomenon generally formed by motivations that oppose people's everyday lives, one established stream of thought proposes the end of tourism (Lash & Urry, 1994). It is argued that the overwhelming power of post-modern media has the potential to erase both traditional and recent distinctions of culture (Baudrillard, 1994), blurring the difference between the authentic and the everyday life and thus suggesting the de-exoticising of touristic encounters (Larsen, 2008) and the dedifferentiation of tourism and everyday life (Coleman & Crang, 2002; Franklin & Crang, 2001; Uriely, 2005). People can become tourists in their everyday lives, experiencing hypermobility through virtual encounter, electronic images and fluidity of signs (Franklin

& Crang, 2001, Harrison, 2011; Scarles, 2009). Within religious tourism, such behaviour encompasses virtual pilgrimage on the internet, which is an emerging religious phenomenon in the post-modern world (MacWilliams, 2002).

However, contrary to such arguments for the rejection of originals in the modern world (Baudrillard, 1981) and the replacement of the quest for authenticity with the longing for pleasure (Ritzer & Liska, 1997), as Belhassen *et al.* (2008) suggest, the virtual is insufficient in satisfying believers' needs, as religiousness cannot be consumed without experiential in-place encounters. Rather, religion, like tourism, is fundamentally about performative, embodied practices; therefore, the positioning of the human body in particular spaces, whether at home or as part of religious tourism, is vital. Religious-oriented tourists, being alienated from the shallowness and inauthenticity of urban life (MacCannell, 1976), travel in search of spiritual and religious connectedness at key religious sites. They travel towards a different place (Dubisch, 1995) that acquires a sacred realm associated with the 'other' and endowed with spiritual magnetism (Preston, 1992), which is linked with the extraordinary that cannot be experienced at home. Belhassen *et al.* (2008) and Rickly-Boyd (2013) moreover, highlighted the importance of performing places as their characteristics and features enhance authentic experience. Immaterial and material engagements through physical immersion in places can, for some religious tourists, render the virtual experience inadequate.

Religion and Tourism: An Overview

The link between religion and tourism has long been observed (Sigaux, 1966; Vukonic, 1996). Religiously motivated tourism is estimated to be as old as religion itself and is thus perceived by some academics as being the oldest form of travel (Kaelber, 2006). Religion and tourism are historically related through the institution of pilgrimage. In particular, vows, which are one of the most frequently reported self-explanations of religious tourists' presence at Greek Orthodox Christian sites, can condition individuals' pilgrimages and visitation patterns to sacred sites including destination choice and frequency of visitation (Terzidou, 2013). The link between religion and tourism is, however, not an exceptional feature of Christianity but a universal phenomenon of religious history. For example, consistent with their theological teachings, Hindu pilgrimages are considered a religious obligation during free time (Singh, 2006 and Chapter 7, this volume). Similarly, Muslims are encouraged to travel to circulate Allah's word, to enjoy Allah's creations and to enrich their existing knowledge (Timothy & Iverson, 2006 and Chapter 4, this volume). This is achieved in part through adherents' pilgrimage to Mecca which is compulsory for every Muslim once in his/her lifetime. Such 'social movement' (Digance,

2006) continues to this day, with many religious centres having refounded themselves as well-known modern tourism-pilgrimage destinations (Sharpley, 2009), such as Santiago de Compostela (Chapter 15, this volume). Until recently, however, relatively little attention has been paid to religion in the tourism literature (Andriotis, 2009; Belhassen *et al.*, 2008; della Dora, 2012; Poria *et al.*, 2003).

Considering previous studies on religious tourism, their primary focus was on the relationship between tourism and pilgrimage, and more precisely between the tourist and the pilgrim, the main players in the relationship between religion and tourism (Cohen, 1998). Attention was placed on the extent to which modern tourism practices can be distinct from, or comparable to, traditional pilgrimage, albeit mainly from a sociological structural-functional perspective (Boorstin, 1964; Cohen, 1979; Graburn, 1989; Smith, 1992). Boorstin (1964), for example, regards pilgrims as serious in their religious pursuit of spiritual fulfilment, whereas tourists' activity in their search for hedonistic and superficial wish-fulfilment are seen as trivial. Singh (2004) observed that tourists to Himalayan shrines were widely concerned with taking as many photos as possible, whereas pilgrims were concerned with resolving their personal problems by communicating with their gods. It is such behaviours that lead Smith (1992) to propose the social approval of pilgrims in contrast to tourists. For instance, devout exhausted Tibetans following the route to the sacred sites are admired by the locals for their devotion, whereas modern tourists are regarded suspiciously and with less sympathy (Singh, 2004).

Such distinction between pilgrims and tourists is further established through Smith's (1992) pilgrim–tourist continuum. In her frequently cited work, Smith (1992) placed both pilgrims and tourists on a continuum according to their motives, with pilgrims at the sacred extreme and tourists at the secular extreme. Between the two extremes, countless possibilities of sacred–secular combinations can exist. In the middle of the continuum where leisure and recreational motives are almost equal to religious motives, travellers are considered to be 'religious tourists'. Smith (1992) suggests that, even though tourists and pilgrims have the same basic travel needs (i.e. time, logistics, financial resources), a distinction can be observed between tourism and pilgrimage within the framework of individual belief and significance associated with each performance. Such a distinction has been most actively promoted by theologians who perceive tourism as linked to globalisation and consumerism (Maguire & Weatherby, 1998) and thus to be a form of escape from everyday life (MacCannell, 1976; Matheson *et al.*, 2014) and from the religious daily activities. In general, the Christian Church and theology express their disapproval towards the secular aspects of tourism by postulating that religious pilgrimage is not tourism, since its motive is predominately of a religious or spiritual nature (Vukonic, 2002). The present-day use of the terms, classifying the 'pilgrim' as a religious, pious traveller and the 'tourist' as a pleasure, relaxation seeker, is thus a culturally erected division drawing upon individuals' motives (Collins-Kreiner, 2010).

Accordingly, within the literature, those who encompass travel for pleasure in their religious itinerary or where the pilgrimage site represents a modernity and change from its original purpose, are usually defined by a term comprising the word 'tourism' (see for example, Poria *et al.*, 2003; Smith, 1992; Vukonic, 1996). In contrast, those who have only religious motives merit the term 'pilgrimage' (see Coleman, 2001; Digance, 2006) or 'travel' (see Singh, 2004) instead of 'tourism', which has been mainly connected to secularism. Nevertheless, as identities, within the framework of religious tourism, are negotiable both on a social and an individual level according to each person's performances, understandings and surroundings (Edensor, 2001; Franklin & Crang, 2001), it is important to move beyond such typologies and social categories (Andriotis, 2009; Ron, 2009) in order to develop an understanding of tourists' behaviour, practices and adopted roles.

Alongside such work, other scholars have attempted to relate the two phenomena within the post-modern world. Cohen (1979: 190), for example, developed a thorough typology of tourists based on their experiences highlighting how, in the case of the 'existential tourist', tourism has more of an affinity with traditional pilgrimage; such a tourist being someone who is 'fully committed to an elective spiritual centre, that is one external to his native society and culture'. Generally, a shift has been noticed in the manner of interpreting tourism, offering new dimensions to the sacred/profane dichotomy. MacCannell (1973), for example, was the first to conceptualise tourists as pilgrims in suggesting that the modern tourist is a secular pilgrim and that tourism is a 'secular substitute for organized religion' (Allcock, 1988: 37). Similarly, Graburn (1989: 22) compared the practice of tourism with that of pilgrimage, concluding that 'tourism . . . is functionally and symbolically equivalent to other institutions that humans use to embellish and add meaning to their lives'. Accordingly, despite music and sport tourism being simply about entertainment and pleasure, the question of whether they constitute a kind of sacred or ritual experience in modern society has attracted considerable academic interest (see Alderman, 2002; Cardwell & Ali, 2014; Gibson, 2005; Kruse, 2003). Moreover, Graburn's (1989) tourists, similar to pilgrims, engage in cyclical passages of time, which are divided into 'profane' and 'sacred' periods; individuals need to renew themselves through 'sacred' tourism for the return to their 'profane' working lives. Nevertheless, even though tourism, within this context, can be compared to pilgrimage, individuals travelling for religious reasons still engage in different ways of practice and becoming compared to other tourists (della Dora, 2012; Terzidou, 2013), being in-between, and thus influenced and mediated by both their belief and tourism simultaneously.

Tourism as Providing the Stage for Religious Becoming

Building upon our overview of pilgrimage and tourism, we argue that both 'sacred' pilgrimage and 'secular' tourism are two unavoidable and inseparable forces in the process of becoming a religious tourist, which is considered dynamic and fluid, rather than fixed as observed above. The religious tourism experience is considered to be much more complex in that it is the result of a series of performances intertwined with religious prescriptions, embodied spaces of production and consumption, inter-subjective interactions and material encounters (Coleman & Crang, 2002; Crouch, 2009; Edensor, 2001; Franklin & Crang, 2001). Most recently, researchers have proposed a dedifferentiation of tourism and pilgrimage and a blurring of self and place, incorporating the spiritual element within individual experiences, which can be sensed in secular sites as in sacred sites (della Dora, 2012; Terzidou, 2013; Timothy & Olsen, 2006).

In many European religious festivities, the simultaneous presence of sacred and profane behaviours often makes it difficult to distinguish pilgrims from tourists (Gartell & Collins-Kreiner, 2006; Sharpley & Sundaram, 2005). According to Nolan and Nolan (1989), dramatic religious performances may occur at the same places where profane activities such as getting drunk and flirting are simultaneously taking place. Similarly, Eade (1992), who examined pilgrimage and tourism at Lourdes observed that pilgrims occasionally cannot be differentiated from their tourist counterparts in the way that they relax and amuse themselves in the evenings. Modern pilgrimage is, indeed, blended with tourism and pilgrims enact a mundane tourist habitus (Edensor, 2007; Jaworski & Thurlow, 2011), involving sightseeing, travelling, visiting different places and buying local memorabilia, leading Cohen (1974: 542) to state that 'the pilgrim is a kind of part-time tourist'.

Rather, one can speak of shifting identities. Pilgrims, like tourists, can be frivolous or rowdy and interested in heritage features without, however, losing their identity as pilgrims (MacCannell, 1973; Pfaffenberg, 1983). Moreover, not all pilgrims are deeply religious, just as secular people can experience peak moments during travel (Jackson & Hudman, 1995) and are open to the same emotions expected (Eade, 1992). Tourists are, therefore, to be viewed with less scepticism and austerity, as the outcome for both tourists and pilgrims may sometimes be alike at sacred places; even though tourism may not be practically related to the sacred, its end result may be (Singh, 2005). Consequently, the use of ideal types to distinguish between pilgrims and tourists (e.g. Smith,1992) disregards the fact that individuals hardly ever conform to strict categories such as 'pilgrims' and 'tourists' because such categories are themselves open to multiple interpretations (Coleman & Elsner, 1995).

Within this view, tourism within the religious context is considered to be something more than simply a destination or a temporary movement

(Mathieson & Wall, 1982), or a space beyond and marginal to the everyday (Graburn, 1989). Rather, tourism achieves meaning for both the believer as a tourist and individual, and the believer as part of a religious group through relationships between roles, stages and places (Terzidou, 2013). Tourism, as an abstract and broader concept than the structured religion (Figure 9.1), facilitates religious experience and allows for on-site performances and encounters equal to those mentioned by Cloke and Perkins (2005) and Cohen (2010), which bring about emotional and embodied experiences that are fundamental to the overall religious experience. Tourism and religion are, therefore, mutually influential and influencing.

While Belhassen *et al.* (2008) stressed the importance of performance at sacred places as their characteristics and features enhance authentic experience, it has been found (Terzidou, 2013) that religious tourists are primarily motivated by the provision of the very stages in sacred places that allow for the performances of anticipations; understood as places as 'affordances' to solve one's problems. Especially within the context of a vow (Terzidou, 2013), it is about the co-performance of places (which are endowed with a deity's grace) and individuals as hybrids (Latour, 2005; Picken, 2010) that function in achieving particular ends. The selection of the sacred places thus plays an important role as pilgrims anticipate direct communication with their Gods and sacredness through material and immaterial manifestations. Similar to medical tourists who seek medical treatment in other places (Abubakar & Ilkan, 2016), religious tourists often select religious destinations within the context of vows based on their anticipated outcomes, with religious places becoming fluid personalised centres of miraculous acts (Terzidou, 2013); for example,

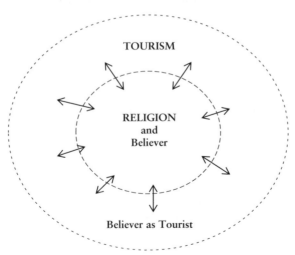

Figure 9.1 The religion–tourism relationship

St Irene Chrysovalantou in Athens is known for curing women with fertility problems, whereas St John the Russian in Chalkida heals headaches.

Nevertheless, the religious tourist experience is not considered as predetermined but comprises a collection of dynamic, unstable and intrinsically multifaceted, complex performances as tourists are entangled (Tribe, 2005) in the human and non-human world (Cloke & Pawson, 2008; Edensor, 2001; Franklin, 2008; Haldrup & Larsen, 2006; Picken, 2010). Both humans and non-humans have affect and agency and the rationale is not merely of being but also of becoming (Crouch, 2003; Scarles, 2009). Through tourism, individuals encounter places, material and people that contribute to their ontological knowledge (Andriotis, 2011) and the making sense of their belief through their actual bodily performance in sacred places (Barsalou *et al.*, 2005; Belhassen *et al.*, 2008; della Dora, 2012). Performance is a form of knowledge (Thrift & Dewsbury, 2000) as people can 'work' their symbolic religious contexts through their bodily engagement with the tangible parts of their religious world and the collective activities, as well as through their encounter with unpredictable situations, new acquaintances and tourist spaces, which enable them to open up and refigure self and space (Dewsbury, 2000) in relation to the religious prescriptions. Within this context, it is assumed in brief that individuals as performers, and human bodies as vessels of belief, are moved through the tourism experience to enliven their belief (Figure 9.2).

In the same way as Scarles' (2009) notes that photographs and photography infiltrate the entire tourist experience, so do the tourist performances of believers' 'light up' and invigorate religious becoming. Indeed, the 'everydayness' of tourism and the 'touristscapes' (Edensor, 2007), alongside mundane recreational activities, such as the time spent on the bus, the daytrips, the restaurants or cafés, become 'special' to some religious tourists, as they entail immanent potential for new appreciations of religion (Terzidou, 2013). Accordingly, while people initially select destinations influenced by exogenous factors (e.g. visuals, texts), personal experiences such as unfulfilled vows may alter their future travel motivations as a result of a series of personal performances (Terzidou, 2013). For example, a pilgrim abandoned her annual pilgrimages to St Raphael on the island of Mytilini in Greece to whom she was committed within the frame

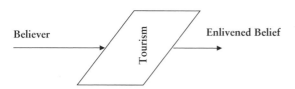

Figure 9.2 Believer as tourist

of a vow, because she blamed him for not having fulfilled her request, although she had visited him with strong belief (Terzidou, 2013).

Hence, religion is not predominately a semiotic, textual field of representation but also a theatre of enactment, performance and agency (Edensor, 1998, 2001), which operates in diverse spaces that are linked through mobilities. Within this context, both sacred places and motivations to visit them are fragile in nature; they are not always fixed in significance for their adherents as proposed by Eliade (1969) with the notion of 'the Centre of the World', but depend on individuals' particular needs, past performances and outcomes in them (Coleman & Elsner, 1995).

Conclusion

In this chapter, it has been argued that religion and tourism are highly connected within the religious context and especially within the context of a vow that requires believers to travel to sacred places as part of a promise. In particular, drawing upon theorists such as Crouch *et al.* (2001) and Edensor (2009), only through a performing and sensing body can people experience and understand their belief, and religious tourism assists in this as it provides a way in which religions are visibly present, transforming religious abstract notions into concrete states exceeding virtual pilgrimages. Rather than merely a set of myths or propositions to which one assents, it is crucial to understand that belief, and in particular becoming a religious tourist, involves a complex configuration of numerable practices, individuals, social bodies and materials that come across each other during a religious trip, and that each aspect of this network enjoys an element of agency (Cloke & Perkins, 2005; Franklin, 2008; Latour, 2005) that contributes to the overall religious experience, either positive or negative. Indeed, what is sacred or secular is something only the performing and experiencing individual can value. Especially within the context of a vow, religious places are not fixed in nature as their significance often depends on the co-performance of the individuals with the places (Terzidou, 2013) in achieving particular ends. Consequently, it is important to capture the nuances of religious tourists' experiences during their travels in order to understand their decision-making process in the selection of religious places.

References

Abubakar, A.M. and Ilkan, M. (2016) Impact of online WOM on destination trust and intention to travel: A medical tourism perspective. *Journal of Destination Marketing and Management* 29 (1), 589–611.

Alderman, D.H. (2002) Writing on the Graceland wall: On the importance of authorship in pilgrimage landscapes. *Tourism Recreation Research* 27 (2), 27–34.

Allcock, J. (1988) Tourism as a sacred journey. *Society and Leisure* 11 (1), 33–45.

Andriotis, K. (2009) Sacred site experience: A phenomenological study. *Annals of Tourism Research* 36 (1), 64–84.

Andriotis, K. (2011) Genres of heritage authenticity: Denotations from a pilgrimage landscape. *Annals of Tourism Research* 38 (4), 1613–1633.

Badone, E. (2007) Echoes from Kerizinen: Pilgrimage, narrative, and the construction of sacred history at a Marian shrine in northwest France. *Journal of the Royal Anthropological Institute* 13, 453–470.

Barsalou, L.W., Barbey, A.K., Simmons, W.K. and Santos, A. (2005) Embodiment in religious knowledge. *Journal of Cognition and Culture* 5 (1–2), 14–57.

Baudrillard, J. (1981) *For a Critique of the Political Economy of the Sign.* St. Louis, MO: Telos Press.

Baudrillard, J. (1994) *Simulacra and Simulation* Ann. Arbour: University of Michigan Press.

Belhassen, Y., Caton, K. and Steward, W. (2008) The search for authenticity in the pilgrim experience. *Annals of Tourism Research* 35 (3), 668–689.

Boorstin, D. (1964) *The Image: A Guide to Pseudo-Events in America.* New York: Harper and Row.

Cardwell, D. and Ali, N. (2014) Nostalgia at the boundary: A study at Lord's cricket ground. In T. Baum and R.W. Butler (eds) *Tourism and Cricket: Travels to the Boundary* (pp. 52–72). Bristol: Channel View Publications.

Cloke, P. and Perkins, H.C. (2005) Cetacean performance and tourism in Kaikoura, New Zealand. *Environment and Planning D: Society and Space* 23, 903–924.

Cloke, P. and Pawson, E. (2008) Memorial trees and treescape memories. *Environment and Planning D: Society and Space* 26, 107–122.

Cohen, E. (1974) Who is a tourist? A conceptual clarification. *Sociological Review* 22 (4), 527–555.

Cohen, E. (1979) A phenomenology of tourist experiences. *Sociology* 13 (2), 179–201.

Cohen, E. (1998) Tourism and religion: A comparative perspective. *Pacific Tourism Review* 2, 1–10.

Cohen, E. and Cohen, S.A. (2012) Authentication: Hot and cool. *Annals of Tourism Research* 39 (3), 1295–1314.

Cohen, S.A. (2010) Chasing a myth? Searching for 'self' through lifestyle travel. *Tourist Studies* 10 (2), 117–133.

Coleman, S. (2001) Pilgrimage: Bringing 'structure' back in. *Anthropology Today* 17 (4), 23.

Coleman, S. and Elsner, J. (1995) *Pilgrimage Past and Present: Sacred Travel and Sacred Space in the World Religions.* London: British Museum Press.

Coleman, S. and Crang, M. (2002) *Tourism: Between Place and Performance.* London: Blackwell.

Collins-Kreiner, N. (2010) Researching pilgrimage: Continuity and transformations. *Annals of Tourism Research* 37 (2), 440–456.

Crouch, D. (2003) Spacing, performance and becoming: Tangles in the mundane. *Environment and Planning A* 35, 1948–1960.

Crouch, D. (2009) The diverse dynamics of cultural studies and tourism. In D.S. Madison and J. Hamera (eds) *The Sage Handbook of Tourism Studies* (pp. 82–97). London: Sage.

Crouch, D., Aronsson, L. and Wahlström, L. (2001) Tourist encounters. *Tourist Studies* 1, 253–270.

della Dora, V. (2012) Setting and blurring boundaries: Pilgrims, tourists, and landscape in Mount Athos and Meteora. *Annals of Tourism Research* 39 (2), 951–974.

Dewsbury, J.D. (2000) Performativity and the event: Enacting a philosophy of difference. *Environment and Planning D: Society and Space* 18, 473–496.

Digance, J. (2006) Religious and secular pilgrimage. In D. Timothy and D. Olsen (eds) *Tourism, Religion and Spiritual Journeys* (pp. 36–48). New York: Routledge.

Dubisch, J. (1995) *In a Different Place: Pilgrimage, Gender, and Politics at a Greek Island Shrine*. Princeton, NJ: Princeton University Press.

Eade, J. (1992) Pilgrimage and tourism at Lourdes, France, *Annals of Tourism Research* 19(1), 18–32.

Edensor, T. (1998) *Tourists at the Taj: Performance and Meaning at a Symbolic Site*. London: Routledge.

Edensor, T. (2001) Performing tourism, staging tourism: (Re)producing tourist space and practice. *Tourist Studies* 1 (1), 59–81.

Edensor, T. (2007) Mundane mobilities, performances and spaces of tourism. *Social and Cultural Geography* 8 (2), 199–215.

Edensor, T. (2009) Tourism and performance. In D.S. Madison and J. Hamera (eds) *The Sage Handbook of Tourism Studies* (pp. 543–558). London: Sage.

Eliade, M. (1969) *Images and Symbols*. New York: Sheed and Ward.

Franklin, A. (2008) A choreography of fire: A posthumanist account. In A. Pickering and K. Guzik (eds) *The Mangle in Practice: Science, Society and Becoming* (pp. 17–45). London: Duke.

Franklin, A.S. and Crang, M. (2001) The trouble with tourism and travel theory? *Tourist Studies* 1 (1), 5–22.

Gartell, J.D. and Collins-Kreiner, N. (2006) Negotiated space: Tourists, pilgrims and the Baha'i terraced gardens in Haifa. *Geoforum* 37, 765–778.

Gibson, H. (2005) Towards an understanding of why sport tourists do what they do. *Sport in Society: Cultures, Commerce, Media, Politics* 8 (2), 198–217.

Graburn, N.H. (1989) Tourism: The sacred journey. In V. Smith (ed.) *Hosts and Guests* (pp. 21–36). Philadelphia, PA: University of Pennsylvania Press.

Haldrup, M. and Larsen, J. (2006) Material cultures of tourism. *Leisure Studies* 25 (3), 275–289.

Harrison, D. (2011) Realizing the virtual. *Metaverse Creativity* 1 (2), 185–195.

Heintzman, P. (2003) Wilderness experience and spirituality: What the research tells us. *Leisure Today* 74 (6), 27–31.

Jackson, R.H. and Hudman, L. (1995) Pilgrimage tourism and English cathedrals: The role of religion in travel. *Tourists Review* 50 (4), 40–48.

Jaworski, A. and Thurlow, C. (2011) Tracing place, locating self: Embodiment and remediation in/of tourist spaces. *Visual Communication* 10, 349–366.

Kaelber, L. (2006) Place and pilgrimage: Real and imagined. In W.H. Swatos (ed.) *On the Road to Being There: Studies in Pilgrimage and Tourism* (pp. 277–295). Leiden: Brill.

Kruse, R.J. (2003) Imagining strawberry fields as a place of pilgrimage. *Area* 53 (2), 154–162.

Larsen, J. (2008) De-exoticizing tourist travel: Everyday life and sociality on the move. *Leisure Studies* 27 (1), 21–34.

Lash, S. and Urry, J. (1994) *Economies of Signs and Space*. London: Sage.

Latour, B. (2005) *Reassembling the Social: An Introduction to Actor-Network Theory*. Oxford: Oxford University Press.

MacCannell, D. (1973) Staged authenticity; Arrangements of social space in tourist settings. *The American Journal Of Sociology* 79 (3), 589–603.

MacCannell, D. (1976) *The Tourist: A New Theory of the Leisure Class*. New York: Schocken.

MacWilliams, M.W. (2002) Virtual pilgrimage on the Internet. *Religion* 32, 315–335.

Maguire, B. and Weatherby, G.A. (1998) The secularization of religion and television commercials. *Sociology of Religion* 59 (2), 171–178.

Matheson, C., Rimmer, R. and Tinsley, R. (2014) Spiritual attitudes and visitor motivations at the Beltane Fire Festival, Edinburgh. *Tourism Management* 44, 16–33.

Mathieson, A. and Wall, G. (1982) *Tourism: Economic, Physical and Social Impacts.* Harlow: Longman Group.

Nolan, M. and Nolan, S. (1989) *Christian Pilgrimage in Modern Western Europe.* Chapel Hill, NC: University of North Carolina Press.

Pfaffenberger, B. (1983) Serious pilgrims and frivolous tourists: The chimera of tourism in the pilgrimages of Sri Lanka. *Annals of Tourism Research* 10, 57–74.

Picken, F. (2010) Tourism, design and controversy: Calling on non-humans to explain ourselves. *Tourist Studies* 10 (3), 245–263.

Poria, Y., Butler, R. and Airey, D. (2003) Tourism, religion and religiosity: A holy mess. *Current Issues in Tourism* 6 (4), 340–363.

Preston, J. (1992) Spiritual magnetism: An organizing principle for the study of pilgrimage. In A. Morinis (ed.) *Sacred Journeys: The Anthropology of Pilgrimage* (pp. 31–46). Westport, CT: Greenwood Press.

Rakic, T. and Chambers, D. (2012) Rethinking the consumption of places. *Annals of Tourism Research* 39 (3), 1612–1633.

Rickly-Boyd, J.M. (2013) Existential authenticity: Place matters. *Tourism Geographies* 15 (4), 680–686.

Ritzer, G. and Liska, A. (1997) 'McDisneyization' and 'post-tourism': Complementary perspectives on contemporary tourism. In C. Rojek and J. Urry (eds) *Touring Cultures: Transformations of Travel and Theory* (pp. 96–112). London: Routledge.

Ron, A. (2009) Towards a typological model of contemporary Christian travel. *Journal of Heritage Tourism* 4 (4), 287–297.

Scarles, C. (2009) Becoming tourist: Renegotiating the visual in the tourist experience. *Environment and Planning D: Society and Space* 27 (3), 465–488.

Sharpley, R. (2009) Tourism, religion and spirituality. In D.S. Madison and J. Hamera (eds) *The Sage Handbook of Performance Studies* (pp. 237–253). London: Sage.

Sharpley, R. and Sundaram, P. (2005) Tourism: A sacred journey? The case of ashram tourism, India. *International Journal of Tourism Research* 7, 161–171.

Sigaux, J. (1966) *History of Tourism.* London: Leisure Arts.

Singh, S. (2004) Religion, heritage and travel: Case references from the Indian Himalayas. *Current Issues in Tourism* 7 (1), 44–65.

Singh, S. (2005) Secular pilgrimages and sacred tourism in the Indian Himalayas. *GeoJournal* 64, 215–223.

Singh, S. (2006) Tourism in the sacred Indian Himalayas: An incipient theology of tourism? *Asia Pacific Journal of Tourism Research* 11 (4), 375–389.

Smith, V. (1992) The quest in guest. *Annals of Tourism Research* 19, 1–17.

Terzidou, M. (2013) Religiousness as tourist practice. Unpublished PhD thesis, University of Surrey.

Thrift, N. and Dewsbury, J.D. (2000) Dead geographies – and how to make them live. *Environment and Planning D: Society and Space* 18, 411–432.

Timothy, D. and Iveson Timothy D, Iverson T. (2006) Tourism and Islam: Consideration of culture and duty. In D. Timothy and D. Olsen (eds) *Tourism, Religion and Spiritual Journeys* (pp. 186–205). Oxford: Routledge Taylor and Francis Group.

Timothy, D.J. and Olsen, D.H. (2006) *Tourism, Religion and Spiritual Journeys.* London: Routledge.

Tribe, J. (2005) New tourism research. *Tourism Recreation Research* 30 (2), 5–8.

Uriely, N. (2005) The tourist experience: Conceptual developments. *Annals of Tourism Research* 32 (1), 199–216.

Vukonic, B. (1996) *Tourism and Religion.* Oxford: Elsevier.

Vukonic, B. (2002) Religion, tourism and economics: A convenient symbiosis. *Tourism Recreation Research* 27 (2), 59–64.

10 Politics, Tourism, Religion and Conflicts: A Suggested Framing Framework

Noga Collins-Kreiner and Deborah Shmueli

Introduction

The aim of this chapter is twofold: (1) to analyse the relationship among politics, tourism, religion and conflicts; and (2) to propose a 'framing' methodology as an approach that provides insight into conflicts stemming from the encounter between religion and tourism. The chapter also considers different sites and case studies that illustrate its observations and arguments, although such detailed discussion is not one of its primary goals.

Religious sites such as cathedrals, temples and mosques are currently attracting an increasing number of tourists worldwide, not only because of their spiritual significance and their capacity as destinations for pilgrimage but also because of the touristic, recreational, educational and cultural purposes they fulfil (Francis *et al.*, 2008; Shackley, 2001; Woodward, 2004). Religious sites offer tourists a wide variety of experiences and activities, including religious services, choir performances, music recitals, art and architecture, and civic and religious ceremonies (Nolan & Nolan, 1992). Not all religious sites are tourism sites, but many evolve as religious-tourism attractions and as meeting points between religion and tourism. Studies have also shown that people visit sites of religious significance for a variety of reasons, which may or may not be related to faith or spiritual needs (Hughes *et al.*, 2013).

Over the past decade, religious-tourism sites have been the subject of intensive scholarly investigation. Some works examine specific sites and seek to better understand how they were demarcated or identified; who enjoys rights of access and ownership; what they mean to individuals and communities; and other questions central to site management (Collins-Kreiner, 2010; Collins-Kreiner *et al.*, 2013, 2015; Kong, 1993, 2001, 2005; Timothy & Olsen, 2006). Conflicts and clashes over political, cultural and social topics often arise around religious sites (Timothy & Olsen, 2006). However, whereas the study of conflict has been addressed in the tourism arena, the conflicts surrounding religion and tourism have received less systematic attention.

How are religious-tourism sites distinct from other tourism sites? Like other tourist sites, religious-tourism sites possess physical and symbolic dimensions and are geographically demarcated. Their distinction, however, lies in their association with places to which one or more religious communities attribute extraordinary religious significance or divine consecration. In recent years, such sites have also received considerable attention with regard to identity formation among minority groups, as scholars have demonstrated how sacred venues serve as a nexus for identity formation, collective memory, self-empowerment and resistance (Brace *et al.*, 2006; Chidester & Linenthal, 1995; Eade & Sallnow, 1991; Friedland & Hecht, 2000; Kong, 1993, 2001, 2005; Napolitano, 2009; Nolan & Nolan, 1992; Tweed, 1997).

Current religious-tourism research focuses on elements of supply and demand such as the management-related aspects of sites and the attributes and motivations of site visitors. Only a few studies explore the relationship among religion, tourism and conflicts on the local, national and international levels (Digance, 2003; Hubert, 1994; Shackley, 2001), leaving us with a dearth of more comprehensive analysis of conflict management and resolution in this arena. As a result, the literature is in need of a theory of conflict within tourism in general (Yang *et al.*, 2013), and within the religious-tourism arena in particular, that addresses factors such as the nature of the conflict, conflict management, conflict resolution and conflict mitigation.

This chapter seeks to generate a better understanding of the linkages between politics, religion, tourism and conflict through a systematic investigation based on 'framing' – a methodology that has been used in a variety of social science disciplines, including conflict management (although little focus has thus far been devoted to conflicts among religion and tourism). Framing analysis is a rigorous conceptual and analytic approach with both interpretive and strategic significance. The purpose of this chapter is to introduce framing concepts and propose a typology that can be effectively used to examine disputes. The methodology provides a comprehensive vocabulary for perceptions – referred to as 'frames' – and offers a detailed and systematic typology of frames based on the literature regarding different case studies.

Religion, Politics, Tourism and Conflicts

Much has been written about the relationship among politics, conflicts and tourism (Butler & Baum, 1999; Butler & Suntikul, 2013; Goldman & Neubauer-Shani, 2016; Pizam, 1999; Pizam & Mansfeld, 1996; Pizam & Tarlow, 1999). The primary research stream that emerged from the late 1990s has addressed post-political conflict situations in relation to business-oriented themes (Hall, 2002; Sönmez & Sirakaya, 2002), travel trade responses to political conflicts (Altinay & Issa, 2006; Cavlek, 2002; Sönmez, 1998), post-conflict tourism markets and the characteristics of new tourists (Butler & Baum, 1999). It also examines new 'attractions' identified soon after political conflict, better known as 'dark tourism' (Collins-Kreiner, 2015; Lennon & Foley, 2000).

According to Hall and O'Sullivan's (1996) working definition, political instability is usually understood as a condition in which political legitimacy, social order and governance are challenged. For a political system to regain stability, it needs to be able to adapt to such challenges. When forces in favour of change are dissatisfied within a political system, non-legitimate activities such as unauthorised protests, violence or even (civil) war are employed as a means of initiating change (Causevic & Lynch, 2013).

Overall, tourism and political stability have been researched from many vantage points, including tourism business and travel trade; public policy and tourism; tourism, peace and world-making; and tourism and terrorism. Elements of supply and demand have also been of major interest to scholars, as evidenced by work on different stakeholders, such as the travel trade and its influence on destination resilience towards instability; tourists and their perception of politically unstable destinations (Cavlek, 2002); public bodies and local governments and their support of tourism renewal (Altinay & Bowen, 2006; Sönmez, 1998); local communities and their stake in the renewal process (Anson, 1999); and the connection between tourism and terrorism (Goldman & Neubauer-Shani, 2016). However, although research dealing with general tourism management and development and politics has increased considerably, work on the relationship between politics, tourism and religion has been lacking (Collins-Kreiner *et al.*, 2015).

Religion and politics are inextricably linked (Park, 1994), and understanding a religion's political vision is now as essential for managing our immediate world as using the internet (Green, 2003). Many sacred places have histories of violence and bloodshed. Conflicts over holy sites frequently spark disputes that are national and ethnic in character and that are often symptomatic of other already existing conflicts. Conflicts in holy places often cause nationalist and ethnic sensitivities to surface and to assume the form of violence that extends far beyond the boundaries of the site itself. An illustrative example of this dynamic is found in the city of Jerusalem, where contests over sacred places are ongoing (see also Chapter 11, this volume). Holy places tend to be dragged into conflicts due to their high value for religious and political combatants alike (Hassner, 2009; Luz, 2005).

For believers, religious sites provide an opportunity to communicate with their gods and to receive and achieve profound insights about the meaning of their faith. This dynamic may lead to competition among religious groups that each desire exclusive control of a particular sacred site. Since these places are valued by the religious, they also attract the attention of political forces. By controlling sacred sites, political forces hope to control believers, the religious movements to which they belong, the hierarchical leadership of these movements and their assets. Conflicts over holy places are difficult to resolve, and conflict can be expected to emerge in holy places that evince high levels of sensitivity (Hassner, 2009; Luz, 2005).

As sites with competing ownership claims over one tangible space, holy places are also an arena in which rival groups struggle for power (Chidester & Linenthal, 1995). Consequently, they are often at the centre of multifaceted struggles involving religion, politics, nationality, ethnicity and territory (Bax, 1995; Bowman, 1991, 2003; Harris, 1997; Herrero, 1999). This dynamic is clearly demonstrated by the sacred sites in the Holy Land, which so often find themselves on the front lines of profane, violent and destructive political conflicts (Luz, 2004, 2005, 2008).

The relationship between conflict and tourism flow has received significant attention in the tourism arena over the past two decades. The conflicts explored in the tourism literature are typically social, cultural, environmental and economic in nature, and most encompass elements of all of these categories. Although the underlying causes of a dispute may be more solidly grounded in one particular category, such differentiation is quite difficult in today's complex world (Dredge, 2010; Poria & Ashworth, 2009; Poria et al., 2003; Singh, 1997; Yang et al., 2013). For example, a study on tourism development in Iran (Zamani-Farahani & Ghazali, 2012) provides information on the state of Islamic religiosity and its sociocultural impact on residents, and affords original insight into the interaction between religion and tourism. This information is of great value to the Iranian authorities, the tourism industry, academics and local communities.

Conflicts that arise from religion are highly emotive, as different groups struggle to define the meaning of place and to negotiate challenges to their own personal and spiritual identities (Naylor & Ryan, 2002). Kong (2001) succinctly sums up this dynamic by noting that just as the sacred is a 'contested category', so sacred space is 'contested space'.

Competing groups' emotional attachment to contested territory transforms the land itself into a sacred place and yields a desire on the part of the involved parties to control, possess and defend their natural and cultural surroundings. As religion and politics are bound together, such contestations are often embedded in politics (Collins-Kreiner, 2008, 2010), and locations of past events may be revered and sacralised even if no physical relic remains (Tunbridge & Ashworth, 1996). Luz (2008), for example, presents a case study of a conflict over the Hassan Bek Mosque in Jaffa, Israel. This conflict was used by a minority group (Muslim Palestinians) in the country to enact resistance and reinforce politics of identity, transforming the place into a nexus of resistance and collective memory formation.

Emmett (2009) shows how, over time and across space, the siting of mosques and churches has demonstrated both conflict and accommodation between Muslims and Christians. These examples are categorised into a typology of 10 different manifestations of intolerance and tolerance – ranging from the destruction to the sharing of sacred sites. Such typologies, it should be noted, may change over time.

As reflected in the literature, conflicts over religious places involve complex layers of social, cultural, political, touristic, economic and psychological forces. To enhance our understanding of such cases and their implications for tourism, the following section offers a framing methodology as an analytical tool that provides insight into the formation of identity surrounding religious sites, how these identities and sites are contested and overall conflicts stemming from the encounter between religion and tourism.

Frames and Framing Analysis

Since its introduction by sociologist Erving Goffman in 1974, the study of frames has been used to understand how people perceive their social world and how the interpretation, or framing, of information affects beliefs and behaviour. The concept of framing has evolved into a useful research method that has triggered considerable work across a wide range of disparate fields over the past decades, including psychology and sociology (Di Masso *et al.*, 2011; Snow *et al.*, 1986; Taylor, 2000), economics (Kahneman & Tversky, 1979), artificial intelligence (Minsky, 1975), negotiations (Neale & Bazerman, 1985; Pinkley, 1990) and conflict management (Kaufman & Gray, 2003; Lewicki *et al.*, 2003; Vaughan & Seifert, 1992). Similar concepts can be found in the fields of management (Creed *et al.*, 2002; Fairhurst & Saar, 1996; Goldart, 1990) and communications (Scheufele, 1999). While some of the above scholars view frames and framing as a social and personal psychological cognitive process, others see it as a deliberate strategic tool of communication.

Cognitively, frames are understood as 'mental lenses', 'filters' or points of view, through which reality is perceived. Frames function as cognitive structures used to screen the multitude of information that people process on a daily basis. People tend to use frames and framing both consciously and subconsciously to make sense of their world, to make decisions and to decide on courses of action. Data consistent with a person's frame is accepted and processed, while inconsistent data is ignored as false or irrelevant. Such selective simplification filters people's perceptions, defining – and to some extent limiting – their fields of vision, leading at times to sharply divergent interpretations of an observed event.

In public disputes in which individuals frequently represent interest groups, organisations and government agencies, personal frames tend to coincide largely with the frames of the group they represent (Shmueli & Ben Gal, 2005). In such disputes, stakeholders may not be acting as individuals. Instead, their values often mirror those of the agencies, organisations and groups with which they identify. Frames shared by a group function much as they do for individuals: that is, by helping assign meaning to observed aspects of a decision-making process while discounting others that appear irrelevant or dissonant with group interests or with information already considered (Shmueli, 2008). The shared nature of frames is perhaps best captured by Curşeu (2011: 90), who conceptualises groups as 'information processing systems' and maintains that 'framing ultimately impacts on intergroup behaviour through the group-level information processing mechanisms'. In this way, framing knowledge can be useful for the practice of public decision-making in contexts with clear physical and spatial consequences. Framing insights can also be used to contend with obstacles to negotiation (Kaufman & Shmueli, 2011).

The remainder of this chapter applies frame analysis to conflicts over religious tourism sites in an effort to provide a helpful perspective for the better understanding of conflict and politics related to religion and tourism.

A Proposed Framework: The Framing of Disputes Surrounding Religious Tourism Sites

Over the past few decades, several new major religious sites have emerged in Israel and are currently at different stages of construction or establishment. Three of these sites were the focus of case studies that provided the data for the research on which this chapter is largely based (Collins-Kreiner et al., 2013). These sites were selected to maximise diversification of the phenomena investigated and include: a site of a relatively new religion (the Baha'i) in a large secular predominantly Jewish city (Haifa); a Muslim mosque in one of the world's most important Christian cities (Nazareth); and a Mormon site in Jerusalem, a city of the utmost importance to Jews, Muslims and Christians (see Figure 10.1).

To generate a comprehensive typology of the frames that influence perceptions of conflicts regarding tourism and religion, we employed grounded theory (Glaser & Strauss, 1967; Strauss & Corbin, 1990) combining attitudes documented in bodies of literature with an empirical dataset gathered from case studies. Our analysis used the 'cognitive approach' to framing, which considers frames as schemata that are stored in people's minds and that underlie their respective discourses surrounding conflicts.

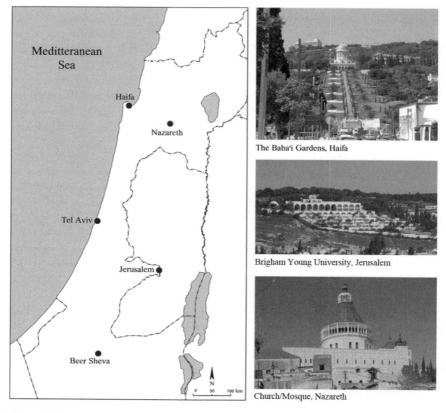

Figure 10.1 Map of Israel and images of three sites

The starting point of our categorisation of frames was a typology that was originally developed in 2003 for environmental conflicts (Lewicki *et al.*, 2003; Shmueli & Ben Gal, 2003). Using this as a base, we identified frames from a close reading of the literature on religious sites and identity of place, with additional frames derived from empirical data. The adaptation to religious sites began by establishing an initial set of frames gleaned from the literature, including Cesari (2005), Emmet (2009), Hassner (2009), Luz (2005, 2008), Shilhav (2001), Sibley (1995) and Watson (2005).

The empirical data was generated by the three aforementioned in-depth case studies on the establishment of significant religious sites in Israel. The dataset included 75 interviews with stakeholders who either had been or were still involved in events surrounding site construction (34 pertaining to the Baha'i Gardens in Haifa, 22 pertaining to the Mormon Centre in Jerusalem and 19 pertaining to the church/mosque in Nazareth). The selected case study methodology involved interviewing stakeholders from diverse organisations and sectors, from different backgrounds and with different levels of knowledge. The interviewees varied in terms of their information sources, motivations, interests and familiarity with the project, and expressed a willingness to participate in the study. Interviews were conducted in Arabic, English or Hebrew (Ben-Gal *et al.*, 2015; Collins-Kreiner *et al.*, 2013; Shmueli *et al.*, 2014).

A list of primary stakeholders was suggested by an interested party in each case study and a perusal of media reports and meeting protocols. A 'snowball' technique was then employed: at the close of each interview, interviewees were asked to identify other stakeholders, and each name mentioned twice was added to the list of interviewees. The dataset for each case study also included national and local media articles, publications, protocols and archival material. The dataset included 2788 coded text pieces and statements. Stakeholder statements, texts from the media and meeting minutes were transcribed and coded using qualitative data processing software (AtlasTi), and recurring themes that appeared to influence stakeholders' perceptions of conflicts were identified as frames. Thirty-six frames that appeared repeatedly in the discourse and appeared to influence perceptions of the disputes were used to code and categorise statements from the interviews and other data (Table 10.1).

For example, in the case of the Mormon Centre in Jerusalem, a statement such as 'There was immense pressure on the Mayor. He didn't know what to do. They [the Mormons] mobilized the entire world', reflects the perception that site developers were influential and powerful, and was coded under the 'Use of Power and Control' frame. A statement such as 'It would have been much simpler if they would have built the Centre somewhere less noticeable', reflects the perception that site location was important, and was coded under both the 'Location' and 'Visibility' frames.

In order to validate the findings, coding was reviewed by the entire research team individually (six all together). In order to create a comprehensive framework that would prove useful for portraying the various competing 'stories', the disaggregated frames were categorised and grouped, initially into six 'frame families': (1) physical characteristics of the site; (2) the site as a cause of physical planning problems, hazards and nuisances; (3) administrative characteristics of the decision-making process; (4) characteristics of the parties involved; (5) the nature of the relationship between stakeholders; and (6) the site's perceived value-based significance (community/social/cultural, political/ideological, religious and economic).

Based on the data and the ideas drawn from the various bodies of literature mentioned above, these six frame families were further aggregated into three 'super-frames': Issues, Process and Values (Table 10.1). Underlying this aggregation is the premise that religious sites are perceived as conflictual when their construction is viewed as a threat, and that a sense of threat arises from sites that are deemed to deviate in one or more

Table 10.1 Relationship among frames and perceptions of deviation and threat

Super-frames	Frame families	Frames	Framing: Perceived as right or wrong due to . . .	Perceived threat
Issues	Physical characteristics of the site	Size, height Visibility Design, shape, aesthetics Access, exclusion Clearly defined boundaries	Physical and spatial issues: Incompatibility/compatibility with the physical environment	Physical quality of life and well-being and/or control over these aspects by the (relevant) community
	Physical planning issues	Planning problems, nuisances and hazards Location as an issue		
Process	Administrative characteristics of the process	Land use and ownership (whether public or private) Timing/pace of development Decision-making processes	Administrative order: Proper procedure, due process	
	Characterisation of the parties involved Nature of the relationships among the involved parties	Stereotypes of parties Who were the parties to the conflict? Use of power, hostility, violence Attitude of trust/distrust Inequality		
Values	Site has community, social or cultural significance	Identity and strength of identity of the surrounding community Sphere of influence (of religious site) Scale of conflict Centre of tolerance Foreign identity perceived positively Contribution to broader ('absorbing') community Inter-group struggle over identity of site Different identity – foreign 'invading' entity Change for the worse (damage, harm) to the 'absorbing' community	Functional social order: Incompatibility/compatibility with the functional social order	Threat to world view Threat to identity Threat to hegemony, sovereignty and/or territorial control
	Site has political, ideological or value-related significance	Inter-group struggle over identity of site Source of power/control Political conflict in guise of religious conflict		
	Site has religious significance	Is the site 'truly' a religious site? Is the site a centre of missionary activity? Gives religion a presence		
	Site has economic, touristic or aesthetic significance	Serves to attract religious pilgrims Serves to attract tourists Increases real estate values No economic contribution		

of the following categories: (1) physical and spatial issues – a site that does not blend in with the landscape, is disruptive from the perspective of planning or aesthetics or is perceived as a nuisance or a hazard; (2) flawed procedure or process – a site that is not built in accordance with procedures that are considered to be legal, proper, fair, etc., or that is perceived to be built at an improper time and/or as a result of inappropriate influences; and (3) value-influenced functional dissonance – a site that is ill-suited to the surrounding community and its institutions and that is perceived as a threat to its prevalent values, religion, culture and dominant social structures of control, property ownership or sovereignty: in other words, a site that is perceived as a meaningful change to the status quo. (Table 10.1 presents the relationship among super-frames, frame families and possible perceptions of deviations caused or threats posed by the sites.)

Understanding Conflicts

Based on our use of Goffman's 1974 model of frame analysis and our own empirical research, we posit that sites are framed as conflictual by parties who view their construction as constituting a threat on three different levels: when the process surrounding site construction is perceived as flawed (the Process super-frame); when site construction is regarded as posing a threat to the status quo from a value-oriented perspective (the Values super-frame); and the perception of site incompatibility with the established physical–spatial order of things (the Issues super-frame).

This typology suggests a model for analysing and understanding the different stories told by people and groups involved in public decision-making processes, in which the decisions adopted might be perceived as endangering the identity of some members of the community. The study also suggests the utility of frame analysis for describing, analysing and explaining tourism processes with both theoretical and practical significance. Theoretically, it represents one of the first applications of frame analysis to tourism research. This approach focuses on the frames, or themes, themselves in order to identify the categories, importance and allocation of different frames, as well as the manner in which they are used by different interest groups to construct their own understanding of conflicts.

On a practical level, the underlying premise of this study is that cognitive perceptions, or framing, play a formative role in shaping the behaviour of individuals and groups. This approach is meant to assist in finding common ground and to facilitate efforts to resolve disputes by generating a better understanding of their dynamics. By communicating their value-based framing, stakeholders are able to couch their interests and arguments in language (or frames) that is understandable to other stakeholders, addressing them on their own terms in order to improve communication and increase the likelihood of a mutually beneficial outcome (Kaufman & Shmueli, 2011). Moreover, the study enabled us to better understand why a site with an identity that differs from that of the host community does, or does not, spark conflict, as much depends on the process itself, as observed in the Baha'i case study in Haifa, Israel (Collins-Kreiner, 2015).

The construction of religious tourism sites has interconnected physical, social, value-laden and political meaning. The proposed typology of frames, frame families and super-frames enables us to discern these various meanings and to understand the relationships among them in an effective and organised manner. The result is a mapping of different perceptions of and insights regarding the factors influencing conflict (or the lack thereof).

Summary

This chapter has proposed a framework based on empirical studies regarding three religious sites in Israel. For this reason, an important direction of future work will be to research conflict as manifested in other religious tourism destinations and to compare and contrast findings in different countries. Frame analysis may be applicable not only to conflicts surrounding religious sites but to public open space planning and new tourism development sites as well, and may differ according to the places in question. Applying the proposed model in other countries will unquestionably facilitate its further development and increase both its scope and accuracy.

Nonetheless, we are still left with a lack of more comprehensive analysis of conflict management and resolution in the religion and tourism arena as a whole, which offers a promising direction for future research. The literature is in need of a systematic theory of conflict that addresses factors such as the nature of the conflict, conflict management, conflict resolution and conflict mitigation. We hope this chapter will attract additional scholarly interest in different types of conflicts, as our goal has also been to enhance our understanding of the inextricable link between religion and politics. As Neusner (2013: 259) reminds us: 'To most of us it seems that religious groups speak a kind of gibberish, intelligible only to themselves, when in fact they mean to make a statement not only to, but about, the social order that encompasses us all'.

References

Altinay, L. and Bowen, D. (2006) Politics and tourism interface: The case of Cyprus. *Annals of Tourism Research* 33 (4), 939–956.

Altinay, L. and Issa, I.A. (2006) Impacts of political instability on tourism planning and development: The case of Lebanon. *Tourism Economics* 12 (3), 361–381.

Bax, M. (1995) *Medjugorje: Religion, Politics and Violence in Rural Bosnia.* Amsterdam: VU University Press.

Ben-Gal, M., Collins-Kreiner, N. and Shmueli, D. (2015) Understanding religious conflicts through framing: The Mormon site in Jerusalem as a case-study. *Journal of Economic and Social Geography (Tijdschrift Voor Economische En Sociale Geografi)* 106 (5), 503–638.

Bowman, G. (1991) Christian ideology and the image of a Holy Land: The place of Jerusalem in the various Christianities. In M.J. Sallnow and J. Eade (eds) *Contesting the Sacred: The Anthropology of Christian Pilgrimage* (pp. 98–121). London: Routledge.

Bowman, G. (2003) Constitutive violence and the nationalist imaginary: Antagonism and defensive solidarity in 'Palestine' and 'former Yugoslavia.' *Social Anthropology,* 11, 319–340.

Brace, C., Bailey, A. and Harvey, D. (2006) Religion, place and space: A framework for investigating historical geography of religious identities and communities. *Progress in Human Geography* 30, 28–43.

Butler, R.W. and Baum, T. (1999) The tourism potential of the peace dividend. *Journal of Travel Research* 38 (1), 24–29.

Butler, R.W. and Suntikul, W. (2013) *Tourism and War*. London/New York: Routledge.

Causevic, S. and Lynch, P. (2013) Political (in)stability and its influence on tourism development. *Tourism Management* 34, 145–157.

Cavlek, N. (2002) Tour operators and destination safety. *Annals of Tourism Research* 29 (2), 478–496.

Cesari, J. (2005) Mosque conflicts in European cities: Introduction. *Journal of Ethics and Migration Studies* 31 (6), pp. 1015–1024.

Chidester, D. and Linenthal, E. (1995) *American Sacred Space*. Bloomington, IN: Indiana University Press.

Collins-Kreiner, N. (2008) Religion and politics: New religious sites and spatial transgression in Israel. *The Geographical Review* 98 (2), 197–213.

Collins-Kreiner N. (2010) Geographers and pilgrimages. *Journal of Economic and Social Geography (Tijdschrift Voor Economische En Sociale Geografi)* 101 (4), 437–448.

Collins-Kreiner, N. (2015) Dark tourism as/is pilgrimage. *Current Issues in Tourism* 19 (12), 1185–1189.

Collins-Kreiner, N., Shmueli, D. and Ben-Gal, M. (2013) Spatial transgression of new religious sites in Israel. *Applied Geography* 40, 103–114.

Collins-Kreiner, N., Shmueli, D. and Ben Gal, M. (2015) Conflicts at religious tourism sites: The Baha'i World Centre, Israel. *Tourism Management Perspectives* 16, 228–236.

Creed, W.E., Langstraat, J.A. and Scully, M.A. (2002) A picture of the frame: Frame analysis as technique and as politics. *Organizational Research Methods* 5, 34–55.

Curşeu, P.L. (2011) Framing effects in small-group and intergroup negotiation: A cognitive perspective. In W.A. Donohue, R.G. Rogan and S. Kaufman (eds) *Framing Matters, Perspectives on Negotiation Research and Practice in Communication* (pp. 71–94). New York: Peter Lang.

Digance, J. (2003) Pilgrimage at contested sites. *Annals of Tourism Research* 30 (1), 143–159.

Di Masso, A., Dixon, J. and Pol, E. (2011) On the contested nature of place: 'Figuera's Well', 'The Hole of Shame' and the ideological struggle over public space in Barcelona. *Journal of Environmental Psychology* 31, 231–244.

Dredge, D. (2010) Place change and tourism development conflict: Evaluating public interest. *Tourism Management* 31 (1), 104–112.

Eade, J. and Sallnow, M.J. (1991) *Contesting the Sacred. The Anthropology of Christian Pilgrimage*. London: Routledge.

Emmett, C.F. (2009) The siting of churches and mosques as an indicator of Christian–Muslim relations. *Islam and Christian–Muslim Relations* 20 (4), 451–476.

Fairhurst, G.T. and Sarr, R.A. (1996) *The Art of Framing: Managing the Language of Leadership*. San Francisco, CA: Jossey-Bass.

Francis, L.J., Williams, E., Annis, J. and Robbins, M. (2008) Understanding cathedral visitors: Psychological type and individual differences in experience and appreciation. *Tourism Analysis* 13 (1), 71–80.

Friedland, R. and Hecht, R. (2000) *To Rule Jerusalem*. Santa Barbara, CA: University of California Press.

Glaser, B.G. and Strauss, A.L. (1967) *The Discovery of Grounded Theory: Strategies for Qualitative Research*. New Brunswick, NJ: Aldine Transaction.

Goffman, E. (1974) *Frame Analysis: An Essay on the Organization of Experience*. New York: Harper & Row.

Goldart, E.M. (1990) *What Is This Thing Called Theory of Constraints and How Should it be Implemented?* Croton-on-Hudson, NY: North River Press, Inc.

Goldman, O.S. and Neubauer-Shani, M. (2016) Does international tourism affect transnational terrorism? *Journal of Travel Research* 56 (4), 451–467.

Green, W.S. (2003) Religion and politics: A volatile mix. In J. Neusner (ed.) *God's Rule: The Politics of World Religions* (pp. 1–9). Washington, DC: Georgetown University Press.

Hall, C.M. (2002) Travel safety, terrorism and the media: The significance of the issue-attention cycle. *Current Issues in Tourism* 5 (5), 458–466.

Hall, C.M. and O'Sullivan, V. (1996) Tourism, political instability and violence. In A. Pizam and Y. Mansfeld (eds) *Tourism, Crime and International Security Issues* (pp. 105–121). New York: John Wiley.

Harris, R. (1997) Gender and the sexual politics of pilgrimage to Lourdes. In J. Devlin and R. Fanning (eds) *Religion and Rebellion* (pp. 152–173). Dublin: University College of Dublin Press.

Hassner, R.E. (2009) *War on Sacred Grounds*. Ithaca, NY: Cornell University Press.

Herrero, J.A. (1999) Mejugorje: Ecclesiastical conflict, theological controversy, ethnic division. *Research in the Social Scientific Study of Religion* 10, 137–170.

Hughes, K., Bond, N. and Ballantyne, R. (2013) Designing and managing interpretive experiences at religious sites: Visitors' perceptions of Canterbury Cathedral. *Tourism Management* 36, 210–220.

Hubert, J. (1994) Sacred beliefs and beliefs of sacredness. In D.L. Carmichael, J. Hubert, B. Reeves and A. Schanche (eds) *Sacred Sites, Sacred Places* (pp. 9–31). London: Routledge.

Kahneman, D. and Tversky, A. (1979) Prospect theory: An analysis of decision under risk. *Econometrica* 47, 263–289.

Kaufman, S. and Gray, B. (2003) Using retrospective and prospective frame elicitation to evaluate environmental disputes. In L. Bingham and R. O'Leary (eds) *The Promise and Performance of Environmental Conflict Resolution* (pp. 1–15). Washington, DC: Resources For the Future Press.

Kaufman, S. and Shmueli, D. (2011) Framing in public decision interactions: Transferring theory to practice. In W. Donohue, R. Rogan and S. Kaufman (eds) *Framing Matters: Perspectives on Negotiation Research and Practice in Communication* (pp. 167–190). Cresskill, NY: Peter Lang Publishing.

Kong, L. (1993) Ideological hegemony and the political symbolism of religious buildings in Singapore. *Environment and Planning D: Society and Space* 11 (1), 23–45.

Kong, L. (2001) Mapping 'new' geographies of religion, politics and poetics in modernity. *Progress in Human Geography* 25 (2), 211–233.

Kong, L. (2005) Religious processions: Urban politics and poetics. *Temenos: Finnish Journal of Religion* 41 (2), 225–249.

Lennon, J. and Foley, M. (2000) *Dark Tourism the Attraction of Death and Disaster*. London: Continuum.

Lewicki, R., Gray, B. and Elliott, M. (eds) (2003) *Making Sense of Intractable Environmental Conflicts: Concepts and Cases*. Washington, DC: Island Press.

Luz, N. (2004) *Al-Haram Al-Sharif in the Arab-Palestinian Public Discourse in Israel: Identity, Collective Memory and Social Construction*. Jerusalem: Floersheimer Institute for Policy Study, Achva Press. (Hebrew.)

Luz, N. (2005) *The Arab Community of Jaffa and the Hassan Bek Mosque: Collective Identity and Empowerment of the Arabs in Israel via Holy Places*. Jerusalem: Floersheimer Institute for Policy Study, Achva Press. (Hebrew.)

Luz, N. (2008) The politics of sacred places: Palestinian identity, collective memory, and resistance in the Hassan Bek mosque conflict. *Society and Space: Environment and Planning D* 26 (6), 1036–1052.

Minsky, M. (1975) A framework for representing knowledge. In P.H. Winston (ed.) *The Psychology of Computer Vision* (pp. 177–211). New York: McGraw Hill.

Napolitano, V. (2009) Virgin of Guadalupe, a nexus of affect. *Journal of the Royal Anthropology Institute* 15, 96–112.

Naylor, S. and Ryan, M. (2002) The mosque in the suburbs: Negotiating religion and ethnicity in South London. *Social & Cultural Geography* 3, 39–59.

Neale, M.A. and Bazerman, M.H. (1985) The effects of framing and negotiator overconfidence on bargaining behaviours and outcomes. *Academy of Management Journal* 28, 34–49.

Neusner, J. (2013) *God's Rule: The Politics of World Religions*. Washington, DC: Georgetown University Press.

Nolan, M.L. and Nolan, S. (1992) Religious-tourism sites as tourism attractions in Europe. *Annals of Tourism Research* 19, 68–78.

Park, C.C. (ed.) (1994) *Sacred Worlds: An Introduction to Geography and Religion*. London: Routledge.

Pinkley, R.L. (1990) Dimensions of conflict frame: Disputant interpretations of conflict. *Journal of Applied Psychology* 75, 117–126.

Pizam, A. (1999) A comprehensive approach to classifying acts of crime and violence at tourism destinations. *Journal of Travel Research* 38 (1), 5–12.

Pizam, A. and Mansfeld, Y. (1996) *Tourism, Crime and International Security Issues*. Chichester: Wiley.

Pizam, A. and Tarlow, P. (1999) From the guest editors. *Journal of Travel Research* 38 (1), 4.

Poria, Y. and Ashworth, G. (2009) Heritage tourism: Current resource for conflict. *Annals of Tourism Research* 36 (3), 522–525.

Poria, Y., Butler, R. and Airey, D. (2003) Tourism, religion and religiosity: A holy mess. *Current Issues in Tourism* 6 (4), 340–363.

Scheufele, D. (1999) Framing as a theory of media effects. *Journal of Communication* 49, 104–122.

Shackley, M. (2001) *Managing Sacred Sites: Service Provision and Visitor Experience*. London: Continuum Press.

Shilhav, Y. (2001) *Territorial Iconography: Geographical Symbols of Jerusalem – A Jewish-Israeli Perspective*. Jerusalem: Jerusalem Institute for Israel Studies. (Hebrew.)

Shmueli, D. (2008) Framing in geographical analysis of environmental conflicts: Theory, methodology and three case studies. *Geoforum* 39, 2048–2061.

Shmueli, D. and Ben Gal, M. (2003) Stakeholder frames in the mapping of the lower Kishon River basin conflict. *Conflict Resolution Quarterly* 21 (2), 211–238.

Shmueli, D. and Ben Gal, M. (2005) Creating environmental stakeholder profiles: A tool for dispute management. *Environmental Practice* 7 (3), 165–175.

Shmueli, D., Collins-Kreiner, N. and Ben Gal, M. (2014) Conflict over sacred space: The case of Nazareth. *Cities* 41 (A), 132–140.

Sibley, D. (1995) *Geographies of Exclusion: Society and Difference in the West*. London: Routledge.

Singh, R.P.B. (1997) Sacred space and urban heritage in India: Contestation and perspective. In B.J. Shaw and R. Jones (eds) *Contested Urban Heritage* (pp. 101–131). Brookfield, VT: Ashgate Publishing Company.

Snow, D.A., Rochford Jr., E.B., Worden, S.K. and Benford, R.D. (1986) Frame alignment processes, micromobilization, and movement participation. *American Sociological Review* 51, 464–481.

Sönmez, S.F. (1998) Tourism, terrorism, and political instability. *Annals of Tourism Research* 25 (2), 416–456.

Sönmez, S.F. and Sirakaya, E. (2002) A distorted destination image? The case of Turkey. *Journal of Travel Research* 41 (2), 185–196.

Strauss, A. and Corbin, J. (1990) *Basics of Qualitative Research: Grounded Theory Procedures and Techniques*. Newbury Park, CA: Sage.

Taylor, D.E. (2000) The rise of the environmental justice paradigm: Injustice framing and the social construction of environmental discourses. *American Behavioural Scientist* 43, 508–580.

Timothy, D.J. and Olsen, D.H. (2006) *Tourism, Religion and Spiritual Journeys*. London/ New York: Routledge.

Tunbridge, J.E. and Ashworth, G.J. (1996) *Dissonant Heritage: The Management of the Past as a Resource in Conflict*. Chichester: Wiley.

Tweed, T.A. (1997) *Our Lady of the Exile: Diasporic Religion at a Cuban Catholic Shrine in Miami*. Oxford: Oxford University Press.

Vaughan, E. and Seifert, M. (1992) Variability in the framing of risk issues. *Journal of Social Issues* 48, 119–135.

Watson, S. (2005) Symbolic spaces of difference: Contesting the Eruv in Barnet, London and Tenafly, New Jersey. *Environment and Planning D: Society and Space* 23, 597–613.

Woodward, S.C. (2004) Faith and tourism: Planning tourism in relation to places of worship. *Tourism and Hospitality Planning & Development* 1 (2), 173–186.

Yang, J., Ryan, C. and Zhang, L. (2013) Social conflict in communities impacted by tourism. *Tourism Management* 35, 82–93.

Zamani-Farahani, H. and Ghazali, M. (2012) The relationship between Islamic religiosity and residents' perceptions of socio-cultural impacts of tourism in Iran: Case studies of Sare'in and Masooleh. *Tourism Management* 33, 802–814.

11 Religious Tourism in Palestine: Challenges and Opportunities

Rami K. Isaac

Introduction

Rinschede (1992: 52) defined religious tourism as a 'form of tourism whose participants are motivated in part or exclusively for religious reasons'. The term 'religious' emerges as a result of the understanding of tourists' motivations. Religious tourism hence involves visiting local, regional, national or international pilgrimage centres and joining religious ceremonies, conferences and celebrations and all other religious oriented meetings that do not take place in the home environment (Rinschede, 1992). According to Hinnells (1984), the concept of religion revolves around a system of recognisable beliefs and practices that acknowledge the existence of a 'superhuman' power that enables people to both address and transcend the problems of life. Religious tourism is therefore connected to this system through the behaviour and motives for visiting sites of religious significance.

Travel for religious reasons dates back to the earliest civilisations, and is possibly the oldest and most predominant type of travel in human history (Jackowski & Smith, 1992; Rinschede, 1992; Timothy & Boyd, 2006). For thousands of years, people have been travelling to places considered sacred to meet or to worship concepts around religion (Coleman, 2004). Religion is important in people's lives, and indeed it has been claimed that human beings have always had a need to believe in a superior entity (Timothy & Olsen, 2006). From the beginning of human societies until modern times accordingly, there have been several cults and beliefs relating to different Gods and superior forces, which were and are worshipped and venerated through statues, representations and buildings (Rojo, 2007).

Every year, millions of people visit major religious destinations around the world (Jansen & Kühl, 2008), both ancient and modern in origin. The majority of religious travellers are adherents of the world's major religions, and identify themselves as Christians, Muslims, Hindus or Buddhists (Gan et al., 2000). Religious tourism has experienced huge growth in the past 20 years (D'Amore, 2009). Many distinguished scholars, such as Bywater (1994), Holmberg (1993), Olsen and Timothy (1999), Post et al. (1998),

Russell (1999), San Filippo (2001) and Singh (1998) have also confirmed the increasing trend of religious tourism.

Destinations such as Saudi Arabia, in which the Islamic holy site of Mecca is located, can expect to experience strong growth in tourism as they continue to encourage religious tourism, although much more can still be done to promote this element of their tourism product. Aside from the current troubled economic situation in Europe, which is one of the principal source markets for religious tourists, the main threat to the overall growth of religious tourism is the uncertain political situation in the Middle East. The political situation in Israel and Palestine will determine to a large extent the flow of tourists to major religious destinations in that region including Bethlehem, Jerusalem in Palestine and the surrounding holy sites, while turbulence in countries such as Egypt, Syria and Libya contributes to a general negative perception regarding peace, stability and security in the region (Mintel, 2012).

This chapter deals with religious tourism to Palestine, and will address the challenges, obstacles, bottlenecks and opportunities of this particular market. The Holy Land has always been the main destination of Christian religious tourists from all over the world. Religious tourism to the Holy Land and its sites, especially to Jerusalem, Bethlehem and Nazareth, is known to have taken place as far back as the 2nd century (Colby, 1983).

Little research has been undertaken on the profile of religious tourists, and indeed there are likely to be differences between the different sub-segments of the market. One view is that religious tourists tend to be less interested in luxury or the quality of their accommodation than leisure tourists in general. The main focus is the destination and being able to visit the sites to which they have travelled. In destinations visited by large numbers of tourists, such as Mecca, many of the hotels have large rooms with over 10 beds in each, catering for groups of visitors who find it quite acceptable to share in this way (see Chapter 18, this volume).

Religious tourists generally spend less than leisure tourists, in part due to their selection of less expensive accommodation, but also because the places they visit do not always charge for admission. Equally, religious tourists tend to spend more time at the places they visit, compared to leisure tourists, who are more inclined to maximise their visits to destinations by travelling to several attractions over the same period of time (Mintel, 2012).

This chapter, accordingly, begins by analysing the various segments and typologies developed conceptually as well as empirically by various authors in the field, followed by an introduction to Palestine and its major religious and sacred sites. The chapter will continue by addressing the revival of visitor arrivals to Palestine despite the political instability and sporadic incidents taking place in Israel and Palestine. Finally, the chapter will address the various challenges and opportunities facing this religious tourism market.

Segments and Typologies of Religious Tourism

Raj and Morpeth (2007) identified that within the eclectic range of topics that comprise religious tourism and pilgrimage studies, there is common agreement on some issues such as the term 'religious space' referring both to the limited space within a shrine, sanctuary, cathedral, etc., and to the geographical space that a pilgrim traverses on his/her pilgrimage. Early efforts to segment this market were done from a general perspective, frequently revolving around attempts to differentiate between pilgrims and tourists (e.g. Cohen, 1992a; Graburn, 1989; Pfaffenberger, 1983). The best known typology is Smith's (1992) pilgrim–tourist continuum, which places pilgrims and tourists at polar opposites of a continuum with an apparently endless combination of sacred–secular motivations a person could imaginably have when deciding to travel to sacred sites. Subsequent to Smith, Santos (2003) developed a comparable typology, also placing tourism and religion at opposite ends of a spectrum, with the grades between the two based on the religious background of travellers, the values they place on various religious spaces and the experiences they expect to have in those spaces. Other forms have focused on more general aspects of religious travel, including Morinis' (1992) six types of pilgrims (devotional, instrumental, normative, obligatory, initiatory and wandering). Other approaches include Cohen's (1992b) distinction between concentric–formal and peripheral–popular sacred sites, Rinschede's (1992) separating of short-term religious travel (religious tourism) and long-term religious travel (pilgrimage) and Singh's (2013) recent comparison on pilgrimage and tourism attributes.

Nevertheless, in recent years the foci of these segmentation theories and models related to the religious tourism market have changed in terms of scale (Ron, 2009). This has come about partially, as Collins-Kreiner and Gatrell (2006) debate, because some tour operator agencies consider religious markets to be a homogeneous set, established upon generic assumptions (e.g. seniors, low-income travellers, prefer package tours) without considering factors such as the religious background of travellers. From an industry perspective, tourism types or market segments are usually based on the activities in which people engage while traveling, rather than on their motives for travel (Timothy & Olsen, 2006).

This perspective of defining religious tourism based on motivation has led to a number of studies related to the division of religious motivations, namely religious and non-religious motivations for travel within contemporary Christian travel (e.g. Collins-Kreiner & Kliot, 2000; Fleischer, 2000; Fleischer & Nitzav, 1995; Nolan, 1987; Nolan & Nolan, 1989, 1992; Olsen, 2006b; Ron, 2009; Weidenfeld, 2006). There is also wide discussion regarding the various tourist motivations relative to two dimensions, along the two axes of pious pilgrim–secular tourist and sacred pilgrimage–secular (Murray & Graham, 1997; Nolan & Nolan, 1989), while Alecu (2011) suggests other ways in which religious tourism can be studied. It is also suggested that religious travel can be essentially of two types: mono-functional travel, in which the sole purpose is religious, and plural-functional travel, in which the religious purpose is combined with a cultural one. It is likewise advocated that religious tourism can be differentiated by the nature of the tourists' religious beliefs, such as Christian tourism – itself divided into Greek Orthodox, Catholic and Protestant tourism, Hindu tourism, Judaic tourism, Islamic tourism and other faith-related travel.

Lately, it has been argued that the religious market has developed into a much larger and more segmented market, with niches ranging from high-end religious travel, volunteer-oriented religious travel to modern-day pilgrimages such as visits to the Karmapa in Tibet (Kurlantzick, 2007). Thus, religious tourism includes travel to a religious destination site, e.g. a trip to the Holy Land travel with a spiritual intent, e.g. a Christian conference, or even leisure travel with a fellowship intent e.g. a faith-based cruise trip (as discussed in Chapter 17, this volume).

Additionally, in recent years, new segments within religious tourism have appeared such as faith-based tourism. Religious or faith-based tourism, however, is not only about pilgrimages. Faith-based travel may take place for life cycle events, for missionary work or humanitarian interest projects as well as for religious conventions and conclaves (Tarlow, 2014). In addition, faith-based tourism, although often dominated by group or affinity groups, is also gaining ground among the individual leisure travel, especially among young people (who compose about one third of faith-based visitors) there are a great number of people who seek spiritual aspects to their vacations. Think through what areas of your community offer a chance to increase self-awareness or spirituality; 20 years ago, faith-based travel was almost non-existent, but today more than 12 cruise operators transport around 3000 people each year on cruises that are themed for Christians and other religious beliefs (Tarlow, 2014).

Approximately 44 million Americans embarked on volunteer holidays with churches and religious groups in 2011, and most of these were domestic trips. Nevertheless, this demonstrates the potential for international travel in the future (Tarlow, 2014). The World Religious Travel Association (2009; cited in the United States Agency for International Development [USAID], 2014) states that the worldwide faith travel market was valued at $18 billion and composed of over 300 million travellers.

Religious Tourism and Palestine

After the Six Day War in 1967, the UN Security Council adopted Resolution 242, which notes the 'inadmissibility of the acquisition of territory by force' and calls for Israel to withdraw from lands seized in the war and the rights of all states in the area to a peaceful existence with secure and recognised boundaries. This implies that the territories of Palestine include the West Bank (including East Jerusalem) and the Gaza Strip (see Isaac *et al.*, 2016).

Understanding the challenges and opportunities of the religious tourism market in Palestine requires some insight into the region in which Palestine is located. The Eastern Mediterranean holds a long tradition of tourism, drawing visitors for cultural, business, leisure and religious purposes. Palestine occupies a unique geographical location, at the crossroads between Europe, Asia and Africa. As a cradle of cultures, it has much to offer with respect to history and antiquities, such as the ancient civilisations of Egypt and Mesopotamia and the numerous Greek and Roman ruins along the Mediterranean coast. Palestine is also where the most important Christian, Muslim and Jewish religious sites are located (Isaac *et al.*, 2016).

Tourism has been making an increasing and steady contribution to Palestinian wealth since 2005 and currently contributes around 14% of gross domestic product (GDP), an increase of 5% since 2007. The number of Palestinians employed in the tourism sector is not insignificant, and includes both male and female Palestinians, although with different genders sometimes dominating distinct subsectors. For example, the accommodation industry is mostly male while the handicraft industry is predominantly female. Approximately 50% of the State of Palestine's tourism revenues come from domestic tourism. Of the other 50%, 85% of those revenues result from international visitors coming for religious purposes and pilgrimages that still form the backbone of the Palestinian tourism economy. Domestic tourism is particularly supported by Palestinians living in Israel. Significantly, the Christian religious and pilgrimage market is the largest tourism niche in Palestine, but margins for this service may be smaller than for other services because these visitors generally adopt low budget/low margin travel programmes. This service is also subject to high seasonal fluctuations around religious feasts, and pilgrimage visitors are less susceptible to influence by marketing as their motivation is spiritual. Therefore, it is challenging to entice these visitors with other non-pilgrimage services or to increase the overall number that visit each year (Palestine Trade Centre, 2014). Furthermore, the performance of the tourism services sector has been hampered by a range of issues, which will be explained further in the subsequent sections. The perception that Palestine is a dangerous place to visit is one example and the inability of the State of Palestine to control its borders or circulation of people within its territory is another.

In spite of these impediments, tourism seems to have picked up a steadier pace in recent years due to a broadening of the range of tourism services available and developments in existing tourism services (for example, the opening of new restaurants, cultural centres, museums and resorts across the West Bank and East Jerusalem). The number of actors in the tourism sector has also increased, and the 2010 decision to establish a Palestine Tourism Board (PTB; a public/private partnership), although not yet operationalised, is important in order to address the limited cooperation and coordination that has existed between stakeholders.

Palestine's religious and sacred sites

The tourism sector has always been a primary sector in the Palestinian economy and indeed an essential source of income. The assets and religious sites of the Palestinian areas are located in Bethlehem, Jericho, Nablus, Hebron and East Jerusalem (Figure 11.1). Bethlehem is located 9 km south of Jerusalem. The most important Christian and Muslim sites in Bethlehem are the Basilica and the Grotto of the Nativity Church, which are sacred for the Catholic, Greek Orthodox and Armenian churches, all of which have ownership rights to the church. The structure of the church as a piece of property is legally owned communally by these three groups. In addition to the above, other sacred sites in Bethlehem are the Churches of St Catherine and St Jerome, the Milk Grotto and the pilgrimage site of Shepherds' Field, St Theodosius' Monastery, Mar Saba Monastery and the Mosque of Omar (2nd Caliph) (Isaac *et al.*, 2016). Jericho (the biblical 'city of palm trees') is located on the West Bank of the Jordan Valley, 8 km north of the Dead Sea. Dating back more than 10,000 years, Jericho is the lowest city and the oldest continuously inhabited site in the world. Besides the historical and ancient sites and its walls, an interesting site in Jericho is the Monastery of Qurantul (the Forty). The monastery, perched on the side of the Mount of Temptation, offers a spectacular panorama of the Dead Sea, the Jordan Valley and Jericho. This mountain was where Jesus fasted for 40 days and was tempted by the devil. Hisham's Palace site is also one of the most impressive residences of the Omayyad period; archaeologists call it 'the Versailles of the Middle East' (Alternative Tourism Group, 2014). The city of Nablus is located in the northern West Bank, 49 km from Jerusalem, and its attractions include the Old City of Nablus (Roman era), Roman ruins at Sebastia (the home of the Nabi Yahya Mosque, a former Crusader cathedral), Jacob's well and Mount Gerizim (home of the Samaritan community). Hebron is a Palestinian city located in the southern part of the West Bank and its most important religious site is the Ibrahimi Mosque (Cave of the Patriarchs). East Jerusalem constitutes the oriental part of Jerusalem. Following the Israeli conquest of the western part of Jerusalem in 1948, the city was divided and a new designation came into being: East Jerusalem. East Jerusalem's attractions include several ancient and historical sites, the most important religious sites being the Dome of the Rock, Al-Aqsa Mosque, Mount of Olives, Garden of Gethsemane, the Church of the Holy Sepulchre and the Church of the Ascension.

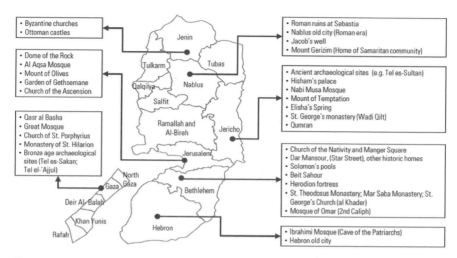

Figure 11.1 Tourism attractions in Palestine (Source: Portland Trust, 2013)

Tourists arrivals

According to MOTA (2016), the number of overnight stays in Palestine for inbound and domestic tourism reached 1,211,561 in 2014 (Figures 11.2–11.6, Table 11.1). The State of Palestine's religious and pilgrimage tourism is closely entangled with that of Israel. Most tourists visit the State of Palestine while visiting Israel and vice versa.

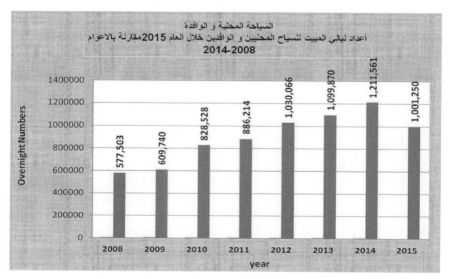

Figure 11.2 Number of overnight stays by inbound and domestic tourists during 2015 compared with 2004–2014 (Source: MOTA, 2016)

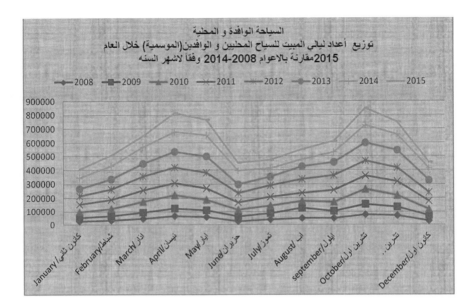

Figure 11.3 Distribution of overnight stays for inbound and domestic tourism during 2008–2015 (Source: MOTA, 2016)

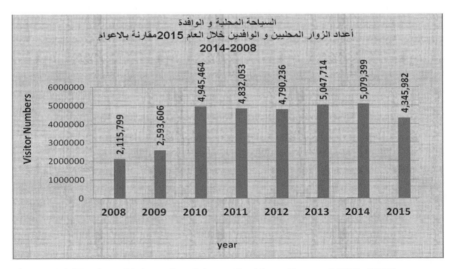

Figure 11.4 Number of inbound and domestic visitors (Source: MOTA, 2016)

Over the years, Bethlehem has continued to see record numbers of both one-day and overnight visitors. It has always been one of Palestine's leading destinations, attracting millions of visitors from various religious markets from around the world. Bethlehem ranks as a 'must see' for all religious, pilgrims and visitors to the Holy Land.

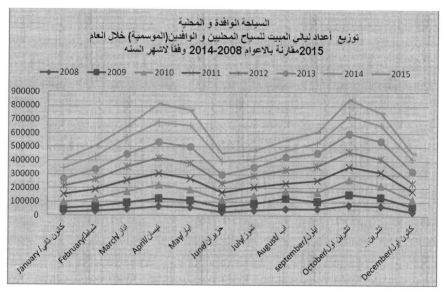

Figure 11.5 Distribution number of inbound and domestic visitors during 2008–2015 by month (Source: MOTA, 2016)

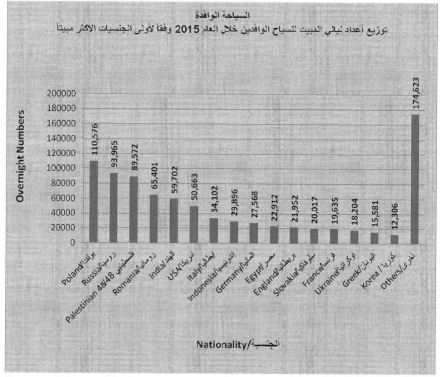

Figure 11.6 Overnights stay by top nationality (Source: MOTA, 2016)

Table 11.1 Distribution of number of inbound and domestic overnights during 2008–2015 by region

	2008	2009	2010	2011	2012	2013	2014	2015
Jericho/اريحا	62510	49798	75054	68531	80108	65673	61457	42328
Hebron/الخليل	1564	2505	2284	3825	3196	2913	2379	2128
Bethlehem/بيت لحم	392523	364053	547502	589360	698274	776169	848124	686971
Jenin/جنين	230	2308	4180	9278	25342	18550	19349	17047
Ramallah /رام الله	35399	60164	73483	86179	100330	103932	122161	106961
Nablus/نابلس	8285	5504	8446	9250	7876	10670	12734	10999
Tulkarm/طولكرم			6150			20	77	211
Tubas /طوباس			18					9
Qalqeliah/قلقيلية						24		21

Source: MOTA, Palestine (2016).

According to MOTA (2016), the three top source markets for overnight stays in Palestine are the Polish, Russians and the Palestinians residing in Israel, the so-called 1948 visitors. As can be observed from Figures 11.1– 11.6 and Table 11.1, tourism in Palestine is booming again. Despite various incidents which have occurred in the region and the ongoing conflict (see Isaac, 2013), new tourism investments are being established every year. New hotels and resorts, museums and attractions are opening up and complementing the destination's appeal by catering to a more diverse range of markets, both local and international (Isaac, 2016).

Challenges facing religious tourism in Palestine

There are a number of important challenges facing and limiting the development of both religious tourism and tourism of all types in Palestine.

The impact of Israeli occupation on religious tourism to Palestine

Israeli restrictions particularly on holy places throughout the occupied territories of Palestine explicitly target religious and cultural heritage, and include damage and demolition of mosques and other significant ancient sites. Continuous military incursions severely damage tourism not only by affecting the destination image but also by creating an unstable business environment for any (future) developments in the tourism sector (Isaac, 2010).

Restrictions on freedom of movement

A number of Israeli-imposed restrictions continue to limit the movement of Palestinians. According to data collected by the United Nations and the Rand Corporation (cited in Lang & De Leon, 2016) there are up to 500 physical impediments or 'closure obstacles' to the ability of Palestinians to move freely, 'including checkpoints, road gates, roadblocks, earth mounds, trenches, road barriers, and earth walls'. These include some 85 fixed and hundreds of 'flying', or temporary, surprise checkpoints. In addition to these physical barriers, Israel imposes a permit system to control Palestinian movement between the West Bank's three territories – Areas A, B and C – as well as East Jerusalem, the Jordan Valley and Israeli settlements. Nearly all recent reports have found that the movement and access restrictions are a key constraint to Palestinian economic development. According to the World Bank (cited in Lang & De Leon, 2016) 'internal closures stifle economic activity by raising the cost of doing business . . . and [have] fragmented the West Bank territory into small and disconnected "cantons"'. Following the late 2015 increase in Palestinian–Israeli violence, Israel established some 38 new obstacles to movement in East Jerusalem, including 16 checkpoints and 20 roadblocks (Lang & De Leon, 2016). Since the 1990s, Israel's various restrictions on movement including a combination of checkpoints, permits and the Separation Wall, have prevented Palestinians in the West Bank from visiting churches and mosques in Jerusalem, while no such restrictions exist for Jewish-Israelis living in illegal West Bank settlements, who can freely access the city whenever they want.

Furthermore, a variety of barriers make it difficult for foreign nationals to travel in the West Bank and Gaza. Israel sometimes prohibits visitors from entering these areas. A recent example is the World Council of Churches meeting in Palestine. After traveling to Ben Gurion Airport in Tel Aviv for a climate justice meeting, the World Council of Churches (WCC) staff and partners were detained or deported in a manner that WCC General Secretary Rev Dr Olav Fykse Tveit termed both unprecedented and intolerable (World Council of Churches, 2016). These restrictions have clear implications for tourism, an industry that is an important source of jobs and revenue for Palestinians. In and around the city of Bethlehem and other centres of historical and religious significance, tourism is a pillar of the local economy – one that has been hit hard by recent security incidents, operations and restrictions. Some estimates (Lang & De Leon, 2016) indicate that due to difficult entry and exit processes for tourists, tourism in the Palestinian areas has been reduced by 20%–60% of its potential. Additionally, based on general econometric models of the impact of visa restrictions, it is estimated that these types of impediments on travel reduce trade and foreign direct investment by up to 25% (Lang & De Leon, 2016).

Weaknesses in reaching Arab tourists

While a relatively large number of tourists visit Palestine from the EU and the United States, the situation is different regarding Arabs, including Muslims and Christians from Arabian countries. Data shows that Arab visits to Palestine comprise only 3% of total tourism in Palestine, partly as a result of the Israeli occupation. Israeli foreign relations with other countries are complex, highly defining and decide what groups and which nationalities have access to occupied Palestine. For instance, visitors crossing the border to Palestine need an Israeli visa, which in many cases is very difficult for Arab visitors such as Syrians or Lebanese to obtain. Therefore, several Arab governments prohibit and even discourage their citizens from visiting Palestine because of the Israeli occupation and the undefined borders with Israel. On the other hand, a large number of Arabs refuse to visit Palestine because of the Israeli occupation as they consider this would imply a form of normalisation. For instance, the main Islamic site (Al-Aqsa Mosque) is under Israeli military occupation and East Jerusalem as a whole is still occupied. This situation discourages and limits the promotional activities by the Palestinian side (government and private sector) (International Chamber of Commerce, 2013).

Weaknesses in reaching domestic visitors

Locally, less than half of the Palestinian population participates in tourism in the Palestinian territory. Palestinians residing in Palestine make up 37.8% of total tourism in Palestine. Most trips are one-day trips with few or no activities conducted and little need for accommodation. The resulting low level of expenditure on accommodation might represent a potential for improvement if the hotels and tourism agents started introducing offers targeting domestic markets.

At the local level, the underperformance of domestic tourism is mostly due to the difficulties faced by Palestinian citizens in moving between cities and reaching a large number of sites, because some tourist sites are located in areas that Israel has placed under full military control and the Palestinian tourism companies face difficulties in accessing these sites.

According to the Paris Protocol,

Tourist buses or any other form of tourist transport authorized by either side, and operated by companies registered and licensed by it, will be allowed to enter and proceed on their tour within the area under the jurisdiction of the other side, provided that such buses or other vehicles conform with the EEC technical specifications [I. currently adopted.] All such vehicles will be clearly marked as tourist vehicles. (Article X, 4; cited in International Chamber of Commerce, 2013)

Based on the mentioned article, tourist buses from the Palestinian side, which are granted licenses by the Palestinian authority, should be allowed to enter and undertake tours in areas under Israeli military control. Moreover, according to Article X, 6, Palestinian tourism companies and agents should have access to tourism-related facilities equal to that enjoyed by Israeli companies and agents. Due to the constant violation of the Paris Protocol by the Israeli government, limitations on movement and access by Palestinian tourism agents, buses and guides have resulted in a relative strengthening of the appeal of the tourism packages offered by Israeli companies leading to a higher preference by the foreign visitor for the Israeli companies. It is extremely important to consider the impediments to free access of movement of tourists across Palestine, especially to the Gaza Strip, because these restrictions have prevented the Palestinian government and police from accessing areas of high touristic value and potential for development. This suggests that the weakness in the Palestinian tourism sector is partially a result of Palestinian institutional weakness and also lack of sovereignty on the part of the Palestinian government, and thus an inability to reach tourist areas to provide for the protection of tourists and the administration and implementation of the rule of law.

Restrictions on religious freedom and related intolerance

The occupied territories of Palestine, Jerusalem, Bethlehem, Hebron and Nablus all hold places of considerable religious significance for Christianity, Judaism and Islam but are vulnerable to the impacts of settlements in various forms throughout the West Bank. Both Jerusalem and Hebron have been targeted by particularly aggressive settlement policies and practices perhaps because of their religious significance. Such settlements disrupt the lives of residents and potential tourists and hinder Palestinian development in these areas.

Points of entry/exit

At the present time (2017), Israel has control over the flow of international tourists and the religious market in particular, including the issuing of visas, flights, lodging and appointing Israeli tour guides within the country (Isaac *et al.*, 2016). Israel and Jordan are the main gateways to the State of Palestine, and all these borders are under Israeli control. In this context, this means that tourism to the State of Palestine remains dependent on Israeli goodwill to a very significant extent.

Tourists who reveal an intention to visit the territories of Palestine risk facing delays at the airport in Tel Aviv or at the Allenby Bridge (border crossing with Jordan). Some would-be visitors are deported without explanation; others are told that they are being sent back because they are security threats to the State of Israel (Alternative Tourism Journal, 2014).

Summary

To sum up, the following are the most important difficulties facing tourism to Palestine:

- The main reason for the tourism sector not reaching its full potential is Israel's unilateral control of the borders and its method of controlling the entry of visitors. This indirectly, through various policies, prevents Arab pilgrims from visiting Palestine and hence prevents an expected 4 million visitors yearly to Al-Aqsa Mosque alone as part of hajj rites.
- Limiting Palestinian tourist guides from working in Israel by not granting licenses either on security grounds or through administrative requirements that are difficult for Palestinian guides to satisfy. This makes it easier for tourist groups to choose Israeli tourist guides in both Israel and Palestine. Currently, only 40 of 300 West Bank guides are allowed to work in Israel.
- The full control over access by Israeli agencies limits the time spent by foreign visitors at Palestinian sites, significantly minimising the economic benefits which could be obtained from tourism.
- Israeli media coverage has resulted in branding Palestine as an unsafe place to visit, hence reducing the number of religious and other visitors to Palestine. The Israeli government, by controlling entry visas, can limit the number of visitors and direct them to areas under Israeli government control.

Opportunities for religious tourism in Palestine

Despite the above problems, there are significant opportunities to develop further religious tourism in Palestine.

Attracting the Arab and Muslim markets

It is well known that Muslims go to Mecca for hajj, with 4 million such visitors arriving in Saudi Arabia in 2016 (hajj period only). One of the main opportunities for the tourism sector in Palestine consists of the need for Muslims conducting hajj rites to visit the Al-Aqsa Mosque in Jerusalem as a complementary part of their hajj. However, several Islamic countries such as Indonesia, Iran, Pakistan and Bangladesh have no relations with Israel and their citizens are prohibited from entering Palestine, as they need Israeli visas. Once Palestine has its own borders, this could open the potential for millions of additional visitors to Palestine each year. Traditionally, Islamic tourism was often associated with the hajj and umrah only. However, recently there has been an expansion of products and services designed specifically to cater to the business- and leisure-related segments of Muslim tourists across the globe. Islamic non-hajj-related tourism is a recent phenomenon in the theory and practice of the global tourism industry, and Islamic tourism is becoming an emerging niche market with 108 million Muslim travellers, accounting for 10%–12% of the global international tourism sector. With an annual growth rate of 4.8%, the Muslim tourism market is growing faster than the global tourism market, which recorded a growth rate of 3.8% in 2013 (Organisation of Islamic Cooperation, 2015). Provided the estimated growth in the Muslim population and positive economic prospects for many Muslim majority countries continue, the Islamic tourism market is forecast to grow to $200 billion with 150 million tourists by the end of 2020 (Crescent Rating, 2015). An additional activity that could attract Muslims and other foreign visitors would be the experience of bed and breakfast in Palestinian homes, which could compensate at least in part for the lack of bed places in hotels, motels and guest houses and provide significant additional income for the local population. Such a development would also provide opportunities for closer contact between tourists and local residents, something often preferred by foreign visitors because such accommodation is much cheaper than hotels. In this regard, it is important to consider that during the celebrations of Bethlehem 2000, many houses in the village of Beit Sahour were organised as bed and breakfasts. Currently, the so-called Alternative Tourism Group uses many home-stay operations to accommodate their guests (Kokaly, 2016, personal communications). Moreover, the emotional importance of Palestine to the Islamic and Arab world is considered an advantage in attracting a large number of visitors, allowing them to gain personal knowledge of Palestine in addition to showing support for the Palestinian cause. This opportunity has been realised in recent years by the Palestinian authority as shown by Rula Ma'ay'a, the minister of tourism, in a statement: 'Visiting Palestine is not a form of normalization with the jailer, but an empathy with the prisoner' (International Chamber of Commerce, 2013).

Innovative tourism products

There are opportunities for Palestine to bundle traditional pilgrimage and religious travel experiences along with activities related to culture and heritage to make unique innovative tourism packages. In addition, Palestine could design long-term strategies and master plans for the further development of the Islamic religious tourism market from the member states of the Organisation of Islamic Countries (OIC, which includes Malaysia, Turkey, the United Arab Emirates, Saudi Arabia, Qatar, Indonesia, Oman, Jordan, Morocco and Brunei).

Conclusion

The aim of this chapter was to reveal the importance of the religious tourism market to Palestine and to demonstrate the many difficulties and opportunities facing this important market in Palestine. The tourism sector in Palestine is one of the most important economic sectors of the

Palestinian economy and would certainly play a role in its recovery process following the eventual end to the Israeli occupation. Economic indicators and the increasing number of tourists and visitors show that the importance of tourism to the Palestinian economy is growing each year, and indeed has the potential to grow faster if the restrictions imposed by the occupation were lifted. Tourism today is a powerful and political tool by which Palestinians are able to convey an important message to the outside world. At the time of writing this chapter (2017), the biggest challenge facing the religious tourism market in Palestine is the Israeli occupation. This has posed many problems for the further development of tourism to Palestine, including the lack of Palestinian control over borders, the immobility of the domestic markets within Palestine, the Segregation Wall which cuts deep into Palestinian territory and the fragmentation of Palestine into different areas of control. Palestinians to date are powerless to plan for the future development of tourism in the absence of a clear indication of when the conflict will end.

References

Alecu, I.C. (2011) Epistemological aspects of religious tourism in rural areas. *International Journal of Business, Management and Social Science* 2 (3), 59–65.
Alternative Tourism Group (2014) *Palestine and Palestinians*. Beitsahour: ATG.
Bywater, M. (1994) Economist intelligence unit. *Travel and Tourism Analyst* 2, 39.
Cohen, E. (1992a) Pilgrimage and tourism: Convergence and divergence. In A. Morinis (ed.) *Sacred Journeys: The Anthropology of Pilgrimage* (pp. 18–35). Westport, CT: Greenwood Press.
Cohen, E. (1992b) Pilgrimage centres: Central and excentric. *Annals of Tourism Research* 19 (1), 33–50.
Colby, S. (1983) Christianity and Christian holy sites in the Galilee. In A. Soffer, A. Shmueli and N. Kliot (eds) *The Lands of Galilee* (pp. 521–528). Haifa: Haifa University and Tel Aviv Ministry of Defence.
Coleman, S. (2004) *Framing Pilgrimages: Cultures in Motion*. London: Routledge.
Collins-Kreiner, N. and Kliot, N. (2000) Pilgrimage tourism in the Holy Land: The behavioural characteristics of Christian pilgrims. *Geojournal* 50, 55–67.
Collins-Kreiner, N. and Gatrell, J.D. (2006) Tourism, heritage and pilgrimage: The case of Haifa's Bahia Gardens. *Journal of Heritage Tourism* 1 (1), 32–50.
Crescent Rating (2015) *Muslim/Halal Travel Market: Basic Concepts, Terms and Definitions*. Singapore: Crescent Rating.
D'Amore, L. (2009) Peace through tourism: The birthing of a new socio-economic order, founder and president. *Journal of Business Ethics* 89 (4), 559–568.
Fleischer, A. (2000) The tourist behind the pilgrim in the Holy Land. *International Journal of Hospitality Management* 19, 311–326.
Fleischer, A. and Nitzav, Y. (1995) *Christian Pilgrims: The Tourism Potential for Peripheral Regions in Israel*. Rehovot: Centre for Development Studies.
Gan, Z., Ma, Y. and Song, B. (2000) Tourism resource of religious culture. In Z. Gan, Y. Ma and B. Song (eds) *Tourism Resource and Development* (pp. 157–176). Tianjin: Nankai University Press.

Graburn, N. (1989) Tourism: The sacred journey. In V.L. Smith (ed.) *Hosts and Guests: The Anthropology of Tourism* (pp. 21–36). Philadelphia, PA: University of Pennsylvania Press.

Hinnells, J.H. (1984) *The Penguin Dictionary of Religions*. London: Penguin Books Ltd.

Holmberg, C.B. (1993) Spiritual pilgrimages: Traditional and hyper real motivations for travel and tourism. *Visions in Leisure and Business* 12 (2), 19–27.

International Chamber of Commerce (2013) Palestine tourism sector. Palestine. See http://www.iccpalestine.com/resources/file/publications/WTO%20&%20the%20 Palestinian%20Tourism%20Sector.pdf (Accessed 1 July 2015).

Isaac, R.K. (2010) Alternative tourism: new forms of tourism in Bethlehem for the Palestinian tourism industry. *Current Issues in Tourism* 13 (1), 21–36.

Isaac, R.K. (2013) Palestine: Tourism under occupation. In R.W. Butler and W. Suntikul (eds) *Tourism and War* (pp. 143–158). Abingdon: Routledge.

Isaac, R.K. (2016) Pilgrimage tourism to Palestine. In R.K. Isaac, C.M. Hall and F. Higgins-Desbiolles (eds) *The Politics and Power of Tourism in Palestine* (pp. 124–148). London: Routledge.

Isaac, R.K., Hall, C.M. and Higgins-Desbiolles, F. (eds) (2016) Palestine as a tourism destination. In R.K. Isaac, C.M. Hall and F. Higgins-Desbiolles (eds) *The Politics and Power of Tourism in Palestine* (pp. 15–34). London: Routledge.

Jackowski, A. and Smith, V.L. (1992) Polish pilgrim-tourists. *Annals of Tourism Research* 19 (1), 92–106.

Jansen, W. and Kühl, M. (2008) Shared symbols: Muslims, Marian pilgrimages and gender. *European Journal of Women's Studies* 1, 295–311.

Kurlantzick, J. (2007) 21st century religious travel: Leave the sackcloth at home. 29 April. See http://www.nytimes.com/2007/04/29/travel/29religion.html?_r=0 (accessed 1 August 2016).

Lang, H. and De Leon, R. (2016) Strengthen the Palestinian economy to keep a two state solution viable. *Centre for American Progress*. See https://cdn.americanprogress.org/wpontent/uploads/2016/04/12143137/PalestinianEcon.pdf (accessed 1 August 2016).

Mintel (2012) Religious and pilgrimage tourism: Market report. London: Mintel International.

Morinis, A. (1992) Introduction: The territory of the anthropology of pilgrimage. In A. Morinis (ed.) *Sacred Journeys: The Anthropology of Pilgrimage* (pp. 1–28) Westport, CT: Greenwood Press.

MOTA is Ministry of Tourism and Antiquities, based in Ramallah, Palestine.

Murray, M. and Graham, B. (1997) Exploring the dialectics of route-based tourism: The Camino de Santiago. *Tourism Management* 18 (8), 513–524.

Nolan, M. (1987) Roman Catholic pilgrimage in the new world. In M. Eliade (ed.) *Encyclopaedia of Religion* (pp. 332–335). New York: The Macmillan Publishing Company.

Nolan, M. and Nolan, S. (1989) *Christian Pilgrimage in Modern Western Europe*. Chapel Hill, NC: University of North Carolina Press.

Nolan, M. and Nolan, S. (1992) Religious sites as tourism attractions in Europe. *Annals of Tourism Research* 19, 68–78.

Olsen, D.H. (2006b) Tourism and informal pilgrimage among the Latter-Day Saints. In D. Timothy and D.H. Olsen (eds) *Tourism, Religion and Journeys* (pp. 254–270). London/New York: Routledge.

Olsen, D.H. and Timothy, D.J. (1999) Tourism 2000: Selling the millennium. *Tourism Management* 20 (4), 389.

Organisation of Islamic Cooperation (2015) *International Tourism in OIC member countries Prospects and Challenges* Ankara: Statistical, Economic And Social Research and Training Centre for Islamic Countries.

Palestine Trade Centre (2014) *Tourism Sector Export Strategy 2014–2018*. Ramallah: Palestine Trade Centre.

Pfaffenberger, B. (1983) Serious pilgrims and frivolous tourists: The chimera of tourism in the pilgrimage of Sri Lanka. *Annals of Tourism Research* 10, 57–74.

Post, P., Pieper, J. and Uden, M.V. (1998) *The Modern Pilgrim: Multidisciplinary Explorations of Christian Pilgrimage*. Leuven: Peeters.

Raj, R. and Morpeth, N. (2007) *Religious Tourism and Pilgrimage Management: An International Perspective*. Wallingford: CABI.

Rinschede, G. (1992) Forms of religious tourism. *Annals of Tourism Research* 19 (1), 51–67.

Rojo, D.M. (2007) Religious tourism: The way to Santiago. Unpublished master's thesis. Bournemouth University.

Ron, A. (2009) Towards a typological model of contemporary Christian travel. *Journal of Heritage Tourism* 4 (4), 287–297.

Russell, P. (1999) Religious travel in the new millennium. *Travel and Tourism Analyst* 5, 39–68.

San Filippo, M. (2001) The religious niche. *Travel Weekly* 60 (18), 12.

Santos, M. (2003) Religious tourism: Contributions towards a clarification of concepts. In C. Fernandes, F. McGettigan and J. Edwards (eds) *Religious Tourism and Pilgrimage: ATLAS Special Interest Group, 1st Expert Meeting* (pp. 27–42). Fátima: Tourism Board of Leiria/Fátima.

Singh, S. (1998) Probing the product life cycle further. *Tourism Recreation Research* 23 (2), 61–63.

Singh, R.B. (2013) Pilgrimage-tourism: Perspective and vision. In R.B. Singh (ed.) *Hindu Tradition of Pilgrimage: Sacred Space and System* (pp. 305–332). New Delhi: Dev Publishers.

Smith, V.L. (1992) Introduction: The quest in guest. *Annals of Tourism Research* 19, 1–17.

Tarlow, P. (2014) The importance of religious tourism market. See http://www.eturbonews.com/50998/importance-religious-tourism-market (accessed 18 May 2016).

Timothy, D.J. and Boyd, S.W. (2006) Heritage tourism in the 21st century: Valued traditions and new perspectives. *Journal of Heritage Tourism* 1 (1), 1–16.

Timothy, D. and Olsen, D. (2006) *Tourism, Religion and Spiritual Journeys*. London: Routledge.

USAID (2014) *Faith and Adventure Tourism Market Profile*. Prepared by Holy Land Incoming Tour Operators Association (HLITOA). Bethlehem: HLITOA.

Weidenfeld, A. (2006) The religious needs of the hospitality industry. *Tourism and Hospitality Research* 6 (2), 143–159.

World Council of Churches (2016) WCC: Israeli treatment of representatives at airport unacceptable. See http://www.oikoumene.org/en/press-centre/news/wcc-israeli-treatment-of-representatives-at-airport-unacceptable (accessed 9 May 2016).

12 Marketing Myanmar: The Religion/Tourism Nexus in a Fragile Polity

David Mercer

> . . . it is clear that the Myanmar junta is using Buddhist heritage conservation projects, especially religious monuments, as a way of legitimizing its own position, strengthening the dominance of the majority ethnic group, and marginalizing the cultures of the Karen and Mon minorities . . .
>
> Logan, 2007: 41

> . . . a Disney-style fantasy version of one of the world's great religious and historical sites is being created by the military government . . . They use the wrong materials to build wrongly shaped structures on top of magnificent ancient stupas
>
> Christian Manhart, UNESCO heritage advisor – quoted in Crampton, 2005

The period since the Second World War has seen the unfolding of two momentous – and interrelated – worldwide trends. The first is globalisation and the second is decolonisation. One obvious manifestation of the former is the now unprecedented level of international connectivity – of people, goods, technologies, religions and ideas. Tourism plays a central role in this process. At the same time, the attainment of independent political status has, for a large number of new state entities, generated a host of deep-seated, and still largely unresolved, political and economic growing pains. This is especially the case where often arbitrary geographical boundaries, drawn up by former colonial powers, have resulted in forced amalgamations of markedly different ethnic and religious groups. Nigeria, Thailand, Malaysia, Indonesia and, of course, the focus of this chapter – Burma/Myanmar – all spring readily to mind as exemplars from a very long list of possible cases. As demonstrated by the disintegration of the former Yugoslavia in the 1990s, as well as violent episodes over the years in such conflicted places as East Timor, Aceh and Bougainville, there is always a level of fragility and impermanence underlying historical attempts at nation-building 'from above'. And often one does not have to dig too deeply to find that religious differences play a major role in the ongoing conflicts. Contemporary Burma – which one commentator (Smith, 1996) has described as the 'Yugoslavia of Asia' – is certainly no exception in this regard, as discussed below.

Ko Ko Thett (2012) reminds us that in the 1920s period of 'high colonialism', the 600-fleet Irrawaddy Flotilla Company (IFC) – at the time, by far the world's largest riverboat company – was transporting as many as nine million passengers a year up and down the river (the Aeryawaddy) that forms the major transport artery in the 'Land of the Pagodas'. But the tragedy for Burma is that, over recent decades, a succession of military-backed governments has consistently failed to recognise the serious damage that internal conflict inflicts on the potentially highly lucrative tourism market, an issue that has now been given precise quantitative expression for different countries in the recent, ground-breaking report, *Tourism as a Driver of Peace* (World Travel and Tourism Council, 2016). Relatedly, the former military junta failed to grasp that ethno-religious *diversity*, its rich architectural legacy in the landscape, as well as the associated intangible heritage (dance performance, ritual/ceremony, festival, art, etc.) can be an enormously powerful drawcard for discerning, international tourists.

'Selling' Buddhism

The evidence from such popular destinations as India, Nepal, Bhutan, Cambodia and Thailand is unambiguous: a significant and growing segment of the world's affluent, middle-class travel market has an insatiable appetite for engaging with cultural and architectural heritage, religious customs and ceremonies, local cuisine, language and lifestyles. Further, the explosion of interest in public events featuring the Dalai Lama, as well as in such movements as *Vipassana* in North America and Australia, points to a growing hunger for Asian-inspired spiritual exploration in an age of hyper-consumerism.

All of these factors were at play in a recent international conference held in Dhaka. This brought together delegates from the so-called 'Buddhist Heartland' countries of South Asia (Bangladesh, Bhutan, India, Nepal and Sri Lanka), and elsewhere, to explore ways in which these countries, in particular, could capitalise on the new-found fascination with Eastern religion in the West, learn from the success of such projects as St James Way in Europe and collaboratively tap into the potentially lucrative 'pilgrimage' market of 500 million Buddhists worldwide (Ministry of Civil Aviation and Tourism, Bangladesh, and World Tourism Organization [UNWTO], 2015). Burma was represented at the conference but the proceedings make it quite clear that, in that forum at least, the five nations mentioned above were the centre of attention for discussion around possible, linked pilgrimage 'circuits'.

More recently, we have witnessed further evidence of collaboration, as well as ongoing differences, between Buddhist nations over historical claims to 'truth' and 'authenticity'. In May 2016, a major gathering of Buddhists from 28 countries was held in Kathmandu and then Lumbini (Nepal) to celebrate the 2560th anniversary of the birth of Buddha. The subsequent 'Lumbini Declaration' urged all Buddhists to acknowledge Lumbini as the rightful birthplace of the Lord Buddha and – at least once in their lifetime – to visit there, as well as three other key (though 'lesser' significant) pilgrimage sites in neighbouring India. As with the Dhaka conference – and clearly with an eye to the potentially huge pilgrim tourism market – there was an explicit message to privilege certain iconic sites and countries above others. Perhaps unsurprisingly, India boycotted the conference. Kong and Woods (2016) have suggested a four-fold classification of *religious competition*, which are *inter-religious, religion-secular, religion-state* and *intra-religious competition*. India's action fits firmly within their *intra-religious* category.

The 'Asian' Century?

With regard to heritage sites endowed with great religious significance, two additional issues have become increasingly clear in the early years of what some have called the 'Asian Century'. The first is the uneasy tension between Western and non-Western attitudes towards the very concept of heritage and heritage management (Aygen & Logan, 2016). The second is the universal problem of mass tourism and its impacts. As Cameron (2016: 330) reminds us, in the first decade of the World Heritage Convention's existence (1972–1982), '. . . tourism was rarely part of the World Heritage discourse'. This is certainly not the case today.

Later in the discussion, we shall touch upon the way in which, for much of the last 50 years, Western European nations and North America effectively shunned Burma as a tourist destination and place for investment. But, as we shall also see, this in turn prompted the Burmese government to engage much more proactively with its 'friendlier' neighbours in ASEAN – a South East Asian regional economic bloc of some 620 million people – into which the country was formally inducted in 1997. All of ASEAN's 10 member states have a rapidly growing middle class with a strong appetite for international travel (Henderson, 2015). The bloc has a large collective Buddhist population. Of significance to the later discussion, too, is the fact that in 1993 Myanmar joined with 39 other Asian countries in signing the somewhat defiant Bangkok Declaration on Human Rights. This was a strong signal to the West that 'Asian values' and sovereignty needed to be respected, and questioned a 'universal' definition of human rights. Relatedly, in May 2014, Myanmar joined with the five 'Buddhist heartland' countries mentioned above to ratify the UN Convention for the Safeguarding of the Intangible Cultural Heritage. The concept of 'intangible cultural heritage' is open to wide interpretation. However,

Logan (2007) defined it as 'heritage that is embodied in people rather than in inanimate objects'. In theory, it could, for example, be used to justify a liberal definition of 'voluntary labour' when applied to pagoda reconstruction and similar work, an issue that is discussed below.

Tourism visitation statistics and their reliability as they relate to Burma will be discussed later in this chapter. However, in passing it is worth noting that in 2014, nearly 50% of tourists in neighbouring Thailand came from outside the country, mainly via land border crossing points. Over 90% of Thailand's population are Buddhist (totalling around 63 million) but unfortunately there are no data differentiating 'pilgrims' from 'secular' tourists. The same applies to adjacent China which now accounts for around 27% of the tourism market share for Burma (UNWTO, 2016). When the new tri-nation highway linking India, Myanmar and Thailand is finally opened there is certain to be a dramatic growth in traffic along that particular 'pilgrim circuit'.

Nation-Building, Religion and Tourism

Gillen (2014: 1308) has roundly criticised mainstream tourism research for its 'neglect . . . in engaging with leisure as a means of building and avowing the validity' of one-party nations. Taking his criticism on board, a recurring theme throughout this chapter is the intimate and complex relationship between nation-building in what – until very recently – has been an authoritarian, one-party state; democracy and human rights concerns; religious (in)tolerance; and the potentially substantial economic opportunities offered by tourism (Blanchard & Higgins-Desbiolles, 2012; Gillespie, 2013; Logan, 2012). This nexus is also of central significance in other ASEAN nations such as Indonesia (Silver, 2007) and Cambodia (Gillespie, 2013).

Recently, for example, as the nominally civilian government (elected in November 2015) desperately struggled to implement a delicate ceasefire agreement with eight different ethno-religious groups, as well as related policies grounded in religious and ethnic *inclusivity*, a senior general in the still enormously powerful Burmese military faction was accused by commentators of inflaming 'religious extremism'. Addressing fresh army recruits at a training school in politically contested Shan State, Snr. General Min Aung Hlaing pledged to safeguard the country's 'Buddhist heritage' for future generations (Wa Lone, 2016). With a total of 570,000 persons self-identifying as Christian, according to the 2014 census, this state has the largest complement of Christians in Burma, a significant minority in a state of 5.8 million people. Recent conflicts there – including injuries to overseas tourists from ubiquitous landmines – have had a significant impact on the popular trekking industry in particular (BBC News, 2016; Macgregor & Thu Aung, 2016).

At one level, the general's remarks are by no means surprising in a country with a longstanding tradition of strongly nationalistic Buddhist activism. In 1961, for example, an attempt was made to enshrine Buddhism as the official state religion in the Constitution. The same document committed the government to allocating 50% of its budget each year to religious matters including supporting the restoration of pagodas, temples and monasteries. The Ministry of Religious Affairs has a specialist agency with a clearly defined charter to nurture and encourage Buddhism and Buddhist teaching: 'The Department for the Promotion and Propagation of Sasana' and all Buddhists can earn 'merit' through *dana* (giving) by worshipping at sacred sites, volunteering their labour for pagoda restoration and making donations. The local media frequently give maximum exposure to senior military and government personnel worshipping at Buddhist temples, giving alms or overseeing pagoda restoration work. In addition, new stupa (or pagoda) construction in Christian and Muslim areas is strongly encouraged, often on confiscated land, while obstacles are frequently put in the way of building churches and mosques.

Perhaps not unexpectedly, then, the July 2013 Asian issue of *Time* magazine caused an outcry in some quarters in Burma when its cover featured a photograph of the radical Buddhist monk, U Wirathu under the headline 'The face of Buddhist terror'. Receiving only muted opposition from authorities (the magazine was summarily banned), the leader of the extremist 969 Movement, U Wirathu constantly travels the country and makes strategic use of social media warning of the 'threat' of Islamic expansion, condemning interfaith marriage and promoting the boycotting of Muslim businesses (Beech, 2013). Even though Muslims make up only 4% of the country's population, the narrative being fuelled is that they are 'taking over'. There are strong parallels here with India's *Hindutva* movement.

Let us now briefly reset the historical clock, initially by some 70 years, to highlight some important historical context for the above, as well as for the discussion that follows.

A New Country is Born

In January 1948, Burma's former colonial power, Britain, decreed that the artificial state entity of the New Union of Burma should share an extensive and complex 2000-kilometer-long border with India, Bangladesh and China to the west and north, and Thailand and Laos to the east. Over the millennia, Burma had experienced wave after wave of different military, linguistic and religious influences from various colonising empires originating in these countries. Some of these (e.g. the Pagan, Khmer and Mongol) had an extensive geographical reach across much of South East Asia and ruled for periods of hundreds of years. Others were more short-lived. But, as at Angkor Wat in Cambodia (also a relic of the Khmer empire), all left often outstanding religious and architectural traces in the landscape that – as we shall see – are of international significance today. Interestingly, too – and in marked contrast to contemporary Burma – many of the earlier empires, like Pagan and Mrauk U, demonstrated remarkable tolerance for religious diversity.

Physically, upon independence in 1948, the country was in a parlous state. Its infrastructure had been almost totally destroyed by both Japanese and British military forces during the Second World War. Nationalisation of all the key economic sectors, including land and hotels, was one of the first acts of the U Nu-led government. Over the ensuing decades, this subsequently turned out to be economically disastrous and Burma rapidly descended into a downward spiral from being one of Asia's most buoyant and productive economies, especially in terms of rice production, to one of the poorest in the world. The rice harvest declined ten-fold in the 60 years after the 1930s.

Even today – often compounded by natural disasters (such as the devastating 2008 Cyclone Nargis) as well as earthquakes and flooding – major physical and institutional infrastructure deficiencies are holding back development, a message that is regularly relayed by such international agencies as the Economist Intelligence Unit and the World Bank Group (2016). For example, only 33% of the population have access to electricity, compared to 60% in Bangladesh and 99% in Vietnam. Based upon 2014 statistics, the most recent *Human Development Report* assigned Myanmar a low Human Development Index score of 0.536 (Norway is 0.994) and calculated its gross national income per capita at US$4,608 compared to Thailand's $13,323 (United Nations Human Development Programme, 2015).

Ethnic and Religious Minorities

Inevitably, the newly defined boundary delineations with neighbouring states, legislated in 1948, resulted in the geographical truncation of centuries-old traditions of population movement, ethnicity and religion that still resonate strongly today. There were a number of peripheral regions and their ethnic groups (like the dissenting Karenni) that, from the outset, felt little or no affinity with the Rangoon-based central government, with the seat of power located often hundreds of kilometres away and separated by rugged terrain with few roads or domestic airports. Thus, the animist and Christian Chin, who make up around 2% of the country's population, have far more in common with their neighbours across the border in India and Bangladesh than with the majority Buddhist Bamar (or Burmese), who account for approximately 88% of the population and are concentrated overwhelmingly in the central and southern parts of the largest country in South East Asia (678,500 square kilometres; population: approximately

54 million). The same goes for both the Kachin and Shan's traditional links with neighbouring China and the Mon's historical connections with Thailand.

At the time of writing, following the extreme violence of 1991 and again in 2012, in which many people died and some 140,000 were displaced, there are newly heightened tensions between Buddhist settlers and the self-identifying Rohingya Muslims in the coastal State of Rakhine (also known as Arakan) on the Bay of Bengal. Several mosques have been destroyed in the latest round of bitter clashes against the one million-strong Rohingya people who have been denied legal recognition in their long-established 'home' country, as well as in neighbouring Bangladesh.

Rakhine State is the second poorest in Myanmar. It also happens to host Mrauk-U, the former capital of the extensive Arakanese Kingdom, and home to one of the world's most significant assemblages of Buddhist pagodas and Muslim mosques dating back to the 15th century. The tropical monsoon state also boasts a range of outstanding coastal resources that, only now, are beginning to be fully recognised and capitalised upon in a new rush of overseas investment by hotel chains such as Hilton in luxury resorts like Ngapali/Thandwe.

However, the continuing actions of radical Buddhist groups such as Ma Ba Tha (Buddhist Association for the Protection of Race and Religion) against the local Muslim population, as well as the government's inaction against the perpetrators, have been roundly condemned by the UN Human Rights Council Special Rapporteur on Myanmar in her latest report (Yanghee Lee, 2016). Failure to resolve this vexed issue is having a substantial impact on the international reputation of the national government and, by extension, on the fledgling tourism industry (International Crisis Group, 2014). Because of the security situation, the major heritage attraction of Mrauk-U, for example, was declared off-limits to tourists between June and October 2012.

The legitimacy of state boundaries can be sorely tested, especially in cases where there are rich natural resources such as wild rivers, mountains and forests, offering considerable tourism potential, as well as timber, hydro-power and, especially, opium and jade, waiting to be exploited. This has been a long-running issue with the seemingly implacable Kachin separatist movement (Meehan, 2011). Kachin is Burma's northernmost province and the dominant religion here is Christianity. Abutting the Himalayas, it is one of the world's most celebrated biodiversity 'hot-spots' and also home to Burma's highest mountain, Hkakabo Razi, at 5881 metres, but the precise boundaries with China were not finally settled until the 1960s. The Kachin Independence Army (KIA) effectively controlled the province for some 30 years but ongoing conflicts with the Burmese army have resulted in massive displacement of the population and mean that the region is often off-limits to international tourists.

The 'Burmese way to socialism'

After 14 years of independence, in the wake of more than a century of British rule, Burma's political landscape changed dramatically overnight. In the first of what eventually would be a number of coups over the ensuing years, it became a military dictatorship in March 1962. This is, of course, not an unfamiliar story for many new, post-colonial countries seeking a degree of political stability. From that time on, through the medium of a coalition between the State Peace and Development Council (SPDC) (renamed the State Law and Order Restoration Council [SLORC] in 1997) and the 350,000-strong Tatmadaw (or 'royal force'), the authoritarian government attempted, with mixed success, to control every aspect of life in the country, including the economy, the media, the constitution and judicial system, the conduct of elections, the suppression of political dissent and so on (Cheeseman, 2015; Crouch & Lindsey, 2014). SLORC's 'three guiding principles' provided the governance foundation: (i) the non-disintegration of national solidarity; (ii) the non-disintegration of the Union; and (iii) the perpetuation of the sovereignty of the state.

Effectively, wealth and power became highly concentrated in the hands of the senior military and their close connections. Serious human rights abuses, including forced labour, became routine and were highly publicised and condemned internationally in numerous reports produced over the years by the United Nations and such watchdog agencies as Amnesty International and Human Rights Watch. Initially, in 1997, uncompromising trade sanctions were put in place by the United States, the European Union and a number of other countries (Henderson, 2003).

The 'Burmese Way to Socialism' represented an unashamedly centralised nation-building exercise on an ambitiously grand scale; a herculean task in such a large and topographically challenging country, home to over 130 different ethno-religious groups. As is so often a characteristic feature of such projects (Sri Lanka, Cambodia and Laos are obvious comparisons), the appropriation and 'selling' of a dominant religion's architectural symbols and ceremonies, both domestically and internationally, was a key component of the government's public relations armoury (Brubaker, 2012). The dominant religion in question is Theravada Buddhism, practised by nearly 90% of the population.

Internal Armed Conflict and 'Cultural Cleansing'

Notwithstanding the military regime's consistently hard-line approach, with an official total of 21 ethnic armed associations (EAOs), and a six decades-long civil war on multiple fronts (most aggressively in Shan, Kachin and Rakhine states), the country has the dubious distinction of heading the list of arenas for the world's longest-running internal armed conflicts (Gravers, 2015; World Travel and Tourism Council, 2016). An additional consequence has been that, especially following the brutal suppression of pro-democracy demonstrations in 1988 (the so-called, 8888 Uprising, in which an estimated 3000 people were killed [Tallentire, 2007]), much resistance was forced either underground or overseas. In the age of the internet, there are now numerous activist blogs, websites and radio stations (e.g. Democratic Voice of Burma) based outside Burma. These engage with both specific ethnic and religious causes (e.g. monnews. org) as well as broader questions relating to the country as a whole (e.g. Tourism Transparency; Burma Centre Prague; Burma Campaign UK; Info Birmanie).

Interestingly, much of the open resistance in 1988 centred in and around the 46-hectare, Shwe Dagon Pagoda (or Paya) complex in Rangoon. Constructed between the 6th and 10th centuries, this impressive gold-plated structure has been described quite simply as 'the most important site of Burmese Buddhism' (Morley, 2013: 611). It clearly has both enormous spiritual and political symbolic significance, as well as being arguably Burma's premier tourist attraction. Since the serious civil unrest of 1988 and again in 2007 (the so-called 'Saffron Revolution'), in an assertive display of state power, the government has engaged in a massive urban gentrification exercise around the complex. A number of exclusive housing precincts, international hotels and modern shopping centres have been built and entire poor neighbourhoods have been razed and their residents evicted. One estimate is that around 200,000 people were displaced from their squatter settlements and forcibly relocated to new towns up to 100 kilometres away (Barnett, 2008). Such 'cultural cleansing' is by no means uncommon in conflict zones across the world. For example, it mirrors the military assault of Croatian nationalists against purportedly 'Muslim' architectural heritage in the premier tourist destination of Mostar in the 1990s (Connor, 2016). Kong and Wood's (2016) heuristic framework for analysing religious competition was introduced earlier. The actions centred on and around the Shwe Dagon Pagoda are clearly illustrative of the *religion-state competition* category of Kong and Wood's (2016) framework, discussed earlier.

Not uncommonly, the boundaries between religion, the demonstration of state power and tourist spectacle can be complex and blurred. In August 2000, and following the 'merit-making' tradition of the Burmese kings centuries earlier, a crowd estimated at around 500,000 greeted the arrival of a giant 600-tonne marble statue of Buddha in Yangon. This newly hewn monument had been transported on a 12-day ceremonial journey down the Irrawaddy River from the original quarry site in the Mandalay region, using three steamers propelling a giant barge. The massive logistical project also involved the construction of new railway connections at both the start and end of the journey. At regular intervals, the barge and the accompanying flotilla of highly decorated vessels made nightly stopovers at settlements along the river where celebrations and devotional offerings took place on a grand scale. Known as the Lawka Chantha Aghaya Labha Muni, this massive structure now sits inside an 11-metre-tall glass case in the spectacular Kyauktawgyi Buddha Temple on Mindhamma Hill in the northern suburbs of Yangon. Simultaneously, this is a place of religious devotion, a major tourist draw and an expression of extraordinary state power and wealth.

A 'Hermit State' Opens Up

In the eyes of many democratic nations and civil society groups around the world, Myanmar for long was considered a 'pariah' or 'hermit' state (Philp & Mercer, 2002). By definition – and to return to the opening remarks on globalisation – 'hermit states' are poorly connected globally, and historically this has been reflected in low international tourism visitation numbers. For 2006, this figure was measured at only around 270,000. By 2010, this had crept up to 792,000, still dramatically lower than visitor numbers to such neighbours as Thailand, Laos or Cambodia (Selth, 2013). UNWTO (2016), for example, reports a total of around 16 million international visitors to Thailand in 2010.

The last five years have seen a few, faltering signs that a suite of democratic reforms is underway and that Myanmar is now gradually 'opening up' to the world. Internet censorship, for example, has been relaxed since 2011, many political dissidents have been released from custody and by 2015 the number of border gateways with neighbouring countries had risen to five. But the real extent of the power shift is unclear (Jones, 2014). Many commentators and potential investors are still wary (partly because of suspicion surrounding the artificially inflated tourist arrival figures presented by the government), and a great deal more needs to be done before international tourists, especially from non-Asian countries, can feel genuinely comfortable about the security situation (International Crisis Group, 2016). It is telling, for example, that in a recent detailed World Tourism Organization (2011) overview of *Religious Tourism in Asia and the Pacific* any mention of Myanmar was noticeably absent. Corruption at all levels is also an ongoing problem. Burma was ranked 147 out of 168 countries in the most recent Corruption Perceptions Index (Transparency International, 2015). The non-governmental organisation (NGO) Tourism Transparency (www.tourismtransparency.org) produces regular online updates of maps showing where international visitors are permitted to travel within the country and also where it is currently deemed unsafe to venture. Not surprisingly, recent maps have promoted a very clear message: 'The Buddhist "heartland" of Yangon-Bagan-Mandalay is safe and welcoming; the peripheral regions of mixed ethnic and religious heritage are frequently problematic and off-limits'.

'Visit Myanmar Year'

The year 1996 witnessed the launch of two highly publicised promotional campaigns, both aimed at an international audience. The first was the military government's much-vaunted 'Visit Myanmar Year' (VMY). In stark contrast, the second – initiated by prominent opposition leader, Aung San Sui Kyi – was branded 'Don't Visit Burma Year'. The deliberate usage of the labels 'Myanmar' and 'Burma', respectively, highlights an ongoing and profound political divide in this deeply conflicted country. 'Burma' was officially redesignated the Republic of the Union of Myanmar by the ruling military government in 1989. But the legitimacy of that regime and the associated name-change have been by no means universally accepted, either by local oppositional parties and ethnic minority groups, or more widely by other countries (Asian Correspondent, 2015). However, over time, the name 'Myanmar' has become increasingly accepted. On 1 September, 2015, for example, the UK's *Guardian* newspaper announced with some fanfare that 'We will from today be using the name Myanmar'. Somewhat provocatively, the National League for Democracy's (NLD) 'anti'-campaign appeared just a few months after Sui Kyi (daughter of Burma's leader in the earlier independence movement, Aung San) was released from a six-year period of house detention. Interestingly, she is an adherent of Theravada Buddhism, the dominant religion in Burma.

Modelled on its predecessor – the highly successful 1987 'Visit Thailand Year' – VMY was a deliberate attempt to 'sell' the country's undeniably rich Buddhist heritage sites, festivals and ceremonies to the world, to attract high-spending overseas visitors to the Yangon, Mandalay, Bagan triangle in particular and, most importantly, to present a strong image of a secure, modern and united nation-state, free of religious intolerance and human rights abuses. At the lavish ceremonial launch of the campaign, Lieutenant-General Khin Nyunt declared that it represented a commitment 'to open our doors to the world' (quoted in Economist Intelligence Unit, 1997: 26). An additional arm to this campaign came in the form of putting forward eight properties for nomination on the prestigious UNESCO World Heritage Site list.

Ultimately, VMY was a public relations failure for the military government and a major victory for the NLD that succeeded in persuading many overseas tour companies and individual travellers to boycott the country. This is a strategy that, for example, had been successfully employed by the International Food and Allied Workers in Guatemala in 1979 to pressure the military regime there to address its appalling record on human rights abuses. There was, accordingly, no eagerly anticipated upsurge in international visitors to Burma, and the ambitious target of 500,000 international visitors was found to be wildly optimistic. The Economist Intelligence Unit (1997) estimated a figure of 184,281 tourists for the first eight months of VMY. Additionally, the World Heritage nominations were summarily rejected and the authorities had to wait almost 20 years for their first successful application in this regard (Pyu Ancient Cities). Three years after VMY, Suu Kyi was still urging the world to stay away:

> I still think that people should not come to Burma because the bulk of the money from tourism goes straight into the pockets of the generals. And not only that, it's a form of moral support for them because it makes the military authorities think that the international community is not opposed to the human rights violations which they are committing all the time. (Daw Aung San Suu Kyi, 1999)

Her call was again taken up in 2008 in the UK when a coalition of supportive groups (including Tourism Concern, the Trades Union Congress and Burma Campaign) pressured the publisher, BBC Worldwide, to cease publication of the *Lonely Planet* guide to Myanmar.

Let us now take a closer look at the actions of the military regime in the lead up to VMY that generated such a strong impetus for a tourism boycott on the part of the NLD and overseas players.

Opposition to VMY

As highlighted by the two quotes at the start of this chapter, the SLORC/SPDC regime placed an enormous emphasis on both 'restoring' and marketing highly selective Buddhist monuments and festivals as symbols of Bamar state power, legitimacy and 'unity' to both a domestic and international audience. Not surprisingly, as we saw in the case of the Shwedagon Paya, sites singled out for particular attention were places of considerable religious significance and symbolic power, as well as being highly popular as tourist and pilgrimage sites. These included Bagan, of which more below, the Mandalay Palace and the 'Golden Rock' Pagoda in Kyaiktyio. The guiding principle was for tourist movements within the country to be strictly controlled and restricted to certain 'sanitised' enclaves, thus allowing for the dissemination of a carefully crafted political message emphasising national unity and growing prosperity grounded in the Buddhist religion. Displaced Buddhists living in poverty near prime heritage sites targeted for 'modernisation' were not treated justly and the main beneficiaries of tourism spending were those with strong military connections (Jones, 2014; Ko Ko Thett, 2012).

The years leading up to VMY saw a major surge in hotel and golf course construction in and near religious sites that are popular with international tourists. Many of these developments were joint ventures with the Japanese Sakura Group and with Singaporean and Chinese investors. As mentioned earlier, a major criticism coming from the NLD, the United Nations and international NGOs was that much of the construction as well as new airport and road development and targeted pagoda 'restoration' was carried out using forced labour. The cleaning of the Mandalay moat (principally to make it attractive for tourists), for example, involved round-the-clock labour by 'volunteers', assisted by 2000 co-opted prisoners in chains (Barnett, 2008). Such work has a long tradition in Burma with bonded pagoda slaves (*hpaya kywan*) in earlier times providing the much-needed muscle power for stupa construction and restoration. This practice was formally abolished in 1947. Yet, at a UN Commission on Human Rights hearing in 1995, the government representative argued forcefully that working on temple reconstruction and other such projects was indeed intrinsic to Burmese Buddhist cultural traditions and should not be categorised as forced labour; those who cannot afford to make financial offerings, it was stressed, donate their labour and gain merit (*dana*) by their actions (Economist Intelligence Unit, 1995).

This hearing came two years after Burma signed the Bangkok Declaration on Human Rights, mentioned earlier. But one year later, the Australian Council for Overseas Aid (1996) released its long-awaited report on slave labour and drew attention to the fact that *non-Buddhists* from ethnic minorities were also commonly recruited to work on Buddhist monuments. Most recently, the Walk Free Foundation (2016) has released its latest report on modern slavery around the world. With an estimated 0.96% of the population classified as 'slaves' (515,100 people), Burma still ranks highly, alongside Cambodia and Brunei, in South East Asia on the Global Slavery Index.

A 'Softer' Tone from the NLD

A little over a decade after the launch of VMY, much had changed in Burmese politics. It was clear that the NLD and Aung San Suu Kyi had overwhelming support throughout the country. Many dissidents were granted amnesty, there was a gradual relaxation of controls on freedom of speech and movement, and, most importantly, in November 2010, Aung San Suu Kyi herself was released from what was to be her final period of house arrest. Within months, the NLD made it clear that it had decided to adopt a much more conciliatory attitude towards the promotion of international tourism. In an official statement on the question in May of that year, the league cautioned that many enterprises were still owned and controlled by individuals and families with strong military connections but that nevertheless . . .

> The NLD would welcome visitors who are keen to promote the welfare of the common people and the conservation of the environment and to acquire an insight into the cultural, political and social life of the country . . . (National League for Democracy, 2011)

Subsequently, there has been considerable growth in both visitor numbers and hotel construction. The UNWTO (2016) reported a record total of just over 3 million overseas visitors in 2014; and hotels and guest houses now number around 1300, up from 619 in 2007. As noted earlier, high visitor numbers from Thailand and China stand out, and have risen greatly; in China's case a 300% increase between 2013 and 2014. Both of these countries have substantial Buddhist populations. At the same time, Europe's share of the tourism market (for 2014) remains very low, at a meagre 6.5% and that of the United States even lower, at 2%.

It is likely that these statistics reflect a lingering anxiety about the political and human rights situation in the country, knowledge that sanctions against certain individuals and corporate entities are still in place and a perception of the ongoing repression of religious and ethnic minorities. It also needs to be stressed that the statistics on 'tourist' arrivals vary markedly on the basis of what precisely is being measured and by whom. The Pacific Area Travel Association (PATA), for example, concluded that 2015 saw 1.2 million overseas tourists in 2015 by comparison with the government's inflated figure of 4.68 million (Kyaw Hsu Mon, 2016).

If there is one place that encapsulates all of the cross-cutting issues, contradictions and paradoxes linking religion, heritage, tourism, modernity and economic development in Burma today it is Bagan. So it is to the recent controversies and debates around this contested site that we now turn.

Bagan

Covering an area of approximately 110 square kilometres, on a bend of the Ayeyarwady River in central Myanmar, Bagan is a one-hour flight north from Yangon and home to more than 3000 Buddhist monuments built largely between the 11th and 15th centuries. There is a 42 square kilometre inner core area of prime archaeological significance for which visitors are charged a $20 entrance fee. Up until the end of the 13th century, it was the capital of a kingdom, Pagan, that saw a succession of some 50 Buddhist kings ruling over an area encompassing most of present-day

Myanmar. The population at its height has been estimated at anywhere between 50,000 and 200,000. Renamed 'Bagan' by the military junta in 1989, it is undeniably one of the world's most significant archaeological sites and has been an important pilgrimage destination for hundreds of years. Increasingly, in addition to being a centre for religious devotion and ritual – like Angkor Wat in Cambodia, Anuradhapura in Sri Lanka and Borobudur in Indonesia – the temple complex has become a major tourist attraction. Bagan is somewhat different in that tourism infrastructure and transport development are still at a relatively embryonic stage, certainly by comparison with Angkor and the associated town of Siem Reap, and it sits in a very arid environment with a long history of earthquakes. Hundreds of quakes hit the site from the 12th century onwards, the most recent being a major seismic event in 1975. Needless to add, serious structural damage, or even total collapse, of buildings has been an all-too-common outcome and today only a fraction of the estimated 10,000 or so original buildings remain. Inevitably, this raises the issue of what, if anything, should be attempted by way of rebuilding of what still exists.

The vast assemblage of brick-built structures (temples, stupas, monasteries and mounds) have been meticulously mapped and catalogued in a comprehensive database by archaeologists over the years and classified by size as 'small', 'medium', 'large' or 'very large'. At the height of the 'construction boom' in the 13th century, it has been calculated that work (for 'merit') began on new, small and medium-sized structures every 11–14 days (Hudson, 2008). Over 2000 buildings have now been attributed to that century. In recognition of the site's potential universal heritage value, a process is currently underway for Bagan to be formally added to UNESCO's World Heritage list for possible nomination in 2019. An earlier (1996) application was rejected on the grounds that a robust legal and management framework to protect the site was not yet in place (Mann, 2016). In addition, as highlighted in the Manhart quote at the start of this chapter, there were, and still are, serious concerns about the poor quality, appropriateness and sustainability of much of the recent reconstruction work that has often been hurriedly carried out by contractors (Parry, 2016; Pichard, 2013).

Earlier, mention was made of the large-scale displacement of residents from around the Shwe Dagon Pagoda complex in Yangon that took place after the 1988 civil unrest to 'modernise' the area and make it more 'attractive' for both overseas tourists and the Burmese elite. Similar action was taken in April 1990 against around 5000 Pagan residents who were forced to demolish their homes and ordered to rebuild some 7 kilometres to the south in what is now known as 'New Bagan'. Dozens of hotels were subsequently built on the newly vacant land that was close to the heart of old Pagan. These include the luxury 27-acre Aureum Palace Hotel complex owned by U Tay Za. Reportedly Burma's richest man, he and his large Htoo Group of companies, with interests in everything from mining to logging, construction, tourism and aviation (Air Bagan; Asian Wings) remain on the US government's sanctions list.

Ancient pagodas were often routinely incorporated into hotel sites from the 1990s onwards, and sometimes given new uses, as restaurants for example. Effectively, what this means is that temples that formerly were always available for worship and ceremony have been 'privatised' and general access denied. Bagan currently houses around 80 hotels of varying standard. In addition, the military regime built a road through the central archaeological zone as well as a golf course. U Tay Za is also responsible for the massive 70-metre 'grain- silo' structure, the Nan Myint Viewing Tower. The tower, which opened in 2005, is as high as the tallest and best-known temples at Bagan (Sulamani, Ananda, Thatbyinnyu, etc.) and, although totally incongruous in both aesthetic and scale, is intended to allow visitors a view of the entire Bagan complex. The other site that is hugely popular as a vantage point is the ancient Shwesandaw Pagoda. Tourists in their hundreds are allowed to climb this temple for a view of spectacular sunsets. Clearly, serious wear and tear is occurring. For this reason, and because of a lack of respect for Buddhist tradition shown by a growing number of visitors, climbing has now been forbidden on many of Bagan's ancient structures.

Commentators such as Chapagain (2013) have highlighted the often contradictory nature of the responses of the Myanmar government to heritage and Buddhism in general. As we have seen, some places are completely erased from the record or are 'reconstructed' with little or no regard for architectural merit. Other structures, by contrast, are treated with the utmost reverence and restored to the highest standards and with no expense spared. In 1990, for example, the same year as the mass eviction from Bagan, there was an elaborate celebration marking the 900th anniversary of the construction of one of Bagan's most revered temples, Ananda. This extraordinary building, known as the 'Westminster Abbey of Burma', had been badly damaged in the 1975 earthquake but had been meticulously refurbished in the meantime, culminating in the gilding of the stupa in 1990.

Similar care and attention has been lavished on the brightly illuminated and air-conditioned Alodawpi ('Wish-fulfilling') Pagoda by former Prime Minister General Khin Nyunt. There is a strong belief that army personnel who worship there will achieve accelerated promotion through the ranks. Other structures, though, long associated with myths of a 'dark' and sinister past, have been deliberately allowed to decay. One of these is the Dhammayangyi Pagoda, believed to have been built by a particularly cruel and murderous king. Kraak (2015) is one of a growing number of researchers, from both 'Western' and Asian traditions (e.g. Nagaoka, 2015), who now openly challenge the 'monument-centric' framing of heritage sites as simply assemblages of structures that can be clinically measured and catalogued in architectural terms. Their view is that the intangible myths and legends associated with these structures are every bit as important to the narrative but, to date, have not been given the attention they deserve. Clearly, such issues are central to the manner in which Bagan is framed for tourist consumption.

A New Direction for Tourism?

There is no doubt that the new government is keen to give a high priority to tourism in its forward planning, and it is possible that we are witnessing the early stages of a major transition in policy thinking. In 2011, for example, workshops were held to start the process of developing a *Responsible Tourism* strategy. A year later, the new policy was officially released (Ministry of Hotels and Tourism, 2012). A *Tourism Master Plan* has also now been launched and two of its guiding principles are to (i) maintain cultural diversity and authenticity and (ii) minimise unethical practice (Ministry of Hotels and Tourism, 2013). Both these provide hopeful signs of a new agenda but as Ko Ko Thett (2012) cautions it is still too early to decide to what extent the power and influence of the Buddhist military elite has been eroded. It will take a major effort of political will to ensure that the ethnic and religious minority regions along Burma's borders benefit from what looks certain to be a significant growth in tourist numbers.

There are certainly some modest signs of a space being opened up for civil society voices to be heard. In 2012, and again in 2014, local Bagan residents who had been displaced demonstrated against the unregulated practice of new hotel developments incorporating pagodas within their boundaries and restricting access to all but hotel guests and staff. In one case, 14 structures are involved ('Fight to save Bagan' at www.nationmultimedia. com/ 3 November 2014). But at the same time, construction work on 20 new or existing hotels is continuing, apparently with minimal controls. In the lead up to possible World Heritage listing, oppositional voices at Bagan are calling for a halt to current construction as well as the demolition of existing hotels that have been built 'inappropriately' within the cultural heritage core of Old Bagan. These grass-roots Buddhist groups are demanding that the 'commodification' and commercialisation of such sacred places be halted or reversed and that Bagan and similar sites be opened up to the community as a whole and revert to what they once were: living and breathing cultural spaces that simultaneously accommodated commerce, ceremony, devotion and daily ritual.

Burma's much-vaunted *Tourism Master Plan* encourages the government to follow Thailand's path, adopt a 'high-growth' strategy and aim for a target of 7.5 million overseas visitors by 2020. However, such a strategy is by no means universally applauded within the country. In February 2016, there was a public rift between the 'pro-growth' Ministry of Hotels and Tourism and the much more cautious Ministry of Culture. The conflict was sparked initially by a small incident involving Burmese tourists. A Yangon-based medical firm, the Lucky Trading Company, held a 'staff cheering party' in Bagan. At one stage, this involved personnel dancing and singing at the top of the popular Pyathagyi Pagoda. The merriment was duly filmed and subsequently 'went viral' via Facebook. The behaviour was promptly condemned as being totally inappropriate and disrespectful of Buddhist values and the Ministry of Culture ordered a ban on the widespread practice of climbing to the top of pagodas. Almost immediately, the Ministry of Hotels and Tourism hit back, arguing that this is a popular activity for visitors who wish to photograph the glorious sunsets and that a blanket ban would do untold damage to the tourism industry (Ei Ei Thu, 2016). The Ministry of Culture then relented and an eventual compromise was reached by restricting such access to only five prominent structures at Bagan, one of which is Pyathagyi.

Though perhaps in one sense a relatively trivial episode, this does encapsulate an unresolved tension at the heart of Burma's tourism future. Does the country go down the 'high-volume' route that, unless carefully managed, has the potential to compromise both deeply held spiritual values and the physical integrity of heritage structures; or does it adopt a quite different approach grounded in respect for all religions and human rights and a development paradigm that is inclusive rather than one that merely continues to benefit Burma's political and economic elite?

References

Asian Correspondent (2015) What's in a name? The great 'Myanmar' or 'Burma' debate. 2 September.

Australian Council for Overseas Aid (1996) *Slave Labour in Burma: An Examination of the SLORC's Forced Labour Policies*. Canberra: ACOA.

Aygen, Z. and Logan, W. (2016) Heritage in the 'Asian Century': Responding to geopolitical change. In W. Logan, M.N. Craith and U. Kockel (eds) *A Companion to Heritage Studies* (pp. 410–425). Chichester: Wiley Blackwell.

Barnett, T. (2008) Influencing tourism at the grassroots level: The role of NGO tourism concern. *Third World Quarterly* 29 (5), 995–1002.

BBC News (2016) Shan villagers feel force of Burmese army anger. See www.bbc.com/news/world-asia (accessed 7 July 2016).

Beech, H. (2013) The Buddhist monks advocating intolerance in Asia. *Time*, 1 July.

Blanchard, L. and Higgins-Desbiolles, F. (2012) A pedagogy of peace: The tourism potential. In G.B. Chen, B. Offord and R. Garbutt (eds) *Activating Human Rights and Peace. Theories, Practices and Contexts* (pp. 227–242). Farnham: Ashgate.

Brubaker, R. (2012) Religion and nationalism: Four approaches. *Nations and Nationalism* 18 (1), 2–20.

Cameron, C. (2016) UNESCO and cultural heritage: Unexpected consequences. In W. Logan, M. Craith and U. Kockel (eds) *A Companion to Heritage Studies* (pp. 322–336). Chichester: Wiley Blackwell.

Chapagain, N.K. (2013) Introduction: Contexts and concerns in Asian heritage management. In K.D. Silva and N.K. Chapagain (eds) *Asian Heritage Management. Contexts, Concerns and Prospects* (pp. 1–29). Abingdon: Routledge.

Cheeseman, N. (2015) *Opposing The Rule of Law: How Myanmar's Courts Make Law and Order.* Cambridge: Cambridge University Press.

Connor, A. (2016) Heritage in an expanded field: Reconstructing bridge-ness in Mostar. In W. Logan, M. Craith and U. Kockel (eds) *A Companion to Heritage Studies* (pp. 254–267). Chichester: Wiley Blackwell.

Crampton, T. (2005) Concrete overlay for an ancient Burmese landscape. *International Herald Tribune*, 22 April.

Crouch, M. and Lindsey, T. (eds) (2014) *Law, Society and Transition in Myanmar.* Oxford: Hart Publishing.

Daw Aung San Suu Kyi (1999) See www.responsibletravel.com/copy/burma-boycott (accessed 10 July 2016).

Economist Intelligence Unit (1995) *Country Report: Myanmar.* Fourth Quarter. Dartford: Redhouse Press.

Economist Intelligence Unit (1997) *Country Report: Myanmar.* First Quarter. Dartford: Redhouse Press.

Ei Ei Thu (2016) Tourism ministry joins fight against Bagan ban. *Myanmar Times*, 24 February.

Gillen, J. (2014) Tourism and nation building at the War Remnants Museum in Ho Chi Minh City, Vietnam. *Annals of the Association of American Geographers* 104 (6), 1307–1321.

Gillespie, J. (2013) World Heritage protection and the human right to development: Reconciling competing or complementary narratives using a human rights-based approach (HRBA)? *Sustainability* 5 (7), 3159–3171.

Gravers, M. (2015) Disorder as order: The ethno-nationalist struggle of the Karen in Burma/ Myanmar – A discussion of the dynamics of an ethnicized civil war and its historical roots. *Journal of Burma Studies* 19 (1), 27–78.

Guardian, The (2015) Editorial: The *Guardian* view on Burma, Myanmar, and faltering steps toward democracy. 1 September.

Henderson, J.C. (2003) The politics of tourism in Myanmar. *Current Issues in Tourism* 6 (2), 97–118.

Henderson, J.C. (2015) The new dynamics of tourism in South East Asia: Economic development, political change and destination competitiveness. *Tourism Recreation Research* 40 (3), 379–390.

Hudson, B. (2008) Restoration and reconstruction of monuments at Bagan (Pagan), Myanmar (Burma), 1995–2008. *World Archaeology* 40 (4), 553–571.

International Crisis Group (2014) *Myanmar: The Politics of Rakhine State.* Asia Report 251, Brussels.

International Crisis Group (2016) *The Myanmar Elections: Results and Implications.* Asia Briefing No. 147, Brussels.

Jones, L. (2014) The political economy of Myanmar's transition. *Journal of Contemporary Asia* 44 (1), 144–170.

Ko Ko Thett (2012) *Responsible Tourism in Myanmar: Current Situation and Challenges.* Prague: Burma Centre.

Kong, L. and Woods, O. (2016) *Religion and Space.* London: Bloomsbury.

Kraak, A.L. (2015) Ruins, Rituals and Sunset Sacrifice: The Contesting Values of Bagan in Myanmar. Paper presented at the ICOMOS Conference, Melbourne, 5 November.

Kyaw Hsu Mon (2016) Government to continue tourism policy of maximum growth. *The Irrawaddy*, 2 August.

Logan, W.S. (2007) Closing Pandora's Box: Human rights conundrums in cultural heritage protection. In H. Silverman and D.F. Ruggles (eds) *Cultural Heritage and Human Rights* (pp. 33–52). New York: Springer.

Logan, W.S. (2012) Cultural diversity, cultural heritage and human rights: Towards heritage management as human rights-based cultural practice. *International Journal of Heritage Studies* 18 (3), 231–244.

Macgregor, F. and Thu Thu Aung (2016) Tourism on the front line. *Myanmar Times*, 17 June.

Mann, Z. (2016) Bagan bids for UNESCO World Heritage status. *The Irrawaddy*, 2 August.

Meehan, P. (2011) Drugs, insurgency, and state-building in Burma: Why the drugs trade is central to Burma's changing political order. *Journal of South-East Asian Studies* 42 (3), 376–404.

Ministry of Civil Aviation and Tourism, Bangladesh, and World Tourism Organization (UNWTO) (2015) Developing Sustainable and Inclusive Buddhist Heritage and Pilgrimage Circuit in South Asia's Buddhist Heartland. Conference Proceedings, Dhaka.

Ministry of Hotels and Tourism (2012) *Responsible Tourism Policy*. Nay Pyi Taw.

Ministry of Hotels and Tourism (2013) *Myanmar Tourism Master Plan 2013–2020*. Nay Pyi Taw.

Morley, I. (2013) Rangoon. *Cities* 31, 601–614.

Nagaoka, M. (2015) Buffering Borobudur for socio-economic development. An approach away from European values-based heritage management. *Journal of Cultural Heritage Management and Sustainable Development* 5 (2), 130–150.

National League for Democracy (2011) *Statement No. 10/05/11*. Rangoon.

Parry, R.L. (2016) Cowboy builders are destroying Buddhists historic Burmese city. *The Times* (London), 27 June.

Philp, J. and Mercer, D. (2002) Politicised pagodas and veiled resistance: Contested urban space in Burma. *Urban Studies* 38 (9), 1587–1610.

Pichard, P. (2013) Today's Pagan: Conservation under the generals. In M. Falser and M. Juneja (eds) *'Archaeologizing' Heritage? Transcultural Entanglements between Local Social Practices and Global Virtual Realities* (pp. 235–249). Heidelberg: Springer.

Selth, A. (2013) Burma's Security Forces: Performing, Reforming or Transforming? Regional Outlook Paper No. 45, Griffith Asia Institute, Griffith University, Brisbane.

Silver, C. (2007) Tourism, cultural heritage, and human rights in Indonesia: The challenges of an emerging democratic society. In H. Silverman and D.F. Ruggles (eds) *Cultural Heritage and Human Rights*(pp. 78–91). New York: Springer.

Smith, M. (1996) Playing the ethnic card: Burma at the cross-roads. *Burma Debate* November/December, 1–7.

Tallentire, M. (2007) The Burma road to ruin. *The Guardian*, 28 September.

Transparency International (2015) *Corruption Perceptions Index*. Berlin.

United Nations Human Development Programme (2015) *Human Development Report*. New York: UNDP.

UNWTO (2016) *Yearbook of Tourism Statistics. Data 2010–2014*. Madrid: World Tourism Organization.

Wa Lone (2016) Snr Gen Min Aung Hlaing pledges to help safeguard Buddhism. *Myanmar Times*, 24 June.

Walk Free Foundation (2016) *Global Slavery Index*. Nedlands, WA: WFA.

World Bank Group (2016) *Opening for Business*. Myanmar Diagnostic Trade Integration Study (DTIS). June. World Bank, Washington DC.

World Tourism Organization (2011) *Religious Tourism in Asia and the Pacific*. Madrid: UNWTO.

World Travel and Tourism Council (2016) *Tourism as a Driver of Peace*. WTTC and Institute of Economics and Peace.

Yanghee Lee (2016) Report of the Special Rapporteur on the Situation of Human Rights in Myanmar. United Nations General Assembly, Human Rights Council, Thirty-First Session. March 18. New York.

13 Religious Tourism and Pilgrimage in Russia

Elina Ostrometskaia and Kevin Griffin

Introduction

The purpose of this chapter is to examine and explore the concept of religious tourism and pilgrimage in Russia in the context of the Russian Orthodox church. The chapter begins by briefly discussing the evolution of literature on religious tourism and pilgrimage, and follows this with a brief history of religious tourism and pilgrimage in Russia and the attempted elimination of religion (with a state policy of 'irreligion') by the USSR. The related communist confiscation of religious property and assets, the persecution of religious leaders and the destruction of monuments resulted in the subversion of religious practice throughout most of the 20th century. However, since the collapse of communism, there has been a vibrant upsurge of religious practice, evidenced in the rebuilding of churches and a growing pilgrimage industry. While approximately 44% of Russians claim no particular religious affiliation, this still results in large numbers of practitioners, mainly following the Russian Orthodox faith, but also including Muslims, Christians, Buddhists and a variety of other belief sets. As the largest country in the world, any attempt to suggest a homogenised religious landscape would be false; however, certain trends and patterns can be observed.

The vastness of the Russian Federation is astounding, measuring 17 million km², with a population of about 146 million inhabitants. Approximately three quarters of this population live in urban centres, the vast majority in the western portion of the state. In 2011, domestic travellers made 96.3 million domestic trips. Outbound travel to the likes of the Mediterranean basin is seeing massive growth, but inbound traffic is very variable. The likes of Moscow and St Petersburg are popular destinations, but many other places are either entirely undeveloped or at the very early stages of development. When religion and pilgrimage are added to the promising tourism infrastructure, an enormous potential is presented. Various challenges exist in Russia in relation to tourism in general, and religious tourism and pilgrimage in particular. This chapter will present some thoughts on the current situation and suggest opportunities and potential areas for development for the future.

Religious Tourism

The origins of various forms of religious tourism have been discussed at length, with many authors claiming that perhaps the practice of pilgrimage is the earliest form of tourism (see Griffin & Raj, 2015). While a number of earlier publications exist (such as influential volumes by Lefeuvre [1980], Nolan and Nolan [1989] and Turner and Turner [1978]), as an academic topic of investigation, much work on religious tourism and pilgrimage traces its roots to Volume 19, Issue 1 of *Annals of Tourism Research*, edited by Valene L. Smith, which was published in 1992. Virtually every academic article, book, conference paper or poster since then has drawn directly or indirectly from one or more of the seven papers in this seminal publication. These papers of 1992 by Eade, Cohen, Rinschede, Nolan and Nolan, Vukonić, Jackowski and Smith, Hudman and Jackson have thus laid the foundations for a rich vein of academic exploration over the past quarter of a century. A less well-known, but equally influential publication was a book of papers produced by the Tourism Association of Leria in Portugal (Fernandes *et al.*, 2003), arising from a small meeting in Fatima in 2003. This gathering of like-minded tourism academics laid the seeds of an organisation which eventually led to the development of the annual International Religious Tourism and Pilgrimage Conference, and a partner project, the much respected online *International Journal of Religious Tourism and Pilgrimage* (see www. arrow.dit.ie/IJRTP).

In recent years, religious tourism has aroused the interest of many researchers and practitioners (Drule *et al.*, 2012; Raj & Griffin, 2015), such that Timothy and Olsen's 2006 statement that religious tourism is one of the least studied areas in tourism research (Kamenidou & Vourou, 2015) may now be a little outdated. Nowadays researchers from many disciplines are studying this topic: historians, theologians, sociologists, psychologists, anthropologists, economists, geographers and many more (Vukonić, 1996). However, despite the burgeoning body of work on religious tourism and pilgrimage, many specific themes and topics still remain highly neglected in the literature. One area of exploration, virtually absent from the English language literature, is an investigation and appreciation of religious tourism and pilgrimage in Russia. While a number of authors have examined Eastern European case studies: Jackowski and Smith (1992) have examined Poland; Clarke and Raffay (2015) have undertaken various investigations in Hungary; Liutikas (2015) has extensively examined pilgrimage in Lithuania; and Rajá (2017) has examined the phenomenon in the Czech Republic, very little work has been undertaken further east in Russia itself.

Religious tourism and pilgrimage

It is suggested in the literature that religious tourism orients itself according to the motivation of the traveller. It is a type of tourism whose participants are motivated either in part or exclusively for religious reasons. It includes visits to religious ceremonies and conferences, and above all, visits to local, regional, national and international religious centres (Rinschede, 1992). Scholars and theologians interested in religious tourism recognise a number of challenges and debates, not least being that surrounding the pilgrim–tourist dichotomy, probably the most debated topic relating to religion and tourism in the literature today (Olsen, 2013). Debate over the similarities and differences between pilgrims and tourists has arisen because many scholars and theologians have lost sight of the fact that the subjects of comparison – the pilgrim and the tourist – are studied as ideal types; as socially constructed either/or propositions that do not accurately reflect modern reality (Olsen, 2010). From a postmodern and poststructuralist perspective, it is difficult to accept anachronistic and abstract universal travel typologies that place binary opposites as an 'everything/nothing' concept where types of travel and travellers fit into tidy categories (Adler, 1989; Bauman, 1996). On the whole, the differences between subgroups of tourism are not clearly definitive, and often one can distinguish transitional forms. Thus, today, it is becoming increasingly recognised that pilgrimage and religious tourism are closely connected with holiday and cultural tourism; and also have a strong affinity with social and group tourism. This acknowledges the fact that nowadays, for many tourists, it is very important to travel with a group of believers who think similarly and who are consequently in the same demographic/social division (Rinschede,1992).

A further consideration in the literature is how pilgrimage assists in developing population mobilities such as trade, cultural exchange and political integration, and also less desirable outcomes such as the spread of illness and epidemics. Pilgrimage inevitably necessitates spatial movement; hence, it stimulates geographers' concerns with distance and issues such as its effect on behaviour and place. It is also an important subject in the geographical world because of its size and spatial influence. Pilgrimages have powerful political, economic, social and cultural implications, and even affect global trade and health. As part of religion, pilgrimage has exerted geopolitical influence for most of human history, often challenging the boundaries separating one civilisation from another, which were drawn in part along religious lines (Collins-Kreiner, 2010; Leppakari & Griffin, 2016).

Pilgrimage may therefore be viewed as a phenomenon cutting across religions and cultures, simultaneously challenging and reinforcing the established patterns and concepts of society. As this happens, the etymology of the word 'pilgrimage' itself is becoming very dynamic; nowadays, the word is more broadly used than ever. It is often used in secular contexts – for example, visits to war sites or graves, to residences of celebrities, visits to churchyards and to funerary sites, and for secular pilgrimage gazing (notwithstanding the religious motives for many such visits by others). There is also a growing market in 'New Age' spiritual travel for pilgrimage, personal growth and non-traditional spiritual practices (Attix, 2002).

All pilgrims, religious or secular, share the trait of searching for a mystical, magical or religious experience – a moment when they experience something out of the ordinary that marks a transition from their mundane secular world of everyday existence to a special and sacred state (Collins-Kreiner, 2010). Drule *et al.* (2012), in their study of the non-religious motivations of 1600 Orthodox people from Romania who visited a monastery, found that visitors were mainly motivated by a need for self-actualisation, i.e. a desire to become a better person. In the various forms of 'pilgrimage', since travelling is a spatial phenomenon, there will always be a dialogue between the cognition of the tourist/traveller/pilgrim and the physical place to which he/she travels. In the same way, there is always a dialogue between the participant, his/her direct, empirical experiences and the social discourses that have shaped the understandings that he/she carries into the encounter. Pilgrimage, in this context, can be viewed as a performative act of religious belief/experience, in which sacred sites play an important role (Belhassen *et al.*, 2008). The intangible nature of this act is profoundly important, and an interesting insight in this regard and in the context of this chapter, is the manner in which Russian pilgrims refer to the spiritual value of a site (a church, a monastery or a village shrine) or an artefact; they often use the term *namolennost*, which can be roughly translated as 'antiquity' or 'absorbed many prayers'. Orthodox authors stress the non-rational nature of *namolennost*, which can be grasped only sensually, like a fragrance or like beauty (Suglobova, 1996).

It is vital to understand the motives and desires of pilgrimage groups to avoid conflict and disappointment. To achieve this, a broad, multidisciplinary approach needs to be considered, involving study in various fields. For example, one needs to understand historical, theological and ontological influences when trying to understand how Protestant pilgrims in the Holy Land tend to be disengaged from both the traditional holy sites and from the canonical narratives about the authenticity of Christian holy places that they are visiting when compared with Orthodox and Catholic pilgrims (Collins-Kreiner *et al.*, 2006). Pilgrims are attached to sacred places because of the roles such places play in their religious belief systems and in the formation of their identities. This holistic approach is equally important in investigating all types of pilgrimage and is not just restricted to Christian practice (Belhassen *et al.*, 2008); see for example, McIntosh *et al.* (2016) for a multidisciplinary volume on pilgrimage in India.

Religious Tourism and Pilgrimage in Russia

Origins

One would expect that research on religious tourism in Russia would be abundant since there are numerous religious sites for visitation, and since it is known worldwide for the architecture and artistic elements of its beautiful monasteries, cathedrals and religious relics. On the contrary, there are very few studies regarding pilgrimage or religious tourism in Russia and it appears that very few academics have dedicated their time to religious tourism and pilgrimage studies in this vast country.

The origins of modern Russian pilgrimage traditions coincide with the adoption of Christianity, and possibly even earlier. For more than a millennium (Christianity arriving to Russia in the late AD 900s), pilgrimage has been an integral part of the spiritual life of Russian people. Despite the Mongolian, and then Ottoman 'Iron Curtain', the Russian people found a way to get to sites such as the Holy Land, Constantinople and Mount Athos. In fact, Russian Orthodox pilgrimage to the Holy Land reached its peak in the second half of the 19th and early 20th century. This was largely connected with the establishment and activities of the Russian Ecclesiastical Mission in Jerusalem, as well as the Imperial Orthodox Palestine Society (IOPS), founded in 1882 (Babkin, 2008). For the first 35 years, the Palestinian society was led by Grand Duke Sergei Alexandrovich and, after his tragic death in 1905, by his wife, Grand Duchess Elizabeth Feodorovna. Using a permanent church and state support, working hand in hand with the Russian Ecclesiastical Mission in Jerusalem, IOPS did much to create the Russian Palestine – a unique island of Russia in the Holy Land. Unfortunately, the events of 1917 destroyed the pilgrimage structure, not allowing pilgrims from any social class to visit such holy places.

During the subsequent Soviet era in Russia, despite the imposition of prohibitions, the cravings and needs of Orthodox people for worshipping holy places did not die, and certain pilgrimage practices continued, albeit on a limited scale. The Trinity-Sergius and Kiev-Pechersk Lavra, the Pskov-Caves and Puhtitsa monasteries were visited by thousands of pilgrims on the main church holidays, and from the late 1950s, pilgrim groups were sent to the Holy Land as an initiative of the Department for External Church Relations of the Moscow Patriarchate. An official pilgrimage delegation of the Russian Orthodox Church went on pilgrimages every year (twice a year to Jerusalem and annually to Mount Athos).

Religious tourism and pilgrimage in modern Russia

Since the early 1990s, after the collapse of the 'Iron Curtain', Russians have had the opportunity to travel abroad, and Russian Orthodox pilgrimage has gradually been revived. The Russian Ecclesiastical Mission in Jerusalem started to take pilgrims from Russia, Ukraine, Belarus and other Commonwealth of Independent States (CIS) countries almost weekly, returning to its traditional functioning as it was created 160 years ago. At home, the Holy Synod ordered the Russian Orthodox Church Department for External Church Relations to lead the work on reviving pilgrimage traditions. In 1999, with the blessing of the Patriarch of Moscow and All Russia, Alexy II, the Pilgrimage Centre of the Moscow Patriarchate was created, its main tasks being to promote the revival of Orthodox Church pilgrimage and the creation of a hotel chain for pilgrims. The first pilgrimage services and organisations were established in the early 2000s in a number of dioceses and in a number of monasteries and temples. (This development is an interesting modern comparison with the medieval Christian monasteries discussed by O'Gorman, Chapter 5, this volume). In 2004, there were 88 of these organisations, of which 11 were diocesan. By the end of 2007, the number of pilgrimage organisations in the dioceses had reached 93, and in parishes and monasteries 276. Thus, today, nearly 70% of the dioceses of the Russian Orthodox Church have pilgrimage services (Babkin, 2008).

Unfortunately, the legal status of pilgrimage in Russia is still not defined; it is not a commercial, but a religious activity. However, despite progress made in organising pilgrimages, a number of foreign and domestic Russian pilgrimages are still organised by commercial tourist firms whose reputation is often ambiguous. Closely linked to this, one of the most discussed problems in Russian pilgrimage is authenticity. It is well recognised that the discussion of authenticity in tourism studies originated with MacCannell (1973, 1976); however, a number of other academics have explored the similarities and differences between tourism and pilgrimage, both in ideology and in practice (Cohen, 1992; Eade, 1992; Raj & Griffin, 2015) and, as mentioned above, both kinds of travel have much in common and are almost impossible to distinguish at times. This both confounds and arises from the idea that both include a search for the authentic; authenticity is a fundamental requirement for pilgrims, but perhaps less essential (though still highly desirable) for secular tourists. Moreover, the authenticity of the experience is inextricably linked to the pilgrim's internal needs, desires and experiences and, thus, the origin of contemporary Russian-organised pilgrimage is highly dependent on the traditions and experiences which post-Soviet travellers bring with them (Kormina, 2010).

In Russia (as elsewhere), religious leaders have repeatedly insisted on separating pilgrimage and tourism. In their opinion, the purpose of pilgrimage is to worship at shrines and it simply cannot be mixed with tourism. While some suggest that religious tourism is a journey or visit to religious shrines for cognitive and educational purposes, this kind of 'tourism' does not include religious practices. For religious leaders, pilgrimage is a worship journey, often associated with fasting, prayer and a certain lifestyle – something entirely different and removed from conventional tourism. This simplistic, uncomplicated view of Orthodox Christianity and, thus, pilgrimage, is understood by many Russians as something naturally inherited. While pilgrimage in pre-Soviet times was completely different from today, there are many common traits and the contrast is not as vivid as it may seem.

Although urban and educated pilgrims developed more secular aims and practices that differed from those of the rural peasants as early as the middle of the 19th century (Chulos, 1999), many traditional pilgrimage practices survive to this day. For example, traditionally, pilgrims used to have an individual goal or vow (*obet, zavet* – both nouns derive from the verb *obeshchat'*, to promise). This tradition of taking vows remained a popular religious practice in rural areas throughout the Soviet period, and since many important religious sites were mostly closed/inaccessible, people directed their vows to their local sacred sites. Many modern tourists are not familiar with such traditions nor many of the small, local sites (Kormina, 2010); however, the pilgrimage movement in Russia is gaining strength. Over the past four or five years the number of pilgrims to domestic shrines has increased significantly – to about 3 million people a year.

The pattern of pilgrimage in Russia

According to the Russian Orthodox Church, tour operators offered over 50 different routes in 2000: around 50,000 people travelled abroad and 2 million made a trip within the country (Khristov, 2005). The number of routes increased to over 90 in 2014, and the main target market for this pilgrimage tourism is religious people, as well as tourists interested in the history of the Orthodox Church. Interestingly, travel agencies have noted that in recent years the number of young people interested in religious tourism has increased, for example in 'Pilgrim' travel agencies, nearly 40% of the tourists are aged 25–35. There is also a growing demand for short-term programmes among pupils, students and alumni, not to mention the students of Orthodox schools.

Modern pilgrims have many opportunities to organise their trip via travel agencies or tour operators. However, there are a few obligatory points: one is that in Russia it is advised to bring a bottle for holy water and a bathing suit for diving into holy springs. Although bathing is widespread in Christian pilgrimage, there are many variations across the world. According to Eade (1992), less than 10% of pilgrims to Lourdes visit the baths. In the Russian Orthodox Church, dipping in holy springs and lakes is an essential experience of the pilgrimage. Pilgrims see bathing as a form of religious, and sometimes life-changing, experience (Kormina, 2010).

Currently, the Russian market for religious travel can be divided into three parts: Russia, CIS (former USSR) and foreign countries. Obviously, the most extensive and varied is the domestic Russian market, the development of which has undergone a number of important phases. One of them is to extend long-established routes. For example, pilgrimage tours to the Trinity Sergius Lavra (monastery) in Sergiev Posad (see Figure 13.1), offered by many firms, have been extended with a visit to the Hotkovskiy Pokrovskiy Monastery (approx. 3 km from Radonezh) in Radonezh – the historic town where St Sergius grew up and where his parents are buried. These tours also now include visits to hermitages of the monastery, for example, one at Chernigov, where philosophers Leontiev and Rozanov are buried.

Other examples of extension are additional sites being added to the traditional pilgrimage to Optina Monastery (located 250 km southwest of Moscow – see Figure 13.2). To this itinerary has been added a visit to Shamordino convent (20 km to the northeast) and Tikhonov Deserts (a further 60 km to the northeast), and as discussed above, this route is under constant development. Alternative pilgrimage routes are currently being developed; the following is a list of some of the more popular sites:

Figure 13.1 Troitse-Sergiyeva Lavra Monastery (Source: https://commons.wikimedia.org/wiki/File%3AСвято,Троицкая_Сергиева_Лавра.jpg. User: Grachev)

Figure 13.2 Optina Monastery (Source: https://commons.wikimedia.org/wiki/File:Optina_khramy_goriz_copy.jpg. User: Denghu)

Figure 13.3 New Jerusalem Monastery in Istra (Source : https://commons.wikimedia.org/wiki/File:Novoierusalimsky_monastyr_1.jpg. User: Unwrecker)

- Diveevo and Murom monasteries (450 km and 300 km east of Moscow, respectively, see next section).
- The Pskovo-Pechersky Dormition Monastery, close to the Russian–Estonian border.
- The white shrines of Vladimir and Suzdal (an impressive set of monuments inscribed on the UNESCO World Heritage List, located in the cities of Vlatimir and Suzdal, which are both approximately 200 km east of Moscow).
- Joseph-Volokolamsk Monastery, located in Volokolamsk (130 km northwest of Moscow).
- The New Jerusalem Monastery (also known as the Voskresensky [Resurrection] Monastery) in Istra (60 km west of Moscow) (see Figure 13.3).

Today, some sites are only rarely considered for pilgrimage visitation despite their enormous touristic, cultural, architectural and religious potential. For example, the little known Svyato-Vvedenskiy Makarievskiy Zhabinskiy Belevskiy Monastery in Belev (Tula district – 300 km south of Moscow) or the Ipatievsky Monastery in Kostroma (330 km north of Moscow), Spaso-Prilutsky Monastery in Volgoda (440 km north of Moscow) or the town of Totma (683 km northeast of Moscow) with its unique 'Totma Baroque' architectural style (see Figure 13.4), or the beautiful Temple of Elijah the Prophet – Ilyinsko-Zasodimskogo church, located in the village of Ilyinsky, 3 km north of Kadnikov city (520 km north of Moscow).

Figure 13.4 The Church of the Entry into Jerusalem: A beautiful example of 'Totma Baroque' (Source: https://commons.wikimedia.org/wiki/File:Тотьма._Церковь_Входа_Господня_в_Иерусалим.jpg. User: Olga1969)

There are routes that, according to tour operators, should develop into popular tours in a few years; for example, the route from Abalaksky Monastery (in Abalak) and nearby Tobolsk (historical capital of Siberia) to Ekaterinburg/Yekaterinburg (fourth largest city in Russia) and then on to Verkhoturye, which includes sites of great importance to the Orthodox Church, and buildings of architectural beauty. This route also includes a visit to the newly built and very beautiful wooden monastery at Ganina Yama (or Ganina Pit), near Yekaterinburg, which has been designated as sacred due to the remains of Tsar Nicholas II of Russia and his family being found here.

Sarov and Diveevo pilgrimage sites

A brief description of one route being developed that is based on historical elements provides an illustration of the influences that are involved in this process. One of the most famous pilgrimage routes today is the Sarov and Diveevo route. This is mostly because of the history of the place, as the name of St Seraphim of Sarov is traditionally associated with several places around the city of Sarov and Diveevo village, including Sarov Hermitage, St Seraphim Diveevo convent, as well as two holy springs. Sarov Monastery was founded at the beginning of the 18th century on the border of Nizhny Novgorod and Tambov provinces (now the boundary of the Nizhny Novgorod region and the Republic of Mordovia – 480 km east of Moscow), on the banks of the river Sarovki, at the site of the Tatar town Sarakly. Its founder, Isaac from Arzamas Spassky Monastery, gathered other hermits in 1706 and built the first church of the Dormition of the Mother of God. Initially, the monastery was famous for its strict rules, and this attracted Prochor Mashnin, who joined the monastery in 1778. Eight years later, he was 'tonsured' with the name Seraphim. From 1794 to 1825, he escaped into the forest on the banks of the river Sarovki, and he stayed there in seclusion, without talking (Figure 13.5). He returned to the same monastery and became famous as a wise old man, who had special gifts of healing and prophecy.

Holy Trinity-Saint Seraphim-Diveyevo (Diveevo) Monastery is located in the village of Diveevo, in the Ardatovsky area. It has a special status among Russian monasteries. It was founded around 1780 by Agathius Semyonovna Melgunov, known as the nun Alexandra, in a location specified by the Virgin. Using the funds she received from the sale of all her property, Alexandra built two large temples: one in honour of the Mother of God – 'Life-Giving Spring' and the other in honour of the Assumption of the Blessed Virgin. After her death in 1789, the founder of the monastery was buried near the walls of the Kazan church. Father Seraphim blessed his spiritual children and instructed them to go to her

Figure 13.5 Saint Seraphim pilgrimage site. Stone where Seraphim prayed for 1000 nights (left); well (centre); and hut where Seraphim lived as a hermit (right) (Source: https://commons.wikimedia. org/wiki/File:Seraphim_of_Sarov_-_pilgrim_spot.jpg. User: Tachs)

grave and the ensuing miracles and healings led to a popular pilgrimage, which continues to this day.

From the 19th century, the memory of St Seraphim of Sarov attracted crowds of pilgrims to visit sites in both Sarov and Diveevo. However, as discussed earlier, after the October Revolution of 1917, all monasteries were closed and while some were repurposed as administrative buildings, museums, etc., others were destroyed or almost ruined. In the 1950s, Sarov was given the code name 'Arzamas-16', designated a restricted area and disappeared from the maps of the city, becoming a research centre for the development of nuclear weapons.

During *perestroika*, church services were resumed and in 1991 St Seraphim's relics were rediscovered in the Kazan Cathedral in St Petersburg (then the Museum of the History of Religion and Atheism) after being hidden by the Soviets for 70 years. This caused a sensation in post-Soviet Russia and throughout the Orthodox world. A crucession (religious procession) escorted the relics, on foot, all the way from Moscow to Diveyevo convent, where they remain to this day. The returned relics have intensified the popularity of the site, and many pay respects at the saint's humble cabin hermitage where he lived in the forest. In addition, a number of freshwater springs around the monastery are known for their healing powers (Figure 13.5).

The most famous Diveevo spring is the one near the village of Satis Tsyganovka; which was consecrated by the deeds of St Seraphim. Legend of this spring tells of soldiers patrolling the border of the protected area in the forest, near Sarov, who saw an old man in white clothes. The old man did not answer the question of what he was doing there, but hit the ground three times with a stick and left. Three springs of water appeared at the site. This happened in the 1960s on the banks of the river Satis. That way, St Seraphim moved his spring to make it more accessible to believers from the village of Tsyganovka. The flow of pilgrims to this spring is growing every year. Orthodox Christians come to pray for the healing of diseases of soul and body. Numerous miracles of God's help at the springs of Seraphim of Sarov strengthen the faith of the people and attract an even greater number of followers/sufferers.

Conclusion

Writing this chapter has been a refreshing exercise for both authors. On the one hand, as an English-speaking academic, one of the authors was fascinated to explore the pilgrimage landscape of an unknown country, to learn about the history, evolution and current state of Russian religious sites. The other author, a native Russian, was interested in contextualising the religious traditions of her cultural heritage and placing Russian pilgrimage in a global context. Sadly, such international collaboration in the area of religious tourism and pilgrimage is rare. Griffin (2012) has previously noted that many authors in this area research and publish within their own religious, cultural, linguistic and ethnic sphere, with little collaboration or reference to 'other'. Work by the likes of Raj and Griffin (2015), and indeed this particular volume of papers, are important steps in tackling this silo-mentality, and for the advancement of overall knowledge in the area of religious tourism and pilgrimage. The authors are particularly proud of this chapter as they were unable to find English language references to a number of the sites (particularly those identified as less visited) discussed herein, and thus, this may in fact be the first exposure of these sites to an English-speaking audience.

If religious-motivated travel is to be taken seriously as a tool for economic development and for the betterment of society (see Raj & Griffin, 2017), more effort needs to be made to expose religious tourists and pilgrims to a wider variety of sites, outside their normal comfort zone, which may challenge their world view. Notwithstanding the geopolitical challenges of the modern age that restrict travel to certain 'others', opportunities to encounter the sacred and the profane in settings which are outside one's normal milieu should be encouraged. The liminality of many of the sites discussed in this chapter is current without question, but, there are enormous potential benefits, in a world where allocentric travellers are seeking ever more challenging and novel experiences. The growing global demand for tourism could be an opportunity for the development of religious tourism and pilgrimage in Russia, and thereby act as a tool for economic growth, for the (re)development of cultural heritage sites and even for the promotion of beneficial dialogue between cultures and societies.

References

Adler, J. (1989) Travel as performed art. *American Journal of Sociology* 94, 1366–1391.

Attix, S.A. (2002) New Age-oriented special interest travel: An exploratory study. *Tourism Recreation Research* 27, 51–58.

Babkin, A.V. (2008) *Special Types of Tourism*. Rostov-on-Don: Feniks.

Bauman, Z. (1996) From pilgrim to tourist: Or a short history of identity. In S. Hall and P. du Gay (eds) *Questions of Cultural Identity* (pp. 18–36). London: Sage.

Belhassen, Y., Caton, K. and Stewart, W.P. (2008) The search for authenticity in the pilgrim experience. *Annals of Tourism Research* 35 (3), 668–689.

Chulos, C.J. (1999) Religious and secular aspects of pilgrimage in modern Russia. Byzantium and the North. *Acta Byzantina Fennica*. 9, 21–58.

Clarke, A. and Raffay, Á. (2015) Religion, local produce and sustainability at religious sites in Hungary. *International Journal of Religious Tourism and Pilgrimage* 3 (2), 33–47.

Cohen, E. (1992) Pilgrimage centres: Concentric and excentric. *Annals of Tourism Research* 19 (1), 33–50.

Collins-Kreiner, N. (2010) Geographers and pilgrimages: Changing concepts in pilgrimage tourism research. *Journal of Economic & Social Geography* 101 (4), 437–448.

Collins-Kreiner, N., Kliot, N., Mansfeld, Y. and Sagi, K. (2006) *Christian Tourism to the Holy Land*. Burlington, VT: Ashgate.

Drule, A.M., Chiş, A., Băcilă, M.F. and Ciornea, R. (2012) A new perspective of nonreligious motivations of visitors to sacred sites: Evidence from Romania. *Procedia – Social and Behavioural Sciences* 62, 431–435.

Eade, J. (1992) Pilgrimage and tourism at Lourdes, France. *Annals of Tourism Research* 19 (1), 18–32.

Fernandes, C., McGettigan, F. and Edwards, J. (2003) *Religious Tourism and Pilgrimage, Proceedings of the First Meeting of the ATLAS Religious Tourism and Pilgrimage Special Interest Group*. Leria, Portugal: Tourism Board of Leria Fátima.

Griffin, K. (2012) Pilgrimage through the eyes of the Irish 'traveller' community. *International Journal of Tourism Policy* 4 (2), 157–173.

Griffin, K. and Raj, R. (2015) The globalization of pilgrimage tourism? Some thoughts from Ireland. In R. Raj and K. Griffin (eds) *Religious Tourism and Pilgrimage Management: An International Perspective* (2nd edn; pp. 57–78). Wallingford: CABI.

Hudman, L.E. and Jackson, R.H. (1992) Mormon pilgrimage and tourism. *Annals of Tourism Research* 19 (1), 107–121.

Jackowski, A. and Smith, V.L. (1992) Polish pilgrim-tourists. *Annals of Tourism Research* 19 (1), 92–106.

Kamenidou, I. and Vourou, R. (2015) Motivation factors for visiting religious sites: The case of Lesvos Island. *European Journal of Tourism Research* 9, 78–91.

Khristov, T.T. (2005) *Religious Tourism*. Moscow: Academia.

Kormina, Z. (2010) Avtobusniki: Russian Orthodox pilgrim's longing for authenticity. In C. Hann and H. Goltz (eds) *Eastern Christians in Anthropological Perspective* (pp. 267–286). Berkeley/Los Angeles, CA; London: University of California Press.

Lefeuvre, A. (1980) Religious tourism and pilgrimage: On the move. *Vatican City: Pontifical Commission on Migration and Tourism* 10 (30), 80–81.

Lepparkari, M. and Griffin, K.A. (2016) *Pilgrimage and Tourism to Holy Citi: Ideological and Management Perspectives* Wallingford: CABI.

Liutikas, D. (2015) Religious landscape and ecological ethics: Pilgrimage to the Lithuanian Calvaries. *International Journal of Religious Tourism and Pilgrimage* 3 (1), 12–24.

MacCannell, D. (1973) Staged authenticity: Arrangements of social space in tourist settings. *The American Journal of Sociology* 79 (3), 589–603.

MacCannell, D. (1976) *The Tourist: A New Theory of the Leisure Class.* New York: Schocken Books.

McIntosh, I., Singhal, N. and Das, A. (2016) Pilgrimages in India: Celebrating journeys of plurality and sacredness. Special Issue of *International Journal of Religious Tourism and Pilgrimage* 4 (6). See http://arrow.dit.ie/ijrtp/vol4/iss6/.

Nolan, M.L. and Nolan, S. (1989) *Christian Pilgrimage in Modern Western Europe.* Chapel Hill, NC: The University of North Carolina Press.

Nolan, M.L and Nolan, S. (1992) Religious sites as tourism attractions in Europe. *Annals of Tourism Research* 19 (1), 68–78.

Olsen, D.H. (2010) Pilgrims, tourists and Max Weber's 'ideal types'. *Annals of Tourism Research* 37 (3), 848–851.

Olsen, D.H. (2013) A scalar comparison of motivations and expectations of experience within the religious tourism market. *International Journal of Religious Tourism and Pilgrimage* 1 (1), 41–61. See http://arrow.dit.ie/ijrtp/vol1/iss1/5.

Poria, Y., Butler, R. and Airey, D. (2003) Tourism, religion and religiosity: A holy mess. *Current Issues in Tourism* 6 (4), 340–363.

Raj, R. and Griffin, K. (2015) *Religious Tourism and Pilgrimage Management: An International Perspective* (2nd edn). Wallingford: CABI.

Raj, R. and Griffin, K. (2017 in press) *Conflicts, Religion and Culture in Tourism.* Wallingford: CABI.

Rajá, J. (2017 forthcoming) Religious tourism and pilgrimage in a non-religious country: The Czech Republic. In R. Raj and K. Griffin (eds) *Conflicts, Religion and Culture in Tourism.* Wallingford: CABI.

Rinschede, G. (1992) Forms of religious tourism. *Annals of Tourism Research* 19 (1), 51–67.

Smith, V.L. (1992) Introduction: The quest in guest. *Annals of Tourism Research* 19 (1), 1–17.

Suglobova, I. (1996) Dragotsennye moi (My precious you). *Pravoslavny Sankt-Peterburg (Orthodox Saint-Petersburg)* (11) 53, November.

Timothy, D.J. and Olsen, D.H. (2006) *Tourism, Religion & Spiritual Journeys.* New York: Routledge.

Turner, V. and Turner, E. (1978) *Image and Pilgrimage in Christian Culture: Anthropological Perspectives.* New York: Columbia University Press.

Vukonić, B. (1992) Medjugorje's religion and tourism connection. *Annals of Tourism Research* 19 (1), 79–91.

Vukonić, B. (1996) *Tourism and Religion.* London: Elsevier Science Ltd.

Part 3: Secular Tourism in Sacred Places

As has been discussed in several of the preceding chapters, one of the major issues that often arises between tourism and religion is the use of sacred places by secular tourists, although one might also note that it is not only secular tourists who are causing problems at sacred sites, as the ever-growing numbers of religious tourists as pilgrims are also creating problems of overuse for the management of these sites as indicated, for example, in Chapter 7.

The first chapter (Chapter 14) in this part, by Serralonga, begins with a review of the literature on religious and spiritual travel in order to provide the context for her discussion of a European Union project aimed at increasing participation in spiritual tourism by young people. The goal of the exercise was to develop links between spiritual tourism and nature-focused tourism through creating specific routes and trails in Europe. The project draws on the examples of existing spiritual routes and the ways in which new routes may support the European Union objectives of greater commitment to peace and unity. The increasing popularity of such routes is one of the reasons for greater visitation to a number of sacred spaces in recent years, and the longest established and most successful in terms of numbers and recognition is the Way of Saint James, or the Camino Santiago de Compostela. Timothy and Olsen (Chapter 15) note the tradition of these pilgrim ways and the increasing promotion and development of routes because of their positive economic effects on the communities and regions through which they pass. They discuss the changing nature of users of the routes, from historic pilgrims on foot or horseback to modern-day walkers, cyclists and others with a combination of motivations and expectations. In Scotland, where there has been considerable development of conventional long distance footpaths in the last two decades, there is currently a proposal to develop a 'Fife Pilgrim Way', running from the northern side of the River Forth across the county of Fife to St Andrews, a former major pilgrimage site in Scotland and previous centre of the Christian church in Scotland (Butler, 2011). The motivation for promoting this route is specifically economic, with proponents claiming it 'will bring significant economic benefits and attract many new visitors to Fife' (Phillips quoted in McRoberts, 2014: 3), and an award of £400,000 from the Heritage Lottery Fund in 2015 (Ferrier, 2015) makes its completion likely. Already dubbed 'A Caledonian camino' (Bradley, 2016: 78), it is but one of nine proposed pilgrimage routes planned in Scotland (Narwan, 2017).

In dealing with the topic of engagement with primarily secular tourism by religious institutions, Curtis (Chapter 16) tackles one of the most sensitive issues facing tourism and religion. To some adherents, sacred spaces and artefacts should not be exposed to engagement with secular tourism but instead, protected and preserved from tourism. Curtis demonstrates how institutions, in his case, the Anglican cathedrals of England, have chosen to deal with tourism and leisure travel, and in many cases make deliberate efforts to engage with and benefit from visitors. These great churches have been opened to a variety of activities, ranging from purely sacred ones and slightly related concerts and festivals, to unrelated performances and exhibitions, in some cases taking advantage of the unique settings offered by the cathedrals in terms of acoustics and aesthetic surroundings. Not surprisingly, some ventures have been more successful than others, but overall Curtis concludes that the exercise has been a success despite the problems that still exist. Not all of the engagements would be acceptable to all faiths or in all situations, but there is much to be learned from religious institutions working with, rather than against, secular tourism.

The implications of the combination of both secular and religious tourism is well illustrated in the discussion by Olsen and Timothy (Chapter 17) on Salt Lake City. That city is both a spiritual home to one faith, and a major tourist attraction to secular visitors also, and represents an interesting example of how tourism can be used to support both the spiritual mission of the faith (Mormon) and aid the economies of the state of Utah and Salt Lake City. In tracing the origins of the Mormon faith and its focus in Salt Lake City, Timothy and Olsen reveal how the current planning and management of the tourist and religious attractions in the city have been developed to avoid conflict and disturbance between the various types of tourists and the residents of the city. The relative success of Salt Lake City in this regard has implications for other cities such as Rome and Jerusalem which share similar problems.

The increasing visitation to sacred sites places an onus on proponents of such growth to ensure that destinations and communities en route are suitably equipped to meet the needs of tourists, particularly religious tourists. Ron examines this issue in the final chapter (Chapter 18) in this part and notes the sometimes demanding nature of such requirements and the ways that hospitality providers can meet these needs. The growth of Muslim tourism in particular raises a number of issues in this regard, and Turkey, among other countries, is benefitting from such growth and making adjustments in several destinations to meet changing demands by a new market as its traditional Western mass tourism market is shrinking because of political and security problems (Butler & Suntikul, 2017; Smith, 2017). There are echoes here of the points made in O'Gorman's chapter on early Christian hospitality, and these difficulties are regularly seen in the problems associated with the world's largest annual pilgrimage, the hajj. As tourism and religion become ever more entwined because of the combined use of sites and facilities, all of the issues discussed in this part will grow in complexity and become more demanding in terms of appropriate management and control.

References

Bradley, I. (2016) Scotland strides on with creation of a Caledonian camino. *The Times*, 6 August, p. 78.

Butler, R.W. (2011) The evolution of tourism products in St Andrews, Scotland: From religious relics to golfing mecca. In Y. Wang and A. Pizam (eds) *Destination Marketing and Management* (pp. 149–164). Wallingford: CABI.

Butler, R.W. and Suntikul, W. (2017) *Tourism and Political Change*. Oxford: Goodfellow.

Ferrier, M. (2015) First steps on Pilgrim Way with funding boost. *St Andrews Citizen*, 2 October, p. 5.

McRoberts, K. (2014) Steps taken to create historic pilgrim way. *St Andrews Citizen*, 14 November, p. 3.

Narwan, G. (2017) To be a pilgrim is becoming popular. *The Times*, 14 April 14, p. 10.

Smith, H.L. (2017) Muslim women ditch burkas for bikinis on Turkish halal beaches. *The Times*, 6 May, p. 45.

14 Spiritual Tourism in Europe: The SPIRIT-Youth Project

Silvia Aulet Serrallonga

Introduction and Main Aims

The main aim of this chapter is to review the literature in order to construct a conceptual framework for spiritual tourism. A further objective is to determine how this type of tourism can be linked with existing products to ensure its integration and success as a product while providing sustainability for territories.

The concept of spirituality has been theorised about since ancient times, but it was not until relatively recently that it emerged as a type of tourism. It remains a term that is difficult to explain due to the great diversity of approaches adopted towards it. According to the dictionary, the word spiritual means 'belonging to the spirit, which is not material' (Enciclopedia Catalana, 2016). 'Relating or belonging to the inner life of the soul'. In fact, the word comes from the Latin *spiritualitas* which, in turn, originated from the Greek word *pneuma*, meaning to breathe.

The concept of spirituality can be found in the Old Testament, St Paul using the word as contrary to the material, referring to the dichotomy between the soul and the body. According to St Paul, a spiritual person is guided by the spirit of God and lives his/her life accordingly (Devereux, 2003). One interpretation of St Paul's text refers to the spirit as the central element of the person:

> Within this concept, which is of Greek origin, three dimensions of the person converge: body, mind and spirit. Spirit is understood as the centre of the person, as the opening to the infinite and the meeting with Mystery, as the ethical realization that infuses corporeality and psyche with direction and meaning. (Alzamora, 2006: 33)

The concept of spirituality has evolved over time in line with the different interpretations and disciplines that have adopted approaches to it; it has also been influenced by the different cultural and religious traditions that have addressed the field. Nevertheless, we can identify some common elements in the definition of spirituality. Some philosophers argue that spirit is the essence of the human being and refers to each individual's search for the meaning of life, something all humans do (Willson *et al.*, 2013: 152). In this sense, we can say that the search for spirituality is natural and universal among all human beings.

The spiritual quest has become a predominant characteristic of society since the final years of the 20th century, a symptom of the collective uncertainty of our age (Sharpley & Jepson, 2011). According to Heelas and Woodhead (2005), contemporary Western society has been defined as the society of 'spiritual revolution', with the emergence of two apparently contradictory phenomena. Religious practice and involvement in religious institutions are decreasing on the one hand, while on the other hand the search for spirituality is growing rapidly via a wide variety of beliefs and practices (such as feng shui and yoga), most of which are based on the idea that what is related to the spirit is not material. In the early 1970s, Easterlin (1974) referred to the fact that economic growth does not necessarily translate into increased happiness or at least does not do so linearly in those countries with a level of income sufficient to cover basic needs. And Marx (1987) spoke of the paradox of use value versus exchange value, pointing out that the former can sometimes be much higher than the latter (for example, water has a very high use value but its monetary value is relatively low, while diamonds have a very low use value but their monetary value is very high), which can also be associated with different theories related to the economics of happiness. According to Willson *et al.* (2013), spirituality affects the upper levels of Maslow's (1971) pyramid of needs, levels where everyone seeks the purpose and meaning to life.

In this regard, various authors argue that the search for spirituality is closely linked to the search for well-being, understood from a multidimensional perspective which includes different aspects of life (Bimonte & Faralla, 2012). They therefore relate it to, among other things, notions of happiness, individual well-being and a holistic global view of life. Spirituality also refers to the search for harmony between 'oneself' and 'others' (including people, animals, the Earth, nature), as well as harmony between 'oneself' and 'God or a higher power'; it is therefore viewed as an element of interconnection (Willson *et al.*, 2013: 153). Spirituality can thus be defined as 'experiencing a meaningful connection to our core selves, other humans, the world and/or a greater power as expressed through our reflections, narratives and actions' (Schulz, 2005: 4).

The starting point for the present text is this contemporary notion of spirituality, understood as the search for a meaning to life and well-being (both physical and intellectual). The main objective of the text is to analyse whether it is possible to develop a range of spiritual tourism products within the context of the European Union (EU) via the case study of a specific project: the EU-funded SPIRIT-Youth project.

In this regard, a second aim of the chapter is to define what might constitute spiritual tourism products and to analyse the potential of this type of tourism in the European context. The chapter presents the first part of SPIRIT-Youth , which consists of conceptualising spiritual tourism. As explained below, SPIRIT-Youth was designed to develop spiritual tourism activities for young people. Within the project framework, two research studies were carried out, one on the concept of spiritual tourism in general, and the other on the specific needs of young people (aged 18–29) at the time of travel. This chapter presents the SPIRIT-Youth project and its objectives.

The first phase of the project consisted in defining the concept of spiritual tourism. This definition is discussed below along with the proposed methodology which consisted mainly of conducting secondary and primary research to gather the aforementioned information. This includes a literature review (i.e. spiritual, cultural and religious tourists' consumer behaviour; spiritual tourism frameworks, the influence of culture and nature on spiritual activities), meeting with key stakeholders and field research. In addition to the field research, a questionnaire was sent out to the Network of European Regions for Competitive and Sustainable Tourism (NECSTouR) members to gather information about the products on offer in Europe.

On the basis of the defined concept of spiritual tourism and the various approaches detected, the project set out to define which criteria need to be met by tourist activities for them to be considered spiritual. In order to define the criteria, focus groups were formed with different experts (academics, tourism companies and institutions) to define these characteristics. As members of the focus groups were from different European countries, the sessions were conducted via a virtual meeting platform. Once the criteria were defined, each of the participating regions proposed a series of spiritual activities, which were evaluated by a committee of experts to determine their suitability. Some of the activities have been included as examples.

Defining spiritual tourism

Although its acceptance within mainstream tourism may be a slow process, spiritual tourism has been among the oldest reasons for travel for many millennia. As stated by Haq and Wong (2009), spirituality has recently become an important area of sociological and business research because some studies see it as a solution to the personal and social exhaustion brought about by our current focus on the materialistic lifestyle. Spirituality has been observed to be affecting various businesses and markets around the world, including tourism. One of the first works to link tourism, spirituality and religion was that published by Cohen (1979), which stated that all human beings are spiritual and establish spiritual connections with the places they visit when travelling. However, since then, few attempts have been made to explore the relationship between spirituality and travel or how tourism experiences are imbued with spiritual meaning by individuals (Willson *et al.*, 2013). Despite there being nothing new about travelling for spiritual purposes, the study of spiritual tourism by academics is only a recent phenomenon.

Spiritual tourism was coined from an academic standpoint only recently, probably because the word spiritual is difficult to define and the label can therefore include different types of supply. Spiritually motivated tourists are an emerging niche (Aulet *et al.*, 2015). According to World Tourism Organisation (UNTWO) estimates, around 330 million tourists visit the main religious sites each year, spiritual motivation being one of the most important reasons for this (Lanquar, 2007). Bywater (1994) also mentioned that spiritual travel occupies an important segment of international tourism and has been growing steadily. As already mentioned, spiritual tourism is a broad concept that involves tangible and intangible products and services. The tangible items include churches, mosques, temples, shrines and other centres with a spiritual focus. The intangible products and services include organised spiritual events, seminars, festivals and gatherings for spiritual reasons (Medhekar & Haq, 2012).

ATLAS defines spiritual tourism as 'a religiously oriented form of tourism, which is emotionally satisfactory and includes visits to the architecturally significant temples, participation in retreats or following pilgrimage routes in Europe' (Fernandes *et al.*, 2013). The UNWTO associates this niche to ecumenical tourism, international exchange and travel of spiritual and cultural interest; it is associated with craftsmanship, archaeology or education, which can be practised as a means of exchanging spiritual values and ensures humans' better understanding of one another. In 2013, the UNWTO organised the first International Conference on Spiritual Tourism for Sustainable Development with a view to enhancing the positive effects of spiritual tourism on the economic and social advancement of communities and societies. The conference placed particular emphasis on the following areas: (a) the understanding and safeguarding of spiritual, religious and cultural values and assets in the context of tourism; (b) the development, management, promotion and interpretation of spiritual tourism products; and (c) socioeconomic inclusion and the empowerment of local communities, in particular of vulnerable groups (UNWTO, 2013).

In this context, a spiritual tourist can be described as someone who visits a place outside his/her usual environment for the purpose of spiritual growth (in relation to God or the Divine), regardless of the main reason for travel (Medhekar & Haq, 2012: 214). The journey undertaken with a spiritual intent may have some unique attributes that may not be present at other tourist destinations. These would include rituals to be conducted at the holy place of visit, a focus on prayer, bonding and chanting with fellow travellers, a long walk to climb a mountain, immersion in holy water, donations, a deep reverence, simple vegetarian food and patience with long queues and inconvenience as well (Jauhari & Sanjeev, 2010: 469).

Few attempts have been made to verify the claim (see, for example, Muir, 1911) that individuals seek or experience spiritual fulfilment through tourism, one of the most interesting being the research carried out by Sharpley and Jepson (2011). Using group discussions, these authors confirmed the argument found elsewhere in the literature that visiting and experiencing natural places provide an opportunity for tourists to engage with the environment not only on a physical level but also on a deeper emotional level. These included: a sense of oneness and connection with the world; feelings of being part of something bigger and infinite; a sense of a greater power and the appreciation of creation; a sense of timelessness and of scale; euphoria; a sense of communitas; a feeling of being blessed; and a sense of renewal (Sharpley & Jepson, 2011: 64).

They identified different elements that helped define spirituality in travel:

- The spirituality of the place. There is an emotional/spiritual response to the physical beauty of the area.
- Solitude/quietness/communitas. Experiencing solitude in the quietness of the place and the sharing of that solitude with others were commonly expressed as contributing to spiritual experiences among the groups studied.
- Being high up/limitless. A number of participants spoke about the relationship between spirituality and the physical challenges that emerge when participating in activities such as climbing a mountain. This is connected with emotional responses.
- Remoteness. The sense of spirituality is inspired by the remoteness or peripherality of the areas and the harshness of life for those living there.

The spiritual dimensions of contemporary tourism have been studied in academia from two perspectives (Sharpley & Jepson, 2011):

- Religious tourism, whose participants are motivated in part or exclusively by religious reasons (including history, architectural and artistic features, activities, management with respect to physical and cultural impacts).
- Tourism as a religion, since MacCannell (1976) suggested that the modern tourist is a secular pilgrim. Leisure time has become a space for the contemplative and the creative. According to Graburn (1989), tourism is used by humans to add meaning to their lives and can be considered a rite of passage (like a modern pilgrimage).

Based on this and further research carried out through a review of the academic literature and different case studies, we can define three blocks or areas of action for the SPIRIT-Youth project:

- Spiritual tourism related to cultural tourism, both artistic and historical interests (a).
- Spiritual tourism related to eco-tourism, natural spaces and rural landscapes (b).
- Spiritual tourism itself, which can be religion oriented (c) or not (d), but related to intercultural and interreligious dialogue such as meditation activities and pilgrimages routes.

A new market is emerging in this respect, comprising new actors and consumers. Indeed, there is a noticeable increase in the number of 'retreats' for those interested in spiritual vacations, while the offer of spirituality courses, personal development and alternative therapies is also growing. Holidays are becoming an important time for personal development, spirituality and creativity. As such, this type of tourism can be associated with creative tourism (self-expression), slow tourism, health and wellness activities and tourism in natural environments, all within a framework of sustainability. And it all also coincides with one of the main motivations of the youth tourism market, which is learning from travel.

Spiritual tourism in cultural orientation

Richards (1996) defined cultural tourism as the movement of persons to cultural attractions away from their usual place of residence with the intention of learning new information and experiences to satisfy their cultural needs.

Authors such as McGettigan (2003) and Haq and Wong (2009) link spiritual and cultural tourism because at the heart of the former lies the desire for intellectual learning, spiritual meaning and well-being, values also found in general cultural tourism. From this standpoint, the interaction between culture and spirituality can be understood as follows:

(a) Culture can be understood as the set of possibilities offered objectively to anyone who wants to become humanely cultivated.
(b) Spirituality is, from a subjective point of view, the area closest to each individual's core, as an invitation to find an inner self.

Pine and Gilmore (1999) discuss how the consumer has the opportunity to be changed by the experience, as reflected in Figure 14.1. Thus, tourism becomes an activity of self-development, able to offer visitors the opportunity to develop their potential through participation in courses

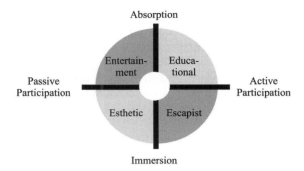

Figure 14.1 The four realms of experience (Source: Pine & Gilmore, 1999)

and learning experiences that are specific to a given destination. These courses and activities may involve elements linked to the identity of the place visited, including both tangible and intangible heritage, and not only visiting spaces such as monuments or museums, but also the experience of arriving there. If the key to spiritual tourism is mental, intellectual or spiritual enjoyment, is all cultural tourism spiritual?

Spiritual tourism in rural areas

Some authors discuss the possibility of tourists engaging with natural or rural places not only on a physical level but also within a deeper, more spiritual context. According to Sharpley and Jepson (2011), this assertion is supported by a number of studies that have explored the spiritual dimension of experiencing particular natural places, such as wilderness areas, forests or the outdoors in general. Spirituality can be experienced in diverse natural landscapes, where sensory awareness and consciousness are increased and this leads to spiritual inspiration and meaningful experience.

Activities in natural places may be classified as appreciative (hiking, sightseeing, bird-watching), consumptive (hunting, fishing, building) or abusive (water-scootering, snowboarding, motor-biking). The proportion of tourists who practise appreciative activities and seek nature-related experiences for spiritual benefits has grown in the last decade (Bimonte & Faralla, 2012). Being high up in the mountains has been found to be the most common source of spiritual feelings, panoramas and being 'on top of the world' or above it (Gifford, 1996), conveying a sense of wonderment, connectedness, smallness/insignificance in the face of the 'greatness' of nature, and a sense of limitless and freedom (Sharpley & Jepson, 2011).

Depending on an individual's needs, purpose and, consequently, preferences, activities may be undertaken with no other reward than the activity itself or with reward accruing as a 'side-product'. In the latter case, depending on their contingent motivational state, individuals may be classified as self-oriented or others-oriented. In the first group, the basic value is individuality, individuals' orientation being towards their own needs, and participation is mainly related to instrumental reasons, e.g. rent-seeking or status. In the second group, the basic value is transcendence, individuals' orientation being towards the needs of others (people, groups, causes), and satisfaction is gained from feeling that one's own participation has had a positive impact on others (although orientation towards others is not necessarily synonymous with altruism) (Bimonte & Faralla, 2012).

At the same time, transcendent or spiritual experiences in nature also produce a state of 'flow', whereby 'the usual distinctions between self and object are lost', allowing for greater connectivity with and immersion in the natural surroundings (Csikszentmihalyi, 1990). The various studies also reveal a correlation between the natural environment and a deep sense of belonging, a sense of place, a profound connection with the world and harmonious feelings (Sharpley & Jepson, 2011).

This idea is related to a concept explored by various geographers, which is the creation of a place. Authors such as Tuan (1977) and Cresswell (2005) refer to the difference between space and place. The place is 'a particular portion of space', which Cresswell (2005: 7) defines as truly meaningful, as a way of seeing, knowing and understanding the world. The concept of space is more abstract. 'What begins as an undifferentiated space becomes a place when we know it better and award it value . . . The ideas of space and place need each other to be defined. If we think of space as something that allows movement, then the place is a pause in the movement; each pause makes the transformation of the space possible' (Tuan, 1977: 6).

There is a 'spiritual geography' of the landscape, shaped by special places, identity, symbolic, prehistoric or historic shrines, hermitages, pilgrimage routes, magical places, etc., with which many people still maintain strong ties. Many protected landscapes carry great importance for local communities and this can manifest itself differently in different cultures, although these landscapes have one common denominator: they inspire respect and affection, strengthen cultural identity and are essential for spiritual well-being. Most are related to sacred symbolisms that are common to different religious traditions: elements such as mountains, stones, forests and trees or water flows are considered sacred places (see also Nelson and Butler [1974] for a discussion on the origin of national parks in this context). This idea is widely explored by different authors, Eliade (1959) being one of the most representative.

The idea of cultural landscapes should also be noted. According to the United Nations Educational, Scientific and Cultural Organisation (UNESCO), cultural landscape 'embraces a diversity of manifestations of the interaction between humankind and its natural environment' (http://

whc.unesco.org/en/culturallandscape/). Cultural landscapes represent the 'combined works of man and nature'. They illustrate the evolution of human society and its settlement over time, under the limitations and/ or physical opportunities presented by their natural environment and of successive social, economic and cultural forces, both external and internal (Mitchell *et al.*, 2009) and positive and negative (Marsh, 1874).

Religiously motivated spiritual tourism

An analysis of possible relationships with other tourist motivations allows different types of spiritual tourism to be identified, with spiritual enjoyment and fulfilment comprising the core. Conceptually, there is a common consensus that religion and spirituality are closely linked. Factors such as increased secularisation in the Western world have meant that, in recent times, 'Spirituality has grown markedly beyond its anchoring in religious traditions' (McCabe & Johnson, 2013).

Religion, in the traditional sense of the word, is not in decline but rather taking on a different form; modern societies remain religious, but religion has become increasingly de-institutionalised. Religious institutions, prescribed theologies and rituals are being superseded by spirituality; more succinctly, spirituality is seen as 'in, and religion is out'. Contrasting with the organised rigidity of traditional religious practice, spirituality, as a (post)modern manifestation of religion, reflects an individualistic search for meaning and harmony and a connection with the world, all of which form part of a 'dynamic process' (Sharpley & Jepson, 2011).

Aulet (2012) explored the relationship between religious tourism, pilgrimage and spiritual tourism. According to this author, religious tourism can be defined as a type of tourism motivated by religion (alone or in combination with other reasons) and includes a religious destination (local, regional, national or international). Apart from visiting the destination, it can be linked to participation in ceremonies and religious activities. The pilgrimage is a spiritual act. It is an individual or collective journey undertaken for reasons of faith to a place that is considered sacred in order to practice religious acts of devotion and penance or to connect with God. Historically, pilgrimage has been defined as a journey in search of the truth (Vukonic, 1996), where people are drawn to sacred places as a result of their spiritual magnetism (Gupta & Gulla, 2010). Pilgrimage requires a sacrifice and spiritual isolation and is an initiation ritual that consists of three phases (separation or marginalisation, death or aggregation and new birth); therefore, the phase of the journey or trip is part of this experience. What pilgrims and religious tourists have in common is that they visit sacred spaces and have an attitude of reverence and respect towards them. They are looking to have an experience that brings them into contact with transcendence and divinity.

There are two key elements to take into account when differentiating religious tourism from other types: motivation and destination. Spiritual tourism may or may not be religiously oriented, is emotionally satisfying and involves enjoyment and spiritual well-being. It can therefore include visits to architecturally significant temples, participation in retreats or pilgrimage routes in Europe and elsewhere. However, it may also include cultural and natural environments and activities for physical relaxation and wellness.

The term 'spirituality' is often used to express commitment to a deep truth that is to be found within what belongs to this world. Thus, spirituality may be thought of simply as a connection between the self and 'this world', implying that a spiritual or emotional relationship exists or is sought between people, 'this world' and specific places. Within the specific context of religion and spirituality, life-as religion, which emphasises a transcendent source of significance and authority, is being subordinated to subjective-life spirituality whereby individuals seek to cultivate their unique subject-lives (Sharpley & Jepson, 2011).

Spiritual tourism without religious motivation

As Mottura (1993) pointed out, spiritual tourism does not necessarily need to be linked to religious sites and religious motivations.

> Art, especially painting, sculpture and music have always been used to express the sacred, but today, dance, theatre, film and literature are also increasingly used to convey spiritual thought. [. . .] A new market is forming, made up of new stakeholders and new consumers: a spiritual market encouraged by the need for demanding knowledge, beyond the regulated religious systems. (Mottura, 1993: 155)

More and more places, both religious and secular, are becoming places of 'retreat' for those interested in spiritual vacations, with increasingly more courses offered in spirituality, personal development and alternative therapies. This growth is explained not only by the fact that people are more aware of their own spirituality, but also due to the practical constraints of everyday life. The harshness of the daily routine awakens people's desire for a spiritual retreat, given that there is a decreasing amount of leisure time in every day schedules, as mentioned above.

Spiritual tourists have classified themselves as 'travellers', 'seekers', 'pilgrims', 'devotees', 'conference/event/festival attendants' and 'adventurers', etc. 'Interestingly, many spiritual tourists have been classified by academic researchers as practising pilgrimage, religious, special interest, cultural or experiential tourists' (Haq & Wong, 2009: 142). This type of tourist looks for sites that evoke a sense of private space that can contribute to his/her mental and spiritual rejuvenation. The specific needs of this segment are very difficult to define as they are very subjective and personal.

McCabe and Johnson (2013) mention transcendence in their study. From a psychological viewpoint, transcendence involves going beyond the ordinary confines of the body; the transcendent spiritual dimension of a person can be seen through a focus on growth or through Abraham Maslow's (1971) self-actualising person, who seeks to improve his/her knowledge of the self and others. In this respect, spiritual tourism is also related to other types such as wellness or creative tourism. According to Richards (2015), creative tourism is a relatively new niche that is being adopted by destinations around the world. The basic reason for this is the growing dissatisfaction with traditional models of tourism development, and the realisation that the creativity of both hosts and tourists is an important potential resource for the sustainable development of tourism, which is in some ways related to the idea of spiritual tourism.

The idea was born in the late-1990s with the aim of giving visitors a more holistic experience that put them in touch with the communities they were visiting and in particular creative local producers. The project enabled destinations to develop a more meaningful and engaging tourism product.

Developing Spiritual Tourism Activities, Some Examples of Good Practices

After analysing the concept of spiritual tourism, the project proceeded to define what criteria or features different tourism activities should have for them to be considered spiritual. To this end, after the literature review had been conducted, several meetings were held between project members and a committee of experts to define these. Four areas or elements were identified that must be taken into account when proposing spiritual tourism activities: carrying capacity, accompaniment, participants' involvement and sense of place.

The first element to consider is related to the feeling of overcrowding. Authors like Sharpley and Jepson (2011) have mentioned elements that clearly identify spiritual experience include solitude and stillness, concepts that are totally opposed to the idea of mass tourism. The UNWTO also mentions that 'Spiritual tourism destination planners and managers need to be very careful when addressing all of these points, especially in terms of carrying capacity, the involvement of people and environmental issues' (Province & Nam, 2013: 13). This does not necessarily mean that they must be places where there are no other visitors (remember that this discussion is about developing tourism activities, so they will attract visitors if they are minimally attractive spaces), but rather that activities should take place at a time when there is a lower influx of visitors (off-peak season and times) and the site should have a good booking management and flow management system. It also means that sites must have the right infrastructure to hold the activity, such as a separate room or space. This is the case with some cathedrals, which have closed-off chapels for those who wish to pray. In this respect, Aulet (2012) mentioned the difficulties generated by managing different types of visitors to sacred spaces due to the different needs and motivations involved.

A second element that was considered important was the presence of a guide or a companion during the activity. This is one of the key factors, as the place needs to talk and transmit its values.

In the foreword to Picazo's (1996) book, Gaspar Espuña defines a guide as:

> The guide is much more than just a companion or, indeed, guide. He or she is an artist who knows how to bring colour and warmth to a landscape, a magician who is able to bring life to ancient stones, a companion who makes long journeys seem fleeting, a professional, in short, who ultimately makes us feel equally at home inside a skyscraper hotel, a Moroccan haima or an African hut

Majó Fernandez and Galí Espelt (1999) add that the guide is also a motivator, a person capable of adapting to different groups, different situations and setbacks, among other things. This means that in addition to having extensive knowledge, they must also have sufficient practical skills. In the case of spiritual activities, the guide is the differentiating element, because he/she must be able to help visitors experience spirituality. Therefore, in addition to experience, as a guide it is essential that he/she has specific training in the spiritual sphere. A key element of the SPIRIT-Youth project are the training sessions for service providers and guides at different destinations. Another important consideration is that the guide is local, so that he/she knows and loves the place and is able to convey that. The last thing required of a spiritual tourism guide, apart from speaking the local language, is being able to speak English as a working language in the EU, bearing in mind that the ultimate goal is a European itinerary.

The third element that is considered is the involvement of participants. As mentioned above, if the goal of spiritual tourism is greater well-being, the attitude of the participants must be active rather than passive. This is clearly a subjective element, as the activity can provide the space and guidance, but there must be personal involvement on the part of the participant. The criterion to consider in this case is that activities establish appropriate systems for obtaining feedback from participants in order to determine their expectations and whether these have been met.

The final element to consider is sense of place. Sharpley and Jepson (2011) speak of the spirituality of the place and the sense of 'remoteness'; that is, finding spaces that are not visitors' usual places of residence and for that precise reason allow them to have an experience that differs from their daily routine. Shackley (2001, 2002) refers to the spirit of the place in holy spaces, in the sense that a visit to a holy place means an encounter with the numinous; this consists in having an experience in a space that makes visitors feel insignificant, excited and involved in an atmosphere that offers the opportunity to have an experience outside their normal lives (see for example the writings of John Muir in the 19th century in Gifford [1996]). Shackley also mentions managing visitors (one of the first elements mentioned as a requirement here). The lower the number of visitors, the easier it is to manage their impact on the space and maintain the 'spirit of place', which guarantees spiritual quality. Monitoring visitors is therefore a very important element in holy places that receive large volumes of visitors.

Another related concept in the sense of place is authenticity. As heritage sites with close links to the cultural identity of the local community, holy sites are places that can offer a spiritual experience. The concept of cultural identity points to a system that can represent the relationships between individuals and their territory. At the core of cultural identity are the oral tradition (language, holy language, stories, songs), religion (group myths and rituals, of which pilgrimages are an example) and formalised group behaviours. Belhassen *et al.* (2008: 686) refer to the fact that a holy space is such because it is 'based on the belief that it bears inherent originality and particular spiritual worth'. The places where these activities take place must therefore be relevant sites in this respect, including both natural and cultural spaces. Much more important than the physical space is the inclusion of intangibles.

The International Council on Monuments and Sites (ICOMOS) discusses the dialectical relationship between tangible and intangible heritage:

> They have a dialectical relationship with one another as the tangible is shown in all its richness while at the same time exposing its intangible soul. The intangible, on the other hand, becomes more accessible in its expression through the support of that which is material. (Carrera, 2003: 1)

Therefore, proposed activities must include both intangible elements and elements clearly related to the local culture and traditions. Table 14.1 shows a summary of the elements identified and their characteristics.

Table 14.1 Criteria for spiritual tourism activities

Element	Characteristics
Carrying capacity/ massification	Small number of participants Flow management to avoid feeling of overcrowding Booking management and planning so as not to exceed carrying capacity
Accompaniment	Person with experience as a guide With specific training Who speaks the local and other languages Who is local
Involvement of participants	Involvement must be requested; they must be 'active' Feedback at the end of the activity Certification
Sense of place	Relevance Level of conservation and protection of the place Inclusion of intangibles Inclusion of traditional elements

Source: Author's own using SPIRIT-Youth data

The SPIRIT-Youth Project

SPIRIT-Youth is a COSME project (COSME-TOUR-2015-3-04) funded by the European Commission's Executive Agency for Small and Medium-sized Enterprises (EASME). According to the European Commission (2016), COSME is the EU programme that addresses competitiveness for enterprises and SMEs. COSME supports SMEs in areas such as facilitating access to funding, supporting internationalisation and access to markets, creating an environment favourable to competitiveness and encouraging an entrepreneurial culture. This specific COSME call was aimed at developing tourism activities out of season in order to help boost the competitiveness of tourism-related SMEs.

The SPIRIT-Youth project is a proposal for stimulating tourism mobility among young people out of season via spiritual tourism. The project's duration was 15 months (from March 2016 to May 2017) and this chapter presents the first results, although the project is not yet finished. It has been designed to develop transnational tourism flows for young people around the concept of spiritual tourism in different countries of the EU. The general objectives of the project are as follows:

(1) to exploit the potential of youth mobility within the EU-27 for leisure purposes, mainly outside the main tourism season, following the principles of sustainable tourism;
(2) to increase innovation and competitiveness in the youth travel sector: a dynamic and key market player in the travel industry;
(3) to contribute to intercultural dialogue, reinforce European cultural identity and foster European citizenship among future generations through sustainable tourism practices.

The idea of the project is to offer a transnational spiritual tourism product to attract mainly but not only the youth tourism market. The product consists of an itinerary across several European countries, with the common theme of spirituality, understood in a global sense. The memorial sites proposed in the itinerary include natural resources as well as landscape, cultural and heritage sites that fit within the concept of spirituality described (retreats, creative tourism activities, personal development courses), with the specific criterion that they must be available during the medium and low season.

The model on which the SPIRIT-Youth concept of itinerary is based is that of the Saint James Way (see also Chapter 15, this volume), borrowing the idea of a certification card similar to that of the Saint James Way passport. The card is stamped after participants complete the different activities. In order to obtain the 'final certificate', each participant must have visited the participant countries and participated in at least four activities in each country.

This proposal is aimed at increasing transnational mobility. The economic potential of the product is based on the assumptions that the aforementioned trends in youth travel match the growing demand for spiritual tourism and adaptation to the specific needs of young people does not require a high budget for SMEs.

The project includes the following seven partners from five different EU countries:

- The coordinator of the project is the Network of European Regions for Competitive and Sustainable Tourism Asbl (NECSTouR), based in Belgium.
- The University of Girona (UdG), Spain, is the academic partner.
- One of the partners is a French Youth Association, Eurocircle, which is a non-governmental organisation that works with youth mobility across Europe.
- Two tourism institutions were included: Stichting VVV Zuid-Limburg (in the Netherlands) and Comune di Prato (in Italy).
- The first two SMEs to become involved in the project were Central de Reserves de Montserrat (Spain) and Equotube SC (Italy).

The project is divided into different work packages (WP).

WP1 was related to the state of the art. The objectives were to define the current state of spiritual tourism in the EU, identify best practices and create a body of knowledge to clarify what is relevant at the present time. A literature review was conducted and field research and case study methodologies were used.

WP2 focused on research into the youth market. The specific objectives were to identify specific needs, interesting activities and different segments of this target market. Quantitative and qualitative methods were used to this end in order to gather data for the market research. Making use of results from the WP1 as well, a quantitative survey was designed and disseminated via Eurocircle by email, using a panel strategy. The results of these activities provided more insight on the specific needs, activities and segments identified in previous stages.

WP3 provided a definition of the tourism product. The objectives were to define the criteria for, and requirements of, each activity, define labelling criteria, identify places and activities in each country and provide standards for sustainability and accessibility, while ensuring the quality of the spiritual experience for all publics. Several meetings and workshops were held among the experts in order to define labelling criteria using the principles of sustainability and to determine those activities that can be considered of spiritual significance and of interest to the target groups. References to accessibility were also included. Each region participating in the project (Limburg, Prato and Catalonia) identified a minimum of 10 activities that met the proposed criteria. In order to ensure objectivity, the activities were validated by an advisory committee composed of external experts.

For WP4, a pilot test was carried out. The objectives were to facilitate cooperation, test viability and increase tourism flows and European citizenship. The duration of WP4 was six months (from October 2016 to February 2017, coinciding with the low season and school holidays in the different countries). From November 2016 to January 2017, three pilot tests were carried out. Each region participating in the project (Catalonia, Limburg and Prato) hosted a group of 25 young people from different parts of Europe in order to test the proposed activities. They had a 'travel diary' to note down their experiences and later provide feedback on the tested products.

WP5 included the drafting of results and evaluating the pilot test. The objectives were to determine the viability of the product and the capacity of the activities. The main aim was to have some guidelines or a handbook at the end of the project on how to design and develop spiritual activities for young people around Europe. Those SMEs offering activities that meet the criteria will be included in a database and allowed to use the SPIRIT-Youth brand. This last step will be developed in WP6 and WP7, which deal with management, communication and dissemination.

Conclusions and Implications

Spiritual tourism does not enjoy the same status in all countries and regions of Europe, some being more developed than others in this respect. Several different product proposals can be found in Italy and Spain in particular, although we have observed a trend in this type of tourism being identified with religious practices or religious heritage. We have also found that most regions do not generally include this type of tourism in their advertising (except in those cases where it has become a star product, such as the Saint James Way). In general, there is little cooperation between different countries in this regard, probably due to a lack of knowledge of the subject matter. The idea of launching a European Route therefore poses quite a challenge.

The aim of the SPIRIT-Youth project is to create a European Route based on spirituality. Launched by the Council of Europe in 1987, Cultural Routes incorporate a journey through space and time to demonstrate how heritage in the different countries and cultures of Europe contributes to a shared and living cultural heritage. The Routes are grassroots networks promoting the principles underlying all the work done and the values upheld by the Council of Europe: human rights, cultural democracy, cultural diversity, mutual understanding and exchanges across boundaries. They act as channels for intercultural dialogue and promote a better knowledge and understanding of European history (Council of Europe, 2014).

The European Institute of Cultural Routes was contacted for this project and has been involved in several SPIRIT-Youth meetings. Besides its role certifying European Routes with the Council of Europe quality label, the institute provides regular advice and training in the field of sustainable governance of the itineraries for its managers. Its contribution to the initial research and definition of this tourism concept is crucial, as it provides the necessary insight with regard to the strengths and weaknesses of the existing routes linking spirituality, which are specifically investing effort in diversifying their target audience and progressively turning to youth tourism.

Among the aims of these Routes are the promotion of European cultural heritage and identity, strengthening the democratic dimension of cultural exchange and tourism, and developing SMEs through the involvement of local and regional authorities, grassroots networks, associations, universities and professional organisations.

In light of this research and taking advice from the European Institute of Cultural Routes, the best way to ensure the viability of this project is to include spiritual activities as a label within existing routes. In fact, several exciting routes related to spirituality already exist. In this respect, the Pilgrimage Routes to Compostela and the Via Francigena are clear examples of routes where spirituality plays an important role. In general, however, the different Council of Europe Routes could also be included, such as the following: the Routes of El Legado Andalusí, the Cluniac Sites in Europe, the European Route of Jewish Heritage, the Saint Martin of Tours Route, Transromanica, the European Route of Cistercian Abbeys, the European Cemeteries Route and the Saint Olav Ways.

The next step will be to determine the main features or requirements for adapting spiritual activities to young people, which is the aim of the SPIRIT-Youth project. According to the WTO (UNWTO & WYSE, 2011), youth travel has grown rapidly in recent decades as living standards in developing countries have risen and young populations travel more and more. The UNWTO calculates that 20% of all international tourists are students and young people. In the coming years, although the youth population will not significantly increase, youth travel will, as young people have more access to disposable income and travel becomes increasingly affordable. The UNWTO forecasts show that by 2020 there will be almost 370 million youth travellers, who will spend over USD 400 billion.

> Young people are invariably at the leading edge of change and innovation (. . .). Young people think outside the box, push boundaries and experiment with the new. In an era of unprecedented challenge for the travel industry, youth travel represents not just an important market segment but also a vital resource for innovation and change. (UNWTO & WYSE, 2011)

In order to guarantee the sustainability of the SPIRIT-Youth project, the key will be not just to have good spiritual activities but ones that are adapted to young people.

References

Alzamora, A. (2006) *La espiritualidad del turismo* (3rd edn). Santa Ponça: Parroquia de Santa Ponça.

Aulet, S. (2012) Competitivitat del turisme religiós en el marc contemporani. Els espais sagrats i el turisme. Universitat de Girona. See http://dugi-doc.udg.edu/handle/10256/7338 (accessed 10 March 2017).

Aulet, S., Vidal-Casellas, D. and Crous, N. (2015) Religious and spiritual tourism as an opportunity for rural tourism: The case of Girona. In G. Bambi and M. Barbari (eds) *The European Pilgrimage Routes for Promoting Sustainable and Quality Tourism in Rural Areas* (pp. 703–714). Firenze: Firenze University Press.

Belhassen, Y., Caton, K. and Stewart, W.P. (2008) The search for authenticity in the pilgrim experience. *Annals of Tourism Research* 35 (3), 668–689.

Bimonte, S. and Faralla, V. (2012) Tourist types and happiness: A comparative study in Maremma, Italy. *Annals of Tourism Research* 39 (4), 1929–1950.

Bywater, M. (1994) Religious travel in Europe. *Travel & Tourism Analyst* 2, 39–52.

Carrera, G. (2003) El patrimonio inmaterial o intangible. *Junta de Andalucía* 1–10.

Cohen, E. (1979) A phenomenology of tourist experiences. *Sociology* 13 (2), 179–201.

Council of Europe (2014) Cultural Routes of the Council of Europe. See http://culture-routes.net/cultural-routes (accessed 31 May 2016).

Cresswell, T. (2005) *Place: A Short Introduction*. Oxford: Wiley-Blackwell.

Csikszentmihalyi, M (1990) *Flow: The Psychology of Optimal Experience*. New York, NY: Harper and Row.

Devereux, C. (2003) Spirituality, pilgrimage and the road to Santiago. In C. Fernandes, F. McGettigan and J. Edwards (eds) *Religious Tourism and Pilgrimage: ATLAS—Special Interest Group First Expert Meeting* (pp. 131–140). Fatima: ATLAS.

Easterlin, R.A. (1974) Does economic growth improve the human lot? Some empirical evidence In David, P.A. and Reder, M.W. *Nations and households in economic growth* p89–125 New York: Academic Press.

Eliade, M. (1959) *The Sacred and the Profane: The Nature of Religion.* Orlando, FL: Harcourt Inc.

Espunas, G. (1996) Forword in Picazo, C. (1996). *Asistencia y guía a grupos turísticos.* P iv Barcelona: Sintesis.

Enciclopedia Catalana (2016) Gran diccionari de la llengua catalana. See http://www.enciclopedia.cat/obra/diccionaris/gran-diccionari-de-la-llengua-catalana (accessed 31 May 2016).

European Commission (2016) COSME. Europe's programme for small and medium-sized enterprises. See http://ec.europa.eu/growth/smes/cosme_en (accessed 22 October 2016).

Fernandes, C., McGettigan, F. and Edwards, J. (eds) (2013) *Religious Tourism and Pilgrimage: ATLAS—Special Interest Group First Expert Meeting.* Fatima: Tourism Board of Leira.

Graburn, N. (1989) Tourism: The sacred journey. In V.L. Smith (ed.) *Hosts, Guests: The Anthropology of Tourism* (2nd edn; pp. 21–36). Philadelphia, PA: University of Pennsylvania.

Gifford, T.(1996) *John Muir: His Life and Letters and Other Writings.* Seattle, WA: Mountaineers Books and London: Baton Wicks.

Gupta, K. and Gulla, A. (2010) Internet deployment in the spiritual tourism industry: The case of Vaishno Devi Shrine. *Worldwide Hospitality and Tourism Themes* 2 (5), 507–519.

Haq, F. and Wong, H.Y. (2009) Is spiritual tourism a new strategy for marketing Islam? *Journal of Management, Spirituality & Religion* 6 (2), 141–156.

Heelas, P. and Woodhead,L. (2005) *The Spiritual Revolution: Why Religion is Giving Way to Spirituality.* Chichester: Wiley.

Jauhari, V. and Sanjeev, G.M. (2010) Managing customer experience for spiritual and cultural tourism: An overview. *Worldwide Hospitality and Tourism Themes* 2 (5), 467–476.

Lanquar, R. (2007) La nueva dinámica del turismo religioso y espiritual. In *Conferencia Internacional sobre Turismo y Religiones: una contribución al dialogo de religiones, culturas y civilizaciones* (pp. 29–31). Córdoba: UNWTO.

MacCannell, D. (1976) *The Tourist: A New Theory of the Leisure Class.* New York: Schocken Books.

Majó Fernandez, J. and Galí Espelt, N. (1999) *El guiatge turístic.* Girona: Universitat de Girona.

Marsh, G.P. (1864) *Man and Nature: Or, Physical Geography as Modified by Human Action.* New York: Scribner.

Marx, K. (1987) *Miseria de la filosofia. Respuesta a la filosofia de la miseria de P.-J. Proudhon.* Mexico: Siglo XXI.

Maslow, A.H. (1971) *The Farther Reaches of Human Nature.* Oxford: Viking.

McCabe, S. and Johnson, S. (2013) The happiness factor in tourism: Subjective well-being and social tourism. *Annals of Tourism Research* 41, 42–65.

McGettigan, F. (2003) An analysis of cultural tourism and its relationship with religious sites. In C. Fernandes, F. McGettigan and J. Edwards (eds) *Religious Tourism and Pilgrimage: ATLAS—Special Interest Group First Expert Meeting* (pp. 13–26). Fatima: Tourism Board of Leira.

Medhekar, A. and Haq, F. (2012) Development of spiritual tourism circuits: The case of India. *Journal on GSTF Business Review* 2 (2), 212–219.

Mitchell, N., Rössler, M. and Tricaud, P.-M. (2009) *World Heritage Cultural Landscapes: A Handbook for Conservation and Management.* World Heritage Papers 26. Paris: UNESCO.

Mottura, P. (1993) Au Seuil du 3ème Millénaire, vers un Tourisme Spiritualiste? Les Cahiers Espaces.

Muir, J. (1911) *My First Summer in the Sierra.* New York: Houghton Mifflin.

Nelson, J.G. and Butler, R.W. (1974) Recreation and the environment. In I. Manners and M. Mikesell (eds) *Perspectives on Environment* (pp. 290–310). Washington, DC: Association of American Geographers.

Picazo, C. (1996) *Asistencia y guía a grupos turísticos.* Barcelona: Sintesis.

Pine, B. and Gilmore, J. (1999) *The Experience Economy.* Boston, MA: Harvard Business School.

Province, N.B. and Nam, V. (eds) (2013) *International Conference on Spiritual Tourism for Sustainable Development. UNWTO: Spiritual Tourism for Sustainable Development.* Madrid: UNWTO.

Richards, G. (1996) *Cultural Tourism in Europe.* Wallingford: CAB International.

Richards, G. (2015) Creative Tourism: New Opportunities for Destinations Worldwide? In World Travel Market Conference.

Schulz, E.K. (2005) The meaning of spirituality for individuals with disabilities. *Disability and Rehabilitation* 27 (21), 1283–1295.

Shackley, M. (2001) *Managing Sacred Sites: Service Provision and Visitor Experience.* London/New York: Continuum.

Shackley, M. (2002) Space, sanctity and service: The English cathedral as heterotopia. *International Journal of Tourism Research* 4 (5), 345–352.

Sharpley, R. and Jepson, D. (2011) Rural tourism: A spiritual experience? *Annals of Tourism Research* 38 (1), 52–71.

Tuan, Y. (1977) *Space and Place: The Perspective of Experience.* Minnesota, MN: University of Minnesota Press.

UNWTO (2013) International Conference on Spiritual Tourism for Sustainable Development | Ethics and Social Responsibility. See http://ethics.unwto.org/event/international-conference-spiritual-tourism-sustainable-development (accessed 29 May 2016).

UNWTO and WYSE, T.W.Y.S. and E.T.C. (2011) *The Power of Youth Travel.* Madrid: UNWTO.

Vukonic, B. (1996) *Tourism and Religion.* Oxford: Pergamon Press.

Willson, G.B., McIntosh, A.J. and Zahra, A.L. (2013) Tourism and spirituality: A phenomenological analysis. *Annals of Tourism Research* 42, 150–168.

15 Religious Routes, Pilgrim Trails: Spiritual Pathways as Tourism Resources

Dallen J. Timothy and Daniel H. Olsen

Introduction

Humans have a long history of travelling for spiritual purposes. As noted in other chapters of this book, ancient and medieval pilgrims travelled for spiritual inspiration, to venerate deities, seek forgiveness for sin or fulfil a religious responsibility. Even the most ancient human beings travelled for spiritual purposes. For example, Göbekli Tepe, Turkey, is widely accepted as the oldest religious structure so far discovered. It was built more than 12,000 years ago and is believed to be a sacred site revered by nomadic peoples who gathered there to undertake sacred rituals, make offerings to the gods and pray to nature deities (Scham, 2008; Schmidt, 2010).

Some 7000 years later, river-based celebrations anteceded today's formal Hindu pilgrimages. Christian pilgrimages were commonplace within a few centuries after the crucifixion of Jesus, and pilgrim travel to the Holy Land was already widespread at the 7th-century Muslim Conquest. Shortly thereafter, alternative sites became important destinations for Christian pilgrims in Europe, particularly Rome, Santiago de Compostela and related places associated with the lives and deaths of saints and apostolic martyrs (Olsen & Timothy, 2006; Timothy, 2011b).

Through the centuries, as pilgrimages developed, the journey towards the sacred centre became more important than arriving at the shrine itself in several religious traditions, particularly within Christianity (Eade & Sallnow, 1991; Santos, 2002; Stausberg, 2010; Turner, 1973). While the aspirational destination was clearly important, the route to get there served a multitude of purposes related to purification, self-sanctification, personal reflection and faith promotion, all of which would prepare the pilgrim spiritually to commune with deity at the eventual destination. An important part of the experience was to withstand, relying on God's help, the difficulties and dangers of the journey, such as rough topography, landslides, accidents, harsh weather conditions, diseases, robbers and wild animals (Sacherer, 2011). The toil and tribulations encountered during the journey simultaneously hardened pilgrims' resolve and softened their hearts. The journey also provided the time and space within which mutual respect, collective worship and spiritual solidarity could develop among co-pilgrims regardless of the standard of living, education, social status or political persuasions at home. Turner (1974) referred to this state of spiritual equality as *communitas*, which was best developed *en route* to the sacred terminus. On pilgrimage, everyone was equal as they sought intimacy with the divine, absolution for sin and fortification of faith.

Through the centuries, certain pilgrimage corridors evolved into set pathways that became well-trodden routes for Christians, Muslims, Buddhists, Hindus, Shintoists and other religious adherents to their respective religious epicentres (Birks, 1978; Funck, 2013; Guichard-Anguis, 2012; Hsun, 2012; Jimura, 2016; Lånke, 2012; Nyaupane & Budruk, 2009; Petersen, 1994; Shair & Karan, 1979; Singh, 2006). Even anciently along these passageways, lodging facilities (e.g. dharamshalas, rest houses, hospices, refuges), guiding services, catering amenities and souvenir vendors developed to capitalise economically on the pilgrims and to satisfy their travel needs (Giotta, 2007; Houlihan, 2000; Shinde, 2007). Today, many ancient pilgrim trails have transformed into important tourist routes that are still used not only by pilgrims but also by non-pilgrim tourists.

This transformation has resulted in a number of issues of importance to trail users and destination planners. This chapter describes the evolution of pilgrimage routes from pious pathways to tourist trails and then examines three critical issues facing faith-based tourism trails today: increases in pilgrimage despite decreases in religiosity, pilgrim trail branding and conflict.

Pilgrim Paths and Tourist Trails

As pilgrim trails became more popular and utilised, they became less spartan, offering relative comfort for the faithful. Many of these routes turned out to be important transportation and trade corridors throughout the 18th and 19th centuries, and many of them today have become important tourism resources and travel itineraries. Lois-González and Santos (2015) and Kevin (2009) suggest that the Way of St James (Camino de Santiago) has found considerable success among religious tourists and non-pilgrim tourists because it offers not only spiritual benefits, cultural values and health and wellness benefits, but it is also a medium for travellers to escape the harried pressures of daily life. Thus, these experiences of 'Otherness' beyond traditional pilgrimage on the Way of St James, the Via Francigena and the West of Ireland pilgrimage walks reflect what Power (2015) refers to as 'post-Catholic' experiences. The same can be said of other faith-based cultural routes that also now serve more general tourism functions.

Like other types of heritage trails, religious routes have become tourism corridors in two primary ways: through organic development or by means of deliberate planning (Timothy & Boyd, 2015). Organic religious trails developed naturally through the years as pilgrims strode through rural and natural areas, villages and cities to arrive at their sacred centres. With increased pilgrim activity and the development of pilgrim guides and maps (Howard, 1980; Webb, 1999), random footpaths and haphazard tracks evolved into formal routes that became widely accepted as the most direct and accessible means of travelling towards the sacrosanct. With the growth of modern-day recreational travel, especially in the 19th and 20th centuries, many of these religious ways came under the domain of mainstream tourism (Fernandes *et al.*, 2012; Murray & Graham, 1997; Morpeth, 2007; Timothy & Boyd, 2015). They frequently navigated pristine natural areas and traversed unique and inspiring cultural landscapes, which were of significant interest to adventure seekers, heritage tourists and nature lovers.

Today, myriad tourist trails throughout the world once functioned as human-made utilitarian corridors for trade, migration, hunting and religious worship. Prominent examples of organic religious trails that are also in demand by non-pilgrim tourists include the Mount Kailash Hindu and Buddhist route in Tibet, which is famous among mountain adventurers; the Inca Trail to Machu Picchu, Peru, an ancient pilgrimage route for the Incas and a modern-day hiking trail for New Age spiritualists and other tourists; the Pilgrims' Way to Canterbury, England; the Via Francigena through France and Italy; and the Way of St James in France and Spain.

The second way in which tourism corridors develop from sacred sites and routes is through intentional efforts to develop tourism trails expressly for economic development and to help preserve or commemorate an element of religious heritage. Unlike most organic religious routes, which originated as ancient pilgrimage ways, most purposive religious trails are themed around the life of an individual (e.g. a deity, a prophet or a saint), a religious architectural style or a series of analogous events. Timothy and Boyd (2015) refer to this deliberate action as purposively planned religious routes (purposive routes). These are essentially networks of similar attractions that are somehow linked tangibly or intangibly to one another based on a common theme. Many faith-based networks, itineraries and routes have been developed for tourism, particularly in Europe. St Patrick's trail, while including areas in Northern Ireland where St Patrick would have roamed, is more a linear network of point attractions associated with the life and ministry of the Irish saint (Boyd, 2013; Simone-Charteris & Boyd, 2010). Russo and Romagosa (2010) provided insight into the Network of Spanish Jewries, which serves the purpose of linking important sites of Jewish heritage throughout Spain in a way that can be visited systematically. The Jesus Trail, a long-distance hiking path in Israel, links together places and shrines associated with the ministry of Jesus. The Saint Martin of Tours Route was fabricated to connect places throughout Europe associated with the life of Saint Martin, including churches and shrines that venerate him. New religious trails are currently being developed today in many parts of Europe (Braga *et al.*, 2014; Horák *et al.*, 2015; Kušen, 2010; Liutikas, 2014; Przybylska & Soljan, 2010) not only for spiritual worship but also as linear resources for economic development.

Likewise, the Buddhist 'Golden Triangle' refers to the locales of the three main events in the life and development of Buddha – Lumbini (Nepal), where he was born; Bodhgaya (India), where he was enlightened; and Kushinagar (India), where he died and entered Nirvana. The town of Sarnath, where Buddha preached his first sermon is also often included in this route. While this South Asian itinerary is still used primarily as a pilgrimage route, it also functions as an important heritage trail for non-Buddhist visitors (Hall, 2006; Medhekar & Haq, 2012).

With the transformation of pilgrim routes into tourist trails and with the formation of purposive religious tourism circuits, several important issues have emerged. The next sections describe three salient contemporary trends and issues facing religious routes in many parts of the globe: increase in the use of pilgrim routes, place branding and conflict.

Decline in religiosity but increase in the use of pilgrimage trails

Although patterns suggest that formal church attendance is declining in the Western world (Chaves & Stephens, 2003; Hirschle, 2010), estimates simultaneously suggest that the number of people utilising pilgrimage routes is increasing. There are at least three reasons for this pattern. First, as noted above, pilgrim trails are today used as linear heritage resources and recreation corridors that appeal to a wider range of travellers beyond pious pilgrims. As cultural and nature-based tourism grows, so does the use of pilgrimage corridors. This sentiment is well reflected in Guichard-Anguis' (2011: 285) assessment of Japan's traditional Kumano pilgrimage trails. She argues that tourism

> has brought tremendous change to the forest and today's visitors have little to do with the pilgrims of the past . . . In this secluded and harsh forested mountain environment, sacred places first appeared many centuries ago. Pilgrims were looking for a relation to the forest which was part of ascetic practice. However, today, the walking boom and wellness concerns create a new perception of the Kumano forest. Visitors enjoy walking not only to keep healthy but also to feel the contact with a Japan of the past in this rather remote part of the country. (Guichard-Anguis, 2011: 285)

As this quote illustrates, pilgrim paths themselves become heritage resources, while the shrines, convents and churches along them gain greater heritage value, even among non-believers.

Secondly, although religiosity may be declining in some regions, it is growing in others (e.g. BBC, 2013). Although there appears to be a direct correlation between increased affluence and secularisation (Hirschle, 2010), 21st-century affluence also enables those who are religious to be able to afford the journey. Religious adherents today are more able to undertake pilgrimage than their forebears were owing to easier global access, cheaper travel, increased affluence, improved access to information and a renewed commitment to their faith in an increasingly secular world.

Finally, there are growing numbers of people who claim to seek spiritual experiences but who are not necessarily religious. This includes New Age spiritualists, as well as other travellers who utilise traditional pilgrimage trails to commune with nature and seek spiritual guidance (Singh, 2009; Timothy & Conover, 2006). Regarding this point, traditional pilgrims and alternative spiritualists are now sharing the same ritualistic trail space wherein 'individuals with various, often contrasting, motivations and expectations walk side by side on this pilgrimage route' (Oviedo et al., 2014: 433). Guichard-Anguis (2011) noted this thread in the pilgrimage forest trails of Japan, and in Europe it is very common (Kevin, 2009; Morpeth, 2008). Many other religions' pilgrim trails are less likely to be shared in the same way, particularly those trails to and within Mecca, since only Muslims may enter the city and participate in the hajj.

Religious routes and place branding/destination image

Pilgrimage routes have an important role to play in developing destination images and place 'branding'. Iconic images of place and place brands can develop organically through time depending on the scale of resources, location, coverage by the media, access to markets, promotional efforts and many other influential variables. By the same token, destinations can be intentionally branded through concerted planning and marketing efforts to develop a recognisable image that will appeal to new market segments.

There are generally two ways in which the marketing concept of 'branding' can be applied to pilgrimage paths and religious trails. The first is the use of famous pilgrimage routes to brand destinations. Some pilgrim paths are so well known, they eclipse all other potential attractions and form the core of an area's tourism economy (Cerutti & Dioli, 2013). The Camino de Santiago is probably the best-known example of this, particularly the parts of the route in the Galicia region of Spain. Galician tourism authorities have long highlighted the city of Santiago and the famous pilgrim route leading to it as the most iconic attraction in the area

(Fernandes *et al.*, 2012; Gonzáles & Medina, 2003; Murray & Graham, 1997; Wright, 2014). Thus, the Camino and the destination have become the 'brand' of Galicia's tourism development efforts.

Similarly, several sections of the Via Francigena (the French road to Rome), a major Christian pilgrimage route, have been developed by local and national governments as a tourism product in otherwise rural and less-developed regions (Cerutti & Dioli, 2013; Ron & Timothy, in preparation; Tencer, 2011). Likewise, much of the brand image of Canterbury, England, is based on the city's famous cathedral and its Pilgrims Way, just as Cusco's image as home to Machu Picchu is inextricably linked to the ancient Inca Trail.

These trends are not limited only to Christian trails. In Japan, for example, the ancient Shinto and Shugendo pilgrimage routes of Kumano are among the most recognised natural and cultural attractions in Wakayama Prefecture, and are promoted heavily as such by local and national governments, as is the Pilgrimage Route of the 88 Temples in Shikoku (Funck, 2013; Chapter 6, this volume).

The second way in which the concept of branding intersects with pilgrimage trails is the labelling of trails with recognised and highly desirable heritage designations. These endorsements reify what is known already by devotees, religious bodies and destination officials – that the routes are important, essential and powerful. In the United States, there are several coveted heritage brands that historic sites and heritage areas strive to achieve. These include but are not limited to National Historic Landmarks, a position on the National Register of Historic Places, National Monuments and National Historic Trails.

While not a pilgrimage route in the traditional sense, the Mormon Trail developed through the forced migration of members of The Church of Jesus Christ of Latter-Day Saints (LDS) from the US Midwest to the Salt Lake Valley in the mid-19th century and is therefore a religious route. Owing to persecution by anti-Mormon foes, and following the martyrdom of the church's founder, most of the Mormons (or LDS) headed West in search of a locale where they could freely practice their religion. Much of their route was established already as the Oregon Trail, but the Mormons forged new branches, and much LDS modern lore is based on the pioneer experiences of their forebears who crossed the plains to what is today Utah and the Intermountain West. Eventually, some 70,000 migrants reached the Great Salt Lake Valley along this 2,092-km trail. The trials, tribulations, celebrations and other experiences of the early pioneers on this trail have become a salient part of the legends and cultural heritage of the Latter-Day Saints (Ron & Timothy, in preparation; Wahlquist, 2014). Each year, thousands of Mormons and non-Mormon history buffs follow the trail or portions of it by car (Hudman & Jackson, 1992; Olsen, 2006), and various family and youth groups regularly organise migration re-enactments on the trail in period dress, pulling handcarts and walking certain distances to commemorate the events of the 1840s and 1850s on this trail (Jones, 2006). Today, the trail has achieved significant national status and is now known as the Mormon Pioneer National Historic Trail. It runs through public and private lands and is managed by the US National Park Service. In addition, many individual sites along the route have been branded National Historic Landmarks.

At the regional level, the Council of Europe established its Cultural Routes Programme in 1987 with the aim of identifying and delineating the most important trans-European cultural routes to promote intercultural dialogue, to protect European heritage and enhance Europeans' quality of life and economic development, to raise awareness of a pan-European cultural identity and to facilitate the development of heritage-based sustainable tourism. To achieve these goals, the Council of Europe established the European Institute of Cultural Routes in 1998 (Grabow, 2010; Timothy & Boyd, 2015; Timothy & Saarinen, 2013). The first cultural route to be listed by the Council of Europe was the Routes to Santiago de Compostela in 1987. As of September 2016, 32 European cultural routes had been selected by the Institute, and predictably, more than one third of these trails are closely associated with religion (Table 15.1). Four of these are organically developed routes that in fact once served, and still serve, as important pilgrimage paths. The remaining eight are purposively linked networks of places that have a common Christian, Jewish or Muslim heritage theme.

Currently, there are eight candidate routes under consideration by the institute, three of which have European religious heritage at their core. Many sites in Europe have a salient part to play in the pan-European cultural identity, and the 'branding' associated with being part of the European Institute of Cultural Routes is a coveted prize for individual sites and locations included in a given itinerary.

At the global scale, many sites of religious and spiritual importance have been inscribed on the United Nations Education, Scientific and Cultural Organisation's (UNESCO) World Heritage List (WHL). However, as of 2016, only four pilgrimage routes have been inscribed with the World Heritage Site (WHS) brand, arguably the most coveted and sought-after heritage trademark in the world (Timothy, 2011a; Timothy & Boyd, 2006). The Routes of Santiago de Compostela: *Camino Francés* and Routes of Northern Spain were listed in 1993. The Routes of Santiago de Compostela in France became a WHS in 1998. Japan's Sacred Sites and Pilgrimage Routes in the Kii Mountain Range were inscribed in 2004, and in 2012, the Birthplace of Jesus: Church of the Nativity and the Pilgrimage Route, Bethlehem, was listed by UNESCO in Palestine.

The Routes of Santiago de Compostela: *Camino Francés* and Routes of Northern Spain are a network of approximately 1500 km of primitive

Table 15.1 Council of Europe cultural routes with a significant religious foundation

Trail	Theme	Year listed	Number of countries	Purposive or organic	Route headquarters
Santiago de Compostela Pilgrim Routes	Pilgrimage route to the tomb of St James. Includes several primary routes from France and Portugal.	1987	8	Organic	Santiago de Compostela, Spain, and several others
Via Francigena	Pilgrimage and trade route to Rome from England, France and Switzerland	1994	4	Organic	Fidenza, Italy
The Routes of El legado andalusi	Some of the routes commemorate the spread of Muslim culture, faith and art through Mediterranean Europe	1997	8	Purposive	Granada, Spain
European Route of Jewish Heritage	Sites of Jewish heritage and influence, commemorating the Jewish contribution to European culture	2004	22	Purposive	Girona, Spain
Cluniac Sites in Europe	Sacred sites association with the Benedictine Reform of Europe	2005	11	Purposive	Cluny, France
Saint Martin of Tours Route	Network of European towns influenced by Saint Martin and sites of his veneration	2005	41	Purposive	Tours, France
Via Regia	Oldest road between Western and Eastern Europe. Had an important pilgrimage component.	2005	8	Organic	Erfurt, Germany
Transromanica – the Romanesque Routes	A network connecting a common Romanesque architectural heritage	2007	8	Purposive	Magdeburg, Germany
European Route of Cistercian Abbeys	Network linking sites associated with the Cistercian Order – key in the development of the church and European states	2010	11	Purposive	Clairvaux, France
Route of Saint Olav Ways	Historic pilgrim trails in Scandinavia and sites associated with King Olav, a martyr and a saint	2010	3	Organic/ purposive	Trondheim, Norway
The Casadean Sites	Network of Casadean sites/congregations that followed the rule of St Benedict	2012	5	Purposive	La Chaise-Dieu, France
Huguenot and Waldensian Trail	Commemorates the persecution and exile of the Huguenots and Waldensians for their religious beliefs	2013	4	Purposive	Marburg, Germany

Source: Compiled from European Institute of Cultural Routes (2016).

pilgrim routes throughout north-western Spain. This WHS consists of the physical routes, churches, shrines, cathedrals, hostels, bridges, monasteries and other infrastructure elements that historically (since the 10th century) and currently serve the needs of pilgrims travelling to the tomb of St James the Apostle. The WHS includes the route from the French border through more than 100 towns and villages that together present a heritage landscape of universal value in the development of Christian pilgrimages in Europe.

Although inscribed separately from the Spanish paths, the Routes of Santiago de Compostela in France WHS commemorates and conserves the four primary trails that pilgrims from throughout Europe were required to negotiate through France. The French routes were key in the religious, cultural and economic development of Europe during the Middle Ages, and like their Spanish counterparts, the routes in France criss-cross important natural and cultural landscapes and take in a wide range of architectural wonders, cities, towns and villages.

Today, millions of tourists visit the shrine of Santiago de Compostela, although every year typically fewer than 200,000 take the traditional pilgrimage route. Route-based travellers can receive a pilgrim passport, or credential, if they walk at least 100 km, and a *compostela*, or a certificate of completion, after arriving in Santiago (Gonzáles & Medina, 2003; Timothy & Boyd, 2015). During the Middle Ages, Santiago became the third most visited Christian pilgrimage destination in the world after the Holy Land and Rome, with some estimates placing pilgrim arrivals at half a million to 2 million per year in ancient times (Stopford, 1994).

In spite of the route's reputation and growing popularity in the Early Middle Ages, its use began to decline significantly in the Late Middle Ages for a variety of reasons. The 16th-century Protestant Reformation discouraged pilgrimage as a superficial manifestation of piousness, rather than an inward cleansing of self (Lånke, 2012). The political instability of the time also made travelling somewhat dangerous, and a widespread fear of the Plague between the 14th and 17th centuries throughout Europe kept many would-be pilgrims at home (Ron & Timothy, in preparation). Because of these and other factors, the Way of St James lost much of its charm, and pilgrimage on the Camino declined considerably. By the mid-20th century, the use of the Way was negligible. In the 1980s, however, the Camino de Santiago began to experience a resurgence of interest when the Council of Europe designated the Way as its first European Cultural Route in 1987. The Catholic World Youth Day of 1989, held in Santiago de Compostela, also brought considerable attention to the shrine and its associated footpaths. Likewise, Jubilee Year 1993 was celebrated in Santiago to memorialise St James Day (Przybylska & Soljan, 2010). The same year, the routes were inscribed on the WHL, additionally spotlighting this heritage importance (Ron & Timothy, in preparation). In 2015, some 262,459 pilgrims arrived at Santiago de Compostela via the trail. Approximately 90% came by foot; the rest came by bicycle, horse or wheelchair. More than one third (38%) of the trail users claim to have been motivated by faith or religion, 54% by a mix of religion and cultural tourism interests, while 8% were motivated to undertake the journey solely for cultural reasons (Oficina del Perigrino, 2016). Tourism in fact was the catalyst for the revival of the Camino (Gonzáles & Medina, 2003) and other Christian routes, such as the St Olav Ways in Scandinavia (Lånke, 2012).

The Sacred Sites and Pilgrimage Routes in the Kii Mountain Range WHS includes three sacred sites that are linked by ancient pilgrimage trails in Yoshino and Omine, Kumano Sanzan and Koyasan (Funck, 2013; Guichard-Anguis, 2011). These religious routes combine the ancient tenets of Shintoism, Buddhism and Shugendo, and have been an important pilgrim path for more than 1200 years (Jimura, 2016). The sacred edifices were the prototypes for many later shrines and temples, and the pilgrimage route has had a profound impact on religious traditions in Japan. The area receives some 15 million pilgrim and non-pilgrim visitors every year who come to enjoy nature and the cultural heritage of the Shinto temples and the traditional trails that have linked them together for centuries (UNESCO, 2016), and the number of tourists continues to grow (Jimura, 2016).

The central focus of the Birthplace of Jesus: Church of the Nativity and the Pilgrimage Route, Bethlehem, is the spot traditionally believed to be the birthplace of Jesus. This locale in Palestine symbolises the beginning of Christianity and is one of the holiest sites on earth for Christians. While the original church was built in AD 339, the current Church of the Nativity was erected in the 6th century and is possibly the oldest Christian church still in use. Tradition suggests that the short pilgrim route from Bethlehem's entrance to the Church of the Nativity follows the path that Mary and Joseph used during their trip to Bethlehem (Atrash, 2016). The path and the pilgrim trail are significant for Christians, and the grotto beneath the church is celebrated as the birthplace of Christ (UNESCO, 2016).

Conflict

When sacred spaces and experiences are shared with profane users and less-than-hallowed purposes, discord is inevitable. The contemplative mindsets of religious adherents consuming their sacred space are often disturbed by picture-taking or boisterous tourists sharing the same space. This conundrum has plagued ceremonies and sacred site for centuries, and it is no less true on pilgrimage paths than it is in any other hallowed space (Timothy & Boyd, 2015).

This has become a challenge as the Kii Mountain pilgrimage routes in Japan have become more geared towards tourist uses in recent years.

Shugendo is a spiritual tradition in Japan that involves nature and mountain worship. The practice of Shugendo requires adherents to master the mountain topography and memorise the mountain passes by making several pilgrimages. The signposts erected and paths established for non-pilgrim users, however, are seen as hindrances to the puritanical customs and learning of the *sendatsu* (senior practitioners and teachers) of Shugendo. Instead of having to learn the landscapes and the mountains through experience, effort and toil, these spaces are now marked and interpreted for tourist consumption, which frustrates the efforts of many Shugendo spiritual practitioners (Jimura, 2016: 387).

Even within the boundaries of a single religion, conflict may occur in relation to the use of a pilgrimage circuit and the sanctification or secularisation of sacred space associated with a trail. For example, in the Muslim holy city of Mecca, pilgrims ambulate a specific route at the sacred sites in and around the Great Mosque of Mecca in order to accomplish their ritualisation processes (Raj & Bozonelos, 2015). While there have long been traditional routes from various parts of the Muslim world to Mecca, most of the conflict occurs at Mecca. The traditional hajj has undergone significant changes in recent decades with tour operators now selling a wide selection of pilgrimage experiences, ranging from three- to five-star packages, which include luxury accommodation and transportation, guide services and assistance with the rituals. To make way for increasing numbers of annual pilgrims, several important and historic (including sacred) sites near the Grand Mosque may be demolished to allow expansion of the mosque and to create room for increased commercial development (Ron & Timothy, in preparation). This 'Vegasisation' of Mecca (Al-Saadi, 2014) has upset many traditionalists and changed many pilgrims' perspectives on their route-based ritual encounters at their holiest site.

Another perspective on conflict is associated with rivalries between competing religious-oriented trails. Perhaps the best contemporary example of this is in Israel where the Jesus Trail and the Gospel Trail vie for prominence (Collins-Kreiner & Kliot, 2016). A group of volunteers and community members in Galilee established the 65-km Jesus Trail footpath in 2007. It focuses on the life and ministry of Jesus. Its purpose is not only to help hikers appreciate the Christian heritage of the Galilee but also to help them learn about the cultural and natural environment of the region (Timothy & Boyd, 2015). The Gospel Trail, started in 2011 by the Israeli Ministry of Tourism, has less of an ecological focus and is more of a cultural heritage and faith-centred hiking trail, with an economic development focus. The two trails run parallel in a few places and meet in several localities. However, they start at different positions in Nazareth and navigate different villages. Much criticism has been meted out to the Ministry of Tourism for creating an analogous trail in Galilee when one already existed (Lewon, 2012; Ron & Timothy, in preparation; Timothy & Boyd, 2015), although some observers suggest that the ministry's trail plans had started before those for the Jesus Trail. The Gospel Trail bypasses many sites that the Jesus Trail includes, thereby offering different narratives and products (Troen & Rabineau, 2014). This also has garnered criticism of the Ministry of Tourism, suggesting that the Gospel Trail has been overly politicised by avoiding the locations of many of Jesus' miracles because they are situated in Arab villages, while the Jesus Trail is more inclusive in that regard (Ron & Timothy, in preparation).

Conclusion

While pilgrimage trails have existed for thousands of years, in recent times they have become an object of tourism development and regional marketing efforts because of their religious, spiritual and cultural offerings, as well as their economic potential. Whether through natural evolutionary processes or by purposive actions to develop a tourism network, religious trails and routes are gaining greater prominence as leisure, New Age, heritage and nature-based tourism resources. Organically evolved religious trails require relatively little investment in terms of infrastructure and development since they represent already established geographic routes that are visible in the cultural landscape. Purposive religious routes, while perhaps requiring a higher level of planning and networking than organic routes do, are also relatively straightforward to develop but nevertheless require a strong regional, often multinational, network of stakeholders and key players to reach sustainable success.

The transition of pilgrimage routes into multi-use trails inevitably results in several unique situations and patterns. This chapter highlights three of these. First is the reality that we are seeing an escalation in the use of pilgrim trails in areas where religiosity appears to be waning (e.g. Western Europe, North America and developed areas of Asia). The second trend is the rise of religious routes becoming major regional or national image promoters and 'brands' for economic development. As well, we are now seeing rising numbers of pilgrim paths being branded with national and international trademarks that set them apart as consequential linear heritage resources of global importance. Finally, the modern-day, multipurpose characteristics of pathways that for centuries or millennia functioned solely as channels of spiritual growth, godly devotion and piety, frequently result in contestation between users, conflict between competing trails and intragroup discord. The common denominator underlying these and many other tendencies is the transformation of traditional pilgrimage routes into corridors for recreational and other touristic purposes through increased access, recognised branding, increased affluence, reduced travel costs, people seeking spirituality over religion and widespread media attention.

References

Al-Saadi, Y. (2014) Mecca's changing face: Rejuvenation or destruction? *Al-Akhbar.* 5 March. See http://english.al-akhbar.com/content/meccas-changing-face-rejuventation-or-destruction?utm_source=freeburner&utm_medium=fee&utm_campagin=Feed% 3A+AlAkhbarEnglish+(Al+Akhbar+English) (accessed 15 July 2016).

Atrash, N. (2016) World Heritage Site in Bethlehem and its potential reflections on tourism. In R.K. Isaac, C.M. Hall and F. Higgins-Desbiolles (eds) *The Politics and Power of Tourism in Palestine* (pp. 79–94). London: Routledge.

BBC (2013) How many Roman Catholics are there in the world? See http://www.bbc.com/news/world-21443313 (accessed 7 September 2016).

Birks, J.S. (1978) *Across the Savannas to Mecca: The Overland Pilgrimage Route from West Africa.* London: Hurst.

Boyd, S.W. (2013) The Causeway Coastal Route and Saint Patrick's Trail: Heritage tourism route development in Northern Ireland. In B. Garrod and A. Fyall (eds) *Contemporary Cases in Heritage* (pp. 204–228). London: Goodfellow.

Braga, C., Soares, M. and Brito, M. (2014) A new pilgrimage in Portugal: Following the steps of Saint Nuno. *International Journal of Religious Tourism and Pilgrimage* 1 (1), 72–82.

Cerutti, S. and Dioli, I. (2013) Via Francigena mountain itineraries: The case of Piacenza valleys. *International Journal of Religious Tourism and Pilgrimage* 1 (1), 83–92.

Chaves, M. and Stephens, L. (2003) Church attendance in the United States. In M. Dillon (ed.) *Handbook of the Sociology of Religion* (pp. 85–95). Cambridge: Cambridge University Press.

Collins-Kreiner, N. and Kliot, N. (2016) Particularism vs. universalism in hiking tourism. *Annals of Tourism Research* 56, 132–137.

Eade, J. and Sallnow, M.J. (1991) *Contesting the Sacred: The Anthropology of Christian Pilgrimage.* London: Routledge.

Fernandes, C., Pimenta, E., Gonçalves, F. and Rachão, S. (2012) A new research approach for religious tourism: The case study of the Portuguese route to Santiago. *International Journal of Tourism Policy* 4 (2), 83–94.

Funck, C. (2013) The roots of Japanese travel culture. In C. Funck and M. Cooper (eds) *Japanese Tourism: Spaces, Places and Structures* (pp. 10–39). New York: Barghahn.

Giotta, S. (2007) Accommodation facilities for pilgrims along the Via Francigena. *Via Francigena* 26, 17–25.

Gonzáles, R.C.L. and Medina, J.S. (2003) Cultural tourism and urban management in north-western Spain: The pilgrimage to Santiago de Compostela. *Tourism Geographies* 5 (4), 446–460.

Grabow, S. (2010) The Santiago de Compostela pilgrim routes: The development of European cultural heritage policy and practice from a critical perspective. *European Journal of Archaeology* 13 (1), 89–116.

Guichard-Anguis, S. (2011) Walking through World Heritage Forest in Japan: The Kumano pilgrimage. *Journal of Heritage Tourism* 6 (4), 285–295.

Guichard-Anguis, S. (2012) Walking the Kumano pilgrimage roads (Japan) and writing diaries: Narratives in Japanese travel culture. In J. Tivers and T. Rakić (eds) *Narratives of Travel and Tourism* (pp. 121–134). Aldershot: Ashgate.

Hall, C.M. (2006) Buddhism, tourism and the middle way. In D.J. Timothy and D.H. Olsen (eds) *Tourism, Religion and Spiritual Journeys* (pp. 172–185). London: Routledge.

Hirschle, J. (2010) From religious to consumption-related routine activities? Analysing Ireland's economic boom and the decline in church attendance. *Journal for the Scientific Study of Religion* 49 (4), 673–687.

Horák, M., Kozumplíková, A., Somerlíková, K., Lorencová, H. and Lampartová, I. (2015) Religious tourism in the south-Moravian and Zlín regions: Proposal for three new pilgrimage routes. *European Countryside* 3, 167–178.

Houlihan, M. (2000) Souvenirs with soul: 800 years of pilgrimage to Santiago de Compostela. In M. Hitchcock and K. Teague (eds) *Souvenirs: The Material Culture of Tourism* (pp. 18–24). Aldershot: Ashgate.

Howard, D.R. (1980) *Writers and Pilgrims: Medieval Pilgrimage Narratives and Their Posterity*. Berkeley, CA: University of California Press.

Hsun, C. (2012) Between religion and state: The Dajia pilgrimage in Taiwan. *Social Compass* 59 (3), 298–310.

Hudman, L.E. and Jackson, R.H. (1992) Mormon pilgrimage and tourism. *Annals of Tourism Research* 19 (1), 107–121.

Jimura, T. (2016) World Heritage Site management: A case study of sacred sites and pilgrimage routes in the Kii mountain range, Japan. *Journal of Heritage Tourism* 11 (4), 382–394.

Jones, M.S. (2006) (Re)living the pioneer past: Mormon youth handcart trek re-enactments. *Theatre Topics* 16 (2), 113–130.

Kevin, T. (2009) *Walking the Camino: A Modern Pilgrimage to Santiago*. Melbourne: Scribe Publications.

Kušen, E. (2010) Modern pilgrimage routes in Croatia. *Tourism* 58 (3), 312–317.

Lånke, B. (2012) The Route of St. Olav Ways: European cultural route and the pilgrimage path to the north. *Via Francigena* 34, 29–33.

Lewon, D. (2012) The Jesus Trail: Hiking from Nazareth to the Sea of Galilee. *Backpacker* 40 (2), 70–80.

Liutikas, D. (2014) Lithuanian valuistic journeys: Traditional and secular pilgrimage. *Journal of Heritage Tourism* 9 (4), 299–316.

Lois-González, R.C. and Santos, X.M. (2015) Tourists and pilgrims on their way to Santiago: Motives, caminos and final destinations. *Journal of Tourism and Cultural Change* 13 (2), 149–164.

Medhekar, A. and Haq, F. (2012) Development of spiritual tourism circuits: The case of India. *GSTF Business Review* 2 (2), 212–218.

Morpeth, N.D. (2007) Ancient and modern pilgrimage: El Camino Frances. In R. Raj and N. Morpeth (eds) *Religious Tourism and Pilgrimage Management: An International Perspective* (pp. 153–160). Wallingford: CAB International.

Murray, M. and Graham, B. (1997) Exploring the dialectics of route-based tourism: The Camino de Santiago. *Tourism Management* 18, 513–524.

Nyaupane, G.P. and Budruk, M. (2009) South Asian heritage tourism: Conflict, colonialism, and cooperation. In D.J. Timothy and G.P. Nyaupane (eds) *Cultural Heritage and Tourism in the Developing World: A Regional Perspective* (pp. 127–145). London: Routledge.

Oficina del Perigrino (2016) Statistics. See https://oficinadelperegrino.com/en/statistics/ (accessed 29 August 2016).

Olsen, D.H. (2006) Tourism and informal pilgrimage among the Latter-Day Saints. In D.J. Timothy and D.H. Olsen (eds) *Tourism, Religion and Spiritual Journeys* (pp. 254–270). London: Routledge.

Olsen, D.H. and Timothy, D.J. (2006) Tourism and religious journeys. In D.J. Timothy and D.H. Olsen (eds) *Tourism, Religion and Spiritual Journeys* (pp. 1–21). London: Routledge.

Oviedo, L., de Courcier, S. and Farias, M. (2014) Rise of pilgrims on the Camino to Santiago: Sign of change or religious revival? *Review of Religious Research* 56 (3), 433–442.

Petersen, A. (1994) The archaeology of the Syrian and Iraqi Hajj routes. *World Archaeology* 26 (1), 47–56.

Power, R. (2015) Walking the spiritual ways: West of Ireland experience of modern pilgrimage. *International Journal of Religious Tourism and Pilgrimage* 3 (1), 46–54.

Przybylska, L. and Sołjan, I. (2010) Polish pilgrimages to Santiago de Compostela: Ways of St. James in Poland. *GeoJournal of Tourism and Geosites* 6 (2), 211–218.

Raj, R. and Bozonelos, D. (2015) Pilgrimage experience and consumption of travel to the city of Makkah for Hajj ritual. *International Journal of Religious Tourism and Pilgrimage* 3 (1), 38–45.

Ron, A.S. and Timothy, D.J. (in preparation) *Contemporary Christian Travel: Pilgrimage, Practice and Place.* Bristol: Channel View Publications.

Russo, A.P. and Romagosa, F. (2010) The network of Spanish Jewries: In praise of connecting and sharing heritage. *Journal of Heritage Tourism* 5 (2), 141–156.

Sacherer, J. (2011) Rolwaling: A sacred Buddhist valley in Nepal. In R.P.B. Singh (ed.) *Sacredscapes and Pilgrimage Systems* (pp. 153–174). New Delhi: Shubhi Publications.

Santos, X. (2002) Pilgrimage and tourism at Santiago de Compostela. *Tourism Recreation Research* 27 (2), 41–50.

Scham, S. (2008) The world's first temple. *Archaeology Magazine* 61 (6), n.p. See http://archive.archaeology.org/0811/abstracts/turkey.html (accessed 12 May 2017).

Schmidt, K. (2010) Göbekli Tepe – the Stone Age sanctuaries: New results of ongoing excavations with a special focus on sculptures and high reliefs. *Documenta Praehistorica* 37, 239–256.

Shair, I.M. and Karan, P.P. (1979) Geography of the Islamic pilgrimage. *GeoJournal* 3 (6), 599–608.

Shinde, K.A. (2007) Visiting sacred sites in India: Religious tourism or pilgrimage. In R. Raj and N. Morpeth (eds) *Religious Tourism and Pilgrimage Management: An International Perspective* (pp. 184–197). Wallingford: CABI.

Simone-Charteris, M.T. and Boyd, S.W. (2010) The development of religious heritage tourism in Northern Ireland: Opportunities, benefits and obstacles. *Tourism* 58 (3), 229–257.

Singh, R.P.B. (2006) Pilgrimage in Hinduism: Historical context and modern perspectives. In D.J. Timothy and D.H. Olsen (eds) *Tourism, Religion and Spiritual Journeys* (pp. 220–236). London: Routledge.

Singh, S. (2009) Pilgrim culture of Tīrthā in India: Enculturation of New Age movements within age-old rituals. In S. Singh (ed.) *Domestic Tourism in Asia: Diversity and Divergence* (pp. 81–106). London: Earthscan.

Stausberg, M. (2010) *Religion and Tourism.* London: Routledge.

Stopford, J. (1994) Some approaches to the archaeology of Christian pilgrimage. *World Archaeology* 26 (1), 57–72.

Tencer, N.J. (2011) Via Francigena: Walking Europe's oldest pilgrimage trail. Tourism-Review.com. See http://www.tourism-review.com/travel-tourism-magazine-walk-the-europes-oldest-pilgrimage-trail--article1485 (accessed 7 September 2016).

Timothy, D.J. (2011a) *Cultural Heritage and Tourism: An Introduction.* Bristol: Channel View Publications.

Timothy, D.J. (2011b) Foreword. In R.P.B. Singh (ed.) *Sacredscapes and Pilgrimage Landscapes* (pp. 1–4). New Delhi: Shubhi Publications.

Timothy, D.J. and Boyd, S.W. (2006) Heritage tourism in the 21st century: Valued traditions and new perspectives. *Journal of Heritage Tourism* 1 (1), 1–17.

Timothy, D.J. and Conover, P.J. (2006) Nature religion, self-spirituality and New Age tourism. In D.J. Timothy and D.H. Olsen (eds) *Tourism, Religion and Spiritual Journeys* (pp. 139–155). London: Routledge.

Timothy, D.J. and Saarinen, J. (2013) Cross-border co-operation and tourism in Europe. In C. Costa, E. Panyik and D. Buhalis (eds) *Trends in European Tourism Planning and Organisation* (pp. 64–74). Bristol: Channel View Publications.

Timothy, D.J. and Boyd, S.W. (2015) *Tourism and Trails: Cultural, Ecological and Management Issues*. Bristol: Channel View Publications.

Troen, I. and Rabineau, S. (2014) Competing concepts of land in Eretz Israel. *Israel Studies* 19 (2), 162–186.

Turner, V. (1973) The centre out there: Pilgrim's goal. *History of Religions* 12 (3), 191–230.

Turner, V. (1974) *Dramas, Fields and Metaphors: Symbolic Action in Human Society*. Ithaca, NY: Cornell University Press.

UNESCO (2016) World Heritage List. See http://whc.unesco.org/en/list/ (accessed 18 August 2016).

Wahlquist, W. (2014) Pioneer trails. In B.S. Plewe, S.K. Brown, D.Q. Cannon and R.H. Jackson (eds) *Mapping Mormonism: An Atlas of Latter-Day Saint History* (pp. 80–83). Provo, UT: BYU Press.

Webb, D. (1999) *Pilgrims and Pilgrimage in the Medieval West*. New York: I.B. Tauris.

Wright, J.B. (2014) The pilgrimage to Santiago de Compostela, Spain. *Focus on Geography* 57 (1), 25–40.

16 Reaching Out – Engagement Through Events and Festivals – The Cathedrals of England

Simon Curtis

Introduction

All religions are characterised by a focus on a calendar of events, yet the degree to which religion permeates the event and festival sector is much overlooked and frequently misunderstood. Traditionally, religious events closely follow the cycle of sacred beliefs which underpin the faiths, but there has also been a strong link with the celebration of the seasons and harvests. In Christianity, Easter and Christmas have formed the backbone of the event calendar for centuries and Lent is preceded by the busy Carnival season, especially in Catholic countries. These religious festivals have become ever more elongated, commercialised and exploited by wider society. This in itself is an interesting and long-standing trend but this chapter will concentrate its analytical eye on the link between the Christian church and the burgeoning event sector of the early 21st century. It will focus on (Anglican) cathedrals in England and investigate the extent to which these great institutions and buildings have harnessed their centuries-old skills and knowledge in the staging of events to explore new ways of reaching out to diverse audiences, whether local residents, tourists or pilgrims. It will reflect on the challenges and tensions that cathedrals must overcome to diversify their event portfolios and consider why events have become a much more significant aspect of their activity and mission. This review is underpinned by the author's professional interest in events and festivals and his own experience in managing a cathedral city destination (Rochester in the south-east of England). This has been supported by secondary research and through a series of interviews and discussions with senior cathedral representative during the summer of 2015. While the case studies are drawn from Anglican cathedrals, the trends and issues revealed have implications for cathedrals in Europe and beyond.

The Church of England Attendance Crisis

Before turning to cathedrals in detail, it is important to note the rather alarming fall in general churchgoing in England in recent decades. The latest statistics from the Church of England via the Archbishops' Council (2015) indicate that just under 1 million people (980,000) attend church services every week in England. On average, attendance is declining at the rate of 1% per year and regular churchgoers now represent just 2% of the adult population. As recently as 1950, the regular attendance figure was estimated at 3 million people, or nearly 8% of the then total adult population of England (Archbishop's Council, 2015).

Within this background of decreasing regular church attendance, the Church of England looks after 16,200 places of worship, of which almost 80% are listed buildings (Church of England, 2015). A growing proportion of these churches are effectively closed and mothballed; others open for occasional special services only. Taking its lead from the Churches Conservation Trust, which now owns nearly 400 redundant (but still consecrated) churches, the Church of England is actively exploring the idea of transforming underused churches into 'festival churches' (Church of England, 2015), essentially managed by local communities for community events and local cultural activity. Indeed, the Churches Conservation Trust have pioneered a number of innovative new uses for its buildings, ranging from a circus school to a well-being centre, to a network of 'glamping' sites where tourists can essentially camp in some comfort under the roof and security of the church.

English churches are rather belatedly reacting to the dramatic and sustained falls in church attendance but face enormous challenges. By comparison, the fate of English cathedrals has been much less severe in terms of regular attendance. Their size, locations and splendour have enabled them to adapt to and exploit new social and cultural trends, not least through the staging of an ever diverse calendar of events.

Cathedrals: A Prestige Collection of Tourist Attractions

There are 42 Anglican cathedrals in England (there are also 21 Catholic cathedrals though these have not been studied in detail as part of this research). Many of the 42 Anglican cathedrals are among the country's leading visitor attractions. The 'Big 6' cathedrals (St Paul's in London, Canterbury, Durham, Salisbury, Winchester and York) were visited by almost 3.5 million people in 2013 (Ecorys, 2014) with total tourist visits to all cathedrals estimated to be 8.25 million. Total visits to the Anglican cathedrals of England, including attendance at regular services, have been estimated at 11 million (Theos and Grubb Institute, 2012). Overall visitor numbers have been gradually increasing since the mid-1990s, mostly due to the burgeoning tourist economy of many of the great cathedral cities.

This has been partly driven by the increasing popularity of choral services (especially evensong), but it is also due to the widening portfolios of events that cathedrals have embraced.

Visitor numbers do vary markedly between categories of Anglican cathedral as shown in Table 16.1. The cathedrals which register most significantly in terms of tourist visits are the 24 cathedrals rated as of national and international significance by Ecorys (2014). These great churches attract nearly 80% of all the tourist visits to all English cathedrals and it is these cathedrals which have most successfully integrated into their local tourist economies.

It is not surprising that such cathedrals have embraced the visitor economy and become fully fledged tourist attractions. It could be argued that they were the earliest tourist attractions and that ancient pilgrims were a forerunner of today's cultural tourist. These cathedrals offer magnificent architectural spectacles, combining exterior precincts of great charm and mystique with interior spaces of remarkable scale and beauty. Visitor motivations are diverse but for many, cathedrals can offer a spiritual experience which lifts them above other cultural attractions. For the cathedrals, tourism offers much needed income through visitor donations and secondary spend at on-site shops and catering venues.

However, while tourists are attracted by the magnificence of these formidable buildings, some potential visitors are either reluctant to step through the cathedral entrance or indifferent to the experience which they offer. This may be related to religious beliefs or, for others, a feeling that cathedrals are rather elitist institutions, representing strict conformity and tradition. Such attitudes may be encouraged by the fact that some cathedrals are surrounded by walls and grand gates and several (albeit a distinct minority) have chosen to charge visitors an entry fee, an uncomfortable barrier for many.

Table 16.1 Visitor numbers to English cathedrals, 2013 (tourist/leisure visits only)[a]

Category	Number of cathedrals	Characteristics	Total visits in 2013
Large international	6	Large in scale; international reputation and significance	3,472,000
Medium-sized historic	18	Medieval origins but more national in scale and significance	2,943,000
Medium-sized modern	2	Twentieth-century cathedrals	199,000
Urban cathedrals	5	Less historic; located in highly dense and large urbanised cities	824,000
Parish churches	11	Smaller cathedrals; converted parish churches	812,000
Total	**42**		**8,250,000**

Source: Adapted from Ecorys (2014).
[a]Excludes regular attendance at daily religious services.

Despite their evident success in attracting visitors in recent decades, cathedrals have become aware that their audiences need to continue to grow and, most importantly, to diversify in profile. They have become more attuned to the advantages of developing and nurturing new audiences and to removing barriers of entry for those reluctant visitors. Events have provided an impetus to achieve this.

Events, Space and Place

For most tourist attractions, events are now an established feature of their strategic planning and management (Weidenfeld *et al.*, 2016). Events are used to create media profile, to attract custom outside the high season, to bring underused assets into production or to enhance the cultural offer of the attraction. They can be expensive and may involve risk, but successful events are regarded as an essential part of the tourist attraction business. The museum sector has led the way in recognising the values of their buildings and unique spaces to generate income from special events and also to be a platform for fundraising (Woodward, 2012). Cathedrals and other great historic buildings, like museums, have adopted more expansive event programmes partly as a natural process of establishing their identity as competitive tourist attractions and exploiting their considerable advantages as event spaces in heritage settings (Di Giovine, 2009).

Setting and spaces have a defining role to play in events; sometimes constraining them but often liberating and defining them. Most of England's great cathedrals enjoy generous spaces in the middle of atmospheric historic cities. The oldest cathedrals in particular are surrounded by precincts with gardens, greens, open spaces and cloisters. While some of the grounds require sensitive use, many of these open spaces provide wonderful event spaces in stunning settings, ideal for summer festivities and as backdrops for weddings and commercial events. The precincts tend to feature a wealth of interesting historic buildings which can be adapted for use as event and activity spaces. Where these are not available, the generous precincts of cathedrals have provided opportunities for sensitive new buildings to be added, and these have often been used as spaces to offer event, hospitality and catering facilities.

Cathedrals are among the largest and grandest of interior spaces which any event organiser could wish for. Naves with high vaulted ceilings, grand arches and galleries can provide breathtaking interiors for events with acoustics which are impossible to replicate in purpose-built event venues. Cathedrals offer prestige combined with authenticity, and add a gravitas to an event which few other venues can compete with. Innovative new portable technologies have meant that the lighting and staging needs of event organisers can be more easily accommodated within cathedrals and that the need to be sensitive within the historic context of the building is now less of a challenge to event operatives and technicians.

Dowson (2015) has highlighted the multiplicity of purposes for Anglican churches and cathedrals to hold events, but it is suggested here that cathedral events can be broadly categorised into three types:

- those associated with the liturgy and the core Christian mission of the church;
- events developed for or by the community and for cultural purposes;
- events developed with a primarily commercial objective.

Each of these is worthy of some detailed exploration.

Liturgical Events

The liturgy of a cathedral refers to the daily cycle of worship and services, a pattern that has been established for centuries. Most cathedrals will typically hold three or four services per day, consisting of communion, prayers and evensong, with extra services on a Sunday. In addition, there will be periodic choir practices and special sermons. Some of these require the closure of the cathedral to visitors, though most only necessitate restriction of access to certain areas. It is this daily performance and ritual within these great buildings that can substantially add to the spiritual experience of visitors. Music and choirs in particular are capable of enhancing the sensory reactions of visitors, temporarily lifting their thoughts above the clutter of the everyday. Such spiritual experiences are not necessarily religious and partly speak of the powerful and shifting combination of music, ritual, light and dark. The experience is akin to the concept of heterotopia (Foucault, 1986) whereby the visitor is taken into a sacred mind space which cannot be experienced in everyday life.

It is easy to underestimate how the ritualised nature of religion has influenced theatre and artistic performance over centuries, which has been well documented by cultural anthropologists such as Grainger (2009). Daily worship involves an element of music, parading, costuming and the creative use of light and sound. They are the natural business of the church, but they require an element of stagecraft. Such intrinsic experience in managing worship and staging services has proved invaluable as cathedrals have diversified into programming events which are additional to their core mission.

Cultural and Community Events

This category of events includes activities related to the role of cathedrals as iconic venues for music and cultural performance, and also reflects their missionary objectives around learning and education and a wider need to reach out to the local community.

Music has always been a central ethos of Christianity and the interiors of cathedrals are among the best acoustical spaces available to orchestras and musicians, whom they have inspired through the ages. Some commentators consider that cathedrals are the greatest expression of the relationship between music and architecture (Goldsmith & Major, n.d.). They work as sonic spaces as much for choirs as they do for jazz bands or modern electronic music. Musical concerts are the primary cultural use for cathedrals and indeed such concerts may be hosted in part for their contribution to raising commercial income through ticketing. Primarily, though, cathedrals are keen to present a varied music programme, not least to ensure that they are contributing to the cultural life of their cities. Cathedrals may develop their own festival of music, a well-known example being the Three Choirs Festival (n.d.) held annually between the three neighbouring cathedrals of Hereford, Gloucester and Worcester. More commonly, cathedrals are keen to play a role as the lead venue for their cities' own arts festivals. In Norwich, for example, the cathedral regularly hosts concerts as part of the two-week-long Norfolk and Norwich Arts Festival in May. Canterbury Cathedral has long been the venue for headline productions for the Canterbury Festival in October, hosting prestige performances of visiting international orchestras, film screenings and theatrical productions.

In addition to their participation in city arts festivals, cathedrals have also increasingly become involved in national cultural festivals such as Heritage Open Days, a four-day festival managed by the National Trust and designed to open rarely seen heritage buildings and sites to the public. Another example is the nationally staged Big Draw Festival held to celebrate drawing as a tool for learning and expression, which has been embraced by several Anglican cathedrals.

After musical events, the second most prevalent event at cathedrals is the temporary 'museum style' exhibition. These may be composed of artworks or be based around items held in the cathedral treasuries and archives. Major national occasions and historical anniversaries are increasingly marked by cathedrals as part of their collaborative cultural missions. Rochester Cathedral held a special service, exhibition and film screenings in 2012 to mark the 200th anniversary of the birth of Charles Dickens who lived close to the city for many years; in 2015, a number of cathedrals (Salisbury, Worcester, Canterbury, Hereford, Lincoln) marked the 800th anniversary of the Magna Carta with special exhibitions; and in 2016, to mark the 400th anniversary of the death of Shakespeare, several cathedrals (Southwark, Lichfield, Hereford, Norwich) staged events ranging from outdoor theatre to exhibitions and talks.

There are examples of some cathedrals pushing the boundaries and taking more programming risks with cultural events. In October 2015, Manchester Cathedral hosted several nights of science fiction films for the Manchester Science Festival; York Minster invited local street artists into the cathedral in 2015 to create original spray paint works which then went on exhibition; the cloisters of Westminster Abbey[1] hosted a fashion show for Italian fashion company Gucci in June 2016.

The extent to which a cathedral is utilized for cultural use, especially exhibitions, is partly determined by its spaces but also by the availability, or lack, of alternative venues in the city (Theos and Grubb Institute, 2012). There is also a strong link to the cathedral educational programme, a means by which it seeks to provide for local schools but also to widen its audience by delivering outreach talks, workshops and projects throughout the city and diocese (the wider district over which a cathedral has ecclesiastical authority).

Despite their reputation as hosts of substantial and high profile events, cathedrals often are also highly active as hosts of much smaller-scale community events. These act as a powerful agent for building relationships within the cathedral community of volunteers and staff as well as the immediate city community and reflect the desire for communities to find a sense of belonging through shared values (Dowson, 2015).

Commercial Events

Anglican cathedrals receive no regular state or public sector funding. Project funding from public conservation agencies such as English Heritage has declined in recent years. Cathedrals are expensive to maintain and conserve, not least as they comprise a range of buildings besides the great churches themselves. They also need to fund their day-to-day running, which includes salaries for their paid staff. The daily running costs of a cathedral is estimated at anything from £12,000 to £20,000 (Maxtone Graham, 2016). Cathedrals are constantly raising funds through the charitable work of their Friends (independent charities with a membership scheme) and volunteers, and at any one time there may be several fundraising campaigns running. Donations are of course important, but the financial challenges mean that any additional income which can be earned from commercial methods has become more significant. Raising revenue commercially can be controversial for a cathedral and this has been demonstrated by some adverse publicity related to charging an entry fee for visitors at cathedrals such as St Paul's in London, and also at Canterbury, York, Ely and Winchester. Raising revenue from commercial activities such as catering, retail and events is far less controversial, provided that all three are sited, managed and delivered in an appropriate and professional way.

All cathedrals are part of and involved in the corporate events market. Conferences, meetings and corporate dinners are the most lucrative of commercial events. Cathedrals actively market themselves as 'venues for hire' to the corporate market, with success being largely an outcome of the quality of the facilities on offer. While the cathedral nave can be used for gala dinners or awards ceremonies, most corporate events require more private meetings spaces and these are typically accommodated in purpose-built facilities (Southwark and Canterbury provide good examples) or within converted historic buildings situated within the precincts. A number of cathedrals have instituted breakfast clubs, using their meeting rooms to build relationships with local businesses who may be persuaded to hold more lucrative dinners and events within the main cathedral at a future date.

The Christmas period is inevitably a busy one in terms of increased worship and community carol singing services, but it also provides opportunities to raise commercial income through the hosting of Christmas markets and events. Winchester Cathedral's generous green has provided a spectacular site for an ice rink and Christmas market over the last decade (Figure 16.1). Such events do of course provide a community resource, and it could be argued that they exemplify a crossover in terms of cultural and commercial events, but the defining objective is a commercial one.

Figure 16.1 Winchester Cathedral: Christmas advertisement

Another example of a crossover event is Chichester Cathedral's Festival of Flowers, a biennial event over three days in June when the ancient medieval cathedral is transformed by up to 100 floral arrangements, accompanied by musical performances, sculptures and a garden fayre within the precincts. Ticket prices for the 2016 event started at £10 and sold out in advance (Chichester Cathedral, 2016).

Graduation ceremonies have become important commercial events for those cathedrals located in cities with universities, which have found that cathedrals provide a suitably prestigious venue for graduates and their families on such a life-marking day (Figure 16.2). The precincts and green spaces of cathedrals provide space for marquees as reception areas following the ceremonies. Some cathedrals host in excess of 10 days of back-to-back ceremonies in any one year.

Figure 16.2 A graduation day at Canterbury Cathedral (Source: Curtis, 2016)

One cathedral which has a well-earned reputation for developing commercial income through events is Liverpool Cathedral. It enjoys the largest internal area of any of England's Anglican cathedrals and has been able to exploit this advantage to host evening dinners and awards ceremonies for up to 1000 guests. It has also hosted special events for companies celebrating corporate success or anniversaries, such as Cunard.

Liverpool Cathedral cut its teeth as an events venue during the city's year as European Capital of Culture in 2008 and has developed a bold and innovative attitude to event programming ever since, including the hosting of occasional rock concerts as part of the Sound City Festival, designed to support breakthrough music artists. It employs a director of enterprise who has asserted that 'enterprise is integral to the mission of the Cathedral – we are providing a safe place to do risky things in Christ's service' (It's Liverpool, 2016).

Case Study: Salisbury Cathedral

Salisbury Cathedral, located in the county of Wiltshire in the south of England, is considered to be one of the 'Big 6' cathedrals and is noted for its tall spire and its vast precinct close, the largest in the UK. It hosts in excess of 1500 services, concerts and other events each year and is committed to working with the local destination management organisation (DMO), Visit Wiltshire, as well as more collaborative working with other major local tourist attractions such as the city museum and Stonehenge, just outside the city (Salisbury Cathedral, 2016). While it does not have an events policy, it does have a visual arts policy and the success of its arts exhibition programme over the last decade has both stimulated linked cultural events as well as inspiring a more open and proactive attitude to events activity. Events are seen as providing a means of diversifying the cathedral audience, and ultimately the regular congregation, and creating useful material for the learning and outreach programme. Staffing capacity has been increased in recent years and there are now two full-time events officers, according to Salisbury Cathedral's director of learning and outreach (Curtis, 2016). This has allowed the development of event skills and expertise within the permanent team.

The most established cultural event at the cathedral is its triennial hosting of the Southern Cathedrals Festival, a choral and musical festival staged annually and in rotation between Salisbury and neighbouring Winchester and Chichester cathedrals. The cathedral is also a core venue for the city's major annual festival, the Salisbury International Arts Festival. Other annual events now include a fashion week, an outdoor contemporary craft and heritage fayre and 'have a go' carving and painting workshops. Occasional historical anniversaries are used as a platform for one-off major events, a good example having taken place in 2015 with the 800th anniversary of the Magna Carta, the most complete version of which belongs to Salisbury Cathedral. A special exhibition based around the iconic manuscript was held together with a series of events, including plays, re-enactments, concerts and debates.

The full event programme was supported by HLF funding and helped the cathedral to achieve record visitor numbers in 2015 (Salisbury Cathedral, 2016).

The cathedral refectory and chapter house are the main focus points for commercial events and certain areas within the close are also available for private marquee hire. The cathedral nave, quire and chapel spaces can be hired by commercial organisations or private individuals, with fees and charges displayed on the cathedral's main website. Additional charges apply for staffing support, staging, lighting and other equipment hire.

The Role of the Heritage Lottery Fund

The Heritage Lottery Fund (HLF) has emerged as an influential and positive funding and guiding organisation to English (and wider UK) cathedrals in recent years. It was created in 1994 as one of the 'good cause' organisations designed to distribute part of the proceeds from the national lottery scheme. It has awarded over £7 billion in funds to heritage buildings and projects since its inception (Heritage Lottery Fund, 2012).

The HLF is aware of the challenging financial needs of places of worship and recognises their need to diversify activity and income generation initiatives. It has a number of different grant schemes; some designed for small and short-term projects, others for major long-term transformative projects. While conservation needs and building repairs often form part of these transformative projects, the HLF encourages cathedrals to develop projects that meet its priorities of encouraging community participation, fostering local partnership, improving accessibility and becoming more financially resilient and sustainable. A great deal of work is required from cathedral fundraisers to develop a large HLF project, with several rounds of bidding taking place. They can be between three and five years in development and require detailed business, activity and conservation planning. Crucially, the HLF encourages cathedrals to increase their staffing capacity as part of the bid and project process.

The HLF increased its share of lottery income after 2013 and a number of major funding projects are now in the formative stage. Canterbury Cathedral's £20 million 'Journey' project is set to receive £12 million from the HLF not only to fund urgent fabric repairs but also to improve intellectual and physical access to the precincts via a new welcome centre and landscaped visitor trails. Lincoln Cathedral's £16 million 'Connected' project has an £11 million HLF grant earmarked for a new interpretation centre and restaurant and the creation of new outdoor event spaces (Heritage Lottery Fund, n.d.).

It is likely that there will be more of these transformative projects taking place at cathedrals over the next decade. For schemes of this type, the HLF sees events and activities as a core element of the projects' outputs and as a mechanism for the cathedrals achieving their objectives related to community reach and increased participation.

Overcoming Challenges and Emergent Themes

Some significant themes have emerged from this review of event activity at Anglican cathedrals. Cathedrals continue to embrace their roles as tourist attractions representing and often leading the identities of their cities. There remain barriers to activity at some cathedrals more than others; nevertheless, there is enough evidence to suggest that cathedrals will be increasingly pushing the boundaries in terms of the frequency and content of non-religious and commercial events in the coming years. Tensions are sure to emerge from time to time but the tolerant attitude which the Anglican church personifies gives English cathedrals a unique ability to adapt to and indeed reflect societal and cultural change. Each of these will be considered in more detail.

Cathedrals often define the cities in which they are located, especially those traditional and ancient English cities which were not heavily industrialised, such as Lincoln, Durham, Wells and Ely. Many of the historic cathedral cities of England are long-established tourism destinations with an infrastructure to exploit such status, including heritage attractions, high-quality public realm and a lively cultural events programme. Cathedrals have increasingly embraced their local tourist industries. They have recognised the commercial opportunities that tourism brings but also appreciate that the tourist audience can unlock funding to invest in their built fabric and their learning missions. Visitors want to discover the stories of the cathedrals' histories and these need to be interpreted and presented in an imaginative way. Tourism thus not only unlocks new revenue possibilities but also unlocks understanding and participation, aspects which the HLF has encouraged with its funding priorities. Cathedrals have also engaged in the wider strategic aspects of tourism and its impact on city image and identity. Many cathedrals are represented on the boards of their county or city DMO and representatives of cathedrals engage with city-wide partnership marketing and regeneration initiatives. They have become much more outwardly focused and involved in partnership and collaborative work across the full spectrum of local culture, community and business.

There are still substantial barriers and restrictions to event activity, and much depends on the individual characteristics, locations and built environment of each cathedral. The main practical barrier for all cathedrals is the daily calendar of worship and liturgy. This does still leave opportunities on certain days and especially during the evenings and of course only tends to impact the main cathedral building and not the surrounding precincts and outer buildings. Some cathedrals are more fortunate than others in possessing generous grounds, spaces and unique heritage buildings which can form exciting indoor and outdoor event spaces.

There are philosophical barriers, usually where the dean and chapter retain a conservative attitude to extending event activity or where they are reluctant to empower their visitor and event staff. There may also be market barriers to event ambitions, where the city has a diverse supply of event venues, where a neighbouring cathedral is relatively close and acts as a competitor venue or if the local corporate market is rather subdued and underdeveloped (especially in small cities such as Wells).

Despite these barriers, there is no doubt that cathedrals are becoming bolder and less risk averse in planning their event programmes. They are more willing to become engaged in city-wide festival activity and they have become convinced of the capacity of events to develop their overall reach and diversify their audiences. The community which surrounds them is a more secular one and, where faith exists, Christianity is increasingly working alongside other faiths. Provided that their core Christian mission and liturgy is protected, there is scope to find new ways of reaching out and connecting to people. The Christian world is a more secular place and Christian institutions have had to adapt to this. In addition, as Ostwalt (2012) has suggested, popular culture is becoming more sacred and individuals find spirituality in a variety of ways and cultural forms, many of which religious sites can embrace and capture. Where the boundaries have been pushed and events have been held that have raised eyebrows, there is little evidence of profanity or sustained controversy. Anglican cathedrals have a tradition for experimentation in architecture, art and music and are likely to be attracted by new forms of cultural expression in the future. Critics have referred to this future transition as a 'spiritual supermarket' but they ignore the fact that post-modern consumption can be motivated as much by community and moral motives as by commerce and materialism (Redden, 2016).

Conclusions

Ultimately, the Christian spirit is about tolerance and the bishops, deans and clergy of English cathedrals recognise that this requires opening up and reaching out in permissive and insecure times. People are seeking spirituality and meaning in their lives, but this can come through a variety of experiences, often not directly related to religious services. Cathedrals are using events to engage the business person, the graduate, the festivalgoer, the jazz music fan and even the fashionista into finding some spiritual value and to perhaps becoming the regular attender, volunteer or friend of the future.

Note

(1)   Westminster Abbey is classified as an abbey church rather than a cathedral.

References

Archbishops' Council (2015) *Cathedral Statistics 2014*. London: Archbishops' Council.
Chichester Cathedral (2016) Festival of flowers 2016. See http://www.chichestercathedral. org.uk/whats-on/festival-of-flowers-2016 (accessed 14 July 2016).
Church of England (2015) Report of the Church Buildings Review Group. See www. churchofengland.org (accessed 8 December 2016).
Curtis, S. (2016) English cathedrals: Events and spiritual capital. *International Journal of Religious Tourism and Pilgrimage* 4 (2), Article 3.
Di Giovine, M. (2009) *The Heritage-scape: UNESCO, World Heritage and Tourism*. Lanham, MD: Lexington Books.
Dowson, R. (2015) Religion, community and events. In A. Jepson and A. Clarke (eds) *Exploring Community Festivals and Events* (pp. 169–186). Abingdon:, Routledge.
Ecorys (2014) *The Economic and Social Impacts of England's Cathedrals*. London: Association of English Cathedrals.
Foucault, M. (1986) Other spaces: The principles of heterotopia. *Lotus International* 48/49, 9–17.
Goldsmith, M. and Major, D. (n.d.) Cathedrals and music. See http://www.npr.org/ programs/specials/milestones/991103.motm.cathedrals (accessed 14 July 2016).
Grainger, R. (2009) *The Drama of the Rite: Worship, Liturgy and Theatre Performance*. Eastbourne: Sussex Academic Press.
Heritage Lottery Fund (2012) *Strategic Framework 2013–2018: A Lasting Difference for Heritage and People*. London: Heritage Lottery Fund.
Heritage Lottery Fund (n.d.) See https://www.hlf.org.uk (accessed 14 July 2016).
It's Liverpool (2016) Live at Liverpool Anglican Cathedral. See http://www.itsliverpool. com/commerce/hymms-liverpool-cathedral (accessed 20 June 2016).
Maxtone Graham, Y. (2016) The price of a cathedral – and how deans pay it. *Spectator Magazine*, 26 March. See http://www.spectator.co.uk/2016/03/the-price-of-a-cathedral-and-how-deans-pay-it (accessed 12 July 2016).
Ostwalt, C. (2012) *Secular Steeples: Popular Culture and the Religious Imagination* (2nd edn). London: Bloomsbury.
Redden, G. (2016) Revisiting the spiritual supermarket: Does the commodification of spirituality necessarily devalue it? *Culture and Religion* 17 (2), 231–249.
Salisbury Cathedral (2016) Strategy 2013–17 and Programme 2016–17. See http://www. salisburycathedral.org.uk (accessed 8 December 2016).
Theos and Grubb Institute (2012) *Spiritual Capital: The Present and Future of English Cathedrals*. London: Theos and Grubb Institute.
Three Choirs Festival Association (n.d.) See http://www.3choirs.org (accessed 12 July 2016).
Weidenfeld, A., Butler, R.W. and Williams, A.M. (2016) *Visitor Attractions and Events*. Abingdon: Routledge.
Woodward, S. (2012) Funding museum agendas: Challenges and opportunities. *Managing Leisure* 17 (1), 14–28.

17 Tourism, Salt Lake City and the Cultural Heritage of Mormonism

Daniel H. Olsen and Dallen J. Timothy

Introduction

Tourism is big business for the state of Utah. In 2014, tourists spent approximately US$7.98 billion in the state and generated US$1.09 billion in tax revenue. The same year, tourism employed 137,200 people directly and indirectly. During 2015, Utah achieved record high visitation, making tourism the state's highest-earning export industry (Fonseca, 2015; Jorgensen, 2015; Larsen, 2016; Leaver, 2016; Nemeth, 2015). Tourists visit Utah to enjoy the state's outdoor recreational resources and experience its cultural heritage. Utah is home to many national and state parks, numerous famous ski resorts and the celebrated Sundance Film Festival, which draw enormous numbers of tourists each year (Leaver, 2016). Utah's rich cultural heritage includes among other things, pioneer trails (e.g. the Mormon and Oregon Trails) and settler communities, Native American heritage, Old West and mining history, numerous archaeological sites and immigrant heritage (Davis *et al.*, 2009).

Salt Lake City (SLC), the state capital, is sometimes called 'the crossroads of the West' because of its contemporary position as a centralised meeting point of major cross-country transportation corridors, including its international airport, which is a major air transport hub for Utah and the broader Intermountain West. More precisely, however, this moniker derived primarily from SLC's historical role as a major junction and nucleus for overland migration routes, explorer trails, communications corridors (e.g. the Pony Express), and eventually the location where the western and eastern portions of the first Transcontinental Railroad were connected in 1869. Secondarily, it is an important crossroads owing to its relative centrality to many of the Intermountain West's national and state parks, ski resorts and other urban centres.

SLC – indeed the entire state of Utah – is also indelibly connected to The Church of Jesus Christ of Latter-day Saints (the LDS Church or Mormon Church) and the centre of what some cultural geographers refer to as the 'Mormon culture region' because of the dominance of the Mormon culture and its influence on the creation of a distinctive human geography (Eliason, 2006; Francaviglia, 1978, 2003; Meinig, 1965; Szasz, 2004; Toney *et al.*, 2003; Yorgason, 2003). As the headquarters and *axis mundi* of the LDS Church, millions of Mormon and non-Mormon tourists visit SLC and Mormon Church-related sites each year. As well, the LDS Church has purposely restored and maintained a number of historic religious sites for the purpose of attracting visitors, making the LDS Church not just the object of the tourist gaze but also a creator of religious and heritage tourism opportunities (Olsen, 2009, 2013, 2016).

This chapter examines the interplay between SLC, tourism and the LDS Church. After a short introduction to the church, the authors briefly discuss how members of the LDS Church function as religious tourists. The chapter then looks at the historical and current context of tourism in SLC and the interplay between the state and city governments and the church in creating a unique religious tourism environment in the western United States.

Mormons as Religious Tourists

The Church of Jesus Christ of Latter-day Saints was founded in 1830 in Fayette, New York, by Joseph Smith Jr. in response to divine revelation and confusion about the contradictory doctrines being taught by other Christian sects of that time. The church grew rapidly in the eastern United States and eventually the Midwest as people were attracted to the primitive principles of Christianity taught by Smith. However, some doctrines and practices that Smith introduced, including baptisms for the dead, modern-day revelation, spiritual manifestations, rejection of the Trinity, abhorrence of slavery, polygamy (eventually prohibited by the church in 1890) and the introduction of a new book of scripture, *The Book of Mormon*, in addition to the Bible, led to antagonistic relations with the non-Mormon community, particularly among other Christian religious leaders. Rhetorical and physical persecution forced the church headquarters to relocate from New York to Ohio, then to Missouri and eventually to Illinois. There, while awaiting trial on falsified charges, Joseph Smith was killed by a mob of armed men (for more information on the history of the LDS Church see Arrington, 1979; Arrington & Bitton, 1992; Bushman, 2005; Givens, 2004; Smith, 1991). While several people vied for control of the organisation, the majority of church members followed Brigham Young, who led them to the valley of the Great Salt Lake and established present-day SLC in 1847 (Arrington, 1985; Turner, 2012).

At the turn of the 20th century, as the first generation of Latter-day Saints began to pass away, church leaders sought to replace their 'living history' with a tangible heritage by identifying, purchasing, marking and restoring historic sites related to the founding of the church and its westward movement (Olsen, 2013). In what Erekson (2005) calls the 'century of commemoration', the church was active throughout the 20th century in its memorialisation and commemoration efforts. After purchasing Carthage Jail (in Illinois), the site of Joseph Smith's martyrdom, church leaders acquired numerous other sites of historical significance in Illinois, Missouri, Ohio, Vermont, New York and Pennsylvania (Olsen, 2013: 229), as well as many sites along the 2092-km Mormon Trail, which was used by some 70,000 LDS immigrants and refugees to arrive in the Salt Lake Valley in the late 19th century (see Chapter 15, this volume). Today, the church continues to acquire properties of historical importance (e.g. Askar, 2014) because of its emphasis on tangible and intangible heritage as a way of building spiritual strength through its pioneering and 'restored gospel' (restorationist) narratives (Figure 17.1). As during the 20th century, properties are acquired today through the generous donations of church members. At many of these historic sites, the church has built visitor centres that are staffed by volunteer missionary guides and interpreters. These sites and visitor centres have a fivefold purpose: to preserve and protect the hallowed places associated with the church's history and development; to provide visitor information to LDS and non-LDS visitors; to liaise with the broader community and construct a positive image in the regions where they are located; to proselytise among non-Mormon visitors and bear witness of Jesus Christ and the restoration of his church; and to help LDS visitors substantiate their own identities and build their faith and testimonies (Olsen, 2013, 2016).

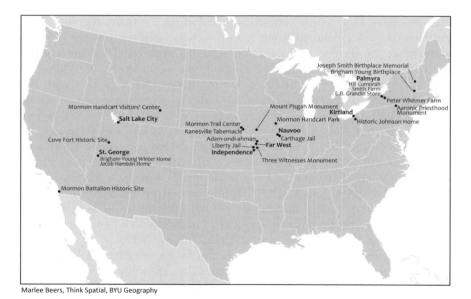

Marlee Beers, Think Spatial, BYU Geography

Figure 17.1 Key Mormon historical sites (Created by Think Spatial, BYU)

As stories of the church's early history and the Mormon pioneers play a prominent role in Mormon collective memory, church leaders and local organisations have initiated a number of events and celebrations to commemorate these stories and to unite members of this growing global faith around sacred narratives of the past (Olsen, 1992). For example, every year on July 24, church members celebrate Pioneer Day, which commemorates Brigham Young's arrival to the Salt Lake Valley on that day in 1847. Although the main celebration is held in SLC with parades, fireworks and other significant events, many towns in the 'Mormon culture region' of the western United States and LDS congregations around the world celebrate this 'greatest of Mormon holidays' (O'Dea, 1957: 82, cited in Olsen, 1996: 160) on a much smaller scale, which usually includes a day of community service (Eliason, 2002; Kuruvilla, 2015; Lloyd, 1997; Olsen, 1996; Smith & White, 2004; Stock, 2009; Welch, 2016).

Some LDS congregations or area units also sponsor youth handcart trek re-enactments of the early Mormon pioneers. The church has developed an official guidebook and a three-part video series to help local leaders organise these treks (Intellectual Reserve, 2015). These pioneer re-enactments are in essence 'a ritual of youth spiritual formation', where young men and women experience first-hand the trials the early pioneers withstood for their faith. These experiences aim to ground participants in a sacred past and 'create a spiritual affinity between the pioneers and contemporary Mormons' (Bielo, 2016: 5, 7). These handcart re-enactments increased in popularity in 1997 when church leaders strongly emphasised the 150th anniversary of the pioneers entering the Salt Lake Valley (Merrill, 2010; Smith, 1999). While local congregations around the world re-enact the handcart trek on private land, the LDS Church presently owns 10 tracts of land dedicated to trek activities in Utah, Wyoming, California, Washington, Florida, Oklahoma and Argentina (Bielo, 2016).

Since the 1930s, local organisations within the LDS Church have sponsored a series of pageants that tell about the church's history, honour the early pioneers and celebrate the life and ministry of Jesus (Bielo, 2016; Bushman, 2009; Gurgel, 1976; LoMonaco, 2009). These pageants, with a couple of exceptions, are generally held outdoors on temporary stages near important church history sites or close to LDS temples. Some pageants focus on local or regional church histories, while others focus on broader doctrinal and historical events (Hunter, 2013). These pageants are especially popular among local Mormon populations, but they are continuing to draw an ever-increasing number of non-Mormon spectators as well and have received attention from the national news media (e.g. Applebome, 2011). Perhaps the most famous of all these spectacles is the Hill Cumorah Pageant in Palmyra, New York. It is held on the hill where Joseph Smith is believed to have received the ancient plates from which he translated *The Book of Mormon*. It involves a cast of 700, and

Table 17.1 Church-sponsored pageants in the United States

Name of pageant	Location	Description	Sources/websites
Mesa Easter Pageant: Jesus the Christ	Mesa, Arizona	Tells the story of Jesus Christ's life and ministry through dance and music. This pageant is considered to be the 'largest annual outdoor Easter pageant in the world'.	Griffiths, 2007; https://www.lds.org/locations/mesa-arizona-temple-visitors-center?lang=eng&_r=1
Nauvoo Pageant	Nauvoo, Illinois	The Nauvoo Pageant is a tribute to Joseph Smith and follows the building of the city of Nauvoo.	Austin, 2015; Whatcott, 2014; https://www.lds.org/locations/nauvoo-visitors-center?lang=eng&_r=1
The Hill Cumorah Pageant: America's Witness for Christ	Palmyra, New York	The pageant depicts the main storylines in *The Book of Mormon*, which involve a family that left Jerusalem around 600 BC and settled in the Americas, and culminates in Joseph Smith finding and translating the ancient record they left behind.	Applebome, 2011; Argetsinger, 2004; Armstrong and Argetsinger, 1989; Bielo, 2016; McHale, 1985; http://hillcumorah.org
Castle Valley Pageant	Castle Dale, Utah	The pageant highlights local the pioneer settlement of the area.	Haddock, 2012; Taniguchi, 2004; https://www.facebook.com/CastleValleyPageant
Clarkston Pageant – Martin Harris: The Man Who Knew	Clarkston, Utah	This pageant outlines the life of Martin Harris, who was key in publishing *The Book of Mormon*. Harris lived in Clarkston during the last few years of his life.	Poppleton, 2013; https://www.facebook.com/ClarkstonPageant
The Mormon Miracle Pageant	Manti, Utah	The pageant portrays three different faith-promoting storylines from church history.	Bean, 2005; Johnson, 2016; http://mantipageant.org/

approximately 50,000 people attend the 70-minute play during its run in July each year (Applebome, 2011; Bielo, 2016). In recent years, these pageants have become high-tech spectacles, complete with intricate costumes, sophisticated lighting and sound systems, stuntmen, original prerecorded music and elaborate special effects (Bell, 2013; Hunter, 2013). Table 17.1 provides a list of these pageants in the United States.

With the LDS Church embracing tourism as part of its evangelical and pastoral mission (Hansen, 2010; Olsen, 2009, 2011, 2013, 2016), many members of the church engage in what might be called 'faith tourism', which is sometimes used as 'a catchword for a non-pilgrimage multifaith style of tourism to religious sites mainly undertaken by Christians' (Stausberg, 2011: 156). Even though there is no formal prescription for undertaking traditional pilgrimages in LDS Church theology (Madsen, 2008; McConkie, 1966; Olsen, 2006, 2013), thousands of Latter-day Saints travel to sites related to the Bible, *The Book of Mormon* and church history, being motivated by a desire to see the sites for themselves and to seek spiritual enlightenment (Hudman & Jackson, 1992; Olsen, 2006).

Owing to the absence of doctrine and obligation associated with formal pilgrimage in the church, the term 'pilgrimage' is not typically part of the LDS religious lexicon, and few Mormon travellers would consider themselves to be 'pilgrims' in the traditional sense of the word.

Hudman and Jackson (1992) and Olsen (2006) have suggested that Latter-day Saints who travel with religious motives can be segmented into four different markets, each of which has its own specialised tour agencies. The first is travel to church history sites (see Figure 17.1). Church members visit these locations 'to engage with the material remnants and reminders of [their religious] history' (Mitchell, 2001: 9). While the LDS Church is not usually forthcoming with visitor statistics, Lloyd (2011, cited in Olsen, 2013: 227) estimated that in 2010 over 4 million people visited church historic sites, with just over 500,000 of those being non-Mormons. Many LDS travel guidebooks have been written to help church members find and interpret historic sites throughout the world and to help them locate other tourist services (e.g. Kimball, 1988; Oscarson & Kimball, 1965; Smith, 2003).

The second LDS market is travel to the Holy Land. In common with other Christian denominations, the LDS Church deems very sacred the lands associated with the life and ministry of Jesus and the early apostles (Galbraith et al., 1996). They are ardent travellers to sites of the birth, ministry and crucifixion of Jesus Christ, as well as the locales in Turkey, Greece and Italy associated with the apostle Paul and his followers (Guter, 1997, 2006; Ron & Timothy, in preparation). In addition to the celebrated sites associated with Jesus, a few LDS-specific tourism sites in the Holy Land are popular among Mormon tourists. Brigham Young University (BYU), affiliated with the LDS Church, built the BYU Jerusalem Centre (see Figure 10.1, this volume) to enhance students' on-site learning about the Holy Land. There, students study the Old Testament, New Testament, ancient and modern Near Eastern studies, Hebrew and Arabic (Olsen, 2006; Olsen & Guelke, 2004). Another Mormon-specific sacred site in Israel is the Orson Hyde Memorial Garden on the Mount of Olives, which commemorates the 1841 visit of LDS apostle, Orson Hyde, who offered a dedicatory prayer over the Holy Land for the gathering of the Jews. As well, the graves of two 19th-century Mormon missionaries in Haifa, who died of illnesses while proselytising among the German immigrant population in that city, are venerated as sacred space by many LDS tour groups in the Holy Land.

The third type of LDS religious tourism refers to travel to *The Book of Mormon* lands. Most Mormon historians, geographers and archaeologists believe that the events recorded in *The Book of Mormon* took place in Meso-America. Several tour operators offer land-based 'Book of Mormon tours' that emphasise the ancient civilisations of Belize, Mexico, Guatemala and Honduras. Other operators offer 'Book of Mormon cruises', where LDS groups travel together, usually accompanied by a well-known scriptural scholar.

On board, they have frequent study meetings and lectures, and once at port in Belize or Mexico, group members are taken to visit ancient Maya ruins that are interpreted from an LDS doctrinal viewpoint (Ron & Timothy, in preparation). Mormon travellers go to Meso-America to gain 'a greater understanding of the cultural and historical context in which [*The Book of Mormon*] was written' (Olsen, 2006: 263).

Mormons travelling to temples represent the fourth type of LDS religious tourism. Mormon temples differ from churches or meetinghouses in that the latter can be found throughout the world and are used on Sundays for worship services and throughout the week for other activities. Temples, on the other hand, are less common and are utilised for extremely sacred ordinances and rites, such as eternal marriages and baptisms on behalf the dead who did not have an opportunity to know the gospel of Jesus Christ during mortality. Temples are the most sacred spaces in Mormonism and are open only to church members, except during open houses immediately following the completion of construction, when members of the general public are invited to visit. Mormons travel to temples to participate in important ordinances and to receive instruction for applying the gospel and teachings of Christ in their own lives (Packer, 1980). As these rituals and covenants are an important part of LDS eschatology, travel to temples is semi-obligatory and thereby closely resembles traditional pilgrimage-like travel (Hudman & Jackson, 1992; Olsen, 2006). Temple construction is directly linked to the growth of the church, which now has more than 15 million members in nearly every country on earth. As of 2017, there were 156 operating temples around the world with four being renovated, 11 under construction and the construction of 14 new temples had been announced (The Church of Jesus Christ of Latter-day Saints, 2017). Most temples are located in urban centres, which requires many church members to travel hundreds of kilometres to engage in temple worship. While temple work is their primary objective, many families and church groups combine their experiences in sacred space with more traditional tourist activities in profane spaces, creating as many Christian pilgrims do, a combined pilgrimage and holiday experience.

In addition to travel to sites related to church history outside of SLC, *The Book of Mormon*, temples or the Holy Land, they also travel to SLC to visit church headquarters – sometimes referred to as the 'Mormon Vatican' (Associated Press, 2006; Szasz, 2004: 50) or the 'St. Peters of the New World' (Bishop & Holzaphel, 1993) – to sightsee, live or study (Eliason, 2006). From a religious perspective, Latter-day Saints consider the Church Campus, and in particular Temple Square, first and foremost a sacred site (Jackson & Henrie, 1983). As noted above, Temple Square is the *axis mundi* of Mormonism, and therefore exerts a strong centripetal force among members of the church (Olsen, 2002) because of its central place in the history and operations of the church and its function as a major centre of worship, ritual and instruction. Many LDS members who travel to SLC visit Temple Square and its surrounding blocks to learn more about their spiritual or religious roots and to enhance their faith. Of particular interest is the Salt Lake Temple, the most famous and iconic LDS temple in the world (Jackson & Henrie, 1983). While the Salt Lake Temple was not the first Mormon temple to be built, it is an emblem of the faith and devotion of the earliest pioneer church members and symbolic of the founding of a permanent homeland for the LDS Church and its members in the Salt Lake Valley.

Mormonism as a Religious Attraction

Apart from Utah's parklands and ski resorts, the LDS Church is the major draw to the state for non-Mormon tourists (Associated Press, 2006) and has been so since the late 1800s. The most salient attraction of all is Temple Square in downtown SLC. To tourism officials and industry leaders, Temple Square is a bonafide cultural heritage tourist attraction and is marketed commercially as such by the city and the state (Bishop & Holzaphel, 1993; Ioannides & Timothy, 2010; Jackson, 1988; Visit Salt Lake, 2016).

While obviously not originally built as a tourist attraction, Temple Square is in fact the flagship of heritage tourism in the state. It is the most visited attraction in Utah with an estimated 4.5–5 million visitors annually, approximately half of whom are not Mormons (Olsen, 2009, 2013). Temple Square thus receives as many visitors as Utah's ski resorts (there were approximately 4.5 million skiers during the 2015–2016 ski season) (McCombs, 2016) and half the number of visitors to Utah's state and national parks (approximately 10 million in 2015) (Leaver, 2016).

When Brigham Young entered the Salt Lake Valley, his first order of business was to mark a location for the temple, for temples, as noted above, are the most sacred places for the Latter-day Saints. Temples also mark an established Mormon presence in an area and act as an ideological and physical centre for the surrounding Mormon community (Hudman & Jackson, 1992; Parry, 1994; Timothy, 1992). The completion of the Salt Lake Temple was seen as a partial fulfilment of Isaiah's (2:2) prophecy in the Old Testament that in the last days 'the mountain of the Lord's house shall be established in the top of the mountains'. Young began to organise the Saints following the Plat of Zion plan developed by Joseph Smith in Nauvoo, Illinois, where land would be divided into a large grid pattern with the temple in the middle to symbolise order and community (Bradley, 2004, 2005; Jackson, 1977). The location of the temple, known as the 'Temple Block', was 10 acres in size, and after ground was broken for the building in 1853 the Temple Block soon became a 'communal centre of mechanical industry' (Cannon, 1959: 251). In addition to the Salt Lake Temple (completed in 1893), the Temple Block was home to the Tabernacle where conferences were held, an assembly hall and a 4.5-meter security wall (Cannon, 1959; Mitchell, 1967; Peterson, 2002; Rasmus, 1992; Zobell, 1967). With the Temple Block anchoring the new city, Young began to establish what he hoped would be a religious utopia.

However, with the connection of the Transcontinental Railway in 1869, and the discovery of precious metals in Utah the same year, thousands of non-Mormons began settling in SLC and the surrounding regions. Additionally, a large influx of non-Mormon tourists began to descend on the 'Mecca of Mormonism'. In fact, SLC soon became the most popular tourist destination in the American West, attracting somewhere between 150,000 and 200,000 tourists per year by the end of the 19th century, most of whom came not just for the natural aesthetics of the Rocky Mountains but also to gaze upon the 'mysterious', 'peculiar' and 'deviant' Mormons (Eliason, 2001; Gruen, 2002; Hafen, 1997; Mitchell, 1997).

This influx of tourists initially concerned church leaders, who believed these outsiders from the eastern United States were there to mock, ridicule and persecute the faith, much as they had done in New York, Ohio, Missouri and Illinois. As a result, some thought was given by church leaders to closing Temple Block (now called Temple Square) to non-Mormon visitors (Bishop & Holzaphel, 1993; Hafen, 1997). However, other leaders believed that by keeping Temple Square open to non-LDS tourists, the church could help dispel misperceptions and falsehoods that were circulating about Mormons (Sorensen, 2005). While a few enterprising church members had already begun offering tours of Temple Square (Johnson, 1971; Nibley, 1963; Young, 1922), the church quickly formalised the way that tours were led around Temple Square. In 1902, a Bureau of Information was opened, and church leaders called 105 volunteers to lead official tours of the site to introduce visitors not only to the buildings on Temple Square but also to the doctrines and teachings of the church (Anderson, 1921). Organ recitals and Mormon Tabernacle Choir performances were held at the Tabernacle (Cannon, 1959) and, believing that Temple Square was 'the greatest field for missionary work that there [was] in all the world' (Johnson, 1971: 27), church leaders created the Temple Square Mission in 1921. This mission, however, would be unlike other proselytising church missions around the world. Here, volunteer missionaries would engage in a 'soft sell' approach to Mormonism, 'where guides would attempt to instil spiritual feelings within the hearts and minds of visitors, and then have full-time proselytising missionaries contact those visitors when they returned home' (Olsen 2009: 128).

With growing numbers of visitors to Temple Square – 1 million in 1948 to 2.4 million in 1970 and 4 million in 1988 (Johnson, 1971; Olsen,

2009) – church leaders continually added to the infrastructure of Temple Square to accommodate increased visitation. Temple Square is now part of the 'Church Campus', a 35-acre area that includes the church's main administrative building (where visitors can go to the 26th floor to get a bird's eye view of SLC) (Otterstrom, 2008), Temple Square and the Salt Lake Temple, the Joseph Smith Memorial Building (formerly the Hotel Utah), the Family History Library (the largest genealogical library in the world), the Museum of Church History and Art, the Tabernacle, the Beehive House (a former home of Brigham Young and former church office building), the Lion House (another Brigham Young home), two other administrative buildings and two visitor centres (Olsen, 2009).

Just north of the Church Campus is a large 20,000-person conference centre (Halverson, 2000). In addition to the Church Campus, there are other buildings and sites related to Mormon history and culture around the city. These include the Brigham Young Monument, the Eagle Gate Monument, the Mormon Pioneer Memorial Building and the 'This is the Place' Monument. This is the Place Heritage Park, located beside This is the Place Monument and not operated by the LDS Church, gives visitors a sense of what life was like in 1880s Utah, complete with tour guides in period clothing and a replica pioneer village (Davis, 2003).

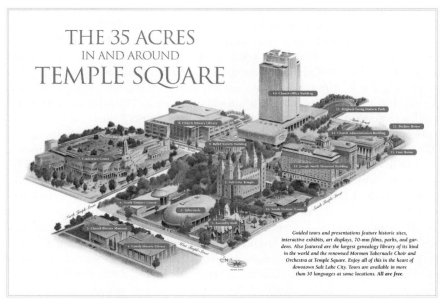

Figure 17.2 Temple Square (Photo: Daniel Olsen)

At Temple Square, the church has also created a number of tourism-specific departments to deal with Church Campus visitors (Figure 17.2).

For example, while the Temple Square Mission continues to be responsible for missionary guide training and to carry out guided tours (see Bremer [2000], Olsen [2009, 2012a, 2012b] and Scott [2005] for more information on the interpretation of Temple Square), there is a Hosting Division that greets visitors entering buildings outside of Temple Square and which hosts prominent non-Mormon visitors. Visitor Activities is a tourism-driven church department that acts as a liaison between the church and local tourism interests, such as the Salt Lake Convention and Visitors Bureau, the SLC Chamber of Commerce and its affiliate, the Downtown Alliance (2016), a non-profit organisation dedicated to building a community of commerce, culture and entertainment. Visitor Activities also maintains a kiosk at the SLC International Airport that gives visitors with long layovers an opportunity to visit Temple Square. The focus of the Temple Square Hospitality Corporation (TSHC) is to bring visitors, both tourists and local residents, to Temple Square. TSHC operates a number of catering businesses, hosts wedding receptions, operates four restaurants and hosts the website www.templesquare.com, which acts as a 'one-stop shop' for information about Temple Square and the surrounding area, including operating hours, how to book a tour of Temple Square, buildings to visit, a listing of upcoming events, places to visit around Temple Square and where to eat (Olsen, 2009: 129-132).

Adjacent to Temple Square is the Family History Library. As noted above, it is the largest genealogical library and family history resource centre in the world, and thus functions as one of the church's most important tourist attractions outside of Temple Square (Josiam & Frazier, 2008; Timothy, 1997, 2008). Genealogy and family history are among the most popular leisure pursuits in contemporary Western society (Meethan, 2008) that stimulate increasing numbers of personal heritage buffs to travel to their ancestral lands and to genealogy centres where they can trace their roots by searching through recorded documents (Higginbotham, 2012; Meethan, 2004; Santos & Yan, 2010; Timothy, 2008). For Mormons, family history research is a religious obligation that enables families to be linked or 'sealed' together in perpetuity (Cannell, 2005; Otterstrom, 2008). Owing to the LDS theological underpinnings of genealogy, the church has developed vast collections of family history documents from all corners of the globe, and volunteers work continuously to digitise the records for public consumption at the genealogy centre or online. Genealogical research at the library, the 'Genealogical Capitol of the World', features prominently as a potential leisure activity in the local tourism marketing media (Visit Salt Lake, 2016). Tens of thousands of people (mostly non-Mormons) visit the Family History Library every week (Ray & McCain, 2009), and demand for its services continues to grow exponentially year by year.

In addition to planning, organising and developing tourism-related infrastructure and services on and around Temple Square, the church has also invested in the surrounding urban milieu (Jackson, 1993). These efforts are in part because of concerns over urban blight and a desire to maintain the area 'in a way that would be proper and befitting to the church itself', the downtown community and Temple Square (Wright & Jorgensen, 1993: 12). For example, in 1974, the first regional downtown mall, the Church-owned ZCMI Mall (Zions Cooperative Mercantile Institution) opened southwest of Temple Square. At this time, the church also became an active partner with other landowners in developing a second major urban shopping centre, Crossroads Mall (Jackson, 1993). Over the next few decades, the church helped community leaders complete most of the *Second Century Plan*, which was developed by community leaders to renew the city's urban core (Burns, 1984). Examples of this include leasing church-owned property to the city for one dollar per year to build a convention centre, and donating money to help expand the new TRAX light-rail system. Recently, the church closed the ZCMI and Crossroads malls and at a cost of US$2 billion, redeveloped the area into the City Creek Centre, a 20-acre multi-use development that includes retail, housing and office space (Ellin, 2013; Shumway, 2015; Watkins, 2012).

With these types of financial and structural investments in SLC's urban core, one might wonder how the church could recoup its investment. Interestingly, the church does not charge admission fees for visits to Temple Square. As Olsen (2009) notes, this is so for a few different reasons. First, almost all tour guides and department leaders are local volunteers or missionaries from all over the world who donate their time and talents to operate tourism at Temple Square. As such, there is relatively low overhead for wages. Second, church members follow the biblical injunction to offer 10% of their earnings in tithes. The church also has a number of for-profit businesses (Shumway, 2015), and this income, combined with tithing contributions, allows church departments to handle all expenses of operating Temple Square without raising money through admission fees or donations. Third, charging an admission fee for entrance to Temple Square might deter some tourists from visiting, which would go against the policy of the square being open for all (Olsen 2011, 2012a).

A review of tourism websites, brochures and other marketing media related to SLC and Utah suggests that Temple Square and other Latter-day Saint tourist sites are underemphasised in official marketing efforts. As Olsen (2008) observed, there are two primary reasons for this. The first is that to many people, Utah is synonymous with the Mormon Church, and as such, the general assumption among tourism promoters is that potential visitors to Utah probably have already heard of the Mormons and that the church and its unique history are already an important reason for visiting

(Rugh, 2006). Thus, using Temple Square and Latter-day Saint culture as a draw may not be the most effective way of spending marketing spaces and budgets. Thus, very few ads are created specifically to promote Mormon attractions and activities.

The second reason LDS iconic sites in Utah appear commensurately infrequently in state and local advertising is that tourism officials are trying to move beyond the pervasive view that Utah and SLC are all about Mormonism, that the state has much more to offer than just religion. Instead, current marketing foci include conventions, national parks, natural experiences, skiing and lesser-known attractions throughout the city and state. Relatedly, tourism officials are attempting to change the prevailing view that Utah and SLC comprise an ultra-conservative religious region without nightlife and alcoholic beverages. With increased efforts to draw in non-Mormon tourists, much of the city's promotional efforts highlight the local nightlife, including bars and restaurants. Tourism sites related to the LDS Church are depicted as only one element of the total array of cultural heritage offerings available in the city and state (Olsen, 2008; Scott, 2005).

Conclusion

Like most other Christian denominations, members of The Church of Jesus Christ of Latter-day Saints are passionate travellers to sacred locales, despite the church not having any official policies or dogmas related to pilgrimage. Although the one aspect of LDS religious tourism that does resemble traditional pilgrimage in some regards is the semi-compulsory temple ordinances administered on behalf of the living and the dead. While the church constructs new temples every year in diverse locations, for a significant number of the 15 million Mormons throughout the world, travelling to a temple may require a substantial measure of hardship: months or years of saving money for the journey, several days of travel using a variety of transportation modes and time away from home and work. Latter-day Saints also visit biblical sites associated with the life and ministry of Jesus Christ and the early apostles in the Holy Land and the Mediterranean, as well as a few Mormon-specific sites also in the Holy Land. Likewise, tours and cruises that focus on *The Book of Mormon* lands are becoming increasingly popular as a way of experiencing the historical and cultural contexts of the events recorded in that holy writ.

Church members are acutely aware of the history of their religion, and many contemporary faith-promoting stories, youth activities, hymns, folklore and pageantry underscore the struggles of the 19th-century Mormon pioneers as they faced persecution in the eastern and Midwestern United States and tribulations on their voyage to the Salt Lake Valley. This collective memory translates into a thriving tourism apparatus focusing on a large network of LDS historic sites and theatrical pageants in the United States that are of interest both to Latter-day Saints and to non-Mormon history aficionados alike. At the terminus of the Mormon Pioneer Trail is SLC.

SLC is home to the headquarters of the LDS Church, the famed Salt Lake Temple and a collection of historic sites and museums. Temple Square, the Family History Library and indeed the entire Church Campus are the most visited attractions in SLC and the state of Utah. Although admission to all LDS sites, including Temple Square, is free of charge, the tourism stimulated by these visits is extremely important for the city and state. As such, unique relationships have developed between city administrators, many of whom are not LDS, tourism development organisations and the church. The Mormon Church realises its role as a tourist attraction, but it views this responsibility from an evangelical and pastoral perspective rather than an economic one. While the church earns no money directly from tourism, it continues to work with local tourism authorities, so that both parties' objectives are met in a closely connected set of symbiotic associations.

SLC is a unique North American city. It is anchored by a religious tourism district rather than by a central business district (Wright & Jorgensen, 1993), although these functions overlap simultaneously within the same bounded spaces. Early visitors to Utah in the 19th century labelled the Mormons a 'peculiar people' in a pejorative sense. Today, it offers a unique set of attractions and spiritual experiences not offered by any other urban area outside of Rome, Jerusalem, Mecca, Varanasi, Lourdes, Santiago de Compostela and Bethlehem, and this is nowhere more apparent than in the distinctive relationships between the church and tourism authorities, as noted above. This, together with the other unique travel patterns mentioned earlier, such as *The Book of Mormon* tours and cruises, and even visits to LDS-specific sacred sites in the Holy Land, makes Mormons as tourists and as the object of the tourist gaze indeed a 'peculiar people' – a biblical moniker referring to the special people of God and a nickname the Mormon Church has cherished for generations.

References

Anderson, E.H. (1921) The Bureau of Information. *The Improvement Era* 25 (2), 131–139.

Applebome, P. (2011) A Mormon spectacle, way off Broadway. *The New York Times*. See http://www.nytimes.com/2011/07/14/nyregion/hill-cumorah-pageant-offers-mormon-spectacle-way-off-broadway.html?pagewanted=all&_r=0 (accessed 13 September 2016).

Argetsinger, G.S. (2004) The Hill Cumorah Pageant: A historical perspective. *Journal of the Book of Mormon and Restoration Scripture* 13, 58–69.

Armstrong, R.N. and Argetsinger, G.S. (1989) The Hill Cumorah Pageant: Religious pageantry as suasive form. *Text and Performance Quarterly* 9, 153–164.

Arrington, L.J. (1979) *The Mormon Experience: A History of the Latter-day Saints.* Chicago, IL: University of Illinois Press.

Arrington, K.J. (1985) *Brigham Young: American Moses.* New York: Alfred A. Knopf.

Arrington, L.J. and Bitton, D. (1992) *The Mormon Experience: A History of the Latter-day Saints.* Chicago, IL: University of Chicago Press.

Askar, J.G. (2014) LDS Church buys farmland, Haun's Mill, Far West, Kirtland property from Community of Christ. See http://www.deseretnews.com/article/865555292/LDS-Church-buys-farmland-Hauns-Mill-Far-West-Kirtland-property-from-Community-of-Christ.html?pg=all (accessed 9 September 2016).

Associated Press (2006) Utah's Big Draw? Mormon 'Vatican'. *Denver Post.* See http://www.denverpost.com/2006/06/27/utahs-big-draw-mormon-vatican/ (accessed 13 September 2016).

Austin, J.H. (2015) Performing the Past: Two Pageant Traditions in Nauvoo, Illinois. PhD dissertation, Indiana University.

Bean, K.R. (2005) Policing the Borders of Identity at the Mormon Miracle Pageant. PhD dissertation, Bowling Green State University.

Bell, J.A. (2013) Ritualized theater: The performing pilgrim's process at the Hill Cumorah Pageant. In J.M. Hunter (ed.) *Mormons and American Popular Culture: The Global Influence of an American Phenomenon* (Vol. 1; pp. 163–181). Santa Barbara, CA: Praeger.

Bielo, J.S. (2016) Replication as religious practice, temporality as religious problem. *History and Anthropology.* doi: 10.1080/02757206.2016.1182522.

Bishop, M.G. and Holzapfel, R.N. (1993) The 'St. Peter's of the New World': The Salt Lake Temple, tourism, and a new image for Utah. *Utah Historical Quarterly* 61 (2), 136–149.

Bradley, M.S. (2004) Colliding interests: Mapping Salt Lake City's west side. *Journal of Urban History* 31 (1), 47–74.

Bradley, M.S. (2005) Creating the sacred space of Zion. *Journal of Mormon History* 31 (1), 1–30.

Bremer, T.S. (2000) Tourists and religion at Temple Square and Mission San Juan Capistrano. *Journal of American Folklore* 113, 422–435.

Burns, E. (1984) Plan and process in Salt Lake City. *Triglyph: A Southwestern Journal of Architecture and Environmental Design* 1, 11–16.

Bushman, C. (2009) The pageant people: A Latter-day Saint appropriation of an art form. In H. du Toit (ed.) *Pageants and Processions: Images and Idiom as Spectacle* (pp. 217–224). Tyne: Cambridge Scholars Publishing.

Bushman, R.L. (2005) *Joseph Smith: Rough Stone Rolling.* New York: Random House.

Cannell, F. (2005) The Christianity of anthropology. *Journal of the Royal Anthropological Institute* 11 (2), 335–356.

Cannon, T.L. (1959) Temple Square: The crossroads of the West. *Utah Historical Quarterly* 27 (3), 247–257.

Davis, J. (2003) LDS heritage sites. In R.H. Jackson and M.W. Jackson (eds) *Geography, Culture and Change in the Mormon West: 1847–2003* (pp. 65–78). Jacksonville, AL: National Council for Geographic Education.

Davis, J., Jackson, M.W. and Jackson, R.H. (2009) Heritage tourism and group identity: Polynesians in the American West. *Journal of Heritage Tourism* 4 (1), 3–17.

Downtown Alliance (2016) About the Downtown Alliance. See http://www.downtownslc.org/about/mission (accessed 14 September 2016).

Eliason, E.A. (2001) Curious gentiles and representational authority in the City of the Saints. *Religion and American Culture: A Journal of Interpretation* 11 (2), 155–190.

Eliason, E.A. (2002) The cultural dynamics of historical self-fashioning: Mormon pioneer nostalgia, American culture, and the international church. *Journal of Mormon History* 28 (2), 139–173.

Eliason, E.A. (2006) Mormon culture region. In S.J. Bronner (ed.) *Encyclopaedia of American Folklife* (pp. 825–829). London: Routledge.

Ellin, N. (2012) Co-creation: From egosystem to ecosystem. In N. Ellin (ed.) *Good Urbanism: Six Steps to Creating Prosperous Places* (pp. 33–53). Washington, DC: Island Press.

Erekson, K.A. (2005) From missionary resort to memorial farm: Commemoration and capitalism at the birthplace of Joseph Smith, 1905–1925. *Mormon Historical Studies* 6 (2), 69–100.

Fonseca, F. (2015) Utah's national parks hit visitation records. *The Salt Lake Tribune.* See http://www.sltrib.com/home/3358254-155/countrys-largest-national-parks-hit-visitation (accessed 23 August 2016).

Francaviglia, R.V. (1978) *The Mormon Landscape: Existence, Creation, and Perception of a Unique Image in the American West.* New York: AMS Press.

Francaviglia, R.V. (2003) *Believing in Place: A Spiritual Geography of the Great Basin.* Reno, NV: University of Nevada Press.

Galbraith, D.B., Ogden, D.K. and Skinner, A.C. (1996) *Jerusalem: The Eternal City.* Salt Lake City, UT: Deseret Book.

Givens, T.L. (2004) *The Latter-day Saint Experience in America.* Westport, CT: Greenwood Press.

Griffiths, L. (2007) Mesa Mormon temple prepares for Easter pageant. *East Valley Tribune.* See https://web.archive.org/web/20070911150555/http://www.eastvalleytribune.com/story/86475 (accessed 13 September 2016).

Gruen, J.P. (2002) The urban wonders: City tourism in the late-19th-century American west. *Journal of the West* 41 (2), 10–19.

Gurgel, K.D. (1976) Travel patterns of Canadian visitors to the Mormon culture hearth. *The Canadian Geographer* 20 (4), 405–418.

Guter, Y. (1997) Mormon-Christian Pilgrimage to Israel–Pilgrim's Experience. Master's thesis, Bar Ilan University (in Hebrew).

Guter, Y. (2006) Pilgrims 'communitas' in the Holy Land: The case of Mormon pilgrimage. In M. Poorthuis and J. Schwartz (eds) *A Holy People: Jewish and Christian Perspectives on Religious Communal Identity* (pp. 337–348). Leiden: Brill.

Haddock, S. (2012) Castle Valley Pageant a community classic. *Deseret News.* See http://www.deseretnews.com/article/865559882/Castle-Valley-Pageant-a-community-classic.html?pg=all (accessed 13 September 2016).

Hafen, T.K. (1997) City of saints, city of sinners: The development of Salt Lake City as a tourist attraction 1869–1900. *Western Historical Quarterly* 28 (3), 342–378.

Halverson, W.D. (2000) *The LDS Conference Centre and its History.* Salt Lake City: DMT Publishing.

Hansen, T. (2010) Spiritual safety tips for frequent travellers. *Ensign.* See https://www.lds.org/ensign/2010/07/spiritual-safety-tips-for-frequent-travelers?lang=eng (accessed 13 September 2016).

Higginbotham, G. (2012) Seeking roots and tracing lineages: Constructing a framework of reference for roots and genealogical tourism. *Journal of Heritage Tourism* 7 (3), 189–203.

Hudman, L.E. and Jackson, R.H. (1992) Mormon pilgrimage and tourism. *Annals of Tourism Research* 19 (1), 107–121.

Hunter, J.M. (2013) Pageants. In J.M. Hunter (ed.) *Mormons and American Popular Culture: The Global Influence of an American Phenomenon* (Vol. 2; pp. 166–167). Santa Barbara, CA: Praeger.

Intellectual Reserve (2015) Handcart trek re-enactments: Guidelines for leaders. See https://www.lds.org/youth/activities/bc/pdfs/stake/Handcart-Trek-Guidelines-June-2015.pdf (accessed 13 September 2016).

Ioannides, D. and Timothy, D.J. (2010) *Tourism in the USA: A Spatial and Social Synthesis*. London: Routledge.

Jackson, R.H. (1977) The Mormon village: Genesis and antecedents of the City of Zion plan. *Brigham Young University Studies* 17 (2), 223–240.

Jackson, R.H. (1988) Great Salt Lake and Great Salt Lake City: American curiosities. *Utah Historical Quarterly* 56 (2), 128–147.

Jackson, R.H. (1993) Sacred space and city planning: The Mormon example. *Architecture & Behaviour* 9 (2), 251–260.

Jackson, R.H. and Henrie, R. (1983) Perception of sacred space. *Journal of Cultural Geography* 3 (2), 94–107.

Johnson, M.K. (1971) A History of the Temple Square Mission of the Church of Jesus Christ of Latter-day Saints to 1970. Master's thesis, Brigham Young University.

Johnson, V. (2016) Manti celebrates 50th season of Mormon Miracle Pageant. *Deseret News*. See http://www.deseretnews.com/article/865656750/Manti-celebrates-50th-season-of-Mormon-Miracle-Pageant.html?pg=all (accessed 13 September 2016).

Jorgensen, T. (2015) Utah tourism drives over $1B in tax revenues. *KSL.com* news report. See http://www.ksl.com/?sid=36882688&nid=148 (accessed 23 August 2016).

Josiam, B.M. and Frazier, R. (2008) Who am I? Where did I come from? Where do I go to find out? Genealogy, the Internet and tourism. *Tourismos* 3 (2), 35–56.

Kimball, S.B. (1988) *Historic Sites and Markers along the Mormon and Other Great Western Trails*. Urbana, IL: University of Illinois Press.

Kuruvilla, C. (2015) Pioneer Day is a Mormon celebration of history and faith. Here's why. *The Huffington Post*. See http://www.huffingtonpost.com/entry/pioneer-day-2015-mormon_us_55af15a5e4b0a9b94852f9ec (accessed 12 September 2016).

Larsen, L. (2016) Utah's travel and tourism industry nets over $1 billion in tax revenue. *Standard-Examiner*. See http://www.standard.net/Recreation/2016/05/26/Travel-and-tourism-Utah-s-top-earning-industry (accessed 23 August 2016).

Leaver, J. (2016) The State of Utah's Travel and Tourism Industry, 2015. Ken C. Gardner Policy Institute, University of Utah, industry report. See http://gardner.utah.edu/wp-content/uploads/2016/05/TourismReport-v7.pdf (accessed 23 August 2016).

Lloyd, R.S. (1997) 'Day of Service' to honour Legacy of 1847 pioneers. *Church News*. See http://www.ldschurchnewsarchive.com/articles/29363/Day-of-service-to-honor-legacy-of-1847-pioneers.html (accessed 28 August 2016).

Lloyd, R.S. (2011) A rich experience in a different kind of mission. *Church News* January 22, 2011.

LoMonaco, M.S. (2009) Mormon pageants as American historical performance. *Theatre Symposium* 17, 69–83.

Madsen, M.H. (2008) The sanctification of Mormonism's historical geography. *Journal of Mormon History* 34 (2), 228–255.

McCombs, B. (2016) Utah ski resorts north record year for visitors. *The Big Story*. See http://bigstory.ap.org/article/e244be9daab64e35aebd25f570a2d3b9/utah-ski-resorts-notch-record-year-visitors (accessed 15 September 2016).

McConkie, B.R. (1966) *Mormon Doctrine*. Salt Lake City, UT: Bookcraft.

McHale, E.E. (1985) 'Witnessing for Christ': The Hill Cumorah Pageant of Palmyra, New York. *Western Folklore* 44, 34–40.

Meethan, K. (2004) 'To stand in the shoes of my ancestors': Tourism and genealogy. In T. Coles and D.J. Timothy (eds) *Tourism, Diasporas and Space* (pp. 139–150). London: Routledge.

Meethan, K. (2008) Remaking time and space: The internet, digital archives and genealogy. In D.J. Timothy and J. Kay Guelke (eds) *Geography and Genealogy: Locating Personal Pasts* (pp. 99–112). Aldershot: Ashgate.

Meinig, D.W. (1965) The Mormon culture tegion: Strategies and patterns in the geography of the American west, 1847–1964. *Annals of the Association of American Geographers* 55 (2), 191–220.

Merrill, T.G. (2010) Remembering the pioneer legacy. *The Religious Educator* 11 (2), 163–173.

Mitchell, H. (2001) 'Being There': British Mormons and the history trail. *Anthropology Today* 17 (2), 9–14.

Mitchell, M. (1997) Gentile impressions of Salt Lake City, Utah, 1849–1870. *The Geographical Review* 87 (3), 334–352.

Mitchell, R.C. (1967) Desert tortoise: The Mormon Tabernacle on Temple Square. *Utah Historical Quarterly* 35 (4), 279–291.

Nemeth, D. (2015) Utah sees rise in tourism from China: New ads aim to keep international visitors coming. *Fox13Now.com* news report. See http://fox13now.com/2015/03/25/utah-sees-rise-in-tourism-from-china-new-ads-aim-to-keep-international-visitors-coming/ (accessed 23 August 2016).

Nibley, P. (1963) Charles J. Thomas: Early guide on Temple Square. *The Improvement Era* 66 (3), 167–168, 202–203.

O'Dea, T.F. (1957) *The Mormons*. Chicago, IL: University of Chicago Press.

Olsen, D.H. (2006) Tourism and informal pilgrimage among the Latter-day Saints. In D.J. Timothy and D.H. Olsen (eds) *Tourism, Religion and Spiritual Journeys* (pp. 254–270). London: Routledge.

Olsen, D.H. (2008) Contesting Identity, Space and Sacred Site Management at Temple Square in Salt Lake City, Utah. PhD dissertation, University of Waterloo.

Olsen, D.H. (2009) 'The strangers within our gates': Managing visitors at Temple Square. *Journal of Management, Spirituality & Religion* 6 (2), 121–139.

Olsen, D.H. (2011) Towards a religious view of tourism: Negotiating faith perspectives on tourism. *Tourism, Culture and Communication* 11 (1), 17–30.

Olsen, D.H. (2012a) Negotiating religious identity at sacred sites: A management perspective. *Journal of Heritage Tourism* 7 (4), 359–366.

Olsen, D.H. (2012b) Teaching truth in 'Third Space': The use of religious history as a pedagogical instrument at Temple Square in Salt Lake City, Utah. *Tourism Recreation Research* 37 (3), 227–238.

Olsen, D.H. (2013) Touring sacred history: The Latter-day Saints and their historical sites. In J.M. Hunter (ed.) *Mormons and American Popular Culture: The Global Influence of an American Phenomenon* (Vol. 2; pp. 225–242). Santa Barbara, CA: Praeger.

Olsen, D.H. (2016) The Church of Jesus Christ of Latter-day Saints, their 'Three-fold mission', and practical and pastoral theology. *Practical Matters* 9, See http://practicalmattersjournal.org/2016/06/29/lds-three-fold-mission/.

Olsen, D.H. and Guelke, J.K. (2004) Spatial transgression and the BYU Jerusalem Centre controversy. *The Professional Geographer* 56 (4), 503–515.

Olsen, S.L. (1992) Centennial observances. In D.H. Ludlow (ed.) *Encyclopaedia of Mormonism* (Vol. 1; pp. 260–262). New York: MacMillan.

Olsen, S.L. (1996) Celebrating cultural identity: Pioneer Day in nineteenth-century Mormonism. *BYU Studies* 36 (1), 159–177.

Olsen, S.L. (2002) *The Mormon Ideology of Place: Cosmic Symbolism of the City of Zion, 1830–1846*. Provo, UT: Joseph Fielding Smith Institute for LDS History.

Oscarson, R.D. and Kimball, S.B. (1965) *The Travelers' Guide to Historic Mormon America*. Salt Lake City, UT: Bookcraft.

Otterstrom, S.M. (2008) Genealogy as religious ritual: The doctrine and practice of family history in the Church of Jesus Christ of Latter-day Saints. In D.J. Timothy and J. Kay Guelke (eds) *Geography and Genealogy: Locating Personal Pasts* (pp. 137–151). Aldershot: Ashgate.

Packer, B.K. (1980) *The Holy Temple*. Salt Lake City, UT: Bookcraft.

Parry, D.W. (1994) Introduction. In D.W. Parry (ed.) *Temples of the Ancient World: Ritual and Symbolism* (pp. xi–xxiv). Salt Lake City, UT: Deseret Book.

Peterson, P.H. (2002) Accommodating the Saints at General Conference. *BYU Studies* 41 (2), 4–39.

Poppleton, J. (2013) Clarkston Pageant returns in August. *HJNews*. See http://news.hjnews. com/allaccess/clarkston-pageant-returns-in-august/article_397c70f4-f033-11e2-8973-0019bb2963f4.html (accessed 13 September 2016).

Rasmus, C.J. (1992) Temple Square. In D.H. Ludlow (ed.) *Encyclopaedia of Mormonism* (Vol. 4; pp. 1465–1469). New York: Macmillan.

Ray, N.M. and McCain, G. (2009) Guiding tourists to their ancestral homes. *International Journal of Culture, Tourism and Hospitality Research* 3 (4), 296–305.

Ron, A.S. and Timothy, D.J. (in preparation) *Contemporary Christian Travel: Pilgrimage, Practice and Place*. Bristol: Channel View Publications.

Rugh, S.S. (2006) Branding Utah: Industrial tourism in the postwar American west. *Western Historical Quarterly* 37 (4), 445–472.

Santos, C.A. and Yan, G. (2010) Genealogical tourism: A phenomenological examination. *Journal of Travel Research* 49 (1), 56–67.

Scott, D.W. (2005) Re-representing Mormon history: A textual analysis of the representation of pioneers and history at Temple Square in Salt Lake City. *Journal of Media and Religion* 4 (2), 95–110.

Shumway, J.M. (2015) Tithes, offerings and sugar beets: The economic logistics of the Church of Jesus Christ of Latter-day Saints. In S.D. Brunn (ed.) *The Changing World Religion Map: Sacred Places, Identities, Practices and Politics* (pp. 1207–1228). Berlin: Springer.

Smith, B.C. (2003) *The LDS Family Travel Guide: Independence to Nauvoo*. Orem, UT: LDS Family Travels.

Smith, C.S. (1999) A legacy of the sesquicentennial: A selection of twelve books. *Journal of Mormon History* 25 (2), 152–163.

Smith, J. (1991) *History of the Church* (7 Vols). Salt Lake City, UT: Deseret Book.

Smith, J. and White, B.N. (2004) Detached from their homeland: The Latter-day Saints in Chihuahua, Mexico. *Journal of Cultural Geography* 21 (2), 57–76.

Sorensen, P.J. (2005) The lost commandment: The sacred rites of hospitality. *Brigham Young University Studies* 44 (1), 5–32.

Stausberg, M. (2011) *Religion and Tourism: Crossroads, Destinations and Encounters*. London: Routledge.

Stock, M.A. (2009) Puppets, Pioneers, and Sport: The Onstage and Offstage Performance of Khmer Identity. Master's thesis, Brigham Young University.

Szasz, F.M. (2004) How religion created an infrastructure for the mountain west. In J. Shipps and M. Silk (eds) *Religion and Public Life in the Mountain West: Sacred Landscapes in Transition* (pp. 49–68). Walnut Creek, CA: Alta Mira Press.

Taniguchi, N.J. (2004) *Castle Valley America: Hard Land, Hard-Won Home*. Logan, UT: Utah State University Press.

The Church of Jesus Christ of Latter-day Saints (2017) Temples. See https://www.lds.org/church/temples/find-a-temple?lang=eng (accessed 17 August 2017).

Timothy, D.J. (1992) Mormons in Ontario: Early history, growth and landscape. *Ontario Geography* 38, 21–31.

Timothy, D.J. (1997) Tourism and the personal heritage experience. *Annals of Tourism Research* 24 (3), 751–754.

Timothy, D.J. (2008) Genealogical mobility: Tourism and the search for a personal past. In D.J. Timothy and J. Kay Guelke (eds) *Geography and Genealogy: Locating Personal Pasts* (pp. 115–135). Aldershot: Ashgate.

Toney, M.B., Keller, C. and Hunter, L.M. (2003) Regional cultures, persistence and change: A case study of the Mormon Culture Region. *The Social Sciences Journal* 40, 431–445.

Turner, J.G. (2012) *Brigham Young: Pioneer Prophet*. Cambridge, MA: Harvard University Press.

Visit Salt Lake (2016) Genealogy. See http://www.visitsaltlake.com/things-to-do/genealogy/family-history-library/ (accessed 16 September 2016).

Watkins, N. (2012) A Step Towards Sustainable: The Meshing of the Mormon Church Headquarters' Environmental Earth Stewardship Practices with Modern Trends of Sustainability. Undergraduate honor's thesis, Utah State University.

Welch, D. (2016) The Mormon Pioneer Day holiday. World Religion News. See http://www.worldreligionnews.com/religion-news/christianity/the-mormon-pioneer-day-holiday (accessed 27 August 2016).

Whatcott, J. (2014) Nauvoo Pageant features British experiences. *Deseret News*, See http://www.deseretnews.com/article/865608318/Nauvoo-pageant-features-British-experiences.html?pg=all (accessed 13 September 2016).

Wright, J.G. and Jorgensen, C. (1993) Change comes to Salt Lake City. *Planning* 59 (6), 10–15.

Yorgason, E.R. (2003) *Transformation of the Mormon Culture Region*. Chicago, IL: University of Illinois Press.

Young, L.E. (1922) The Temple Block Mission. *The Relief Society Magazine* 9 (11), 559–563.

Zobell, A.L. (1967) Opening the Tabernacle. *The Improvement Era* 70 (9), 10–13.

18 Religious Needs in the Tourism Industry: The Perspective of Abrahamic Traditions

Amos S. Ron

Introduction

The religious needs of tourists and travellers have been with us forever, but the main body of academic research literature concerning these needs is only about a decade old (e.g. Polyxeni *et al.*, 2012; Weidenfeld, 2006; Weidenfeld & Ron, 2008). For example, when people travelled in biblical times they had to observe a variety of religious rules and regulations concerning food (Timothy & Ron, 2016: 108), accommodation (Goodman, 2007), keeping the Sabbath and more. In addition to the formal rules and regulations, they also had spiritual needs, such as prayer, which assisted them in overcoming their objective and subjective fears and anxieties concerning travel.

A distinction should be made between religious tourists and pilgrims on the one hand (Ron, 2009), and the spiritual and religious needs among tourists who travel for a variety of other reasons, such as family vacations, cruise tourism and business tourism, on the other hand. Whereas the former travel to sacred sites, the latter travel to other sites, but they still have religious needs and concerns. There is far more research on pilgrims and religious tourists (e.g. Coleman & Elsner, 1995; Stausberg, 2011; Timothy & Olsen, 2006) than there is on the religious needs of the ordinary 'non pilgrim' tourist.

An important source in this context is Olsen (2013). According to him,

> the religious tourism market is changing and becoming more complex . . . and with the view that religious site managers and religious tourism promoters and operators need to better understand the religious motivations and expectations of various types of visitors to their sites so as to better meet the needs of various visitors. (Olsen, 2013: 43)

The solution, as suggested by Olsen, lies in carrying out a segmentation according to religion and territory, or in identifying the special needs of tourists (Weidenfeld, 2006: 143).

This chapter aims to focus on the 'non pilgrim' tourist by identifying and relating to three major religious needs that are common in tourism and hospitality: food, ritual and atmosphere. The three needs will be analysed and segmented according to the historical appearance of the three monotheistic faiths, i.e. Judaism, Christianity and Islam. Dealing with other faiths is beyond the scope of this chapter.

Food

Many religions have dietary rules and regulations that indicate precisely to the followers which foods and beverages are edible and which foods are not (Polyxeni *et al.*, 2012; Simoons, 1994; Timothy & Ron, 2016: 106–112). Being a tourist and an observant follower can be very challenging at times, but the good news is that the dietary laws are often common knowledge for both the host and the guest, and overcoming these obstacles has its rewards for all.

Judaism

The Jewish faith is highly regulated foodwise. According to Timothy and Ron,

> Orthodox Jews adhere to a set of food laws known as *kashruth*, which is based on ancient scripture from the books of Leviticus and Deuteronomy. These kosher dietetic laws hinge on three principles: kosher foods . . . can be eaten, blood cannot be consumed, and meat and milk products cannot be served together in the same dish or even during the same meal . . . In addition to the kosher animals and preparation methods of the kashruth, glatt kosher additionally includes eating meat only from animals with smoot or defect-free lungs. However, today glatt kosher is commonly used as a generic term for an even stricter code of kashruth . . . Split-hooved ruminants (e.g. cows, goats and sheep), most domestic fowl, and scaled fish are generally kosher. Pork, carnivores or birds of prey, non-scaled fish, and shell fish are not kosher and cannot be consumed or cooked in a kosher kitchen . . . Jewish law also requires that all blood must be removed, and the slaughtering of animals must be done by an authorized religious authority . . .
>
> Certain feasts, holidays and other celebrations in Judaism also call for special foods to be prepared and eaten. During the eight days of Passover, unleavened bread is the only grain product that can be eaten . . . Rosh Hashanah, Succoth, Yom Kippur and Hanukkah are important celebrations that are commemorated with special meals . . . (Timothy & Ron, 2016: 108)

There are a number of academic sources on the interface between Jewish observance and tourism. Klin-Oron (2005) wrote on the vacations of

Haredi (Ultra-Orthodox) Jews in Israel, and Cahaner (2009) on the spatial aspects of Haredi Jews in Israel, including many references to tourism. In addition, there are several academic publications on the issue of kosher food and travel (Cahaner & Mansfeld, 2012; Cahaner *et al.*, 2012 [chapter 9], 2015; Cohen Ioannides & Ioannides, 2006; Ioannides & Cohen Ioannides, 2002; Mansfeld & Cahaner, 2013; Mansfeld *et al.*, 2016; Maoz & Bekerman, 2010).

From the various academic and non-academic sources, the challenges faced by the Jewish traveller emerge quite clearly, while there are at least six types of solutions:

(a) *Staying at a kosher hotel:* In Israel and elsewhere, there are kosher hotels, usually owned by Jews, and often located in areas that are popular among Haredi Jews, such as the Catskills in the United States (Brown, 1998; Johnson, 1990).

(b) *Staying at an 'ordinary' hotel, but eating in kosher restaurants:* Many cities in Western countries have kosher restaurants that cater both to local Jews and to Jewish travellers (Kashrus Magazine, 2016).

(c) *Buying kosher food from an appropriate dealer:* The Greek island of Corfu, for example, has no kosher restaurant, but the kosher consumer who wishes to visit the island can order kosher food through a Jewish restaurant in Athens, and it can be delivered to the non-kosher destination (Pollack, 2011).

(d) *Bringing kosher food from home:* A simple solution for the Haredi consumer is to bring packed and preserved kosher food (Cahaner & Mansfeld, 2012: 310; Mansfeld *et al.*, 2016: 397). This solution is useful for short trips, but one can also suit long-term travellers, who stock up as they go along.

(e) *Home swaps:* Home exchanges are common among Haredi travellers (Cahaner, 2009: 148). This practice helps save money and overcomes the problem of a non-kosher kitchen.

(f) *Renting an Airbnb place that has a kosher kitchen:* The Ultra-Orthodox Jewish market is growing rapidly, and consequently organisations such as Airbnb (often located in Jewish neighbourhoods) are stepping in (Klein, 2015).

Islam

Understanding the relationship between Islam, food and tourism is important, because Muslims represent more than 20% of the world population, and it is estimated that 70% of Muslims obey their dietary code. In Islam, food is broadly classified into two groups: halal (permissible) and haram (prohibited) (Bon & Hussain, 2010: 47). According to Polyxeni *et al.* (2012), the Qur'an prohibits the consumption of pork and its derivatives; alcohol; various kinds of jellies that are made from pork fat; and products that have emulsifiers, such as canned goods. Furthermore, according to the Qur'an, the consumption of sarcophagus animals and sea creatures that do not have scales and fins (e.g. calamari, shrimps and lobster) is prohibited. Finally, even animals that are permitted to be eaten must be killed and prepared following a specific ritual, referred to as the Islamic canons (Polyxeni *et al.*, 2012: 131). A very detailed list of halal and haram animals was compiled by Bon and Hussain (2010: 50–51).

The topic of halal tourism has received a great deal of academic attention in the past few years. The vast amount of literature can be classified into three main types: general-introductory, by country and by theme. Some of the general sources on halal tourism are Bon and Hussain (2010), Jafari and Scott (2014), Mansfeld *et al.* (2000), Polyxemi *et al.* (2012) and Weidenfeld and Ron (2008). Sources by country include analyses and predictions relating to France (Wright & Annes, 2013); Japan (Adidaya, 2016; Samori *et al.*, 2016); Malaysia (Henderson, 2016; Samori *et al.*, 2016; Shaari *et al.*, 2013); Morocco (Carboni & Janati, 2016); New Zealand (Razzaq, 2016; Razzaq *et al.*, 2016); Singapore (Henderson, 2016); and Turkey (Boğan *et al.*, 2016; Duman, 2012; Elaziz & Kurt, 2017), as well as examples from other countries. The thematic issues refer to marketing (Izberk-Bilgin & Nakata, 2016), challenges (Battour & Ismail, 2016), opportunities (Mohsin *et al.*, 2016) and terminology (El-Gohary, 2016). Most of the publications emphasise the lucrative potential of halal tourism, but a distinction can be made between Muslim and non-Muslim countries.

In most cases, the literature relating to Muslim destinations emphasises the very high potential, whereas the emphasis on non-Muslim countries is more critical, and even contested. For example, research on the halal potential in New Zealand claims that an analysis of 367 accommodation websites found only three sites that were geared towards halal tourism (Razzaq *et al.*, 2016: 92). In France, halal tourism is more common, but at the same time halal food is perceived as '. . . a threat to the very essence of French republican ideals' (Wright & Annes, 2013: 388), an example being that during an official Iranian visit to France, lunch between the French and Iranian leaders was cancelled after President Hollande refused to take wine off the menu for his meeting with his Muslim counterpart, Rouhani (Sparks, 2016).

Cultural differences regarding food can be an obstacle, as a Muslim tourist to Euro Disney in Paris shared with the TripAdvisor community: 'Visited Disney in ugust. In short there is nowhere that caters for halal food in or around the resort . . . Only option i found was an area in outside paris called Gare du nord. which is a few miles away and requires a few train hops' (The halal problem at Disneyland Paris, 2014). This post, and others echo the dietary challenges of being a foreigner in a culturally contested environment, and in this particular case may reflect French antipathy to catering to non-indigenous French customs and sensitivity over its traditional food and cuisine.

Summing up, food is a very important aspect of travel, and travellers are often sensitive to alimentary issues that are culturally sensitive. Based on the above-mentioned examples, we can suggest a sensitivity scale within the context of Abrahamic traditions, where Judaism would be the most sensitive, Islam would be sensitive, but to a lesser degree, and Christianity would be the least sensitive.

Christianity

In the Book of Acts (11:7-9), Peter has a vision, in which he hears a voice saying to him '. . . Arise, Peter; slay and eat. But I [Peter] said, Not so, Lord: for nothing common or unclean hath at any time entered into my mouth. But the voice answered me again from heaven, What God hath cleansed, *that* call not thou common'. Consequently, Christianity is less sensitive to food regulations in comparison to Judaism and Islam. However, Christianity is highly diversified denomination-wise, with several thousand denominations (Miller *et al.*, 2009), some of which have dietary restrictions and days of fasting, which of course can have an effect on Christian travellers.

The most common and widely spread food regulation in Christianity is Lent (n.d.), observed by Eastern Orthodox, Roman Catholic, Anglican, Lutheran and Methodist churches, in which observant Christians abstain from meat and eat fish instead, while some observe a purely vegetarian diet. The Lent period refers to the last 40 days preceding Easter. In most cases, the implications for the Christian traveller are minimal, and most of the relevance is to the tourism food services such as restaurants and airlines, which come up with Lent menus, as demonstrated by a hotel in St Petersburg (Lent menu in hotel's restaurants, n.d.).

The Church of Jesus Christ of Latter-day Saints (Mormons) observes dietary laws, known as the *Word of Wisdom* (Doctrine and Covenants: section 89), which prohibit the consumption of alcohol, tea, coffee and tobacco. The attitude towards alcohol in Christian denominations varies between prohibition (Methodists, Pentecostals and Baptists), tolerance (Lutherans and Presbyterians) and encouragement (Anglicans and Catholics) (Syanberg *et al.*, 2015: 57–58).

In sum, of the three religions discussed in this chapter, Christianity is the least sensitive to restrictions concerning alimentation, and consequently, the Christian traveller can easily merge into surrounding culinary situations and traditions.

Ritual

According to the Merriam-Webster dictionary, ritual in the context of religion is defined as 'an act or series of acts regularly repeated in a set precise manner' (Ritual, n.d.) The more common rituals in monotheism include prayers, days or periods of complete or partial fasting, periodical readings from sacred scriptures, attending houses of prayer (e.g. synagogues, churches, mosques), taking the Holy Communion (for Christians) and many more rituals that may fall within the scope of tourist activities.

Prayer

In Judaism, the observant followers pray three times daily, always in the direction of Jerusalem. Tourism activities do not clash with the prayer, but the direction of Jerusalem may sometimes be unknown. Islam has a somewhat similar attribute (five times daily, always towards Mecca), and in order to show the direction of Mecca, many hotels that cater to Muslims (Sharia-compliant hotels and others) have a 'Mecca Sticker' in each bedroom. These stickers (sometimes tiles) have a marked arrow pointing in the direction of Mecca for the purpose of worship (Henderson, 2009: 207). This arrow serves two purposes: it indicates the direction of Mecca and that the hotel is 'Muslim friendly'. The difference between the two photos in Figures 18.1 and 18.2 (both taken in East Jerusalem) is that the sticker in Figure 18.1 is on the desk, while the sticker in Figure 18.2 is in the drawer. Obviously, the first sticker is more visible, indicating the Muslim ownership of the hotel, and the more discrete sticker indicates that the hotel owners are non-Muslim – in this case, they are Christian. These arrows are widespread in Muslim-friendly settings, reflecting the estimated figure that 63% of Muslims pray daily (Cetin & Zeki Dincer, 2016: 21).

In Christianity, prayers are usually less structured, sometimes spontaneous (depending on the denomination) and usually not restricted timewise or direction-wise, and therefore are less considered by the tourism industry.

Fasting

Monotheistic faiths have days of complete or partial fasting, which is certainly a challenge for the fasting tourist. Judaism has six days of fasting in a year, the most famous being the Day of Atonement (Yom Kippur) (Fast days: Days of opportunity, n.d.). Most Christian denominations observe Lent (see above), Orthodox Christians have their periodical fast days (The fasting rule of the Orthodox Church, n.d.) and many Mormons fast on the first Sunday of each month (Mauss, 1972).

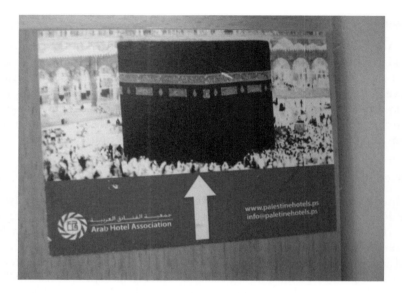

Figure 18.1 Mecca sticker on a desk in a Muslim-owned hotel in East Jerusalem

Figure 18.2 Mecca sticker in a drawer in a Christian-owned hotel in East Jerusalem

But from the perspective of fasting and tourism, Islam undoubtedly provides the greatest challenge because of the month-long fast of Ramadan, which is one of the five pillars of Islam (Al Jahwari, 2015: 126). During that period, Muslims must abstain from all food and drink from sunrise to sunset. The fast is applicable to all except infants, the mentally ill, the elderly, travellers (during their trip and if they are to keep the fast later), pregnant women, women who have recently given birth and those who have their period – they must fast again once their period has ended (Polyxeni *et al.*, 2012: 131). According to the Muslim lunar calendar, the month of Ramadan is the ninth month, but according to the Gregorian solar calendar the fast is earlier each year by 10–11 days due to the difference in calendars (Olsen & Ron, 2013: 9). Having meals only between sunset and sunrise means eating can take place at odd hours, depending on the location and time of year, and hotels need to perform accordingly in order to serve their Muslim clientele.

Readings

Various religions encourage periodical (daily, weekly) readings from sacred scriptures. The tourism industry, especially the hospitality industry, can easily cater to such needs by placing the relevant scriptures (preferably in the relevant languages), religious calendars and lists of local religious activities in hotel bedrooms (Battour *et al.*, 2011: 530; Collins-Kreiner & Kliot, 2000; Weidenfeld, 2006). In Judaism, daily and weekly readings, following the Jewish calendar, are very common, as it is among most Christian denominations. For example, Christadelphians read three chapters of the Bible every day (Notes on daily bible readings, n.d.).

Islam also encourages periodical readings from the Qur'an. According to Mujtaba (2016: 173): 'Reciting Qur'an is a commendable deed whole year around, but during the fast [of Ramadan] it assumes a far greater significance. It is narrated from the holy prophet Muhammad (pbuh) that everything has its own spring season, and the spring of the Qur'an is the month of Ramadan'.

Attending places of prayer and worship

While travelling, many worshippers like to have a place to pray and worship. Airports are a relevant example: tourists often have long hours between flights, which is why some airports have constructed such spaces. Athens International Airport is a good example. The Greek Orthodox travellers have their church (Figure 18.3), and the others have a worship area devoid of any element that could be offensive to some, such as a cross or icons (Figure 18.4).

Some hotels also include designated spaces for prayer. For example, according to the CEO of a synagogue furniture manufacturing company, they recently built synagogues in five hotels in Israel, including some well-known deluxe hotels (Upgrade and construction of synagogues in hotels, n.d.). Many hotels advertise synagogues within walking distance, and Expedia, for example, advertises 175 hotels within walking distance of Jerusalem's Great Synagogue.

Figure 18.3 Greek Orthodox Church at Athens International Airport

Figure 18.4 Interfaith worship area at Athens International Airport

The cruise ship industry is developing rapidly, and according to the *Daily Telegraph*, more and more cruise lines provide spaces for worship while at sea (Archer, 2012). In this context, Di Foggia *et al.* (2012: 171) point to the provision of Muslim places of worship on cruise lines around Dubai. Moreover, some cruise companies train staff specially to meet the growing need of vacationers for church services (Cruise Ship Priest Program, n.d.).

Atmosphere

One of the more important aspects of the tourism experience is the atmosphere at the destination. Defining it is not simple, and the number of definitions almost equals the number of definers. Oktay (2016: 706) reviewed much of the research literature on atmosphere in the context of customer loyalty. A relevant definition for our purposes is 'the effort to design buying environments to produce specific emotional effects in the buyer that enhance purchase probability' (Kotler, in Oktay, 2016: 706). In many cases, the word 'atmosphere' does not stand alone. Roth and Langemeyer (1996) refer to *homely atmosphere* and *special atmosphere*; Oktay (2016: 706) refers to *service atmosphere*; and Urry (2007: 41) refers to *authentic atmosphere*. However, in the context of religious needs, the term *appropriate atmosphere* (Urry, 2002: 246) is the most suitable, and the aim of this section is to describe, analyse and interpret the appropriate atmosphere.

Strangeness vs. familiarity

In his seminal paper on the varieties of tourist experiences, Erik Cohen (1972) classified types of tourists according to their inclination/openness/readiness to being exposed to strangeness and familiarity. In the context of religion, we can also observe a continuum of attitudes towards other religious environments while touring. On the one hand, there are those who prefer to be surrounded by religious familiarity, and on the other hand, there are those who are attracted to religious strangeness while travelling. The first type will be motivated by reasons such as a preference for a religious comfort zone, easy access to permissible food and similarity of dress code, whereas the latter type will be attracted to different customs, traditions and philosophies. In contemporary Jewish Israeli society, there are good examples of both types: the Ultra-Orthodox Haredi Jews who seek seclusion (Mansfeld & Cahaner, 2013), and the young secular Israeli backpackers who travel to India and other destinations, and encounter non-Jewish religious experiences (Noy & Cohen, 2005).

Hotels

Hotels provide more than just accommodation. They are also cultural agents and culture brokers, and provide hospitality that can be addressed in cultural perspectives (Lashley, 2015). As such, they mediate between hosts and guests. The hospitality industry has developed hotels that cater to followers of specific faiths. This chapter will demonstrate this from the perspectives of Islam (Sharia-compliant hotels) and Judaism (glatt kosher hotels).

Sharia-compliant hotels

According to Henderson (2010: 246–247), 'Sharia' is an Arabic word meaning 'the clear, well-trodden path to water', which regulates everyday behaviour. The Sharia reflects a fivefold classification of human actions: obligatory, recommended, permitted, disliked and forbidden. Thus, Sharia-compliant hotels are a term relating to hotels that are built and operated in accordance with this classification.

According to Stephenson (2014: 157), for a hotel to be classified as Sharia-compliant it would have to contain features associated with five key components:

(1) *Human resources:* Traditional uniforms for staff; dress code for female staff; prayer time provision for Muslim employees; restricted working hours for Muslim staff during Ramadan; staff (and guest) adherence to moral codes of conduct.
(2) *Private rooms:* Separate floors with rooms allocated to women and families; markers indicating the direction of Mecca; prayer mats and copies of the Qur'an; conservative TV channels; geometric and non-figurative patterns of decoration (e.g. calligraphy); beds and toilets positioned facing away Mecca; toilets fitted with a bidet shower or health faucet; and halal-friendly complimentary toiletries.
(3) *Dining and banqueting facilities:* Halal food; dining quarter provision for women and families, in addition to communal area provision; art that does not depict human or animal form; and no inappropriate music.
(4) *Other public facilities:* No casino or gambling machines; separate leisure facilities (including swimming pools and spas) for both sexes; female and male prayer rooms equipped with the Qur'an; toilets facing away from Mecca.
(5) *Business operation:* Ethical marketing and promotion; corporate social responsibility strategies (linked to Islamic values) and philanthropic donations; and transactions and investments in accordance to principles and practices associated with Islamic banking, accounting and finance.

Such hotels are easier to operate in Muslim environments, but they can also be found in non-Muslim countries such as Australia, New Zealand, Japan, Korea, China, the United States, the United Kingdom and many more (Bahli, n.d.).

Glatt kosher hotels

A glatt kosher hotel is a hotel that has adopted a stricter standard of kashrut. One can distinguish between kosher hotels and glatt kosher hotels. Whereas the first term implies mainly the availability of kosher food, the latter term also has the cultural and sociological connotations of a very conservative clientele who prefer to be together, also because of the religious atmosphere (Diamond, 2002; Loewe, 2004).

By comparison to the Sharia-compliant hotel, the kosher and the glatt kosher hotels are more flexible. A regular hotel can be temporarily transformed into a kosher or glatt kosher hotel for high holidays, weekends, etc.; according to Diamond (2002: 498–499), in the United States 'Starting in the 1960s and . . . booming in the 1980s and 1990s, a new form of kosher hotel appeared. This model involved entrepreneurs temporarily taking over non-kosher hotels and resorts and providing kosher services for a limited period of time, often over the Passover holiday. Passover was a particularly popular (and profitable) time for the kosher hotel business because of the holiday's comprehensive food restrictions'.

Common elements in such hotels are:

(1) *A kosher kitchen:* The hotel kitchen must have proper inspection, according to the desired degree of kashrut.
(2) *Kosher food throughout the hotel facilities:* The kosher inspection applies to dining rooms, swimming pool snack bar, lobby and room service. Guests are requested not to bring food from the outside.
(3) *Shabbat elevator:* According to Loewe (2004: 300) 'The Shabbat or Sabbath elevator is one of several . . . inventions which allows Orthodox Jews to observe Sabbath regulations, but avoid the suffering or deprivation that strict adherence to Jewish law would otherwise entail. According to Jewish law, Orthodox Jews are prohibited from riding in elevators, using electrical appliances, or turning lights on and off, because using electricity is analogous to building a fire, and building fires is strictly forbidden on the Sabbath. The Sabbath elevator, however, circumvents the need to push buttons or "operate" the device. It is pre-programmed to stop at the floors where Orthodox hotel guests stay on the Sabbath'.
(4) *A place to pray:* Some hotels have a synagogue on their premises, while temporary synagogues can be improvised in the hotel meeting halls.
(5) *Appropriate dress code of employees:* The conservative dress code is essential, but the employees can be non-Jews.
(6) *Separation between men and women in swimming facilities:* If spatial separation is not applicable, there will be separate times – i.e. hours for men and hours for women.

Cruise ships

The cruise industry is developing rapidly, and one of the more interesting phenomena is religious segmentation – in other words, more and more people choose a cruise tour because of its cultural and religious compatibility. The following two examples are from the Latter-day Saints (Mormon) and Muslim contexts.

Latter Day Saints

According to Olsen (2006), Latter-day Saints cruises are becoming more popular. Surfing through Mormon tour companies' websites reveals that many Mormons prefer to join a cruise with other Mormons on board. The reasons can be the destinations but no less important is the educational component of daily lectures and concerts while on board (Alaska – The Last Frontier, n.d.; Book of Mormon Cruise March 1–8, 2009). Participants report that these cruises are 'spiritual and educational, in addition to being fun and relaxing' (Book of Mormon Cruise March 1–8, 2009). There is no data concerning such tours, but the assumption is that like other cruise products, the numbers are rising.

Islam

Cruises for Muslims are also an emerging phenomenon. According to Kessler (2015), the Salaam Cruise Company brands the cruise as a halal vacation experience, which includes not only food, but also appropriate activities including Islamic lectures by world-leading scholars and speakers, and destinations, such as mosques, where applicable. Unlike the Salaam cruise destinations which include the Bahamas (Abu Ibrahim, 2013), Iran's cruise destinations are more conservative: its first cruise ship since the 1979 Islamic Revolution recently completed its maiden trip and docked in the Persian Gulf resort island of Qeshm (Iran's first ever cruise ship completes maiden voyage, 2017).

Conclusion

Comparing the three religions

In this chapter, the choice was to focus only on the three Abrahamic traditions (Judaism, Christianity and Islam). Demographics indicate a significant difference in size between the three faiths – Christianity being the largest (32%), followed by Islam (23%) and Judaism (0.2%) (The global religious landscape, n.d.). The difference in size is not the only significant variable. Another important variable is the proportion between active (observant) and inactive members. It is estimated that about 70% of Muslims follow the dietary code (Bon & Hussain, 2010: 47) – which is probably very high compared to Christianity and Judaism. Moreover, the median age of Muslims is 23 years, of Christians is 30 years and Jews have the highest median age of 36 years, whereas the median age of the world's overall population is 28 years (The global religious landscape, n.d.).

One of the implications of these statistics is that the halal tourism industry is growing, which is probably one of the reasons for the abundance of academic and industry-related literature on Islam and tourism, in general, and Islam and halal tourism, in particular.

Based on the research discussed here, it was decided to present the differences between the three traditions along two sensitivity scales. Regarding food, Judaism would be the most sensitive, Islam would be sensitive but to a lesser degree, and Christianity would be the least sensitive. Regarding atmosphere, Islam would be the most sensitive, followed by Judaism. In both elements (food and atmosphere), Christianity would be the least sensitive. As for ritual, it is difficult to suggest a clear sensitivity scale.

Future research

Despite the focus on three religions only, several topics were not covered by this research, which could be covered by future research. A partial list would include four issues:

(1) *Periods of travel*: All three religions have their own calendar, which implies (both formally and informally) when to travel and when to refrain from travelling. In Judaism, for example, there is a period of three weeks in the summer during which it is recommended not to travel.
(2) *Guidebooks:* Apart from the ordinary guidebooks that describe a destination, some guidebooks focus on a destination with an emphasis on a particular religious background, such as Spain for the Muslim traveller.
(3) *Tour guides:* When tourists reach a destination, often they use the services of a tour guide, who can refer to their religious background. One example is from Ephesus, in Turkey. Despite the archaeological and historical background, the Christian traveller expects the (usually) Muslim guide to refer to the New Testament.
(4) *Dress code:* Followers of certain religions have their typical and normative dress code, to which the host societies are not always sensitive. A good example would be the French attitude towards the Bourkini. From the Muslim point of view, a conservative dress code is required even at the beach, but from the French point of view, it is a violation of French law.

We are encountering an increasing rate of segmentation in many aspects of life, and religious needs are no exception. One can only assume that this trend will continue to develop. Based on the demographics presented above, it is expected that the phenomenon of Sharia-compliant hotels and specialised cruise tours in particular will increase.

References

Abu Ibrahim (2013) Salaam cruise: The Muslim vacation getaway. See http://muslimmatters. org/2013/01/21/salaam-cruise/ (accessed 16 April 2017).

Adidaya, Y.A. (2016) Halal in Japan: History, issues and problems: The effect of the 'Halal boom' phenomenon on Japanese society and industry. MA thesis, University of Oslo.

Al Jahwari, D.S. (2015) An integrative model of Muslim students' religiosity and travelling behaviour to gaming destinations. PhD thesis, College of Hospitality, Retail and Sport Management, University of South Carolina. See http://scholarcommons.sc.edu/ etd/3214 (accessed 7 April 2017).

Alaska. See http://www.cruiselady.com/cruise/alaska (accessed 16 April 2017).

Archer, J. (2012) Do cruise lines provide a place of worship? *The Telegraph.* See http://www. telegraph.co.uk/travel/cruises/articles/Do-cruise-lines-provide-a-place-of-worship/ (accessed 9 April 2017).

Bahli, S. (n.d.) 'Shariah compliant hotel' or 'Muslim friendly hotel': Searching for a balance. See   https://www.academia.edu/22372230/_SHARIAH_COMPLIANT_HOTEL_ OR_MUSLIM_FRIENDLY_HOTEL_SEARCHING_FOR_A_BALANCE_ Introduction (accessed 15 April 2017).

Battour, M. and Ismail, M.N. (2016) Halal tourism: Concepts, practices, challenges and future. *Tourism Management Perspectives* 19, 150–154.

Battour, M., Ismail, M.N. and Battor, M. (2011) The impact of destination attributes on Muslim tourist's choice. *International Journal of Tourism Research* 13 (6), 527–540.

Book of Mormon Cruise (March 1–8, 2009). See http://www.webbtours.com/ brochures%5CBook%20of%20Mormon%20Cruise%2009.pdf (accessed 16 April 2017).

Boğan, A.G., Batman, O. and Sariişik, M. (2016) An evaluation depend on the conceptual framework of halal tourism and applications in Turkey. See https://www. academia.edu/25702923/Helal_Turizmin_Kavramsal_%C3%87er%C3%A7evesi_ ve_T%C3%BCrkiyedeki_Uygulamalar_%C3%9Czerine_Bir_ De%C4%9Ferlendirme_An_Evaluation_Depend_on_the_Conceptual_Framework_ of_Halal_Tourism_and_Applications_in_Turkey (accessed 2 April 2017).

Bon, M. and Hussain, M. (2010) Halal food and tourism: Prospects and challenges. In N. Scott and J. Jafari (eds) *Tourism in the Muslim World (Bridging Tourism Theory and Practice, Volume 2)* (pp. 47–59). Bingley: Emerald Group Publishing Limited.

Brown, P. (1998) *Catskill Culture: A Mountain Rat's Memories of the Great Jewish Resort Area.* Philadelphia, PA: Temple University Press.

Cahaner, L. (2009) The development of the spatial and hierarchic structure among the ultra-orthodox population in Israel. PhD thesis, University of Haifa.

Cahaner, L. and Mansfeld, Y. (2012) A voyage from religiousness to secularity and back: A glimpse into 'Haredi' tourists. *Journal of Heritage Tourism* 7 (4), 301–321.

Cahaner, L., Yozgof-Aurbach, N. and Sofer, A. (2012) Ultra-orthodox in Israel – Space, society and community. Reuven Chaikin Chair in Geostrategy, University of Haifa (in Hebrew).

Cahaner, L., Jonas, A. and Mansfeld, Y. (2015) Between myths and risk perception among Haredi tourists. *Journal of Acta Touristica* 27 (1), 7–31.

Carboni, M. and Janati, M.I. (2016) Halal tourism de facto: A case from Fez. *Tourism Management Perspectives* 19, 155–159.

Cetin, G. and Zeki Dincer, M. (2016) Muslim friendly tourism (MFT): A discussion. *Journal of Tourismology* 2 (1), 65–67.

Cohen, E. (1972) Toward a sociology of international tourism. *Social Research* 39 (1), 164–182.

Cohen Ioannides, M.W. and Ioannides, D. (2006) Global Jewish tourism: Pilgrimages and remembrance. In D.J. Timothy and D.H. Olsen (eds) *Tourism, Religion and Spiritual Journeys* (pp. 156–171). London: Routledge.

Coleman, S. and Elsner, J. (1995) *Pilgrimage: Past and Present in the World Religions.* Cambridge, MA: Harvard University Press.

Collins-Kreiner, N. and Kliot, N. (2000) Pilgrimage tourism in the Holy Land: The behavioural characteristics of Christian pilgrims. *GeoJournal* 50 (1), 55–67.

Cruise Ship Priest Program (n.d.). See http://www.aos-usa.org/store/pg/40-About-the-Cruise-Ship-Priest-Program-clone.aspx (accessed 9 April 2017).

Di Foggia, G., Lazzarotti, V. and Pizzurno, E. (2012) The economics and management of innovation in travel and tourism services. *UTMS Journal of Economics* 3 (2), 167–179.

Diamond, E. (2002) The kosher lifestyle: Religious consumerism and suburban Orthodox Jews. *Journal of Urban History* 28 (4), 488–505.

Duman, T. (2012) The value of Islamic tourism: Perspectives from the Turkish experience. See http://www.iais.org.my/icr/index.php/icr/article/viewFile/13/12 (accessed 2 April 2017).

Elaziz, M.F. and Kurt, A. (2017) Religiosity, consumerism and halal tourism: A study of seaside tourism organizations in Turkey. *Tourism* 65 (1), 115–128.

El-Gohary, H. (2016) Halal tourism, is it really halal? *Tourism Management Perspectives* 19, 124–130.

Fast days: Days of opportunity (n.d.). See http://www.chabad.org/library/article_cdo/aid/609607/jewish/Fast-Days.htm (accessed 8 April 2017).

Goodman, M. (2007) *Judaism in the Roman World: Collected Essays.* Leiden/Boston, MA: Brill.

Henderson, J.C. (2009) Islamic tourism reviewed. *Tourism Recreational Research* 32 (2), 207–211.

Henderson, J.C. (2010) Sharia-compliant hotels. *Tourism and Hospitality Research* 10 (3), 246–254.

Henderson, J.C. (2016) Halal food, certification and halal tourism: Insights from Malaysia and Singapore. *Tourism Management Perspectives* 19, 160–164.

Ioannides, D. and Cohen Ioannides, M.W. (2002) Pilgrimages of nostalgia: Patterns of Jewish travel in the United States. *Tourism Recreation Research* 27 (2), 17–26.

Iran's first ever cruise ship completes maiden voyage (2017) Travel Wirenews. See http://travelwirenews.com/irans-first-ever-cruise-ship-completes-maiden-voyage-53954/ (accessed 16 April 2017).

Izberk-Bilgin, E. and Nakata, C.C. (2016) A new look at faith-based marketing: The global halal market. *Business Horizons* 59 (3), 285–292.

Jafari, J. and Scott, N. (2014) Muslim world and its tourisms. *Annals of Tourism Research* 44, 1–19.

Johnson, K. (1990) Origins of tourism in the Catskill Mountains. *Journal of Cultural Geography* 11 (1), 5–16.

Kashrus Magazine (2016) Kosher travel guide. See http://www.kashrusmagazine.com/magazine.php?do=180 (accessed 11 March 2017).

Kessler, K. (2015) Conceptualizing mosque tourism: A central feature of Islamic and religious tourism. *International Journal of Religious Tourism and Pilgrimage* 3 (2), 11–32.

Klein, D. (2015) Using Airbnb to stay in (frum) Jewish neighborhoods. See http://yeahthatskosher.com/2015/07/using-airbnb-to-stay-in-frum-jewish-neighborhoods/ (accessed 11 March 2017).

Klin-Oron, A. (2005) Sun, sea and shtreimels – Haredi vacations in Israel. MA thesis, The Hebrew University of Jerusalem.

Lashley, C. (2015) Hospitality and hospitableness. *Research in Hospitality Management* 5 (1), 1–7.

Lent (n.d.) See https://en.wikipedia.org/wiki/Lent (accessed 25 March 2017).

Lent menu in hotel's restaurants (n.d.). See http://cpairport.ru/en/hotel-info/events/lent-menu/ (accessed 25 March 2017).

Loewe, R. (2004) From Moscow to Curaçao: Orthodoxy, evasion, and competition in Jewish life. *Reviews in Anthropology* 33 (3), 299–315.

Mansfeld, Y. and Cahaner, L. (2013) Ultra-orthodox Jewish tourism: A differential passage out of a socio-cultural bubble to the 'open space'. *Tourism Analysis* 18 (1), 15–27.

Mansfeld, Y., Jonas, A. and Cahaner, L. (2016) Between tourists' faith and perceptions of travel risk. *Journal of Travel Research* 55 (3), 395–413.

Mansfeld, Y., Ron, A. and Gev, D. (2000) *Muslim Tourism to Israel–Characterization, Trends and Potential.* Center for Tourism, Pilgrimage, and Recreation Haifa: University of Haifa.

Maoz, D. and Bekerman, Z. (2010) Searching for Jewish answers in Indian resorts: The postmodern traveler. *Annals of Tourism Research* 37 (2), 423–439.

Mauss, A.L. (1972) Saints, cities, and secularism: Religious attitudes and behaviour of modern urban Mormons. *Dialogue – A Journal of Mormon Thought* 7 (2), 8–27.

Miller, F.P., Vandome, A.F. and McBrewster, J. (2009) *Christian Denomination.* Saarbrücken: VDM Verlag.

Mohsin, A., Ramli, N. and Alkhulayfi, B.A. (2016) Halal tourism: Emerging opportunities. *Tourism Management Perspectives* 19, 137–143.

Mujtaba, U. (2016) Ramadan: The month of fasting for Muslims, and tourism studies: Mapping the unexplored connection. *Tourism Management Perspectives* 19, 170–177.

Notes on daily bible readings (n.d.). See http://www.dailyreadings.org.uk/ (accessed 8 April 2017).

Noy, C. and Cohen, E. (eds) (2005) *Israeli Backpackers: From Tourism to a Rite of Passage.* New York: State University of New York Press.

Oktay, E. (2016) A study of the relationship between service atmosphere and customer loyalty with specific reference to structural equation modelling. *Economic Research-Ekonomska Istraživanja* 29 (1), 706–720.

Olsen, D.H. (2006) Tourism and informal pilgrimage among the Latter-day Saints. In D.J. Timothy and D.H. Olsen (eds) *Tourism, Religion and Spiritual Journeys* (pp. 254–270). London: Routledge.

Olsen, D.H. (2013) A scalar comparison of motivations and expectations of experience within the religious tourism market. *International Journal of Religious Tourism and Pilgrimage* 1 (1), 41–61.

Olsen, D.H. and Ron, A.S. (2013) Managing religious heritage attractions: The case of Jerusalem. In B. Garrod and A. Fyall (eds) *Contemporary Cases in Heritage: Volume 1* (pp. 51–78). Oxford: Goodfellow.

Pollack, T. (2011) Keeping kosher in Greek isles. See http://yeahthatskosher.com/2008/07/greek-isles-greece/ (accessed 11 March 2017).

Polyxeni, M., Mylonopoulos, D. and Kondoudaki, A. (2012) The management of tourist's alimentary needs by the tourism industry. The parameter of religion. *International Journal of Culture and Tourism Research* 5 (1), 129–140.

Razzaq, S.A. (2016) Halal, New Zealand! An exploratory study into the halal-friendliness of accommodation providers in New Zealand. MC thesis, University of Canterbury, New Zealand.

Razzaq, S., Hall, C.M. and Prayag, G. (2016) The capacity of New Zealand to accommodate the halal tourism market: Or not. *Tourism Management Perspectives* 18, 92–97.

Ritual (n.d.). See https://www.merriam-webster.com/dictionary/ritual (accessed 7 April 2017).

Ron, A.S. (2009) Towards a typological model of contemporary Christian travel. *Journal of Heritage Tourism* 4 (4), 287–297.

Roth, P. and Langemeyer, A. (1996) Cultural tourism in Germany. In G. Richards (ed.) *Cultural Tourism in Europe* (pp. 122–133). Wallingford: CABI.

Samori, Z., Salleh, N.Z.M. and Khalid, M.M. (2016) Current trends on halal tourism: Cases on selected Asian countries. *Tourism Management Perspectives* 19, 131–136.

Shaari, J.A.N., Khalique, M. and Malek, N.I.A. (2013) Halal restaurant: Lifestyle of Muslims in Penang. *International Journal of Global Business* 6 (2), 1–15.

Simoons, F.J. (1994) *Eat Not This Flesh: Food Avoidances from Prehistory to the Present* (2nd edn). Madison, WI: The University of Wisconsin Press.

Sparks, I. (2016). See http://www.dailymail.co.uk/news/article-3419814/Lunch-French-Iranians-CANCELLED-President-Hollande-refused-wine-menu-meeting-Muslim-counterpart-Rouhani.html (accessed 3 April 2017).

Stausberg, M. (2011) *Religion and Tourism: Crossroads, Destinations and Encounters.* London/New York: Routledge.

Stephenson, M.L. (2014) Deciphering 'Islamic hospitality': Developments, challenges and opportunities. *Tourism Management* 40, 155–164.

Syanberg, J., Withall, A., Draper, B. and Bowden, S. (eds) (2015) *Alcohol and the Adult Brain (Current Issues in Neuropsychology)* (1st edn). London/New York: Psychology Press.

The fasting rule of the Orthodox Church (n.d.). See http://www.abbamoses.com/fasting.html (accessed 8 April 2017).

The global religious landscape (n.d.). See http://www.pewforum.org/2012/12/18/global-religious-landscape-exec/ (accessed 17 April 2017).

The halal problem at Disneyland Paris (2014). See https://www.tripadvisor.com/ShowTopic-g2079053-i21935-k7721885-The_halal_problem_at_Disney_land_paris-Disneyland_Paris_Seine_et_Marne_Ile_de_France.html (accessed 3 April 2017.

Timothy, D.J. and Olsen, D.H. (eds) (2006) *Tourism, Religion and Spiritual Journeys.* London: Routledge.

Timothy, D.J. and Ron, A.S. (2016) Religious heritage, spiritual aliment and food for the soul. In D.J. Timothy (ed.) *Heritage Cuisines: Traditions, Identities and Tourism* (pp. 104–118). London: Routledge.

Upgrade and construction of synagogues in hotels (n.d.) (in Hebrew). See http://www.melonaim.org/?CategoryID=0&ArticleID=5539 (accessed 9 April 2017).

Urry, J. (2002) Gaze. In J. Jafari (ed.) *Encyclopaedia of Tourism* (p. 246). London: Routledge.

Urry, J. (2007) *Mobilities.* Cambridge: Polity Press.

Weidenfeld, A. (2006) Religious needs in the hospitality industry. *Tourism and Hospitality Research* 6 (2), 143–159.

Weidenfeld, A. and Ron, A.S. (2008) Religious needs in the tourism industry. *Anatolia: An International Journal of Tourism and Hospitality Research* 19 (2), 357–361.

Wright, W. and Annes, A. (2013) Halal on the menu? Contested food politics and French identity in fast-food. *Journal of Rural Studies* 32, 388–399.

19 Tourism and Religion: Themes, Issues and Conclusions

Richard Butler and Wantanee Suntikul

Summary

In this volume, as editors, we have tried to illustrate the many facets of the tourism–religious nexus, primarily from a tourist perspective. The vast amount of literature on religion, religious tourism and pilgrimage has already been discussed by many of the contributors to the volume, and it is not our intent to return to this material. We have emphasised that the focus of this volume is on the relationships, problems, difficulties, conflicts, issues and benefits that occur when tourism and religion interact. This situation is almost inevitable as religious artefacts, sites and symbols are also often major tourist attractions, and thus tourists will visit such locations, often whether they are 'marked' as tourist attractions or not, and even when there is little or no formal provision made for visitors. When such situations are combined with what may be thought of as inappropriate behaviour by tourists or excessive numbers of tourists at these locations, or what are seen as unacceptable restrictions placed on visitors by those in charge of such features, then the potential for conflict and disagreement is high. When this situation is complicated and exacerbated by political and other influences on the management and accessibility of these features, any potential issues and problems become magnified and the effects may extend far beyond the footprints of the sites themselves. Such conflicts are not confined to those between secular and religious elements, but also include disagreements, sometimes becoming violent, between religious groups, as witnessed by violence between Christian sects over the management of the Church of the Holy Sepulchre in Jerusalem a century ago and disagreements between Shia and Sunni leaders over participation in the hajj in Mecca in recent years.

Several major themes emerge from the discussions. One is the increasing level of interaction between religious and secular interests at religious sites. A second is the increasingly secular use of such sites. Compounding these issues is the involvement of politics and ideology in the management and control of religious sites of tourism significance, and underlying some of the actions taken by those in control is the need or desire for economic gain from tourism. All of these potential problems are exacerbated by the dynamic nature of tourism and the continuously increasing numbers of tourists globally, to whom sacred sites, by virtue of their architecture, history, grandeur, heritage and visibility, are places to visit, often unrelated to any spiritual or religious motivation.

The first part of this volume discussed examples of the involvement of different faiths with tourism, beginning with King's chapter on indigenous rights and viewpoints on sacred sites. O'Gorman noted the role of the Christian church in providing hospitality to travellers, initially pilgrims and other religious travellers, a role increasingly driven by economics in recent years. Raj and Kessler and Kanvinde and Binumol discussed the appeal and role of mosques and temples and motivations for visiting these structures, while Wong noted how the religious guardians of a sacred site responded to coping with visitors of all types. Collins-Kreiner and Luz and Nakanishi reflected on how changes in technology and viewpoints have changed the way the faithful in Judaism and Shintoism now visit their sacred sites. All of these chapters reflected the dynamic nature of visitation to religious sites and the changing motivations of many visitors.

Subsequent chapters dealt with aspects of religiosity and the religious element in travel and tourism, particularly in the context of pilgrimage, a subject dealt with specifically by Ostrometskaia and Griffin in the context of Russia and the effects of political change there on religious observance. The issue of spirituality and travel was examined by Terzidou, Scarles and Saunders, and in passing by several other contributors. In the latter cases, it is clear that travel to sacred sites is an integral part of all faiths and thus interaction with, and being part of, tourism is almost inevitable. In places like Santiago de Compostela, which is not a only a key pilgrimage site but also a major tourist attraction, the amount of contact between these groups has been increased by the growing popularity of the Camino, a phenomenon that is occurring and being developed in other areas in Europe and elsewhere, as the chapter by Timothy and Olsen revealed. As described by Serrallonga, the promotion of spiritual tourism and the development of routes for spiritual travellers are also driven by political goals including encouraging the growth of European unity. Inevitably such developments bring secular and religious tourists into contact with each other in the context of religious sites and structures, with many implications.

From the political perspective, Mercer clearly demonstrated how religion and tourism can be used in a much less attractive manner, namely to enable maintenance of control by a dominant religious majority over people of minority faiths in Myanmar, where the development of tourism to religious centres determined by the military government saw the relocation of local residents, the imposition of forced labour, and violence against minority groups, resulting in an international tourism boycott of the country. While the enormous and spectacular legacy of religious temples in Myanmar is a great tourist attraction, the religious intolerance of the government and its subsequent actions proved too great a deterrent and these policies have since been amended as the military control of power has diminished. It serves as a sad reminder of how the combination of politics, tourism and religion can have negative repercussions for local residents (Butler & Suntikul, 2013). The political aspect of visitation to religious sites is a topic also discussed by Collins-Kreiner and Shmueli in the context of framing specific problems in this area, and as Isaac demonstrated, is a major factor in the problems facing the development and maintenance of tourism to holy sites in Palestine.

Problems of Interaction between the Secular and the Religious

Increasingly, religious institutions are taking a more proactive role in their relationships with tourism and leisure for a variety of reasons. Some see such increased involvement as being part of their missionary function, while others see financial benefits to allow them to maintain and improve the fabric and operation of buildings and other structures.

As Olsen and Timothy showed with their examination of Salt Lake City, religious groups can use secular tourism as well as religious pilgrimage to obtain economic benefits for their faith and the secular regions of the city and state and successfully combine the secular and religious elements of tourism. Curtis demonstrated a similar success for English cathedrals in attracting increased visitation and income, thus aiding the preservation of the fabric and operation of some of the great churches of England, albeit by welcoming users, many of them secular, with a wide range of backgrounds and motivations.

One striking example of this deliberate involvement with tourism and leisure is demonstrated by Winchester Cathedral in England. Each winter, the cathedral authorities erect an ice rink and a Christmas market next to the cathedral (see Figure 16.1) and promote these widely on their website (www.winchester-cathedral.org.uk) along with a lengthy list of additional activities which can be enjoyed at the cathedral. As they noted, this set of activities attracts a considerable number of people to the building and helps support the cost of the upkeep of the cathedral (around £10,000 a day). Agencies offering accommodation and other services to travellers are beginning to appreciate the economic benefits of catering specifically to the needs of religious tourists, as Ron illustrated in his chapter, and great efforts have been made to make the hajj both more comfortable and secure for the faithful with commercial and religious developments in Mecca. Despite the potential importance of tourism-generated income for religious sites in terms of maintenance and preservation, there has been little academic study of this topic, but in the future it is likely to assume even more importance than at present.

One key issue of the primarily secular use of religious properties is the avoidance of conflict between religious and secular users. While Wong explained the attitudes of Buddhist monks in dealing with secular visitors to temples, in many cases conflict can be avoided by scheduling secular activities at times that do not conflict with religious ceremonies. It is not always possible to avoid some level of disagreement or conflict, however. In the Orkney Islands, off the north coast of mainland Scotland, the Island Council felt obliged to take measures to avoid problems caused by tourists who were disturbing religious services and funerals in St Magnus Cathedral in Kirkwall, the island capital. Tourists were reported ignoring signs indicating the cathedral was closed because of private funerals, taking photographs of private ceremonies, removing orders of service sheets as souvenirs and even attempting to lift the lid of a coffin (Horne, 2016).

Viero (2003), in his study of interaction between local residents (users of the cathedral in Santiago de Compostela) and tourist visitors to the cathedral, found that residents could be categorised on the basis of their response to, and behavioural adjustment resulting from, contact with non-religious users of the cathedral. They *embraced* tourists, in the sense of accepting and approving of them; engaged in *boundary maintenance*, whereby they avoided tourists by voluntarily adjusting their visitation to the cathedral to be there when tourists were absent; while the third group engaged in what he termed *forced adjustment*, feeling they had little option but to change their times of visit to the cathedral and visit less often because of the presence of tourists. Interestingly, he discovered little negative feeling towards tourism in general in the town, but the last two groups expressed discontentment with tourists as individuals because of their behaviour and presence in the cathedral. There are clear similarities in the reported attitudes and behavioural responses of residents in that study to the work of Ap and Crompton (1993) and Dogan (1989) on resident attitudes to tourists in general. It is important to note that residents felt disturbed by the presence of tourists in other, secular, parts of Santiago de Compostela also, indicating that the drawing power and impact of the cathedral extended beyond the confines of the building itself. The powerful attraction of many important religious sites and artefacts reaches distant markets and clearly has effects beyond their immediate footprint, bringing into communities some visitors at least, who may have very different attitudes and patterns of behaviour to those of local residents. Such has been the case from the time of the Crusades and even earlier.

Notwithstanding the comments above, it is clear that many religious organisations are actively engaging in tourism promotion and development. Mention has already been made of the role of religious institutions in offering accommodation to visitors, beginning with O'Gorman's chapter, and this has extended in many other ways. Italian convent organisations have taken in paying guests for many years, and provide a different experience to conventional accommodation for visitors to Florence, Rome and Venice among other tourist cities (Ogden, 2017), while at least 20 temples cater for tourists in Korea under the title 'Templestay'. This programme is designed as a cultural programme allowing visitors to 'experience the 1,700-year-old traditions of Korean Buddhism' (www.Templestay.com, n.d.) and is supported by a video created by the Cultural Corps of Korean Buddhism (2013). In order to improve the pilgrim experience and mitigate the impact of so many travellers, the Green Pilgrimage Network (2014), which began in 2011, 'inspires pilgrim places to (amongst other actions) promote responsible tourism (and) accommodate pilgrim visitors sustainably'. In Cyprus, the Church of Cyprus (2008) has combined with the Cyprus Tourism Organisation to create the 'Cyprus Island of Saints Pilgrimage Tour'. A similar development has taken place in Paraguay where the 'Ruta Jesuitica' blends culture, history and spirituality, also in conjunction with the national tourist organisation (Camara Paraguaya de Turismo de las Misiones Jesuiticas, n.d.). At the time of writing (2017), the anniversary of the beginning of the Protestant Reformation is being celebrated in Germany, especially in Wittenberg in Saxony-Anhalt, where Martin Luther is supposed to have nailed his theses to the church door. The region and related sites have become known as 'Lutherland', and a Playmobil miniature toy figure of Luther has become the fastest selling of such items, outselling *Peppa Pig* and characters from *Frozen* and *Ninja Turtles*. The development of associated tourist attractions has included 'eat like Luther' menus in restaurants, hiking trails following his journeys called 'Luther Tours', museums in various towns associated with him and accommodation being provided in Erfurt monastery where he studied (Greaves, 2015).

Thus, the combined marketing of religious phenomena (inanimate, constructed and human) is continuing apace. The media, in all forms, shares considerable responsibility for the significant rise in religious-related travel. Page (2010) reported a massive increase in the popularity of, and subsequent visitation to, a shrine in Kashmir following a reference to it in the *Lonely Planet* guide. The shrine, of a medieval Muslim preacher, was claimed to be the burial place of Jesus. Such was the increase in visitation that the shrine was closed to Western visitors because of local resident resentment. The manager commented 'It is the work of people associated with the tourist trade. They are misleading visitors....' (cited in Page, 2010: 42). The great passion for taking 'selfies' and other photographs has also resulted in problems with tourists being charged with offences and even imprisoned for inappropriate behaviour in sacred locations. Four tourists who posed naked on a sacred mountain top in Malaysia were blamed for a subsequent earthquake which killed 18 people (Alexander, 2015). Previously, in other areas, tourists were deported from Cambodia for taking nude pictures in Angkor Wat, and others detained for being naked at Machu Picchu in Peru.

In general, problems occurring in the context of contact between the secular and the religious arise because of two major problems. One relates to the numbers of visitors and a second to the behaviour of visitors. Numbers present a problem, not only of secular but also of religious tourists, as has been demonstrated at the hajj, where the large numbers involved (several million) annually result in deaths and injuries stemming primarily from overcrowding at the sacred site in Mecca. In other locations, it is mostly the numbers of secular tourists who overcrowd and even distort the use and experience of sacred sites for others by their presence. In many cases, the problems resulting from inappropriate behaviour of mostly secular tourists at sacred sites stem from lack of knowledge of what is appropriate behaviour and lack of information on the same topic. There is no doubt, however, that deliberate disregard for the sacred nature of specific sites and the wishes of the local residents and faithful also provokes dislike and even antagonism towards visitors. More rigid enforcement of temporal constraints, not allowing visits to a site during religious practice for example, would alleviate some issues. In other situations, physical constraints may be necessary, such as preventing access to parts of a site. The banning of secular visitors completely from sacred sites would be a last step and in many cases would run contrary to the welcoming mission of most faiths, as well as missing the opportunity both to invite participation in the particular faith and to obtain much needed financial support for the physical fabric of many sites. Analogies to the problems facing those responsible for managing and protecting natural areas such as national parks are easy to see, and the comments made in the second chapter, by King, in the context of the management of Uluru and Kata Tjuta National Park to meet the concerns of local Aboriginal residents and owners of the site are very valid in this context. For example, the removal of the chain that supports and thus encourages visitors to climb Uluru would also remove much of the temptation and feasibility of inappropriate or undesired behaviour. Inclusion of all viewpoints, cooperation between all parties and a willingness to compromise when that does not threaten or endanger the specific site or artefact are all essential for the effective and appropriate management and use of such sensitive sites.

Pilgrimage: From Religious to Secular

As several authors in this volume have noted, pilgrimage is a complex phenomenon and over recent decades in particular has taken a variety of forms, again reflecting the dynamic nature of tourism. These forms have ranged from the traditional strictly penitent religious format to secular forms of travel that have been dubbed 'pilgrimage' in the popular and tourist media. *Schott's Almanac of New Tourism* (Schott, 2008) listed 13 modern trends in tourism and travel; pilgrimage was listed as one of the trends, along with climateers, staycations and debauchery. Schott (2008: 11) mentions religious pilgrimage to conventional sacred sites such as Lourdes, but also notes 'pagan pilgrimages' to alternative festivals and gatherings including musical events, lifestyle events and extreme sporting occasions. It is not only extreme sporting events that attract so called pilgrims. The term has become common in usage to describe travellers visiting specific sites of importance to the heritage of sporting activities. The 'spiritual' homes of cricket, Lord's ground in London and Rupertswood in Australia (the location of the origin of The Ashes, an iconic trophy contested for over a century between Australia and England) are two sites that are visited by cricket pilgrims on a regular basis (Baum & Butler, 2014). The Old Course at St Andrews is universally accepted as 'The Home of Golf', being the oldest golf course in existence, and the home of the Rules of Golf for most of the world, and is commonly referred to as 'the Mecca of Golf' (Butler, 2011). The British Golf Museum in St Andrews is one of the top 20 tourist attractions in Scotland and as one of the authors has frequently observed personally, many golfers visiting St Andrews talk of being 'pilgrims' to the 'home of golf'. Key locations for other sports achieve similar sacred status: Celtic Football Club in Glasgow, founded by an Irish priest in the 19th century, plays at Parkhead, but to fans the ground is known as 'Paradise', while rugby commentators talk of the 'sacred turf' at Twickenham, the home of English rugby. This endowing of sporting locations with a sacred image is not solely a British phenomenon. 'Halls of Fame' for various sports are found in a number of countries and are seen by fans as places of pilgrimage, and increasingly many sporting venues open their premises to visitors when sport is not being played there, in the same manner as cathedrals and temples are opened to secular visitors when not in religious use.

Having observed Real Madrid fans make the sign of the cross on entering the tunnel to the playing field at the Bernabéu Stadium in Madrid, it is not unreasonable to make a comparison with the faithful entering a church or temple. The website selling tickets to the stadium concludes by stating that visitors can 'Finish your exploration of Santiago Bernabéu by paying homage to the team's on-site museum' (www.realmadrid.com/en). On a tour of the stadium, the comparison with visiting a holy place is strong: visitors are shown the trophies (relics) won by the club; photographs of the players (saints) adorn the walls of the dressing room; the tunnel (nave) leads to the playing field (altar); and one can acquire both souvenirs (relics) and photographs taken with replicas of the trophies or players. One pays for the privilege of entering this iconic building (indulgencies) and is certainly somewhat overawed on emerging at the end of the tour. As with secular visitors to religious sites, it is doubtful if the experience results in conversion to becoming an adherent of the faith or a fan of Real Madrid, but to those already so inclined, such a visit is indeed a pilgrimage.

Whether such visits should be considered as pilgrimages or whether they have any religious significance is less important in the context of tourism than the fact that the motivation to visit such places makes them appropriate to consider in that context. In the same manner, fans of specific films and television programmes display pilgrim-like behaviour in visiting the settings of their favourite programmes. Visits to film site locations have been examined at considerable length (see for example Beeton, 2010) and the phenomenon of 'movie-induced tourism' is clearly acknowledged. Similar phenomena exist for television programmes: Highclere Castle, the setting for *Downton Abbey*, the London scenes for *Sherlock Holmes* fans and the Scottish Highlands the setting for Hogwarts in *Harry Potter* films and *Outlander*, have all experienced greatly increased visitation since they appeared in popular media, and attract fans wishing to visit the settings, both real and fictional, of the programmes. Music has not escaped this trend, as shown by the continued popularity of the town of Salzburg, both for its Mozart connections, and as the setting for parts of *The Sound of Music*, while the most popular music-related site in terms of visitation is Graceland, the former home of the late Elvis Presley. The popularity of Graceland, along with visitation to places like Père Lachaise cemetery in Paris ('tombstone tourism' – Daly, 2017), the burial place of Jim Morrison, Maria Callas, Frédéric Chopin and Oscar Wilde, show how visiting a memorial to a deceased artist has become very clearly another form of pilgrimage, in these cases perhaps more worthy of the term. Visitation to such sites as graveyards, and indeed, many churches, mosques, temples and other sacred sites marking the resting place of deceased saints, prophets and other religious people, take us to links between religion and 'dark tourism'.

'Dark tourism' (Sharpley & Stone, 2009) is now a well-established subform of tourism, and although whether visitation to all places associated with death is 'dark' or not is open to debate, it is clear that visits to graves and death sites are perhaps appropriately considered as part of the tourism–religion nexus. Winter (2009, 2011) has discussed the nature of visitation to WW1 battlefield and cemetery sites in Flanders, and this phenomenon has been sensitively reviewed by Miles (2016) in his volume on *The Western Front*. There is little doubt that for many such tourists engaged in 'battlefield tourism' there is a large element of spirituality in their experience. Those visiting sites where family members or people known to them died are inevitably affected by the experience, and even those who have had no direct personal link with the dead, rarely remain unmoved at such locations as the Menin Gate (a WW1 monument inscribed with the names of over 54,000 men who died with no known grave), the USS *Arizona* site in Honolulu or any of the many large cemeteries preserved as monuments to the war dead throughout the world. The entries in visitor books at such places serve as confirmation of this (Winter, 2011), as many visitors describe their visit as a 'pilgrimage'. In a similar vein, visits to former concentration camps and memorials to the Holocaust should also be seen as forms of pilgrimage, with inappropriate behaviour of some visitors being the cause of considerable concern and distress to others. The spectrum of dark tourism developed by Stone (2006) is relevant here, as at the one end, such visitation falls clearly into pilgrimage, where the motivation is spiritual, if not religious, while at the other end, it is conventional tourism to visit an object or site of curiosity, perhaps associated with an event or person that had meaning to the visitor. Figure 19.1 illustrates the overlap between three subsets of tourism – religious, dark and conventional – with typical destinations placed in the appropriate sectors.

Thus, in Figure 19.1, Mecca might be placed at M, clearly falling into religious tourism, the Somme Battlefield Cemetery (SB) as both religious and dark tourism, Auschwitz (A) as dark tourism, Lord's cricket ground (L) as primarily conventional tourism but with a religious-like connotation, Graceland (G) being both conventional and dark tourism, Jerusalem (J) as being relevant to all three types of tourism and Disneyworld (D) as being clearly conventional tourism. As with most tourist activities, it is likely that few, if any, of such visits would be taken in isolation if part of a vacation, although the desire to visit a specific site may be a major factor in the decision to visit a specific region. Thus, unlike a formal traditional pilgrimage for religious purposes such as the hajj, such trips might represent only one or more elements of a more conventional tourist holiday.

In this increasingly secular (at least in the West) world, pilgrimage has come to mean much more than religiously inspired and devoted, if not obligatory, travel. Tourists are visiting sites and settings in recognition of, and admiration for, people, situations and places for which they have strong feelings and sometimes a personal connection. To them it would appear natural to think of such trips as pilgrimages despite the lack of

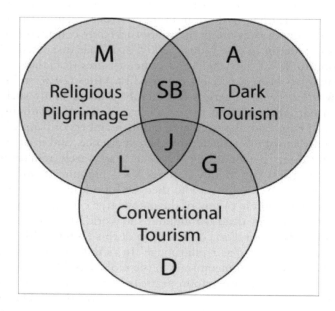

Figure 19.1 Religious, dark and conventional tourism

direct religious connections. When these locations are also the setting for religious pilgrimages, the potential difficulties and issues are clear.

Conclusions

Tourism and religion will almost certainly remain inextricably linked in the future just as they have been for centuries past. Religious observance generally requires travel by the faithful, sometimes at a local scale to the nearest church, mosque or temple, sometimes over considerable distances to shrines, cathedrals, central mosques and temples, and sometimes very lengthy travel to specific sites such as the Holy Land for Christians, to Jerusalem for the Jewish faithful, to designated sites associated with Buddha or other divinities in Asia and to Mecca for Muslims. In these cases, such travel increasingly requires the use of conventional tourism facilities: accommodation, transportation and other infrastructure and services. Inevitably, therefore, the pilgrims come into contact with conventional tourists, many of whom will be interested in and desirous of visiting the same sites, but for secular, not religious, reasons in most cases. Sacred sites, from shrines, burial grounds and places of worship to places of birth, life and death of sacred figures are all major tourist attractions in their secular role, a role which may be opposed by adherents of particular faiths. Thus, the potential will always exist whenever the two groups of travellers, both those at each end of a religious–secular continuum and those at other points on such a scale, come into contact with each other at specific sites. One can only hope that some of the points made in this volume, some of the examples given and some of the discussion of conflicts that have arisen, prove useful to those in charge of pilgrimages, sacred sites and tourism in general, to prevent disagreement and conflict and thus ensure the preservation of these special sites and access to them by all who wish to experience their significance.

References

Alexander, L. (2015) Gap-year girl held over naked stunt. *The Times*, 11 June, p. 3.

Ap, J. and Crompton, J.L. (1993) Residents' strategies for responding to tourism impacts. *Journal of Travel Research* 32 (1), 47–50.

Baum, T.G. and Butler, R.W. (2014) *Tourism and Cricket: Travels to the Boundary*. Bristol: Channel View Publications.

Beeton, S. (2010) The advance of film tourism. *Tourism and Hospiatltiy Planning and Development* 7 (1), 1–6.

Butler, R.W. (2011) The evolution of tourism products in St Andrews, Scotland: From religious relics to golfing Mecca. In Y. Wang and A. Pizam (eds) *Destination Marketing and Management* (pp. 149–164). Wallingford: CABI.

Butler, R.W. and Suntikul, W. (2013) *Tourism and War*. London: Routledge.

Camara Paraguaya de Turismo de las Misiones Jesuiticas (n.d.) *Ruta Jesuitica*. Itappua: BOLF.

Church of Cyprus (2008) *Cyprus Island of Saints A Pilgrimage Tour.* Nicosia: Cyprus Tourism Organisation.

Cultural Corps of Korean Buddhism (2013) *The Essence of Korean Buddhist Culture.* Seoul: Templestay Information Centre.

Daly, J. (2017) The grave but lucrative business of tombstone tourism. *The Irish Independent,* 6 March, p. 11.

Dogan, H.Z. (1989) Forms of adjustment: Sociocultural impacts of tourism. *Annals of Tourism Research* 16 (2), 216–236.

Greaves, M. (2015) Martin Luther is a central figurine again in Germany. *The Times,* 22 August, p. 80.

Green Pilgrimage Network (2014) *Green Pilgrimage Network.* Assisi: Green Pilgrimage Network.

Horne, M. (2016) Cathedral bans tourists from funerals after selfies taken. *The Times* 15 October, p. 22.

Miles, S. (2016) *The Western Front Landscape, Tourism and Heritage.* Barnsley: Pen and Sword Books.

Ogden, M.A. (2017) My nights with the nuns. *The Times,* 19 February, pp. 6–7.

Page J. (2010) Tomb tourists told he's not the Messiah. *The Times,* 2 April, p. 42.

Schott, B. (2008) Schott's Almanac of New Tourism. *The Times,* 19 July, p. 11.

Sharpley, R. and Stone, P.R. (2009) *The Darker Side of Travel: The Theory and Practice of Dark Tourism.* Bristol: Channel View Publications.

Stone, P.R. (2006) A dark tourism spectrum: Towards a typology of death and macabre related tourist sites, attractions and exhibitions. *Tourism: An Interdisciplinary Journal* 54 (2), 145–160.

Templestay (n.d.) See www.templestay.com (accessed 5 November 2016).

Viero, A.G. (2003) Residents' Opinions of Tourism in Sacred Places: The Case of Santiago de Compostela, Spain. MSc thesis, University of Surrey.

Winter, C. (2009) Tourism, social memory and the Great War. *Annals of Tourism Research* 36 (4), 607–626.

Winter, C. (2011) First World War cemeteries: Insights from Visitor Books. *Tourism Geographies* 13 (3), 462–479.

Websites

https://www.viator.com/tours/Madrid/Entrance-Ticket-to-Bernabeu-Tour/d566-2140BERNABEU?pref=02 (accessed 10 January 2016).

www.winchester-caathedral.org.uk (accessed 3 December 2016).

Index